A Treasury of Brooklyn

A Treasury of
BROOKLYN

Edited by
MARY ELLEN *and*
MARK MURPHY *and*
RALPH FOSTER WELD

WILLIAM SLOANE
ASSOCIATES, INC.
Publishers . . . New York

First Printing, 1949

Typography and Format Designed by
LEONARD W. BLIZARD

Manufactured in the United States of America by H. Wolff

Published simultaneously in Canada by
George J. McLeod, Ltd.

Contents

Acknowledgment

The Editors wish to thank all those who have been helpful in the long preparation of this book. Particularly, our gratitude goes to the Long Island Historical Society and its Librarian, Miss Edna Huntington, and to Miss Sarah Moore.

Introduction

BROOKLYN seems well on the way to becoming an American legend, yet, oddly, one without a text. It has somehow reached a place in our literature and folklore where it is that thing some grammarians contend is impossible: a one-word cliché. The way the word "Brooklyn" on a radio program causes the fellow with the signs to lift one that says *Laughter* reminds us of the Old Star Theater in Brooklyn when burlesque was playing there. A red-nosed comedian could always get a laugh by saying he was from Canarsie. The following week in Cleveland, he would get exactly the same kind of laugh by saying he was from Ashtabula or Sandusky. Now, God knows, he's saying Brooklyn.

The state of affairs since the death of vaudeville and the spread of the American Army over the world in the recent war probably have had a lot to do with the fame of Brooklyn. We remember proudly the sort of casual anarchy combined with a proficient combativeness that hundreds of thousands of Brooklyn boys introduced into the Army. Some Texans used to claim that there were a lot more Texans in the Army than ever saw Texas before 1941. Most of the middle-eastern seaboard in those war years seemed to take on the protective coloration of Brooklyn. During the war, Brooklyn quite often was described as the Forty-ninth State, and of late some of the funny people have taken to calling it a State of Mind. For decades it was called among other things the Borough (once the City) of Churches, or of Homes and Churches, or of Churches and Cemeteries—Dodgers-Town, Manhattan's Bedroom, and even Borough of Braggarts.

Many of these descriptions are, or were, perhaps moderately accurate, but we think that the best way to describe Brooklyn is to say that it is a division of Greater New York containing nearly three million people living within eighty-one square miles bounded by Newton Creek, the Borough of Queens, Jamaica Bay, the Atlantic Ocean, the Narrows, New York Harbor, and the East River. As a single community it ranks fifth in the United States in industry, third in population, and first in foreign trade.

Yet none of this explains the town or its peculiar attraction for the people who live in it. Where Manhattan—here in Brooklyn we call *that* place New York—for all its diverse populations and range in social scale from the poorest to the richest, has a certain homogeneity, Brooklyn has little. People who have lived in Brooklyn for any time describe themselves as coming from Brownsville, Williamsburg, Bay Ridge, Greenpoint, Bedford-Stuyvesant, Flatbush, the Hill, the Heights, Park Slope, Borough Park, Bensonhurst, or whatever area they live in, and each section has a proper name and a character of its own. In the days before the housing shortage, the people of Brooklyn did not move each fall as did the people across the river, the people in the slums because often they couldn't and those who lived in nice places because they didn't want to.

The way the people of Brooklyn attain an identity with where they live, whether in the bitter slums of Brownsville or the mansions of Park Slope, is perhaps one of those curious extensions of history. The present community is made up of what was a collection of farming towns with a trading center near a river bank. And some of that feeling for land, for one particular spot on earth, even if now five stories above it, that pervaded, say, the Walloons who settled Flatbush, seems to remain here yet.

Anyway, Brooklyn is not ineffably comic. It contains bleak slums and beautiful old houses, hundreds of those apartment buildings with marble façades and casement windows, and thousands of little two-story houses with gardens in the back. It is the town of Henry Ward Beecher and Frankie Yale; of the abolitionists (moderate), the temperance movement, and Murder, Inc.; of the Children's Museum and Greenwood Cemetery; of the Long Island Historical Society and Coney Island. After all, Brooklyn is a place where people are born, live, and die. It depends on how you look at it, how you feel, or what time of day it is, whether it is stupid, charming, malicious, kind, or cruel—and it can be all of these.

The writings collected here are intended to be an account and in some way an explanation of this strange place which is a city and yet not a city but which has left its stamp on the people who live in it.

THE EDITORS

Brooklyn, 1949

The Place and the People

THE COLONIAL HISTORY of Brooklyn has the usual elements, except that the Dutch farmers were always careful to pay the Indians something for the land they took. The Hollanders settled on the sandy, flat land at first because it resembled home to them, and the island was not cleared of trees until the Revolution, when the wood was chopped into fuel.

They built churches, fought Indians, started schools, and taught the catechism, reading, writing, and the casting of accounts. We have selected here some passages from the historians of the town's early days that show, we think, a little of what things were like. They are not meant to be an exact telling of the tortuous civil and ecclesiastical history of the seventeenth and eighteenth centuries in our borough.

In reading them, one should keep in mind that to the Europeans who settled this land religion and politics were inseparable. The Dutch who set the patterns of the five towns—Flatlands, Flatbush, Brooklyn, Bushwick, and New Utrecht—fol-

lowed the superb tenets of Amsterdam and tolerated most religions. The sixth town—Gravesend that is considered by historians when they write of the colonial history of Brooklyn was
founded by an Englishwoman, Lady Deborah Moody, who
found with the Hollanders a religious freedom she could never
have attained in New England.

THE STRAWBERRY RAID

by RICHARD DENTON

Long-Island, the West-end of which lies Southward of
New-York, runs Eastward above one hundred miles, and is in
some places eight, in some twelve, in some fourteen miles broad;
it is inhabited from one end to the other. On the West is four
or five *Dutch* Towns, the rest being all *English* to the number
of twelve, besides Villages and Farm houses. The Island is most
of it of a very good soyle, and very natural for all sorts of *English* Grain; which they sowe and have very good increase of,
besides all other Fruits and Herbs common in England, as also
Tobacco, Hemp, Flax, Pumpkies, Melons, &c.

The Fruits natural to the Island are Mulberries, Persimons,
Grapes great and small, Huckelberries, Cranberries, Plums of
several sorts, Rosberries and Strawberries, of which last is such
abundance in June, that the Fields and Woods are died red;
Which the Country-people perceiving, instantly arm themselves
with bottles of Wine, Cream, and Sugar, and instead of a Coat
of Male, every one takes a Female upon the Horse behind him,
and so rushing violently into the fields, never leave till they have
disrob'd them of their red colours, and turned them into the
old habit.

From A Brief Description of New York, Formerly Called New Neth-
erlands with the Places thereunto Adjoining together with the Manner
of its Scituation, Fertility of Soyle, *etcetera*.
*Printed for John Hancock, at the first shop in Pope's-Head Alley in
Cornhill at the Three Bibles, and William Bradley at the Three
Bibles in the Minories, London, 1670.*

Some of the earliest descriptions of Brooklyn are in a book with the interesting title "Journal of Our Voyage to the New Netherland, begun in the name of our Lord & for His glory, the 8th of June, 1679, and undertaken in the small Flute-ship, called the Charles, of which Thomas Singleton was Master; but the superior Authority over both Ship and Cargo was in Margaret Filipse, who was the Owner of both, and with whom we agreed for our Passage from Amsterdam to New York, in New Netherland, at seventy-five Guilders for each Person, payable in Holland. Our Names were registered, that of my Friend as P. Vorstman, and my own as J. Schilders."

Vorstman was actually Jaspar Dankers and Schilders was Peter Sluyter. They were disciples of Jean de Labadie, by that time dead, who years before had proclaimed himself possessed of the spirit of John the Baptist. The Labadists, a contentious sect, traveled over the world, and finally died out in Maryland. The journal was discovered in an Amsterdam bookshop and translated by Henry Cruse Murphy, a prominent Brooklyn lawyer, politician, and scholar of the last century.

Sluyter, after telling of the voyage, describes how he and his companion crossed from New York to Long Island.

from . . .

JOURNAL OF OUR VOYAGE . . .

by PETER SLUYTER

Here we three crossed over, my comrade, Gerrit, our guide, and myself, in a row-boat, as it happened, which, in good weather and tide, carries a sail. When we came over we found there Jan Teunissen, our fellow passenger, who had promised us so much good. He was going over to the city, to deliver his letters and transact other business. He told us he would return home in the evening, and we would find him there. We went on, up the hill, along open roads and a little woods, through the first village, called Breukelen, which has a small and ugly little church standing in the middle of the road. Having passed through here, we struck off to the right, in order to go to *Gouanes*. We went upon several plantations where Gerrit was acquainted with most all of the people, who made us very welcome, sharing with us bountifully whatever they had, whether it was milk, cider, fruit or tobacco, and especially, and first and most of all, miserable rum or brandy which had been brought from Barbadoes and other islands, and which is called by the Dutch *kill-devil*. All these people are very fond of it, and most of them extravagantly so, although it is very dear and has a bad taste. It is impossible to tell how many peach trees we passed, all laden with fruit to breaking down, and many of them actually broken down. We came to a place surrounded with such trees from which so many had fallen off that the ground could not be discerned, and you could not put your foot down without trampling them; and, notwithstanding such large quantities had fallen off, the trees still were as full as they could bear. The hogs and other animals mostly feed on them. This place belongs to the oldest European woman in the country. We went immediately into her house, where she lived with her children. We found her sitting by the fire, smoking tobacco incessantly, one pipe after another. We enquired after her age, which the children told us was an hundred years. She was from Luyck (Liege), and still spoke good Waalsche (old French), with us. She could reason very well sometimes, and at other times she could not. She showed us several large apples, as good fruit of that country, and different from that of Europe. She had been about fifty years now in the country, and had above seventy children and grandchildren. She saw the third generation after her. Her mother had attended women in child-bed in her one hundred and sixth year, and was one hundred and eleven or twelve years old when she died. We tasted here, for the first time, smoked *twaelft* [1] (twelfth), a fish so called because it is caught in season next after the *elft* [2] (eleventh). It was salted a little and then smoked, and, although it was now a year old, it was still per-

[1] The striped bass.
[2] The shad.

· 4 ·

fectly good, and in flavor not inferior to smoked salmon. We drank here, also, the first new cider, which was very fine.

We proceeded on to *Gouanes*, a place so called, where we arrived in the evening at one of the best friends of Gerrit, named Symon. He was very glad to see us, and so was his wife. He took us into the house, and entertained us exceedingly well. We found a good fire, half-way up the chimney, of clear oak and hickory, of which they made not the least scruple of burning profusely. We let it penetrate us thoroughly. There had been already thrown upon it, to be roasted, a pail-full of *Gouanes* oysters, which are the best in the country. They are fully as good as those of England, and better than those we eat at Falmouth. I had to try some of them raw. They are large and full, some of them not less than a foot long, and they grow sometimes ten, twelve and sixteen together, and are then like a piece of rock. Others are young and small. In consequence of the great quantities of them, everybody keeps the shells for the purpose of burning them into lime. They pickle the oysters in small casks, and send them to Barbadoes and the other islands. We had for supper a roasted haunch of venison, which he had bought of the Indians for three guilders and a half of *seewant*, that is, fifteen stuivers of Dutch money (fifteen cents), and which weighed thirty pounds. The meat was exceedingly tender and good, and also quite fat. It had a slight spicy flavor. We were also served with wild turkey, which was also fat and of a good flavor; and a wild goose, but that was rather dry. Every thing we had was the natural production of the country.. We saw here, lying in a heap, a whole hill of watermelons, which were as large as pumpkins, and which Symon was going to take to the city to sell. They were very good, though there is a difference between them and those of the Caribby islands; but this may be owing to its being late in the season, and these were the last pulling. It was very late at night when we went to rest in a Kermis bed, as it is called, in the corner of the hearth, along side of a good fire.

30th, *Saturday*. Early this morning the husband and wife set off for the city with their marketing; and we, having explored the land in the vicinity, left after breakfast. We went a part of the way through a woods and fine, new made land, and so along the shore to the west end of the island called *Najack*.[3] As we proceeded along the shore, we found, among other curiosities, a highly marbled stone, very hard, in which we saw Muscovy glass lying in layers between the clefts, and how it was struck or cut out. We broke off a small piece with some difficulty, and picked out a little glass in the splits. Continuing onward from there, we came to the plantation of the *Najack* Indians, which was planted with maize, or Turkish wheat. We soon heard a noise of pounding, like thrashing, and went to the place whence it proceeded, and found there an old Indian woman busily employed beating Turkish beans out of the pods by means of a stick, which she did with astonishing force and dexterity. Gerrit inquired of her, in the Indian language, which he spoke perfectly well, how old she was, and she answered eighty years; at which we were still more astonished that so old a woman should still have so much strength and courage to work as she did. We went from thence to her habitation, where we found the whole troop together, consisting of seven or eight families, and twenty or twenty-two persons, I should think. Their house was low and long, about sixty feet long and fourteen or fifteen feet wide. The bottom was earth, the sides and roof were made of reed and the bark of chestnut trees; the posts, or columns, were limbs of trees stuck in the ground, and all fastened together. The top, or ridge of the roof was open about half a foot wide, from one end to the other, in order to let the smoke escape, in place of a chimney. On the sides, or walls, of the house, the roof was so low that you could hardly stand under it. The entrances, or doors, which were at both ends, were so small and low that they had to stoop down and squeeze themselves to get through them. The doors were made of reed or flat bark. In the whole building there was no lime, stone, iron or lead. They build their fire in the middle of the floor, according to the number of families which live in it, so that from one end to the other each of them boils its own pot, and eats when it likes, not only the families by themselves,

[3] Fort Hamilton, which is surrounded, in a great measure, by a marsh, and hence is here called an island.

but each Indian alone, according as he is hungry, at all hours, morning, noon and night. By each fire are the cooking utensils, consisting of a pot, a bowl, or calabash, and a spoon also made of a calabash. These are all that relate to cooking. They lie upon mats with their feet towards the fire, on each side of it. They do not sit much upon any thing raised up, but, for the most part, sit on the ground or squat on their ankles. Their other household articles consists of a calabash of water, out of which they drink, a small basket in which to carry and keep their maize and small beans, and a knife. The implements are, for tillage, a small, sharp stone, and nothing more; for hunting, a gun and pouch for powder and lead; for fishing, a canoe without mast or sail, and without a nail in any part of it, though it is sometimes full forty feet in length, fish hooks and lines, and scoops to paddle with in place of oars. I do not know whether there are not some others of a trifling nature. All who live in one house are generally of one stock or descent, as father and mother with their offspring. Their bread is maize, pounded in a block by a stone, but not fine. This is mixed with water, and made into a cake, which they bake under the hot ashes. They gave us a small piece when we entered, and although the grains were not ripe, and it was half baked and coarse grains, we nevertheless had to eat it, or, at least, not throw it away before them, which they would have regarded as a great sin, or a great affront. We chewed a little of it *with long teeth,* and managed to hide it so they did not see it. We had also to drink out of their calabashes the water which was their drink, and which was very good. We saw here the Indians who came on board the ship when we arrived. They were all very joyful at the visit of our Gerrit, who was an old acquaintance of theirs, and had heretofore long resided about there. We presented them with two jewsharps, which much pleased them, and they immediately commenced to play upon them, which they could do tolerably well. Some of their *patroons* (chiefs), some of whom spoke good Dutch, and are also their medicine-men and surgeons as well as their teachers, were busy making shoes of deer leather, which they understand how to make soft by continually working it in their hands. They had dogs, fowls and hogs, which they learn by degrees from the Europeans how to manage better. They had, also, peach trees, which were well laden. Towards the last, we asked them for some peaches, and they answered: "Go and pick them," which showed their politeness. However, in order not to offend them, we went off and pulled some. Although they are such a poor, miserable people, they are, nevertheless, licentious and proud, and given to knavery and scoffing. Seeing a very old woman among them, we inquired how old she was, when some young fellows, laughing and jeering, answered twenty years, while it was evident to us she was not less than an hundred. We observed here the manner in which they travel with their children, a woman having one which she carried on her back. The little thing clung tight around her neck like a cat, where it was kept secure by means of a piece of daffels, their usual garment. Its head, back and buttocks were entirely flat.

Journal of Our Voyage *by Peter Sluyter published by The Long Island Historical Society and reprinted with their permission.*

The American Revolution might well have ended in Brooklyn on August 27 and 28, 1776. Except for a lucky break in weather, and the caution and indolence of Sir William Howe, the bulk of Washington's armies would have been captured. The Battle of Long Island, as the engagement which occurred on the twenty-seventh has been called, was one of the most inept fights ever engaged in by American troops.

Washington's soldiers were badly defeated. Some of the American generalship seems after a hundred and seventy years of hindsight truly appalling. The American forces were split between Manhattan and Brooklyn; actually no attempt should have been made to defend Long Island in the face of superior British forces; flanks were unprotected, not even watched in one tragic instance; raw troops, who knew neither when to attack nor when to retreat, were placed in front lines. Men died in swamps and creeks fleeing before the English and the Hessians. The latter had been told that Americans scalped and tortured their prisoners, and so they gave little quarter. A band of 400 Marylanders, of the type known as the "Finest Flower of," died as gallantly as Americans have died anywhere so that other soldiers might escape.

The retreat, however, was masterly, the kind of withdrawal that is a victory. Washington on the night of the twenty-seventh and the morning of the twenty-eighth mobilized every boat he could find along the shores of Brooklyn, New York, and New Jersey, and under the cover of fog Colonel Glover's regiment of Marblehead fishermen got the Americans to safety. The fog was highly unusual for that time of year and reminds one of the unexpected clear weather that broke over Europe two days before Christmas in 1944.

WASHINGTON TO THE PRESIDENT OF CONGRESS

Sir, Inclination as well as duty would have induced me to give Congress the earliest information of my removal, and that of the troops, from Long Island and its dependencies, to this city the night before last; but the extreme fatigue which myself and family have undergone, as much from the weather since, as the engagement on the 27th, rendered me and them entirely unfit to take pen in hand. Since Monday, scarce any of us have been out of the lines till our passage across the East River was effected yesterday morning; and, for forty-eight hours preceding that, I had hardly been off my horse, and never closed my eyes; so that I was quite unfit to write or dictate till this morning.

Our retreat was made without any loss of men or ammunition, and in better order than I expected from the troops in the situation ours were. We brought off our cannon and stores, except a few heavy pieces, which, in the condition the earth was, by a long continued rain, we found upon trial impracticable; the wheels of the carriages sinking up to the hubs, rendered it impossible for our whole force to drag them. We left but little provisions on the island, except some cattle, which had been driven within our lines, and which after many attempts to force across the water, we found it impossible to effect, circumstanced as we were.

I have enclosed a copy of the council of war held previous to the retreat, to which I beg leave to refer Congress for the reasons, or many of them, that led to the adoption of that measure. Yesterday evening and last night, a party of our men were employed in bringing our stores, cannon, and tents, from Governors Island, which they nearly completed. Some of the heavy cannon remain there still, but I expect they will be got away to-day.

In the engagement on the 27th, Generals Sullivan and Stirling were made prisoners. The former has been permitted, on his parole, to return for a little time. From my Lord Stirling I had a letter by General Sullivan, a copy of which I have the honor to transmit, that contains his information of the engagement with his brigade. It is not so full and certain as I could wish; he was hurried most probably, as his letter was unfinished; nor have I been yet able to obtain an exact account of our loss; we suppose it from seven hundred to a thousand killed and taken. General Sullivan says Lord Howe is extremely desirous of seeing some of the members of Congress; for which purpose he was allowed to come out, and to communicate to them what has passed between him and his lordship. I have consented to his going to Philadelphia, as I do not mean, or conceive it right, to withhold or prevent him from giving such information as he possesses in this instance. I am much hurried and engaged in arranging and making new dispositions of our forces; the movements of the enemy requiring them to be immediately had; and therefore I have only time to add, that I am, with my best regards to Congress, &c.

Geo. Washington.

New York, August 31, 1776

The residents of Brooklyn, as a whole, were not much interested in the Revolution. Stiles in his history of Brooklyn writes: . . . it is proper to notice the very limited extent to which Kings County militia participated in the battle. Previous to its commencement, they were ordered into service within the lines at Brooklyn, under the command of Lieut.-Col. Nicholas Cowenhoven, of Flatbush, and Major Barent Johnson, of Bushwick, the father of the late worthy Gen. Jeremiah Johnson. [General Johnson participated in the War of 1812.] Many of them, however, embraced the earliest opportunity to join the British army on Staten Island, and others concealed themselves. As a consequence of this universal defection, the regiment was reduced to about two hundred men, and, after the battle, was still further reduced, by desertions, to about one hundred and fifty. This remnant left the island with the rest of the army, under command of Major Johnson, and marched to Harlem, where they dispersed without leave and returned to their homes, where many of them were captured by Tories and incarcerated in the prisons at New York. [Stiles in a footnote in his 1867 edition says that Major Johnson accompanied the army to Jersey, where he was captured by the British and returned home on a parole, given by Howe, in January 1777.] This was not surprising, when we consider the example set them by their colonel, who left his command within the lines and went privately to Flatbush, where he was seen, shortly after, in company with two British officers. For this he was, upon his return to camp, placed under arrest and sent to Harlem for trial by the Committee of Public Safety. The witnesses were, however, conveniently 'spirited away,' through the management of friends, and there being no one to appear against him, the colonel was released. After his return to his home in Kings County, he was engaged in certain transactions in the British commissary and barrack departments, and, with many others, was indicted before the Circuit Court, at Albany, at its October term, in 1837, for treason against the State, but by the good management of Alexander Hamilton, he escaped trial.

For seven years Brooklyn was an occupied, garrison town, and the bulk of the people did their best to remain loyal to King

George. The leaders in Kings County who had been mildly associated with the rebellion declared in a formal statement to Governor Tryon: "We, the members of the Provincial Congress, the County Committee, and the Committees of the different townships, elected for and by the inhabitants of Kings County, feel the highest satisfaction in having it in our power to dissolve ourselves without danger of the County being desolated, as it was by repeated threats, some short time ago. We do hereby accordingly dissolve ourselves, rejecting and disclaiming all power of Congress and Committees, totally refusing obedience thereto, and revoking all proceedings under them whatsoever, as being repugnant to the laws and constitution of the British Empire, and undutiful to our sovereign, and ruinous to the welfare and prosperity of this County. We beg leave to assure your Excellency we shall be exceedingly happy in obeying the legal authority of government, whenever your Excellency shall be pleased to call us forth, being from long experience well assured of your Excellency's mild and upright administration."

The British treated Long Island as occupied territory; elections were forbidden; the civil courts were suspended, with "justice" being imposed arbitrarily by royal functionaries or soldiers; prices were fixed on farm produce, and the farmers were likely at any time to be impressed into working as carters or woodcutters. All the fine trees on the island were cut down to provide fuel for the Hessian camps, and when the wood ran out astonished Dutch farmers saw their land dug up for peat. Churches, except those of the established Church of England, were used as prisons, hospitals, storehouses, and barracks. The Tories looted the land of anyone slightly suspect, and divided the properties of Americans who had joined the Revolution. Whalemen along the Connecticut shore were authorized to cruise in Long Island Sound against British vessels, and a few of them took to making forays on the island, robbing both Whigs and Tories.

The British paid off moderately well, giving gold when they felt like paying for produce, but there were so many robber bands on the island that the farmers usually had to bury their money and pray. Some men got wealthy providing supplies to the English, and 11,000 Americans died in fetid prison ships anchored in the Wallabout where the Navy Yard is now.

Charles Loosley and Thomas Elms, a couple of papermakers, were among the most arrant profiteers in the village during the occupation. They had pleaded with the Continental Congress not to be pressed into military service, because, they said, the infant nation was certainly going to need paper. God knows they knew governments and armies. When the British moved into New York after Washington withdrew from the city, the paper men set up a tavern. Later they took over a gloomy big stone building known as the ferry tavern, near the foot of Fulton Street in Brooklyn. This had belonged to the town, and before the Revolution had been run by Thomas Waldron, the ferry master. He was an active Whig, the commandant of a troop of light horse, and had fled the island to fight with the Americans.

Loosley and Elms named the place the King's Head, and did a fine business. They set a good table, ran lotteries, bullbaitings, horse races, fox hunts and illuminations. Rivington's Gazette, which supplied Tory reading matter to New York, in the issue of January 24, 1778, had an account of a celebration of the Queen's birthday: As the loyalty even of individuals ought, at this time, to be properly encouraged, you will infinitely oblige the public and a number of your readers, by inserting a description of the grand and elegant illumination at the King's Head Tavern, on last evening, in honor of her Majesty's birthday; and it is the desire of the public, as Messrs. Loosley and Elms have ever shown their attachment to the British Government, and a detestation of the present rebellion, that, through the channel of your much-esteemed paper, their conduct may be known and approved of in Europe, as well as by the loyalists in New York. The tavern was illuminated with upwards of two hundred wax-lights. In the centre were the royal arms of Great Britain, and above it, statues of the present king and queen, under a canopy of state elegantly decorated, which shone, like their majestie's virtues, conspicuous to the world. The view of the reduction of Mud Fort (on one side) by his majesty's ships, Roebuck and Vigilant, gave that joy which Britons always feel on the success and honor of their country. On the other side, their generous indignation was roused by a view of those men (the Congress) whose ambition has almost ruined this unhappy country, and reduced its inhabitants to the greatest distress. It was very apropos of the painter to place the devil at the President's elbow, who tells him to persevere, with so significant a grin as seems to indicate his having no manner of doubt of their making his house their home in the infernal regions. The statue of Mr. Pitt, without its head, was placed near the Congress, as being one of their kidney, and gave a hint of what ought, long ago, to have been done. The verses over the tavern door were very proper on the occasion, and well illuminated. In short, everything was well conducted and the *tout ensemble* had really a fine effect. Much is due to Messrs. Loosley and Elms for their patriotic spirit, which meets the approbation of every man who is a friend to his king and country.

On another occasion, Loosley and Elms, who seems to have had a quite cozy friendship with Rivington, advertised in his journal: "PRO BONO PUBLICO.—Saturday next being the birthday of His Royal Highness the Prince of Wales, Loosley, agreeable to an honest old custom, wishes to see his royal and constitutional friends—dinner at 3. The evening to conclude with fireworks and illuminations. A good band of music. REBELS approach no nearer than the heights of Brooklyn." *Loosley and Elms were thought to have made much money, but somehow it didn't last, for soon after the signing of the provisional treaty of peace, a sale was advertised for the benefit of the creditors of Charles Loosley. Among the items that went under the block were* "mahogany and other bedsteads, feather beds and mattresses, dining, tea, and card tables; an elegant clock in mahogany case; a curious collection of well-chosen paintings and pictures; large pier and other looking-glasses, in gilt and plain frames; table and tea sets of china, plate, etc.; a capital, well-toned organ, made by one of the first hands in London; a billiard table in thorough repair; near twenty globe lamps, fit for hall or passage, etc.; wagons, horses, cows, etc.; two tenements adjoining the house; a flagstaff with ensigns, pendants; and several hundred transparent and tin lamps, fit for an illumination." Loosley followed the exodus of Tories to Nova Scotia, and people in Brooklyn heard years later that he was running a tavern at Port Roseway. As the loyalists left New York, their departure was speeded by the people behind singing such songs as:

> When Lord Cornwallis first came o'er
>   The cannon roared like thunder;
> If he should return once more,
>   It will surely be a wonder.
> The refugees and Tories all,
>   Asking mercy at our hands,
> Upon their bending knees do fall,
>   To let them stay and enjoy their lands. . . .

The period of adjustment after peace was long, bitter, and hard. A few minor changes had to be made in the processes of attracting trade. On the old road to Fort Greene there had been a hay scales which throughout the revolution had exhibited high on its front a profile of King George III. When peace came, the owner of the scale inscribed some words below the picture, and for many decades the medallion was considered a very good likeness of Benjamin Franklin.

Brooklyn's part in the war of 1812 was that of furnishing a few soldiers and sailors, but in August 1814 it did look as though Long Island might be invaded for the second time by the British. The people of New York and Brooklyn got shovels and spades and worked in shifts putting trenches and redoubts in Fort Greene. The British didn't come. There has been left from those exciting days, though, a song by Samuel Woodworth, author of "The Old Oaken Bucket" from which we are reprinting two verses.

THE PATRIOTIC DIGGERS

by SAMUEL WOODWORTH

Johnny Bull beware,
   Keep at proper distance,
Else we'll make you stare
   At our firm resistance;
Let alone the lads
   Who are freedom tasting,
Recollect our dads
   Gave you once a basting.
     Pickaxe, shovel, spade,
       Crowbar, hoe, and barrow,
     Better not invade,
       Yankees have the marrow.

Grandeur leaves her towers,
   Poverty her hovel,
Here to join their powers
   With the hoe and shovel.
Here the merchant toils
   With the patriot sawyer,
There the laborer smiles,
   Near him sweats the lawyer.
     Pickaxe, shovel, spade,
       Crowbar, hoe, and barrow
     Better not invade,
       Yankees have the marrow.

When Henry R. Stiles came to Brooklyn from Connecticut, he may have appeared to the men who hired him as one of the carpetbagging historians common in the nineteenth century. He worked for a couple of years as librarian of the Long Island Historical Association, and then set about writing a history of Brooklyn. There must have been hundreds of men throughout the country engaged in that kind of work, shabby fellows, with the dirt of libraries on them, hustling a buck. Libraries are full of their work—histories of counties, histories of towns, all set to a pattern. First they tell of land grants, then of Indian wars, next some history consisting of who succeeded whom as township supervisors, and then a lot of biographies, a great big bunch of live obituaries on the people who subscribed for the books.

In 1867 appeared the first volume of Stiles's *A History of the City of Brooklyn*, the second volume came out in 1869, and the third in 1870. The books were published by subscription and should have been just as shoddy as the usual run of such stuff. They weren't, though. Stiles was good; he wrote well, and he seems to have been an indefatigable researcher. The biographies he ran of his contemporaries did have considerable eulogy in them, but you can't blame a man for making a living. In his seeking out the curious, and how people lived and what their relations were to one another, he was superb. He recorded church fights, lawsuits, eccentricities, as well as acts of civic virtue. He seems to have become enthusiastic about his subject, for he put his carpetbag away. He wrote a history of bundling and its origins, an account of the years it took to find a decent burial place for the Americans who died in the British prison ships, and several genealogies, including one of the Stiles family.

In 1871, *The City of Brooklyn* was published. It was an almost model guidebook and has been attributed to Frank Ballard and Stiles. We are very fond of the prefatory note:

There are persons still living who obtained, when young, their sum total of knowledge about Brooklyn, from that painstaking and authentic work, Rev. Dr. Jebediah Morse's *American Gazetteer*. Making every allowance for the conciseness compulsory upon the compiler of a work of that character, it must seem to these individuals after only seventy years have passed, almost ludicrous to remember that they once read (and perhaps verified by actual observation) that Brooklyn was "a township in Kings County, New York, on the West side of Long Island, containing 1,603 inhabitants, of whom 405 are slaves and 225 are electors, by the state census. In this place are a Presbyterian church, a Dutch Reformed church, a powder magazine, and some elegant houses, lying chiefly in one street. It is separated from New York by East river, which is nearly a mile broad; and forms an agreeable object from the city." This was all that Dr. Morse could conscientiously say of Brooklyn in 1798. And in the American edition of *Rees Cyclopedia*, "revised, corrected, enlarged, and adapted to this country by several literary and scientific characters"—published at Philadelphia early in the present century—the same description appears, word for word, with an addendum that: "by the last census the inhabitants amounted to 2,378. This place is well situated for ship-building, having the advantage of very deep water along its shore."

The *Encyclopedia Americana*, of which the eminent Dr. Francis Lieber was chief editor, published in 1830, honored Brooklyn with notice as "a post-town of New York, in Kings County, on the west end of Long Island, separated from the city of New York by East river. Population in 1810, 4,402, in 1820, 7,175. The village of Brooklyn, within the township, is incorporated and has a pleasant and somewhat elevated situation, opposite to the city of New York, from which it is three quarters of a mile distant. It is a flourishing village, compactly and handsomely built, having various manufactures and an extensive trade, and contained in 1825, 8,800 inhabitants and five houses of public worship. To the east of the village is a tract of land called the *Wallabought*, which is the site of a navy yard and public storehouses, belonging to the United States. Between Brooklyn and Flatbush on the south, a severe battle was fought during the Revolutionary war, between the British and Americans, in which the latter were defeated with great loss."

These two authorities are quoted as supplying a fit foundation for the pride with which the citizens of Brooklyn may now look upon their beautiful home; transformed, as it has been, within a single generation, from insignificance into metropolitan importance by their public spirit, social unity, and practical morality. The village of 1825, with its 8,800 inhabitants and 5 houses of public worship, and without a single noteworthy characteristic, has now become the third city in the Union in population, and, rejoicing in world wide celebrity as the "City of

Churches," has gained a position of influence, and donned a robe of varied beauty, entitling it to admiration and study as one of the most attractive and loveable of American cities. That Brooklyn has so long been without a Guide Book, presenting in popular form and in descriptive detail, its many attractions, is matter of surprise and regret. It is to supply this deficiency that the present publication has been undertaken; and, in the hope that it may serve a useful purpose in unveiling to the general public beauties hitherto too modestly concealed, we dedicate to the citizen and the stranger the first "Guide Book to Brooklyn" worthy of the name, ever issued from the press.

In the second volume of his History of Brooklyn *Stiles did another job of guidebook writing—of the town, how it looked and who was in it, fifty years before. He wrote it as a series of walks, pointing out houses and lanes, and pausing now and then for gossipy descriptions of people. In some of the following pages there are a number of excerpts from these walks. They took up some 160 pages in Stile's quarto volume, and so a number of excellent sections had to be left out if we were ever going to get this book past the first Jackson Administration.*

Several times Stiles mentions Alden Spooner, who founded the Star, Brooklyn's first important newspaper. Spooner once noticed how the town was expanding, and wrote dejectedly in 1830: "Beauty in architecture, solidity in structure, taste and neatness in public grounds, have been entirely disregarded. There are a few ornamental fronts, but scarcely one well designed and proportioned edifice within the limits of the town. The houses generally are run up with a most frugal economy of brick and mortar, or scantlings and planks, as the case may be. One may look in vain for a public square, a well shaded avenue, or even a sufficient cemetery. The whole object seems to have been to cover every lot of eighteen feet with a house, to project and open unneeded as well as unheard of streets, and to tumble the hills into the valleys."

from . . .

A HISTORY OF THE CITY OF BROOKLYN

by HENRY R. STILES

Brooklyn, as seen from the New York side of the river, during the first third of the present century [nineteenth], presented features of simple rural beauty, strongly in contrast with its present imposing aspect. Around the "Old (now Fulton) Ferry," there was a clustering of houses, taverns, stables and shanties, which had grown up since the earliest establishment of a ferry at that point, and which formed the nucleus of a considerable business activity. From the ferry-slip (with its horse-boat, its one steamboat and its row-boat accommodations; but, with no such accommodation as the present ferry-house affords, and with no bell save the resonant throat of the ferryman), the old country road, the "king's highway" of the colonial and revolutionary periods, straggled crookedly upward and backward, out past the old Dutch church, out through Bedford Corners, and away beyond Jamaica, even to Montauk Point; being, in fact, the great highway of travel of Long Island itself. As far as the junction of this old road (now Fulton street), with the new road (now Main street), which came up from the "New Ferry" (as it was even then called, although it had been established some twenty years), it was tolerably well lined with buildings of various shapes and sizes. Pert looking Yankee frame edifices rudely intruded their angularities among the humpbacked Dutch houses quaintly built of stone, or with small imported Holland bricks. Yet one and all wore such an unpretentious and neighborly look, under the brooding shadows of the noble trees, with which the village abounded, that it was plainly evident, even to the most casual observer, that no premonition of the future greatness, so soon to be thrust upon them, had as yet disturbed the minds of their occupants. . . .

In the middle of the [Fulton] street, about fifty or sixty feet east of the flagstaff, stood the old market, a long, shabby, wooden structure, the head of which was about opposite Carll's stables, near Elizabeth street. It was slightly raised above the level of the street, had a rounding roof, and contained six stalls or stands, one of which is remembered to have been occupied by Burdet Stryker, another by John Doughty, another as a fish stand, etc. The locality was a sort of rendezvous for all the butchers, of whom, from time immemorial, there had been a large number resident in Brooklyn. Many of them had their slaughter houses near by; and every morning came down to the ferry stairs with their wheelbarrow loads of nicely dressed meats, which they trundled aboard the boats, barrows and all, and were ferried over to the city where they had stands in the "Fly Market." The old market, also, was the great resort of the sportive blacks, who formed no inconsiderable portion of the population of Brooklyn, at that early day. They were much employed by the butchers and others, and were fat, sleek and happy fellows, generally on the best of terms with their masters and "all the world beside," and full to overflowing of the waggery and tricks for which the Dutch negroes have always been noted. At the market, also, these negroes celebrated their annual "Pinkster" holiday, which corresponded to their masters' "Paas" festival. "Paas," now almost obsolete and kept in remembrance only by a little childish egg cracking, occurred on Easter and Easter Monday, and was a "high day" among the Dutch, who feasted and rollicked to their heart's content. But, as it was evidently impolitic to allow the negroes the opportunity of being "elevated" on the same day with their masters, who were apt to need their sober services and attention, the following Monday (Whitsuntide) was allowed to the slaves as their especial festival. It was, indeed, their annual saturnalia. The village was fairly black with them; they came trooping into Brooklyn from the island, men, women and children, sometimes as many as two hundred. They danced for eels around the market; they sang; "tooted" on fish horns; played practical jokes on one another; and, everywhere, throughout the village, might be heard the cackle of obstreperous laughter by which the negro is wont to give relief to his overplus of happiness. In short, "Pinkster" was a scene of the broadest good humor—where every sort of common game and of uncommon drollery was in requisition, and drinking was by no means neglected. As a necessary consequence of "Pinkster," the negroes generally got "as jolly drunk as lords," and on the following morning as many as twenty-five or thirty would usually be brought up before old Squire Nicolls on a charge of "disorderly conduct." The squire, however, knowing that "Pinkster" came but once a year, and appreciating the peculiar weaknesses of the negro character, always treated the culprits with leniency; and, summarily confiscating whatever funds remained in their pockets after their "spree," dismissed them until such time as the recurrence of their annual festival should again bring them under his judicial notice.

"In regard to Paas," an old Brooklynite writes us that "its observance as a day for the cracking of eggs was kept up with great vigor in Brooklyn, until about 1830. Boys were to be observed on the corners of the streets, carrying their winnings in their hats and trying the hardness of the eggs upon their teeth. The eggs were often boiled and colored, although this latter process did not improve their hardness. Goose eggs and guinea-hen's eggs [having hard shells] were sometimes used clandestinely, or to deceive the uninitiated; and the excitement of this small gambling is remembered to have equaled, in a small way, that to be witnessed at the gold board in Broad street, New York."

To return to the market, however. The old building finally became so dilapitated as to be considered a nuisance, and was torn down one night, in 1814, by a party of young men and boys. It was a public institution, and the "market fees" were always collected by *William Furman*, one of the overseers of the poor, and who occupied a large double frame house, with a long, high piazza in front, which stood upon the site of the present City Rail Road Company's elegant edifice. The house then stood right in front of the ferry stairs, which led down on the lower side of the slip; and, in the basement nearest the water, Mr. Furman kept an oyster house, where, for the moderate charge of *twelve and a half cents*, one could be furnished with as many fine roasted oysters as he could eat at a sitting. . . .

His son, *Gabriel Furman*, Esq., a talented lawyer and historian of Brooklyn, was born in the house which we have described, in the first month of the present century; and, upon the completion of his earlier studies, read law with Elisha W. King, Esq., of New York, whose office he entered in 1823, and with whom he was a favorite student. Here he developed qualities of steadiness, method and good analytical powers; well suited, in the opinion of eminent lawyers, to the successful practice of his profession.

Published by Subscription, 1867

Gabriel Furman, whom Stiles wrote about and, like other historians of Brooklyn and Long Island, quoted extensively, wrote almost daily. He would get up early, wander around, and about noon write about where he had been in the morning. Sometimes he might as well have stayed home. Take the entry for March 1, 1822:

This month came in with a beautiful warm day—Took a walk in the afternoon up Red-Hook lane, and down by Isaac Cornell's—saw four men ploughing and one sowing—In the course of my walk saw several ploughed fields—on returning by Pierreponts saw parts of two skeletons of some men, in the bank, where they had been digging to mend the road—one of the skulls was quite entire—took part of the lower jaw of one of them, to which some very sound teeth were affixed—I expect they are the remains of some soldiers or sailors who were buried there during the Revolution, as the British Hospital and Fortifications were close by—It is not an uncommon thing [to] dig up skeletons in Brooklyn.

Then, occasionally, he would turn up fine stories like this:

THE OLD TULIP TREE

At the beginning of the present century a very large tulip, or white wood tree, existed in Brooklyn, on the bank of the East river, a short distance northeasterly from the Main street ferry. It was a very old tree and hollow, large enough inside to hold eight men comfortably; and was a splendid sight in the spring when in blossom, with its large flowers evaporating their perfume over most of the then little settlement of Brooklyn. Under this tree was a beautiful green sward, and the tree being full of large leaves it cast a most extensive and grateful shade in the warm season. It was so well known in the city of New York, that it was usual among the old-fashioned inhabitants of that city, to make up parties of three or four families, to cross the East river in their own boats, carrying their provisions with them, directly after their early dinner hour of twelve or one o'clock, and to pass the long summer afternoon in laughing, talking, smoking, and drinking under the shade of this tree. The women would boil their tea kettle in the hollow of the tree; and then between four and five o'clock they would sit down to drink tea, with the smooth grass for their tea-table, after which the men would again smoke their long pipes, and after some social chat, and planning another excursion into the country (as it was then called, but how different now!), they would return to the city about sunset, without the fear of being run over by steamboats in their long and slow row across the river, amusing themselves with looking at the gentlemen playing at bowling upon the smooth lawn in the front of the Belvidere club-house, on the height of land south of Corlears Hook; and wondering whether the fishermen in the small boats, anchored a little way from the beach, between the foot of George street (now Market street) and Corlears Hook, had caught any fish; also admiring the gorgeous beauties of the sunset; but at times they would hasten their speed as they looked upon this splendid scene, because the lower cloud that the sun has just disappeared behind, and tinged its edges with living gold, exhibited a very black and ominous appearance, as if it had a thunder shower in its bosom, which idea became strengthened by seeing, almost directly after, the crinkling lightning playing along its surface; and they were also startled by the rushing past them of several porpoises, every few minutes showing their curved backs far above the surface of the water, which, smooth and still as if it were glass, reflected upon its surface all the heights of land, the wharves, buildings, and even lamps of the neighboring city, all which they say to each other is a sign that the storm is near at hand; but they reach home in safety just as the first drops of rain begin to fall. Such parties as these were of very frequent occurrence during the summer. Some may feel an interest in knowing what became of this interesting tree, so identified as it was with many of the purest and most pleasurable enjoyments of our ancestors. One Sunday morning, in the early part of summer, about forty years ago, when the few people who lived at "Brooklyn ferry" (as a large part of the present city was then called) were at church, an alarm of fire was given by the only bell in the place (the Dutch church was then at Brooklyn parish, or Brooklyn proper), which was the fire bell hanging on the Old Ferry road. All ran out to see where the fire was, and observing a smoke in that direction, they passed on until they discovered it was the great tree in flames. For a long time no one dared go near it, under the apprehension that a powder magazine, which then stood in the vicinity, would blow up. The tree was so large and the smoke so great, that for near an hour the inhabitants were much alarmed lest the fire might be communicated to the magazine, and all their houses, if not their lives, destroyed by the explosion, they believing a large quantity of gunpowder to be stored there. After some time, four or five of the most courageous taking pails, and dipping water from the river, threw it into the hollow of the tree and extinguished the fire. It was supposed to have originated from the carelessness of some fishermen, who, having cooked their breakfast there, as was then not an unfrequent occurrence, had neglected afterwards to put out the fire with as much care as was usual. This, however, did not destroy the old tree; it still continued in leaf, and was resorted to during the warm season by the Knicker-bockers for their accustomed tea and smoking parties. But when the gales and storms came in the autumn, the tree was so much weakened by the loss of the wood which had been burnt from the inside, that it was blown down, to the great regret of all the inhabitants of Brooklyn and also of New York, to whom, and especially the latter, it had long been a very pleasant resort.

And now back to Stiles:

from . . .

A HISTORY OF THE CITY OF BROOKLYN

The immense sign [of Coe S. Downing's tavern], projecting over the sidewalk, attracted much attention from strangers, not only from its size, but from its peculiar inscription, which at least one English traveler has immortalized by inserting, *verbatim et literatim*, in his printed travels:

COE S. DOWNING'S STAGE
& LIVERY STABLE.
HORSES AND CARRIAGES TO BE LET.
FLAT-BUSH AND BATH—HEMPSTEAD—JERUSALEM—HEMP-
STEAD HARBOUR—COW NECK—WESTBURY—MUSQUETOE
COVE—JERICHO—OYSTER BAY—HUNTINGTON—EASTWOODS—
DIXHILL—BABYLON AND ISLIP, STAGE HOUSE. . . .

Then, directly opposite Hicks Street, was a small brick building, at one time, the residence of Diana Rapalje, without some notice of whom no history of Brooklyn would be complete. She was the daughter of Garret Rapalje and a descendant of the first white female child born in New Netherland. In early life a favorite in the presidential circles at Washington, she was, in her later days (we will not say *decline*, for her bearing was erect and firm to the last), a stately exhibitor of the fashions of '76; and, as was natural, from her earlier associations, considerable of a politician in her peculiar way. Her erratic doings, from middle age to the close of life, indicated that moderate form of insanity which is termed eccentricity; and which, in her case, manifested itself in many absurd, amusing, and (to those concerned in litigation with her), troublesome forms. It was said that she had loved and had been disappointed, and that, from that time, pride and self-reliance drove her to seclusion and made her disrespectful of the customs and usages of society, in many minor points. Yet, in certain matters of etiquette, no queen could be more haughty.

"Her house," says Alden J. Spooner, Esq., in a pleasant chapter of reminiscences in the *Evening Post*, June 27th, 1868, "passed for haunted. It was a great trial-point of courage to pass by this house, and few boys were bold enough to stand over the way at night and look up at it. The utmost expected from small boys of reasonable pluck, was, that they should race past in a close huddle for mutual protection, and look back furtively over the shoulder. When at some distance, the frightened herd would stop and fearfully look back. Almost all saw something floating over or around the house, shadowy and peculiar, of the traditionary white, and it bore the form of a woman. On one or two occasions I would be sworn I saw the spectre sitting on the top of the house, and I am willing to swear it now, but I came, afterwards, to know that the ghosts which frightened the boys and me were Diana's self, who had a habit of sitting on the roof on summer nights for the sensible purpose of cooling herself. The ancient and respected family of the Rapaljes long enjoyed the reputation of having produced the first-born white child on Long Island; and by boys, who care nothing about dates, Diana was supposed to be this very person. To be sure, this supposition would make her upwards of two centuries old, but, to the boys, there was nothing impossible with Diana. She had always been about the same person in the memory of the oldest inhabitant.

"She traversed the then village of Brooklyn, here and there picking up now a chip to light her fire, and then a codfish from the cheapest store to replenish her kettle. These she would deposit in her ample Dutch pockets, and march through the streets with the tail of the fish waving in the rear.

"Once, in crossing the Brooklyn ferry some ladies were excessively startled, and sprang from their seats in frightful apprehension. A snake was seen wriggling upon the floor. Diana witnessed the alarm with supreme contempt and soon relieved it. 'It is only one of my eels,' she said, pulling some others from her pocket, which she had bought in Fly Market, and whose comrade was attempting an escape. It is needless to say she restored him to her eelymosynary receptacle.

"At another time the clarion tones of chanticleer came from the bosom of the same dignified lady sitting smoothly erect in the same cabin. Lest people might suppose she was exercising her own lungs upon the chromatic scale, she opened her shawl and exposed a roystering bird of the genus rooster, which she informed the company was intended for chicken soup.

"To save the expense, she laid down the cobble stones in front of her residence with her own fair hands. To a friend who afterwards reproached her with 'How could you do it?' she replied: 'Nobody recognized me; *I did it with my back to the street.*' This seems to be a recognition of the fact that most persons passed on the other side of the way."

Her sister married John Fisher, and a few months after her decease, in March, 1824, he married Diana. Both sisters had been distinguished, in early life, for their beauty and accomplishments, and were recognized belles, not only on Long Island, but in the best circles of New York and Washington. John Fisher was a Hessian "redemptioner," who came to Brooklyn soon after the close of the revolutionary war, in such an abject condition of poverty that, it is said, the supervisors seriously discussed the propriety of allowing him to remain in the place lest he should become a burden on the town. Their fears, however, were groundless, for John was industrious and shrewd, and, little by little, amassed considerable money and with it a better social position. He was a communicant in the Episcopal church (St. Ann's) of which he was said to be the politest member, his pew being ever open to strangers. He, also, erected the three brick buildings in Front street (Nos. 9, 11, 13), at a time when such erections were a noticeable improvement in Brooklyn. At the time of his marriage to Diana Rapalje, he was old, paralytic and imbecile, and some occurrences took place afterwards, which constitute a part of the romance of the Kings Co. Surrogate's office, and Chancery reports. After his decease, in June, 1827, she married the Hon. Lemuel Sawyer, of North Carolina, and who represented that state in Congress. He was a man of considerable literary ability, the author of "Wall street, or a Quarter before Three," an excellent farce which met with much success at the Old Park Theatre in New York; but possessed neither means, health, nor business tact. The marriage, however, was one of those which are regulated more by prudential considerations than by affection. Sawyer was in much need of money; so he matched his family against her wealth; while Diana's avowed reason for her choice was that "Sawyer was a lawyer and she wanted a man to match James B. Clarke." [1] The parties subsequently maintained merely the outside appearance of diplomatic courtesy, seasoned occasionally with litigation concerning bits and scraps of property. They lived apart, she residing in one of the Fisher houses on the corner of Front and Dock streets, and on its doorstep frequently sat the "Virginia Honorable," her husband, clad in a dilapidated and faded plaid cloak, having been driven out of paradise by the angel who sometimes appeared at the door, waving her flaming—tongue. She died, January 30, 1849, in her eighty-second year, and was buried in Greenwood.

Diana Rapalje's house was afterwards purchased by Col. Alden Spooner, who occupied it as a residence and as the printing office of the *Star*.[2]

Very nearly opposite to the present Johnson Street was the residence of John Valentine Swertcope, one of those Hessians who had been left (perhaps not unwillingly) upon our shores by the receding wave of British domination, after the declaration of peace in 1783. With his long gray beard, his soldierly tread and strongly marked features, he was certainly the quaintest and most original character in the village. In the British service he had been an armorer; and, very naturally, found some employment in furbishing and repairing the guns, pistols, etc., of his

---

[1] One of her first husband's (John Fisher's) sisters, Eleanor, married James B. Clarke, Esq., and another, Marie, married Peter Clarke. Upon the death of Fisher his will was contested by the Clarkes, although without success.

[2] In one of these buildings, nearly opposite Hicks street, it is said on credible authority, that Talleyrand, the eminent French diplomatist, resided awhile, during his stay in America. It is related of him that he frequently jumped into the market-wagons as they passed along the road on their way home and thus made excursions into Flatbush, Gravesend, and other county towns around Brooklyn. He is, also said to have been the introducer, into this country, of the Russian turnip.

neighbors in Brooklyn. Although his income from this source could have been but slight; yet by industry and thrift he gradually amassed a very snug little property, so that he was commonly reputed to have found a buried treasure. Be that as it may, he was able, in course of time, to purchase from the De Bevoise brothers, a strip of land off from the end of their farm, upon which he erected a dwelling house, and, adjoining it on the north, a gunsmith shop, which was mostly used by his son John. Old Swertcope, among other contrivances, invented an air-gun, the balls of which were clay pellets, and this weapon was an object of great curiosity, and of no small fear, to the boys especially, in their predatory excursions into the old man's orchard. A story is still extant, of an English cockney sportsman, who while hunting around the remains of the old fort on the Heights, raised his gun to fire at a robin, which, to his surprise fell dead before his eyes, 'ere he had even time to aim at it; and when old Swertcope's gaunt and grizzly figure emerged from among the bushes, the amateur sportsman incontinently took to his heels, firmly convinced that the apparition was none else than "St. Nick" himself. Two of these curious guns were sold among Swertcope's effects, after his death, and one was purchased at a pretty high figure by a gentleman who did not understand the secret of its management. Swertcope's son offered to impart the method for a price which the purchaser was not willing to pay, and so "Swertcope's air-gun" must henceforth be remembered among the "lost arts." Much of Swertcope's time was occupied in attending to his fine garden and orchard, where he used to prowl about, in apple season, with whip in hand and a dog at his heels, ready to pounce upon the boys who were skirmishing around his trees. He also did a considerable business in the distilling of *rose-water*. Roses, at that time, were raised in great abundance in the gardens of Brooklyn; and many persons were accustomed to send their annual crop of rose-leaves to Swertcope, who returned to each customer one-half the yield in rose-water; reserving the other half as payment for services in distillation. Having procured from the De Bevoises' some of their fine strawberry plants, of which fruit they had previously held the monopoly in the New York market, he very soon, by his good management, succeeded in dividing with them the reputation and the business of the best berries. In addition to these, he derived no inconsiderable income from the sale of a superior kind of bitters, which he manufactured; and he might be seen almost every morning, wending his way to the ferry, with a basketful of bottles of these bitters, which he peddled off in New York, before his return to Brooklyn.

He was said to be somewhat of a miser, and the large amount of money which he amassed, all in specie, was kept in a heavy iron bound box, under his bed; and its key during his last illness was always placed under his pillow. The late George Hall used to relate that having occasion to visit him, a little before his death, some one called at the house to obtain payment of a small bill, and the sick man directed his daughter to get the necessary amount out of the trunk. As she was engaged a little too long in searching for a coin, the sick man became impatient and suspicious, and raising himself up in bed, exclaimed, "Come away! Come away! vat you doin mit your tam money-rousin?" . . .

On the southerly corner of Sands street, was John Harmer's patent floor cloth factory. Subsequently, about 1819, he erected a new factory in Middagh, near Fulton street. Harmer was an Englishman, a singular genius, and a great infidel, always talking and boasting about his infidelity. He was a friend and great admirer of Thomas Paine, author of *The Age of Reason*; and, in the latter portion of that writer's life he had him to live with him in Brooklyn. Harmer was a man of considerable property, and was the means of inducing Francis Guy, the painter, to come to this place. His daughter, Mrs. Lavinia Smith, is one of the figures represented in Guy's picture. . . .

On a high hill near the line of the present Bridge street was a large establishment called "Mount Prospect Tavern," a great resort of the New York rowdies who used to come over in rowboats from the city, accompanied by their girls, and hold high carnival here. Drunkenness, fighting, noise and profanity had "full swing" here, unchecked by any fear of the New York authorities or village constables. . . .

After leaving the old road [Fulton Street] we pass vacant lots until we come to old St. Ann's church, which then fronted on Sands street, with its side doors on Washington street. It was, at the time of which we speak, the new St. Ann's, the first permanent home which the Episcopalians of Brooklyn had attained, after nearly a quarter of a century's buffeting about among private houses, barns, and old barracks. It was erected in 1805, during the rectorship of the Rev. John Ireland. Heavy in form, constructed of rough stone, overlaid with a coat of plaster and painted of a dark *blue* color, it would probably be considered, now-a-days, as a miracle of ugliness. Even then, the smallness of its windows and the *tout ensemble* of its exterior gave point to the jocular remark of an irreverent wag of a rival denomination, that, he "had often heard of the *church militant*, and its *canons*, but he'd never before seen its *port holes.*" The ground upon which it stood had been given, for the purpose, by Mr. and Mrs. Joshua Sands, whose benefactions ceased only with their lives, and it was a deserved as well as graceful compliment to the latter, which combined her name with that of an ancient saint, in the naming of the edifice. . . .

The Military Garden . . . reached its maximum reputation . . . during the *regime* of Mons. John François Louis Du Flon, a rosy-cheeked, cheery Swiss, who is still most pleasantly remembered by many of our citizens, who are to the manor born. A native of Neufchatel, in Switzerland, married in 1803, to an energetic and estimable lady, who still survives him, he became, soon after settling in New York city, a clerk to Mr. John Jules, an importer of French goods. In course of a few years he accumulated quite a handsome little property, which he was induced, in April, 1822, to invest in the purchase of this property. Although neither he nor his wife had been bred to this occupation, they soon developed the tact and enterprise, which proved that they could keep a hotel, and which secured them hosts of friends. Mr. Du Flon was induced by the Freemasons, who had hitherto been occupying lodge rooms in Lawrence Brower's tavern, to erect a larger building [the Military Garden which stood on the present site of the Borough Hall] . . . in which suitable accommodations could be furnished to the craft. This he did, and it was the beginning of a series of pecuniary embarrassments, which finally ended in his succumbing to a foreclosure of mortgage by John Schenck, his principal creditor. Poor Du Flon found, as many another public spirited man has done, that the friends who are ready with fine suggestions, are not so ready with the cash to back them; and that the public is very willing to have some one lead the march of improvement, provided they are not holden for the result. Yet Du Flon was a general favorite; his pleasant Garden, with its superior ice-cream, its tastefully appointed viands, its attractions of flowers and shrubbery—for he and his wife had the characteristic of their countrymen, a passion for floral pleasures—his own urbanity and cheerfulness of disposition, made his place the resort, *par excellence*, of the best village society; while his hall, from its superior size and accommodations, afforded an excellent place for the balls, amateur concerts, and traveling shows, which from time to time stirred into momentary excitement, the otherwise unruffled pulse of the community. When General Lafayette visited Brooklyn, during his visit to America, in 1824, he received his friends at the Military Garden, and as he grasped Poppy Du Flon's hand (for such was the respectfully-familiar nickname given him by his fellow villagers), he recognized in him the sick man whom he had attended, among others, at a lonely house on the frontier, during the Revolutionary war, and whom he had sat up with, watched and nursed for several days. Both gentlemen were affected to tears. Poppy Du Flon's life was unobtrusive, but useful; and his death, which occurred March 4, 1853, in his eighty-eighth year, was lamented by all. He left a wife, still living [1869], and eight children, all but two of whom settled in and around Brooklyn. . . .

Adjoining [the Middagh estate], and running in the same direction with the southerly line of the Hicks estate, was a strip of land, its western end on the river, and its east end reaching nearly to Henry street, which belonged, at the time of which we speak, to Mr. *Henry Waring*.

This excellent gentleman was born in that portion of New York, now known as Greenwich, Conn., on the 11th of October, 1773. On his maternal side, he was descended from an ancient Scotch family, the Millingtons—his mother being the daughter of Lady Anne Millington—and, on his father's side he came from an old North-of-Ireland family. His father served with considerable distinction as captain of an artillery company during the Revolutionary war, being mustered out of service at Newburgh, at its close. Henry was the eldest son; and in early life, left his parents, came to New York, and engaged himself as clerk to Bedient & Hubbell, merchants, near the old Fly Market. With this firm he continued until 1793, when he went to sea, and subsequently commanded a vessel, owned by Folkert Eden, and engaged in trading between New York and the West Indies. In 1795, he was taken prisoner by a French sloop-of-war, and a prize crew was placed upon his vessel, which was ordered to Martinique. While on the voyage thither, he and a man named Bills, rose upon the prize crew, retook the vessel, placed the crew (seven in number) in the forecastle, and steered for the island of Jamaica. Unfortunately, however, when within ten days sail of that place, he was spoken and boarded by a Spanish frigate. The suspicions of the boarding officer being aroused by finding the vessel in the hands of only two men, he instituted a search; found the seven Frenchmen imprisoned in the forecastle, liberated them and restored to them the possession of the vessel. Waring and Bills were then taken to the island of Eustatia, and were there imprisoned for several months, when they were exchanged and sent to New York. Soon after his return, a privateer, mounting seven guns, and named the *Adelia*, was fitted out by private subscription among the merchants of New York, and he was placed in command. His first cruise was successful, taking one or two prizes. When the United States navy was reorganized, he was offered a commission, but declined it, because his old friend and messmate (Commodore) Chauncey received a higher position than was offered to himself. He then formed a mercantile partnership in New York with a son of his old employer, Eden, and transacted business under the firm style of Waring & Eden. On the 11th of February, 1796, he was married, in his native town, to Susan Peck. Soon after this, his partner Eden, died, and he then engaged in business with Mr. Gideon Kimberly, under the firm name of Kimberly & Waring. . . .

[There] was a tract of 14 acres, extending from the East river to the old road (Fulton street) and in width from Love lane, to a line a little north of the present Pierrepont street. This strip of land was owned by the brothers *Robert* and *John De Bevoise*, whose grandfather Jacobus purchased it from Joris Remsen in 1734.

Robert the elder brother, was a stout, strong, broad-faced man; but having, unfortunately, lost his nose and palate, in consequence of a cancerous disease—was, although really of a kindly disposition, quite an object of terror to the village urchins—which was, by no means, lessened by the savage disposition of twenty or thirty dogs which he kept around the house. John De Bevoise was a strong contrast to his brother Robert—being thin, pale and consumptive. Both were bachelors, and being well off, occupied their time alternately in fishing and gardening. Their dwelling, a small, ancient and rather dilapidated Dutch edifice, which stood on the line of Columbia street, about 160 feet north of the line of Pierrepont, was graced by the presence of an exceedingly beautiful girl, who filled the place of a daughter to the two old men, whose name she bore. Sarah De Bevoise, had many admirers, and the private lane which led down to the house, between the De Bevoise and Pierrepont estates, is said to have received its name of Love lane, from the numerous love-lines, initials of Miss De B. and her love-lorn swains, which were scribbled and cut upon its fence by the young men of the village. She was much petted by her aged protectors, who built for her especial use a little parlor or dolly-house, near the main residence, where she might receive her guests, in more befitting style than she could in the old-fashioned, double-roomed and plainly-furnished farm-house. She married first Mr. Samuel Van Buren, and after his death, Mr. Edward McComber . . . and is still living in New York city.

It is related of old Bob De Bevoise that his ground was enclosed by a high board fence; and, as the trees were thick on the line of the fence, when the posts gave away, from time to time, he nailed the boards to the trees. But the winds stirred the trees, and thereby loosened the boards again; so that, finally, it became a regular Sunday morning job with Bob to nail up his fences, and his neighbors, without reference to almanac, could always tell when sabbath came, by the continual hammer, hammer, hammering which resounded along the line of partition. To Bob De Bevoise, also, belongs the honor of first gratifying the New Yorkers with the taste of garden cultivated strawberries. Previous to the beginning of the present century, this delicious fruit had been known to the New York market, only by the few wild berries which were brought in by women from Tappan and New Jersey. But, about 1800-1802, Robert De Bevoise commenced their systematic cultivation for the market, sending them to market in crockery bowls, at two shillings per pint bowl; and, by refusing to sell any of his plants (people, at that day, were too honest to steal them) secured, and, for about three years, retained the monopoly in the city. He then, as a great favor, gave some of his plants to old Swertcope, the Hessian, who had purchased an adjoining farm, and he, too, in a short time made it a profitable business. The cry of "Hot Corn!" now so frequently heard on summer evenings in the streets of Brooklyn, is associated with the De Bevoise family. Furman says, "at this season of the year, when I was a boy of about seven or eight years of age (1807-8); in the evening, an old colored woman, familiarly known as, De Bevoise's Black Peg, or rather Margaret, or Peggy, the slave of Robert De Bevoise, made her appearance in the main street, then called the Old Ferry road, now Fulton street, crying 'Hot corn, nice hot corn! piping hot!' This was the cry of Peg, for a time; until corn getting a little too tough from the ripening effects of the sun (for then we did not have green corn all the summer through, coming, as it now does, from the West Indies and the south, in the latter part of May and June, and from the north in September, but we had to depend alone upon what was raised in King's county), and the large bell pears having attained nearly their full size, she stewed them whole until they were soft, and then poured molasses over them while they were hot, and carried them through the streets as 'baked pears,' and very palateable they were, as I well recollect; but this cry has gone out of vogue; I have not heard it for years." The selling of hot corn and baked pears were the perquisites of Black Peg. In his later jottings, Furman says, under date of 1836, that he has noticed corn sold for some five or six days past, in the streets of New York and Brooklyn, especially in the evenings, and principally by negroes. He especially mentions a negro "whose stand is about the Fulton market, New York, has quite a rhyme for selling his articles, which I have so frequently heard, as to remember:

> " 'Hot corn! hot corn! I have to sell,
> Come buy my corn, I'll treat you well,
> My corn is good and that I know,
> For on Long Island it did grow." '

and adds that "Long Island is famous for the best green corn in the New York market."

When, in 1816, the village was incorporated, and streets and lots began to be plotted over the old farm lines, Robert De Bevoise took alarm, and expressed a determination to move out of the reach of the modern improvements. Hearing of this, his next neighbor, Mr. Hez. B. Pierrepont, inquired his price, and, $28,000 being named, immediately accepted the offer, much to old Bob's astonishment, who supposed he had placed it at so high a figure that no one would buy. He continued to reside on the place, however, for two years after the sale, and then removed to the neighborhood of the Black Horse tavern, and built a dwelling, still standing, and known as the Abbey, in Fulton avenue.

Soon, however, streets and houses made their distasteful appearance in the vicinity, and he "pulled up stakes" and settled at Bedford. Again the city jostled him, and, in despair, he fled to Jamaica, L. I., where he died some years after. . . .

[On] Red Hook Lane . . . in a retired and beautiful spot, near the line of the present Carroll, between Clinton and Henry streets, was a small cottage occupied, for many years in the early part of the present century, by the well known actress, Mrs. *Charlotte Melmoth*. She was a native of Great Britain, had been duped into a sham marriage, while at boarding school, by a Mr. Pratt (known in the literary and theatrical circles of that day as Courtney Melmoth), and with him went upon the stage, playing in several companies both in England and Ireland. After their separation, she continued to bear his assumed name, and played a season at Covent Garden, in 1774, and at Drury Lane, in 1776. In England, however, she does not seem to have met with the distinguished success which she enjoyed at the Edinburgh and Dublin theatres, where she was an acknowledged favorite for many years. Her first appearance upon the American stage (although she had given readings during the previous winter), was on the 20th of November, 1793, at the old John street theatre, in New York. She was then past the prime of life, but her face was still handsome and her figure commanding; although, unfortunately, so bulky as to restrict her to a very limited range of parts. Still, she came before the New York play goers, of that day, with the deserved reputation of being the best tragic actress, which any—except it were the traveled few—had ever enjoyed the opportunity of seeing. Her character, on this eventful occasion, was that of *Euphrasia*, in Murphy's elegant tragedy of the Grecian Daughter, but her unfortunate dimensions, Dunlap says, "were far beyond the sphere of *embonpoint*, and when Euphrasia invites Dionysius to strike her, instead of her emaciated father, crying, 'Strike here! here's blood enough!' an involuntary laugh broke from the audience, which nearly destroyed not only all illusion, but the hopes of the actress." Her merit, however, carried her through with great applause, and she long remained a favorite. She often played the Grecian Daughter, at this period, but never repeated "Here's blood enough!" By degrees she relinquished the youthful characters, and took up a line of more matronly ones, in which she displayed powers rarely equaled. She was, also, admirable in comedy; Dunlap remarks of her that "she had rather too much of the Mrs. Overdone; and, from a natural deficiency of the organs of speech, could not give utterance to that letter, which her countrymen generally sound double, the letter r." Mrs. Melmoth was much esteemed for her excellent private character, and, compelled at length by advancing age to leave the stage, she purchased this cottage in the quiet and beautiful Red Hook Lane, and took boarders. Stuart the artist, was, for a while, an inmate of her family and his board bills seem to have been paid, in part, at least, with some of his inimitable portraits, which adorned Mrs. Melmoth's parlor, and one of which, that of Judge Egbert Benson, has recently found its appropriate resting place upon the walls of the Long Island Historical Society. At this time, also, or subsequently, Mrs. Melmoth kept a school for young ladies and children at her residence, her pupils mostly belonging to the Cutting, Cornell, Pierrepont, (John) Jackson, and Luquer families; some of these children, now men and women grown, are still living and enjoy very pleasant and respectful memories of their old school-mistress, with whom they boarded during the week, returning to their respective homes on Saturday to spend the sabbath. The nearest neighbor was Mr. Suydam's, where they took turns in going daily for milk wherewith to furnish the suppan and milk, which was a favorite article of food. Mrs. Melmoth's family consisted of herself, her friend Miss Butler, and two aged Dutch negro slaves, a man and a woman. In person, Mrs. Melmoth is recollected as fleshy and heavy, somewhat dignified in manner, but kind in word and deed. She always spoke with emphasis, and, says one of her old scholars, "When she read, she declaimed"— as, indeed, might have been expected from her early vocation. She was esteemed by her patrons as peculiarly successful in advancing her pupils in reading and elocution. After a residence of some ten or twelve years in Brooklyn, she died here, in October, 1823, aged 72 years, much regretted by her friends, and was interred in the burial ground of St. Patrick's Cathedral, New York city.

After her decease, the house was converted into a tavern, which became a favorite resort for the dissipated young men of the town, who there indulged in drinking, eating oysters, raffling for turkeys, geese, etc., their orgies being carried on with a freedom to which the retired character of the spot was peculiarly conducive. In *Furman's Manuscript Notes*, we find the following story, circumstantially told on the authority of an eye witness, Joseph Moser, which connects this house with the haunted house [near by]. . . . One night while a party of young roysterers were assembled at the tavern, having what is best described as a high old time, it was suddenly discovered that the supply of brandy had given out. As a new supply of the desired fluid could only be procured by going down to Brooklyn ferry for it, it immediately became an important question who would go for it; inasmuch as nearly all present shared an apprehension (which, however, they were not willing to own), about passing the haunted house alone at that time of night, it being past eleven o'clock. At length, a young man named Boerum, volunteered his services, boasting that *he* was not afraid of a ghost and (with forced hardihood) declared even his desire to meet it. Mounting his horse, therefore, he started for the ferry, after the brandy. An hour elapsed, and, still another, but he returned not. His boon companions, becoming uneasy in consequence of his prolonged absence, finally resolved to go, all together, and seek him. Mounting, not in hot haste, however, they turned their horses' heads towards the village and on approaching the haunted ground, they found young Boerum's horse standing against the fence not far from the house, and, when they reached the spot itself, their companion was discovered lying senseless in the road, with features horribly distorted. He was taken back to the tavern, where he lingered for two or three days, in a speechless condition, and then died. That he had been no further than the spot where he was found was evident from the fact that the bottle was empty, and that he had not been seen or heard of that night by any one at the ferry, or in the village. . . .

"Denton's Pond" says Mr. Field "was the subject of a curious contract about 1709, between its original proprietors, Abram and Nicholas Brower, and Nicholas Vechte, the builder and occupant of the old 1699, or Cortelyou house. With the strong predilection of his race, for canals and dikes and water communications, old Vechte added the traits of eccentricity and independence. His house stood on a bank a few feet above the Salt meadow, at a distance of a hundred yards from the navigable waters of the creek. To secure access to them, from his kitchen door, Vechte dug a narrow canal to the creek, but the ebb tide often left his boat firmly sunk in the mud, when he wished to reach the city market with the produce of his farm. He, therefore, contracted with the Browers to supply him with water from their [Denton's] pond, and a channel was dug, in furtherance of his scheme, to a water gate, through which his canal was to be flooded. The old Dutch farmer was accustomed to seat himself in his loaded boat, while it was resting in the mud of the empty channel, and hoist his paddle as a signal to his negro servant to raise the gate. The flood soon floated his boat, and bore him out to the creek, exulting with great glee over his neighbors, whose stranded boats must await the next flood. The contract for this privilege, as well as another, by which Vechte leased the right to plant the ponds with oysters, are in possession of Mr. Arthur Benson." . . .

The next house stood on the east side of the [Gowanus] road, between the present Twentieth and Twenty-first streets, and was occupied by *Anthony Hulse*, the owner of a large farm adjacent. Tony Hulse, as he was commonly called, was the terror of the children of the neighborhood, in consequence of his cross and surly disposition, but his wife ruled him with a rod of iron. In such good subjection did she hold him that he was never allowed to come to the table and eat with the family, and, at meal times, poor Tony sat in the chimney corner and made his meal of bread spread with lard instead of butter. On one occasion, it is related, when his neighbors, old Peter Wyckoff and wife, were visiting them and were invited to tea, Peter, as he took his seat at the table, said "Come! Tony," on which Tony looked up with astonishment at his wife Altie, saying "may I? may I?" On another occasion he sharply rebuked a young married lady, a next door neighbor, who called in to see his daughter Marie, by asking "What! are you on the road again spinning street yarn? Why

don't you stay at home and spin and make butter as Rite (Marie)
does?" After his wife's death, the old man revenged himself for
past deprivations, by the exactions and tricks which he practiced upon this same daughter Marie, who kept house for him—
on one occasion, "scaring her half out of her wits," by the sim-
ulated rupture of a blood vessel, which he produced by slyly
chewing poke berries, and spitting out the juice. Tony's house,
now demolished, was a one-story, low-roofed building, without
a kitchen wing, and with a small front porch and stoop, on which,
in fine weather, the old man spent much of his time. A little
beyond his dwelling, on the same side of the road, between
Twenty-third and Twenty-fourth streets, stood, and yet stands,
a one-story house, erected before the Revolution, for his son
John, who left it before this date, in consequence of the old
man's refusal of a sufficient portion of his farm, for the support
of his family. Cornelius Doremus, a very decent man, was afterwards employed by Tony to cultivate the farm, and occupied the
house which had been John's. When Doremus first came, the
old man was so well pleased with him, that he called him, by
way of endearment Cornelisje. After awhile, when the novelty
had worn off, he called him "Corneil"; but, finally, being childish
and hard to please in his old age, he commonly spoke of his
farmer as "Corneil, from the devil."

Crossing a bridge over a small run of water which drained [a]
swamp, you came to the house of George Bennett, on the west
side of the road a little beyond an elevation, known as Blokje's
Bergh. This house was built shortly after the Revolution, and
when about building, George, who had been up the North river
to purchase lumber, on returning in the night, while following a
foot path, a near cut from the turnpike to the Gowanus road near
the head of Freecke's mill pond, was beset by two highwaymen—
but he had the cunning to drop his purse before they laid hold
of him, and thus baffled them in their object. They, however,
left him gagged, in which state he made his way to Tom Bais-
ley's, whom with difficulty he aroused, and, on searching recovered his purse. George Bennett's house is yet standing, on Third
avenue near Twenty-fifth street, having had an additional story

placed under it. He had no children, was grasping, a great boaster, and his yarns were frequently stretched to an interminable length. In going to the rear of his farm, which was over a mile long, he generally followed the cow path on the line between his own and his brother Wynant's farm; and invariably employed himself on such walks, by throwing stones (which were abundant), as he went along, over the fence on to Wynant's side. This aroused the indignation of Wynant's sons, whose land had stones enough of its own, and they in turn, and in self-defense, employed their spare time in throwing them back again; and thus, endlessly went on this fraternal war of the stones. Old Gowanus folks yet remember the oyster war which arose from George's assumed claim to all the oysters in Gowanus cove, in defense of which claim he engaged the services of a stout German as fighting man, who got seriously worsted in a passage at arms with some of the Dutch farmers, as did George also, in the litigation which followed. For many years George Bennett, in addition to farming, carried on the fishing business, keeping a seine and a gang of men with a hut on Bompje's hook, which lay opposite his house. About this time there was a great deal of searching for Capt. Kidd's buried treasure; all the little island of upland in the meadows between Red hook and the main land being dug over. One night a small sloop lay at anchor near Bompje's hook, disappearing before morning; a hole was found dug near the fish hut, with the imprint at its foot of what resembled the bottom of a chest. In addition to this were the footmarks of men lifting it out and the marks of its having been slid or dragged down to the water's edge. George and his men, of course, naturally concluded that valuable treasure had been taken away from the vicinity of their hut, and grievously lamented the fact; but it is probable it was a sham got up to create a sensation and make George uneasy. . . .

The old Van Pelt mansion [was] a low roofed one-story house then occupied by *Henry Van Pelt*; and, also, [there was] a small modern built house occupied by *Tunis Van Pelt*, both located near the bay and Forty-seventh street, the former now gone, the latter yet standing. Henry, or Hank as he was commonly called, was a cripple from his youth, his legs being in such a state that he was under the necessity of walking on his hands and feet like a quadruped, his hands being protected by gloves. He used to have a very low wheeled wagon, easy of access, in which he rode, and was quite a regular attendant of the Dutch church of Brooklyn, of which he was a member. He lived and died a bachelor. The father of these Van Pelts was Wynant, who divided his farm among four sons. They were but indifferent farmers, and made their living chiefly by fishing. In Wynant's days it was customary for old men to wear skull-crowned beaver hats, with a very broad brim, and so well made that a hat would last its wearer for years. It is said that, on one occasion, when the family were on rather short allowance, the old man, who always dined as was customary in that day, with his hat on, took it off as usual when about to say grace, and held it before his face, and when he had finished—for the grace was a long one—he was astonished and naturally very indignant to find that his stalwart sons had cleared the table of all the eatables.

Published by Subscription, 1867

And now . . .

BROOKLYN IS MY NEIGHBORHOOD

by CARSON MCCULLERS

Brooklyn, in a dignified way, is a fantastic place. The street where I live has a quietness and sense of permanence that seem to belong to the nineteenth century. The street is very short. At one end, there are comfortable old houses, with gracious façades and pleasant back-yards in the rear. Down on the next block, the street becomes more heterogeneous, for there is a fire station; a convent; and a small candy factory. The street is bordered with maple-trees, and in the autumn the children rake up the leaves and make bonfires in the gutter.

It is strange in New York to find yourself living in a real neighborhood. I buy my coal from the man who lives next-door. And I am very curious about the old lady living on my right. She has a mania for picking up stray, starving dogs. Besides a dozen of these dogs, she keeps a little green, shrewd monkey as her pet and chief companion. She is said to be very rich and very stingy. The druggist on the corner has told me she was once in jail for smashing the windows of a saloon in a temperance riot.

"The square of the hypotenuse of a right triangle is equal to ——"

On coming into the corner drug store in the evening, you are apt to hear a desperate voice repeating some such maxim. Mr. Parker, the druggist, sits behind the counter after supper, struggling with his daughter's homework—she can't seem to get on well in school. Mr. Parker has owned his store for thirty years. He has a pale face, with watery grey eyes and a silky little yellow mustache that he wets and combs out frequently. He is rather like a cat. And when I weigh myself, he sidles up quietly beside me and peers over my shoulders as I adjust the scale. When the weights are balanced, he always gives me a quick little glance, but he has never made any comment, nor indicated in any way whether he thought I weighed too little or too much.

On every other subject, Mr. Parker is very talkative. He has always lived in Brooklyn, and his mind is a rag-bag for odd scraps of information. For instance, in our neighborhood there is a narrow alley called Love Lane. "The alley comes by its name," he told me, "because more than a century ago two bachelors by the name of DeBevoise lived in the corner house with their niece, a girl of such beauty that her suitors mooned in the alley half the night, writing poetry on the fence." These same old uncles, Mr. Parker added, cultivated the first strawberries sold in New York in their back garden. It is pleasant to think of this old household—the parlour with the coloured glass windows glowing in the candlelight, the two old gentlemen brooding quietly over a game of chess, and the young niece, demure on a footstool, eating strawberries and cream.

"The square of the hypotenuse——" As you go out of the

drug store, Mr. Parker's voice will carry on where he had left off, and his daughter will sit there, sadly popping her chewing-gum.

Comparing the Brooklyn that I know with Manhattan is like comparing a comfortable and complacent duenna to her more brilliant and neurotic sister. Things move more slowly out here (the street-cars still rattle leisurely down most of the streets), and there is a feeling for tradition.

The history of Brooklyn is not so exciting as it is respectable. In the middle of the past century, many of the liberal intellectuals lived here, and Brooklyn was a hot-bed of abolitionist activity. Walt Whitman worked on the *Brooklyn Daily Eagle* until his anti-slavery editorials cost him his job. Henry Ward Beecher used to preach at the old Plymouth Church. Talleyrand lived here on Fulton Street during his exile in America, and he used to walk primly every day beneath the elm-trees. Whittier stayed frequently at the old Hooper home.

The first native of Brooklyn I got to know when first I came out here was the electrician who did some work at my house. He is a lively young Italian with a warm, quick face and a pleasant way of whistling operatic arias while on the job. On the third day he was working for me, he brought in a bottle of bright home-made wines, as his first child, a boy, had been born the night before. The wine was sour and clean to the tongue, and when we had drunk some of it the electrician invited me to a little supper to be held a week later at his house on the other side of Brooklyn, near Sheepshead Bay. The party was a fine occasion. The old grandfather who had come over from Italy sixty years ago was there. At night, the old man fishes for eels out in the Bay, and when the weather is fine he spends most of the day lying in a cart in the back-yard, out in the sun. He had the face of a charming old satyr, and he held the new baby with the casualness of one who has walked the floor with many babies in his day.

"He is very ugly, this little one," he kept saying. "But it is clear that he will be smart. Smart and very ugly."

The food at the party was rich, wholesome Italian fare—

provalone, cheese, salami, pastries, and more of the red wine. A stream of kinsmen and neighbours kept coming in and out of the house all evening. This family had lived in the same house near the Bay for three generations, and the grandfather had not been out of Brooklyn for years.

Here in Brooklyn there is always the feeling of the sea. On the streets near the water-front, the air has a fresh, coarse smell, and there are many seagulls. One of the most gaudy streets I know stretches between Brooklyn Bridge and the Navy Yard. At three o'clock in the morning, when the rest of the city is silent and dark, you can come suddenly on a little area as vivacious as a country fair. It is Sands Street, the place where sailors spend their evenings when they come here to port. At any hour of the night some excitement is going on in Sands Street. The sunburned sailors swagger up and down the sidewalks with their girls. The bars are crowded, and there are dancing, music, and straight liquor at cheap prices.

These Sands Street bars have their own curious traditions also. Some of the women you find there are vivid old dowagers of the street who have such names as The Duchess or Submarine Mary. Every tooth in Submarine Mary's head is made of solid gold—and her smile is rich-looking and satisfied. She and the rest of these old habitués are greatly respected. They have a stable list of sailor pals and are known from Buenos Aires to Zanzibar. They are conscious of their fame and don't bother to dance or flirt like the younger girls, but sit comfortably in the centre of the room with their knitting, keeping a sharp eye on all that goes on. In one bar, there is a little hunchback who struts in proudly every evening, and is petted by every one, given free drinks, and treated as a sort of mascot by the proprietor. There is a saying among sailors that when they die they want to go to Sands Street.

Cutting through the business and financial centre of Brooklyn is Fulton Street. Here are to be found dozens of junk and antique shops that are exciting to people who like old and fabulous things. I came to be quite at home in these places, as I bought most of my furniture there. If you know what you are about, there are good bargains to be found—old carved sideboards, elegant pier-glasses, beautiful Lazy Susans, and other odd pieces can be bought at half the price you would pay anywhere else. These shops have a musty, poky atmosphere, and the people who own them are an incredible crew.

The woman from whom I got most of my things is called Miss Kate. She is lean, dark, and haggard, and she suffers much from cold. When you go into the junk-shop, you will most likely find her hovering over a little coal stove in the back room. She sleeps every night wrapped in a Persian rug and lying on a green velvet Victorian couch. She has one of the handsomest and dirtiest faces I can remember.

Across the street from Miss Kate, there is a competitor with whom she often quarrels violently over prices—but still she always refers to him as an "adela Menchen," and once when he was to be evicted for failure to pay the rent she put up the cash for him.

"Miss Kate is a good woman," this competitor said to me. "But she dislikes washing herself. So she only bathes once a year, when it is summer. I expect she's just about the dirtiest woman in Brooklyn." His voice as he said this was not at all malicious; rather, there was in it a quality of wondering pride. That is one of the things I love best around Brooklyn. Every one is not expected to be exactly like every one else.

Reprinted from March 1, 1941, Vogue, *copyright 1941, Condé Nast Publications Inc.*

THE BROOKLYN MAN

An Editorial in the New York Tribune, January 1, 1892

We have long held that Brooklyn men display a really phenomenal capacity for getting into trouble. We cannot account for it, either. Brooklyn men, as we see them about in town in the daytime, seem peaceable and quiet. When they get off of this end of the Bridge in the morning there may be a slightfuly confused air about them, but this is apt to be seen in any one when he arrives in a great city like New-York. The Brooklyn man does not have that hunted look seen on the face of the dweller in the suburban villages which comes from the ever-gnawing fear that he is going to miss his train, for the Bridge stands always ready for the Brooklyn man's retreat at any moment. But when he mounts the Bridge at half-past 5 o'clock in the afternoon to return home, there is an air of resolution, with perhaps a touch of gaminess, about him which convinces us that the Brooklyn man must be an entirely different sort of a person at night in Brooklyn. Whether this comes from the night or from being in Brooklyn, we cannot say, since it is never possible to catch a Brooklyn man in town after 7 p.m. Any how, we believe that at home after sundown the Brooklyn man is a sly dog.

The latest instance in which a Brooklyn man has got into trouble involves one Ludwig Thoms and a certain William Eggers. Mr. Eggers charges Mr. Thoms with attempting to draw a pistol on him. Thoms, it appears, is a teacher in some sort of a denominational school, and Eggers is a trustee of the school. The other day Eggers called upon Thoms and told him that his services as teacher had become a superfluity. At this Thoms, so Eggers says, "placed his hand on his pistol pocket." Mr. Egger conceived his life to be in danger and ran from the house. Subsequently he got out a warrant for the arrest of Thoms. The officer found him seated at the piano vigorously singing "Home, Sweet Home" in German. He was just making some remarks down in his throat in regard to his lowly thatched cottage when the officer placed him under arrest and took him to the Lee Avenue Police Court. Here Thoms indignantly explained that in making the move which the frightened Eggers interpreted as warlike he had simply been reaching for his handkerchief.

This suggests that Brooklyn should profit by the experience of Arkansas. For many years the Arkansas gentleman habitually carried his tobacco in his pistol pocket. The habit greatly raised the State rate of mortality, as frequently when a man reached for his tobacco the personal friend with whom he was conversing would misinterpret the move and shoot him down. After a while it became customary in Arkansas before reaching for tobacco to wave the hand slightly and remark, "terbacker!" This did very well, but the form was sometimes forgotten, especially in the heat of debate in the Legislature, which finally impelled this body, after losing several good speakers, to pass a law requiring all persons to carry their chewing tobacco in their left-hand vest-pocket. Brooklyn, we say, must borrow from Arkansas. Brooklyn men must, when they don't "mean business," remark "handkerchief!" in an explanatory tone. A better plan yet would probably be to have a city ordinance compelling all men to carry their handkerchiefs elsewhere. The position of the Brooklyn handkerchief must not menace the safety of the public. It is altogether likely that, in the case before us, had Eggers been armed he would have replied to the supposedly hostile move of Thoms. It is no credit to Brooklyn that she allows such chances for causing misunderstandings to exist. We do not apprehend any trouble from Brooklyn men in New-York, as we believe they never bring their pistols across the Bridge, but we do not want to hear of the Brooklyn men having difficulty, even at home.

Always, it seems, the Brooklyn man has taken his religion, politics, and systems of education as matters worth arguing about. For instance, back in the first decade of the eighteenth century, the Dutch had quite a fight about pastors, and there was a split that lasted until after the Revolution, even determining the Whig and Tory factions in that conflict.

This embarrassed note was printed in Furman's Antiquities of Long Island and is from a period before the Revolution:

To the Secretary at New York
Sir,—I am in expectation of a complaint coming to his Excellency by Coll. Beeckman against me, and that his Excellency may be rightly informed of the matter, my humble request to you is, that if such a thing happen, be pleased to give his Excellency an account thereof, which is as follows: A Ffriday night last, the Justices of the County and I came from his Excellency's; Coll. Beeckman happened to come over in the fferry

boat along with us, and as we came over the fferry, Coll. Beeckman and we went into the fferry house to drink a glass of wine, and being soe in company, there happened a dispute between Coll. Beeckman and myself, about his particular order that he lately made to Mr. Ffreeman, when he was President of the Councill, without the consent of the Councill; Coll. Beeckman stood to affirm there, before most of the Justices of Kings County, that said order, that he made then to Mr. Ffreeman as President only, was still in fforce, and that Mr. Ffreeman should preach at Broockland next Sunday according to that order; whereupon I said it was not in fforce, but void and of noe effect, and he had not in this County, any more power now than I have, being equall in commission with him in the general commission of the peace and one of the quorum as well as he; upon which he gave me affronting words, giving me the lie and calling me pittifull fellow, dog, rogue, rascall, &c. which caused me, being overcome with passion, to tell him that I had a good mind to knock him off his horse, we being both at that time getting upon our horses to goe home, but that I would not goe, I would fight him at any time with a sword. I could wish that these last words had bin kept in, and I am troubled that I was soe overcome with passion and inflamed with wine. The works of these Dutch ministers is the occasion of all our quarrells. And this is the truth of the matter, there was no blows offered, nor noe more done. Mr. Ffreeman has preached at Broockland yesterday accordingly, and the church doore was broke open, by whom it is not yet knowne. Soe I beg your pardon ffor this trouble, crave your favour in this matter, and shall always remaine.

Sir, your ffaithful and humble servant,

H. Ffilkin.

From Antiquities of Long Island *by Gabriel Furman, T. W. Booten,* 1874.

Life in Brooklyn

Many people have written about Brooklyn, some of them not quite knowing what to make of it. Any selections of "life in Brooklyn" are actually "life in certain parts of Brooklyn." It is a town that in the past was often called a place of housewives and children, and it is an area of hundreds of communities, thousands of ideas, thousands of attitudes.

from . . .

THE CITY OF BROOKLYN

by JULIAN RALPH

We read about the European capitals, treated with the skill of artists, clothed with the glamour of tradition, and colored by the fancy that grows richer with the distance of its subject. But what has London to show like that daily congestion at the Brooklyn bridge? What crowds in Paris are to be measured with this? What European city has even one of the many strange conditions that produce this scene? Here come the elevated railways that carry three-quarters of a million souls a day, the surface vehicles of the million and six hundred thousand people of Manhattan, the streets leading from the densest population in America, all meeting in one little square, all pouring out people, and all the people streaming into a great trumpet-like mouth of iron in order to be shot across a hanging cobweb of metal threads into a city that has not its mate or counterpart on earth—Brooklyn! It is like a city in some things. It is a vast aggregation of homes and streets and shops, with a government of its own. Yet many things it has not got—things with which many a little town could put it to the blush. And every other city earns its own way, while Brooklyn works for New York, and is paid off like a shop-girl on Saturday nights.

"Stop shoving so!" "Look out who you're pushing!" "Don't try to run over me, I say." These are notes from the chorus of the solid mass of persons that crowd up the stairs to the bridge cars. On the upper platform the trains sweep away regiments at a time. Burly bridge policemen are there, urging every one forward, and at times—until the newspapers cry out, periodically— putting their hands on their betters and wedging them into the cars, through three doors at once, as revolvers are charged. There are fourteen other ways to Brooklyn, all by ferry-boats, and at the time of which I write all these are crowded. They are not mobbed, like the bridge, to be sure, but they are packed with people so that you can only see the rims of the decks as you see the edge of a grocer's measure that has been filled with pease. At first the big bridge hurt the business of the ferry companies, but after a while it built up a surplus and paid them back, just as our elevated roads in time increased the traffic of the horse-cars. In a word, then, everything that is going to Brooklyn at nightfall is crowded. That is even true of the drays which start empty for the bridge that carries forty-one millions of passengers in a year, and for the ferries, one company of which collects thirty-six millions of fares annually.

What is Brooklyn, to which all these persons go? It would be a quarter of New York, like the east side or Harlem, if it were not for the East River, and the political division of the soil into two counties. It is the home of the married middle people of New York, Manhattan Island being the seat of the very rich, the very poor, and the unmarried. It has been called the sleeping-room of the metropolis. It is far more and far better than that. It will become a proud part of the Greater New York of the time to come. And that will be before the realization of the rest of the boast of the fatalists, that "whatever is is."

Nine hundred thousand persons call Brooklyn "home," though, as a rule, they write New York opposite their names on the hotel registers when they travel. All the people of the Greater New York do that. The Brooklyn people inhabit a great fan-shaped city whose handle is out by Jamaica, Long Island, while the sticks of the fan reach to the edge of New York Harbor and the East River from near the Narrows to Newtown Creek on the way to the Sound. In this great area are several tenement districts and three considerable shopping centres, but, in the main, Brooklyn is made up of hundreds of miles of avenues and streets lined with little dwellings. These are the homes of men who work in New York, and earn between $1500 and $3000 a year. Speaking generally, these men are far more interested in New York than in Brooklyn. They do not know in which ward of Brooklyn they live, they cannot name the sheriff or their members of Assembly, and in politics the only local episodes that stir them are the contests for the mayoralty.

As New York is recruited from the country, so is Brooklyn. Many a countryman who comes to New York and prospers never masters the metropolis, or feels at ease or safe in it. Sooner or later such ones move to Brooklyn, where there is elbow-room and a hush at night, and where they see trees and can have growing flowers. Those who are married when they come, and the great self-respecting majority of the poor who marry afterward, are certain to settle in Brooklyn, or, in far fewer numbers, in the other suburban towns. They must choose between cozy homes and crowded tenements. There lies the secret of the suburb, whose growth is only matched by a few cities, which are all in the West. It is customary to say that we New-Yorkers move to Brooklyn, or settle there, to save money. That is true, but comfort and self-respect are in the same dish of the scale with the saving for all whose incomes are small. It is possible for a clerk to own a house in Brooklyn; it is easier for a clerk to fly than to own one in New York. But the people go to Brooklyn to rent houses, not to buy them. They pay the landlords one-fifth of their incomes, or $25 to $50 a month, and that is about half what they would pay to live relatively well in New York— in tenements and flats, mind you, whereas they have houses across the river. Once in Brooklyn, in the evening, these men stay there. They do not go to New York for their dissipation. They do not maintain great social clubs. Few patronize the Brooklyn theatres. The fun these men have is what their wives provide for them.

The women are very different. Just as the few old rich families on the Heights (in Brooklyn) used to despise New York as a "shoddy" town and a Babel, so the great mass of wives in the miles of dwellings look down upon the metropolis. It must clothe and feed them, but it may not have their love. They regard it as a cold and monstrous place, where people live for years next door to other people without getting acquainted, where the un-American rich have set up social boundaries, where nice children may not play out-of-doors without maids to watch them, where the morals of growing boys and girls are in danger, and where young wives sit cooped up in barracklike tenements, without society—unless their country cousins come to town to see them. On the other hand, these women are intensely interested in Brooklyn. Their husbands buy the *Eagle*, *Times*, *Standard-Union*, or *Citizen* (Brooklyn newspapers), and find them Greek, but their wives digest their paragraphs with gusto. It is a woman's town. By day there are no men in those endless miles of dwellings. They have gone to New York to make six trips in as many days, and to bring back millions of money in pay envelopes on the sixth day. The women have the city to themselves, and rule over the children, maids, nurses, shade trees,

flowers, and pretty door-yards. Thus encouraged, each studies
her own neighborhood. Each remembers how the others called
on her when she moved to Brooklyn, and each calls on those
who come after her.

The wives cut a great figure there—a lovely figure, of course—
and one that reveals wholesome and normal conditions. Everything tends to widen their freedom—the quiet city, the saving in
rents, the absence of the men, and the fatigue or the desire for
entertainment, either or both, of the men at night. Therefore
the women have had the opportunity to build up a very pretty
rivalry for self-improvement. They get the latest books from the
libraries. They go to cooking-school in order to shine at dinners
of their own preparing. They flock to dancing-school that they
may triumph at their own parties. They prepare papers to read
in other houses so that the others may read papers at theirs.
There is no whim of feminine fashion that is set spinning in
New York but whirls when it gets over to Brooklyn—always provided that it does not cost too much or require going to the
theatre. The women are the very backbone of the churches, in
which they sing and hold fairs, and by means of which they
figure in circles that are proud of them. Is it any wonder that
they cannot tolerate New York, where the shopkeepers won't
send a purchase around the corner without pay in advance,
where the pews are private property in the best churches, and
where a lady feels herself of no account in the hurly-burly? In
Brooklyn the police understand who owns the town, and the
car-drivers pull up in the middle of a block. Besides, if my lady
has no carriage, she observes that her neighbors also use the
horse-cars.

I have said that the women provide dissipation for their husbands at night. That is a curious feature of Brooklyn life. It has
no Ward McAllister, no Four Hundred—nothing that those
names imply. It is true that there used to be a smart set on the
Heights, and there are others in Clinton Avenue, in New York
and Brooklyn avenues, and on the Park Slope, but then no one
has ever decided that one is any better than another. Instead
of one crowning triumph of caste, society there is divided into

church coteries as a basis, and out of these grow many sorts of little circles, each combination being reproduced over and over again, beyond calculation, in the same district, and in the many districts which in Brooklyn are quite as distinct as if they were separate cities. The lesser circles of which I speak are bowling clubs, whist clubs, euchre clubs, poker clubs, literary guilds, musical coteries, amateur dramatic companies, and dancing classes. Poker is played for small stakes in many circles in Brooklyn—solely, I trust, because it has charms to keep the men at home; but bowling is a passion with the Brooklyn folk. Investigate what set you will, and it is almost sure to include a bowling club in its ramifications and adjuncts. A page of the Brooklyn *Eagle* almanac is devoted to the bowling matches of seventy clubs, but those are the clubs of skilful, earnest players, and do not form a drop in the bucket of the clubs formed by neighborhood coteries all over the town. . . .

Prospect Park, is one of those great triumphs of civic enterprise whose class includes Central, Forest, Fairmount, and Druid Hill parks, in four of our older cities. Prospect Park is not one of the largest of these. It comprises only 516 acres, but every rod of it is the subject of taste and care, and its drives, ponds, playgrounds, and various other ornaments are all of the finest. The people have been adding to its attractions in notable ways quite recently. At its entrance they have erected a great soldiers' and sailors' monument that has the form of a memorial arch of granite, the design of Mr. John H. Duncan, of New York. It is of great size and massive appearance, but the piers are hollow, and stairs within them lead to a hall at the top, where it is proposed to maintain a museum of war relics. Another new and interesting ornament in the Park is the statue of James S. T. Stranahan, by Frederick MacMonnies, the sculptor and artist, whom Brooklyn claims as one of her sons. This is a bronze statue of a man who is yet living among those who have paid this high and singular compliment to him as the creator of their park and boulevard system. He also earned the public gratitude for lending the force of his earnestness and influence to quicken the building of the bridge across to the metropolis. He is aged now, though sound in limb and mind, and is closing a life that shines with many and striking virtues. He has been the chief constructive character of the city, an apostle of annexation, a member of the Greater New York commission, was for many years the president of the Park Board, and was once a member of Congress. Active as is his record, his single aim seems ever to have been to enrich the public, and self-interest never marred his work or weakened the love of his neighbors. Prospect Park has other statues, of Lincoln, J. Howard Payne, Moore, and Washington Irving. But perhaps the sculptured figure which attracts the most attention from visitors is that of Henry Ward Beecher, which rises above the flagging in front of the City Hall. Brooklyn has six others parks and three noble boulevards. These parks are all small, but one of them is, in my opinion, the most beautiful of all the small parks of the United States; at least, it ranks next to Battery Park, whose beauty is solely that of its situation at the point of Manhattan Island. This beautiful Brooklyn pleasure-place is Washington Park, best known by its old name of Fort Greene. It contains only thirty acres, but they are high upon the Hill, and overlook the first and fourth cities of America, the first of our harbors, the local navy-yard, and many other notable sights. By day the view is majestic, by night, it is gorgeous. . . .

The city has no hotels worthy of its size, and needs none. It has not one morning newspaper. It has no vicious section or houses of evil savor, no gambling-dens, no speculative exchanges. New York supplies all these things for it. But it has several evening newspapers, of which the leading ones are the *Eagle* (Democratic) and the *Times* (Republican), the last-named journal being published in the Eastern (or Williamsburg) District. The *Eagle* is admired by journalists all over the country as the best example of a purely local newspaper. It publishes all the news of the world; but its first aim is to record the affairs of Brooklyn, and this it does with remarkable thoroughness, and with such fairness that even in political contests it publishes full reports upon both sides. It is clean and dignified, and has prospered to the point of owning a model building which is one of the "sights" of the town. The *Times* is such another journal, deserving of praise for the same characteristics.

I have said that the men of Brooklyn do not support great social clubs. I was referring to the average and typical citizen who works in New York, and whose kind inhabit the long reaches of quiet and shady streets. The other class, whose professional and mercantile careers keep them in Brooklyn, as well as the well-to-do men of all sorts who possess the leisure, are supporting several clubs, such as the Brooklyn and the Hamilton, in old Brooklyn; the Lincoln, Oxford, and Union League, on the Hill; the Montauk, of the Park Slope; the Hanover, in the Eastern District; the Algonquin, of South Brooklyn; and the Crescent, an organization of a large number of young men with country quarters and a fondness for out-of-door life. The old club of the old residents is the Brooklyn, and the Hamilton is of the same class, but is more youthful and alert. There are twenty-five lesser clubs which I have not mentioned, but of the above it may be said that all are admirable and important, though not one is decidedly prosperous in the degree which marks the prosperity of clubs in the more masculine great cities. A peculiarity of some of these clubs—which they borrow from the character of the city—is the manner in which the members refer to their wives, and, in the old Brooklyn Club, to their personal servants, with the knowledge that these personages are known to the other members. The ladies share the club life to a slight extent, four of the leading clubs having restaurants and rooms for ladies, after a well-established fashion which obtains in New Orleans and Chicago, and which has crowded the toe of one boot into New York club life as I write. "Interest your wife, and she will let you join," is the principle upon which this evolution is working.

Brooklyn has always had a sharp taste for music, and feasts itself upon a varied programme of good quality during every winter. The Brooklyn Philharmonic is an organization of citizens, but not of musicians, which for many years has employed one orchestra or another to give concerts over there. For many years Theodore Thomas played for it; but since his orchestra could no longer be had, the plan of the Philharmonic has slightly changed, and in inducing the Boston Symphony Orchestra to play in Brooklyn, it gives only its moral support to the venture. The more active musical society now is the Seidl Society. One purpose of this society is to bring Anton Seidl and his orchestra over there for a course of concerts, but the society is unselfishly working to cultivate the musical taste of the people beyond its clientèle and their friends. The Brooklyn Choral Society of three hundred voices gives winter concerts after the manner of the Handel-Haydn Society of Boston, the famous oratorios being excellently rendered by them. The Apollo Club, of three or four score voices, forming a male chorus, and led by Mr. Dudley Buck as conductor, gives several concerts a year before fine assemblages that fill the Academy of Music. The Amphion Society, in the Eastern District, is such another organization. The Euterpe Society, under the direction of C. Mortimer Wiske, is a society of musicians maintaining an orchestra of gentlemen and ladies, some of whom are professionals. A male chorus is also formed of this membership, and the concerts of the society are admirable. The conductor, Mr. Wiske, is also the director of the work of the Choral Society. Brooklyn has two dozen other musical clubs. The Arion Society and the Saengerbund are leading German organizations, of which there are many. Their concerts and masquerade balls are great events, in the estimation of the large German element in the city. The Germania is their social club.

Brooklyn is famous for its amateur dramatic and operatic clubs, of which it has more than twenty. Some of these are composed of cultivated persons, some have seen members win distinction on the stage, and all contribute greatly to the winter pleasures of the town. Strangely enough, where this is true the theatres are second-rate at the best, and the legitimate drama is but slightly successful. Lawrence Barrett liked Brooklyn, and used to say that he meant to build up a clientèle there. In time he had a following, but not a great one. The city is too close to New York, and its play-goers prefer the fresher plays and greater variety of the metropolitan stage. In Brooklyn the preparation of the average citizen for a night at the theatre is the donning of a hat and overcoat or a bonnet and wrap. There is no display of fashion or of beauty much adorned. Musical farces and opéras comiques draw best there. The place has half a dozen theatres, the finest being the Academy of Music, and the Amphion Academy in the Eastern District; but the greatest success there has been that of a firm who built a variety theatre upon the site of that old forgotten market-house to which the bodies of the dead were taken from the ruins of the ill-fated Brooklyn Theatre. . . .

In no city that I have yet studied is there such an enthusiasm for education as in Brooklyn. From that, again, one sees how thoroughly it is a city of homes, and how closely allied to the hearth-stone are all the interests which prosper, while all that languish are certain to be those which are apart from or antagonistic to home influences. Whatever a mother would concern herself about is what thrives in Brooklyn, and everything else is poor or despairing. The schools are wonderful: the effort toward the polish of pretty and refining accomplishments is epidemic; the churches have made the town famous; the shopping stores are second only to those of New York's; the parks are all that they should be. But the clubs and theatres are second rate; the bar-rooms are mere kennels; the hotels and restaurants are few and poor, and the wholly vicious resorts are none at all. Brooklyn is the only female among our cities—the sister city to New York. Like a good woman, she offers little to the chance visitor, impelled to come by idle curiosity, and nothing to the roué. But if you live in her house, as one of her family, you are well off indeed. . . .

Harper's New Monthly Magazine, *April, 1893*

It is somewhat indicative of the character of Brooklyn that its society dates in the calculations of most historians of the subject from an event in February and March 1864 called the Sanitary Fair. All of the wealthy and old families—not necessarily inclusive groups—of Brooklyn and Long Island supported the festival, which raised some $300,000 to aid the sick and wounded of the Northern armies. The Fair would correspond to a Red Cross drive of the present day, and the name derived from the money's being turned over to the United States Sanitary Commission.

Even after that, Brooklyn society remained on the sedate side. We won't describe it here, because the pieces we are including are intended to do that. We will quote, though, from a History of the City of Brooklyn put out by the Eagle in 1893:

from . . .

HISTORY OF THE CITY OF BROOKLYN

Regarding the modes of entering any one of the charmed circles [of Brooklyn society], there have been three keys to unlock the ivory gates: church, charity, and grandfather. Wealth has never played much of a part, nor has it been of the slightest value to the young man or the debutante. Some of the most conspicuous leaders have been men of ridiculously small income; some of the most popular "rosebuds" have known what it was to be poor. But among the descendants of the old-time merchant princes on the Heights, family and caste have been everything. It was a great matter to be a genuine old Brooklynite and for years it practically settled the question of admission to the inner circle. Outsiders, no matter who they might be, were regarded askance. Even now the portals of the Heights mansions open with care as to who is to be be admitted. Of the men who socially have rule from the river to Court and Fulton streets today there is but one who is not a Brooklynite of many years residence. The exception made in his favor is so remarkable that it only goes to prove the rule. He is a southerner of irreproachable family and has won his position here through his unfailing kindness, his perfect manhood, and his executive ability. In every other section of the town the evolution of society has been along very different lines. The church first brought people together. The Sunday-school class began it, the church sociable in private houses continued it and the step from this to little dances of an independent order was very slight. Even today the surest way for a young man to gain his *entrée* into social life is to join the young people's association of some energetic church congregation. In characteristics, little if any difference is to be noticed between the members of the various sets. One further trait of Brooklyn social life, one particular characteristic, is to be specially commented upon—the youth of its leaders. In this regard Brooklyn resembles a big, unwieldy country town. As a rule, men and women marry early in life on this side of the East river. They settle down to housekeeping and give the city the reputation of being a town of homes. It is seldom after marriage that they drop back into the old social routine. In New York, in Boston, in Philadelphia, the brides frequently lead the "rose-buds" in point of attraction; but in Brooklyn the most charming young married woman feels that she has played her social part. She gives a tea or two, is seen occasionally at a dance, perhaps, but on most occasions leaves the field to the younger girls.

From time to time some person or other in Brooklyn has tried to take its society dead seriously. Among the most recent has been Guy Pierrepont, who publishes the Brooklyn Blue Book, *and before the war printed something called Guy Pierrepont's Weekly Society Bulletin. We are running a talk-of-the-town story the New Yorker had about Pierrepont, and also some selections from his columns of a few years ago.*

We recently paid a neighborly interborough call on another remarkable publication, the *Brooklyn Blue Book*, and there talked to Mr. Guy Pierrepont, also known as the Blue Blood Boswell of Brooklyn Heights and, occasionally, as Mr. James Stuart Gillespie, Jr., his real name. Mr. Pierrepont's office is on Montague Street, on the premises of Osborn & West, Hats

& Gowns, just this side of the sewing room. We had to stare straight ahead as we approached his desk to avoid the gaze of a Brooklyn miss, in disarray, who was being pinned up by an elderly lady in an open-fronted fitting nook abeam of our course. Mr. Pierrepont was attired in a light blue suit, blue-and-red tie, and bright red cotton socks ringed with green. After we had introduced ourself, he handed us a copy of the *Brooklyn Blue Book*, a slim volume (blue), and informed us that he has been the publisher of it since 1940. "The *Brooklyn Blue Book*, of course, goes back to 1858," he said, "and is much older than the *Social Register*. [This statement would seem to contain the elements of a controversy. According to the Long Island Historical Society, the *B.B.B.* was started in 1895, nine years after the birth of the *New York Social Register*.] It had to be discontinued in 1929," Mr. Pierrepont said. "Too many names." He lifted his eyebrows, shrugged his shoulders delicately, and pointed to a thick blue volume on his desk. "Twenty thousand families," he said. "*Anyone* could get in. My book last year listed fourteen hundred and six families. Not one gets in unless it passes a board. I selected the board myself. No one knows who they are except me. They don't even know each other. All very socially prominent." Pierrepont's families must be nominated by two people already in the *Blue Book*, then approved by a majority of his board, whose members are canvassed by mail. "As you can imagine, there's quite a dither when my notices go out concerning who's selected," he said.

Mr. Gillespie was born in Noroton, Connecticut; attended Duke University; and in 1938 and 1939 worked for the late Maury Paul. He then repaired to Brooklyn, which he felt was being neglected socially; took his present name, that of an old Brooklyn family to which the late J. Pierpont Morgan was related; and began to issue a two-cent potpourri of gossip and hints on etiquette called *Guy Pierrepont's Weekly Society Bulletin*, a periodical that is no longer published. Brooklyn's society, he told us, is unlike Manhattan's in that it's homey. "People here visit each other. Just because you have money doesn't guarantee your being accepted *here*." We hung our head in regional shame, and Mr. Pierrepont said that social acceptability in Brooklyn is predicated largely on membership in Miss Hepburn's Assemblies and Mrs. Fields' Literary Club. He obtained his original list chiefly from these groups and his secret arbiters. "You might be interested to know that Borough President Cashmore is not listed," he said, laughing lightly.

The lady who had been fitting the Osborn & West customer joined us and was introduced as Miss Anna Juliette Osborn. "We certainly missed the *Blue Book* in those years when it wasn't published," she said in a high, wandering voice, after removing some pins from her mouth. "Not that it was any good anyway. Still, I don't know how we ever lived without it." Mr. Pierrepont told us that Miss Osborn got the *Blue Book* out from 1942 until he was released from the Navy last year. She bowed and returned to her fitting nook. "The *Brooklyn Blue Book* differs in many ways from the *Social Register*," its publisher went on. "It costs three dollars less, and we list *all* the children—not just misses from twelve to seventeen and misters from fourteen to twenty. We also list engagements, and I plan to include an article on the Brooklyn War Memorial in the next edition." "How do you like your black lace waist, Mrs. Weston?" we heard Miss Osborn say in the next room. "Oh, Miss Osborn," Mr. Pierrepont called, name some famous Brooklyn people." Miss Osborn named the late Justice Harlan Stone, Charles Evans Hughes, Edward Bok, and Henry Ward Beecher, and we jotted these names down trustingly. "I don't know if they were ever listed, of course," she said, through pins. Mr. Pierrepont looked along his eyelashes in our direction. "The first Mrs. John Jacob Astor was a Brooklyn girl," he said. "So is the wife of John Jacob Astor the Third. You may be interested to know that Mayor O'Dwyer is not listed."

Pierrepont used to do considerable complaining about the little slights one is likely to receive in a rather onerous business. We will explain that we are printing Mr. Pierrepont as we read him, and are not placing (sic)'s all through it.

from . . .

GUY PIERREPONT'S WEEKLY SOCIETY
BULLETIN, APRIL 23, 1942

WHEN ALL IS SAID AND done, it can honestly be said that
the only people who receive unfavorable notices in this column
are the ones who deserve it. Maybe there are one or two who
passibly don't agree with that statement but I'm writing for the
people who do, for the ones who enjoy what I have to say and
who have a broadminded sense of humor. However, my reac-
tions to certain things are probably the same as yours would be
if the incidents happend to you.

For instance, the George C. Tilyou Jr's, were sent an information blank to be filled out for the forthcoming Blue Book of
Brooklyn. In so much as they didn't bother to answer it, a personal telephone call was made in order to accertain whether or
not they had received it because it has turned out in so many
cases that the mails have been sent to the wrong addresses. Well,
Mr. Tilyou answered the phone and demanded to know what
the Blue Book was, if you please (as if anyone didn't already
KNOW) and that he didn't want to have his name in it.

But, and this is the fifty dollar question, since when have the
George C. Tilyou's Jr. become so IMPORTANT socially that they
can efford to tell the Blue Book committee what to do? As a
matter of cold, hard fact the Tilyou's arn't socially prominent
in Brooklyn and never have been. I have yet to see any member
of the family at any of the events of the season and I fail to
see this attitude, especially in view of the fact that the Tilyou
family made their fortune right here at Coney Island, Brooklyn,
U.S.A. and should be interested in Brooklyn if for no other
reason.

The next time the Tilyou's are invited to be included in the
Blue Book they probably won't be quite so hasty . . . but that
will be a long, long time. In the meantime the 1942 edition will
carry on without them.

AND WHILE I'M ON THE SUBJECT of rude socialites, I might

add the name of Mrs. Edward Deems Jr. of 128 Willow Street who has most annoying habit of slamming the telephone receiver in your ear if she's not interested in what you have to say.

The former Beatrice Fries was not interested, evidently, in what I had to tell her over the phone, but I'm sure she will be interested in what I have to say in print. There is absolutely no excuse for rudeness. In the first place, Mrs. Deems is very much interested in the doings of Brooklyn but like Mrs. Cartwright, who also is not adverse to having some pleasant publicity, they seem to think that simply because they have been asked to fill out a form for the Blue Book, it is necessary to "put on this not interested" act.

From Guy Pierrepont's Weekly Society Bulletin, 1942. Reprinted with permission of the author.

In the introduction of the 1946 Bluebook, Mr. Pierrepont gave some pretty strong advice to his customers:

Brooklyn's first peacetime winter season since 1941 heralded a resumption of social life and activity, which of necessity was on a small scale but nevertheless apparent. Society, after nearly four years of vigorous war work with numerous organizations, was gradually putting away the uniforms and donning evening clothes and beginning to think about "doing things" again. This might surprise some Brooklynites who continue to insist there isn't any society left and Brooklyn isn't what it used to be but a brief resume of the current social season certainly would not give that impression.

We still have with us that little clique with a "Manhattan" complex who can't wait to move out of Brooklyn on one hand but continue to be part and parcel of every major social event on this side of Brooklyn Bridge. They are under the impression that its "smart" to talk about Brooklyn when actually most Brooklynites aren't at all interested. For it's a well known fact that most of our inner circle who crossed the bridge to enter larger social fields were simply lost in the shuffle. Park Avenue isn't too elated when a prominent family kicks over its Brooklyn traces and joins their group. You can count on one hand the number of Brooklyn families who made good in New York society and as far as I know, the late Violet Tangeman was the only Brooklynite to ever crash the Newport gates. So if you're toying with the idea of joining the Astor's for dinner I'd think about it twice.

From The Bluebook of Brooklyn, 1946. *Reprinted with permission of the author.*

from . . .

THIS NEW YORK OF MINE

by CHARLES HANSON TOWNE

Then, before I had finished college, the whole family decided to migrate to those hills which I had left behind me; and I remained alone in New York with that older brother of whom I have spoken. We took some quarters in a small bachelor apartment in East Twenty-eighth Street, and I felt very grown-up and important, living thus. My brother was a member of the crack Seventh Regiment; and I used to wonder how he could so joyfully give up an evening a week to go and drill when he might have been as free as I. He was a young lawyer, very successful in after years in his profession, and he wanted to make a lawyer of me. But I began to dream of becoming an editor and a writer.

Before that I had brought out a magazine called the Unique Monthly. Long afterwards I realized how unconsciously humorous the title was; but not then. I typed it out on my brother's Remington, very neatly. I wrote all the stories, articles, and verses myself; and found a boy of my own age who drew the pictures for it. I would leave the space for his childish illustrations, and then rent the single copy out to my companions in the neighborhood—we were still living in Harlem then—for three cents. I studiously copied Golden Days and the Youth's Companion; invented imaginary correspondents whose questions I answered, and took so much pride in my editorial work that within a few months my typing was perfection. I couldn't get out such a paper today.

On Saturdays and Sundays I would go to the country round about; or roam through Central Park. There was a Dancing Academy to be attended. One had to learn how to waltz. Every dance one attended perfected one's steps. And every dance on the program was different. There was the mazurka, the schottische, and the square dances—would that we had them still, with their fun and frolic, their long glides and turns, their freedom and their sense of the community spirit. Now, when I see people dancing in a cabaret or a night-club, on a floor so crowded that it reminds me of nothing so much as the words of the Lord's Prayer printed on a pinhead, I sigh for the less tumultuous dance-floors of my youth, when one could scamper down them without perpetually bumping into a hundred couples.

Of course one found a girl to take about. At a party one evening at which lemonade was served—I never had a drink of real liquor until I was twenty-one, and neither did many a lad I knew—I saw a young damsel of about my own age. She was so lovely that before anyone else had a chance, I asked her if I might not see her home. (How many ladies does one see home nowadays?) She promptly and emphatically said that she would be pleased to have me act as her escort. I took this as a personal tribute; a compliment I never expected. I did not suspect the reason of her readiness until the hour came to go. Then, as we stepped through the door, I asked her where she lived.

I can hear her answer yet; and I still remember the start it gave me, the sinking of the heart I experienced.

"I live in Bensonhurst," she said.

There was nothing to do but take her there.

But there were no subways then. We marched to the Third Avenue elevated road and went to City Hall. Then over the Brooklyn Bridge. It was midnight; and that was an unseemly hour for me then. I was fascinated by her knowledge of the tangle of Brooklyn trolley-cars when we reached that suburb of New York. It seemed to me hours that we rode, and rode, and rode. My liking for her waned with every swerve of the car, every bump and twist and turn of that ambling vehicle; yet I kept up a polite conversation, and feigned a zest I was far from feeling. Into the country we finally fared. I heard streets called out of which I had never heard. Houses were closed, shutters drawn. Decent folk were long since in bed. New York, behind me, was also asleep. "Brooklyn is New York's bedroom," I recalled that a wit had said; and here was I, wide awake in it. Then I think we both must have dozed off a bit. Awakened by a sudden lurch, we heard the conductor cry, "Bath Beach." The next would be our stop. How good to know that!

At the door of her house, I tried to say a hasty good-night. But the young lady seemed loath to part.

"Won't you come in?" she invited, much like the young ladies in the advertisements of today.

It was cold. I was chilled through; but I knew enough not to go within. I thought of the long, dreary trip home. Did women have no sense? "No." I said, firmly.

But as I turned down the path, she called to me. I went back. "We're moving to Brooklyn next week," she said. "I hope you'll come and see me there. Greene Avenue. It's not so far from New York."

Weakly, I said yes; that I would be pleased.

Toward dawn I reached East Twenty-eighth Street, and fell into one of those slumbers which, no matter how brief, refresh the young and healthy.

When I think of how short that journey would be today, I smile. But then—the lessons we learn in our youth!

Only, I didn't quite learn my lesson. Haunted by the girl's prettiness, I wrote to her, reminding her of her promise to let me come and see her in Brooklyn. She answered that her family were giving a musical in their Greene Avenue home to celebrate their occupancy of the new house. And again I found myself on the elevated and in a trolley one evening on my way to keep my engagement.

Those were the days of the long, narrow drawing-room, or "parlor." I found a room filled with people unknown to me.

Dressed in my new tuxedo—the first I had ever owned—I felt important and very New York-y. We would call it now a "superiority complex." Then, it was just plain vanity; and that is, despite the psychoanalysts, what it is today.

I felt that I was entering the social whirl; that I had "arrived," when I could be asked, at my youthful age, to a soirée of such proportions and of such obvious elegance. Only, I secretly wished that I had made my entrance in Manhattan, instead of by this back entrance, as it were. For all New Yorkers, in their secret hearts, looked down upon Brooklynites. There was no Greater New York then; there was just—New York. And Brooklyn was as much of a hinterland as Hoboken or Paterson. "The city of churches," it was called. That seemed to be its one claim to distinction and fame. Its quiet, well-ordered homes—little I knew, or cared, about these. Its first families, some of them infinitely better than those over the bridge—I gave them no thought, no consideration in the scheme of things. They had Henry Ward Beecher, and T. DeWitt Talmage; but what New Yorker would take the pains to go and hear them, when there was Dr. John Hall in New York—and on Fifth Avenue, at that; and Dr. Parkhurst in Madison Square. Oh, we were better, and finer, and more aristocratic—there wasn't a shadow of doubt as to that.

And so, young though I was, I looked about me at these gentle people, and rather pitied them. Was I not living in bachelor quarters in the greatest city in the United States? A little snob —that's what I was. And I deserved the social crash that was so soon to be my lot.

I found myself standing close to the piano which adorned the parlor, close to the folding-doors, heavily draped, which separated it from the square and formal back parlor. In both rooms the guests assembled and we were to have supper in the basement dining-room below. A Negro butler had opened the door for us. That was a touch which overwhelmed me; and he had directed us all to the rooms upstairs where we were to leave our hats and coats. I found, to my chagrin, that most of the older men wore tail-coats and high collars and white ties; but I felt that this was "showing off." Yet if I had possessed such clothes, I knew that I should have worn them. I had never dreamed that this affair would be so formal.

A lady was to accompany the first singer—a tenor of distinction. As I stood so close to her, she whispered, "Would you mind turning the music for me?" I wouldn't, and I did. I felt that she recognized the intelligence in my boyish face.

It was a German song; and though I could not read the music, I *could*, thanks to Miss Frank, read the words, so I knew just when to turn the page. I felt delightfully conspicuous as I leaned forward to do my duty, just as the tenor reached a high note.

Never did sheet music slip and separate and disappear like that! A crashing chord from the lady pianist; a breathless pause—too long—from the tenor; and out of the corner of my eye I saw the pages of the song whirling down that long parlor, as the singing of it whirled into oblivion. I was frightened. Then I grew cold, and numb. I can see that long lane of faces yet—those elegant Brooklynites whispering among themselves of the bleak disaster. They are vague to me now, even as they were vague to me then; but I thought I saw, not pity, but disgust, on many a curved lip.

I do not know what happened next, or how I got out of that room. I know only that I never had supper in the basement; that somehow I must have found my hat and coat, and somehow passed through those portals which I had entered blithely and snobbishly. I found myself again in a trolley making for the bridge. But the trip home is a dream—or, rather, a nightmare—to me. The journey to Bensonhurst was nothing compared to this endless trek back to New York.

Needless to say, I never saw that girl again. And it was years before I could bring myself to visit Brooklyn.

From This New York of Mine, *copyright,* 1931, *by Charles Hanson Towne, and reprinted by permission of Rinehart & Company, Inc. Publishers.*

However, there has been as much study for the sociologist as for the society writer. . . .

from . . .

TROPIC OF CAPRICORN

by HENRY MILLER

It was in the kitchen where the secret confabulations were held, frightening, odious sessions from which they always reappeared with long, grave faces or eyes red with weeping. Why they ran to the kitchen I don't know. But it was often while they stood thus in secret conference, haggling about a will or deciding how to dispense with some poor relative, that the door was suddenly opened and a visitor would arrive, whereupon the atmosphere immediately changed. Changed violently, I mean, as though they were relieved that some outside force had intervened to spare them the horrors of a protracted secret session. I remember now that, seeing that door open and the face of an unexpected visitor peering in, my heart would leap with joy! Soon I would be given a big glass pitcher and asked to run to the corner saloon where I would hand the pitcher in, through the little window at the family entrance, and wait until it was returned brimming with foamy suds. This little run to the corner for a pitcher of beer was an expedition of absolutely incalculable proportions. First of all there was the barber shop just below us, where Stanley's father practiced his profession. Time and again, just as I was dashing out for something, I would see the father giving Stanley a drubbing with the razor strop, a sight that made my blood boil. Stanley was my best friend and his father was nothing but a drunken Polak. One evening, however, as I was dashing out with the pitcher, I had the intense pleasure of seeing another Polak go for Stanley's old man with a razor. I saw his old man coming through the door backwards, the blood running down his neck, his face white as a sheet. He fell on the sidewalk in front of the shop, twitching and moaning, and I remember looking at him for a minute or two and walking on feeling absolutely contented and happy about it. Stanley had sneaked out during the scrimmage and was accom-

· 73 ·

panying me to the saloon door. He was glad too, though he was a bit frightened. When we got back the ambulance was there in front of the door and they were lifting him in on the stretcher, his face and neck covered with a sheet. Sometimes it happened that Father Carroll's pet choir boy strolled by the house just as I was hitting the air. This was an event of primary importance. The boy was older than any of us and he was a sissy, a fairy in the making. His very walk used to enrage us. As soon as he was spotted the news went out in every direction and before he had reached the corner he was surrounded by a gang of boys all much smaller than himself who taunted him and mimicked him until he burst into tears. Then we would pounce on him, like a pack of wolves, pull him to the ground and tear the clothes off his back. It was a disgraceful performance but it made us feel good. Nobody knew yet what a fairy was, but whatever it was we were against it. In the same way we were against the Chinaman. There was one Chinaman, from the laundry up the street, who used to pass frequently and, like the sissy from Father Carroll's church, he too had to run the gauntlet. He looked exactly like the picture of a coolie which one sees in the school books. He wore a sort of black alpaca coat with braided button holes, slippers without heels, and a pig tail. Usually he walked with his hands in his sleeves. It was his walk which I remember best, a sort of sly, mincing, feminine walk which was utterly foreign and menacing to us. We were in mortal dread of him and we hated him because he was absolutely indifferent to our gibes. We thought he was too ignorant to notice our insults. Then one day when we entered the laundry he gave us a little surprise. First he handed us the package of laundry; then he reached down below the counter and gathered a handful of lichee nuts from a big bag. He was smiling as he came from behind the counter to open the door. He was still smiling as he caught hold of Alfie Betcha and pulled his ears; he caught hold of each of us and pulled our ears, still smiling. Then he made a ferocious grimace and, swift as a cat, he ran behind the counter and picked up a long, ugly-looking knife which he brandished at us. We fell over ourselves getting out of the place.

When we got to the corner and looked around we saw him standing in the doorway with an iron in his hand looking very calm and peaceful. After this incident nobody would go to the laundry any more; we had to pay little Louis Pirossa a nickel each week to collect the laundry for us. Louis's father owned the fruit stand on the corner. He used to hand us the rotten bananas as a token of his affection. Stanley was especially fond of the rotten bananas as his aunt used to fry them for him. The fried bananas were considered a delicacy in Stanley's home. Once, on his birthday, there was a party given for Stanley and the whole neighborhood was invited. Everything went beautifully until it came to the fried bananas. Somehow nobody wanted to touch the bananas as this was a dish known only to Polaks like Stanley's parents. It was considered disgusting to eat fried bananas. In the midst of the embarrassment some bright youngster suggested that crazy Willie Maine should be given the fried bananas. Willie Maine was older than any of us but unable to talk. He said nothing but *Bjork! Bjork!* He said this to everything. So when the bananas were passed to him he said *Bjork!* and he reached for them with two hands. But his brother George was there and George felt insulted that they should have palmed off the rotten bananas on his crazy brother. So George started a fight and Willie, seeing his brother attacked, began to fight also, screaming *Bjork! Bjork!* Not only did he strike out at the other boys but at the girls too, which created a pandemonium. Finally Stanley's old man, hearing the noise, came up from the barber shop with a strop in his hand. He took crazy Willie Maine by the scruff of the neck and began to lambast him. Meanwhile his brother George had sneaked off to call Mr. Maine senior. The latter, who was also a bit of a drunkard, arrived in his shirt sleeves and, seeing poor Willie being beaten by the drunken barber, he went for him with two stout fists and beat him up unmercifully. Willie, who had gotten free meanwhile, was on his hands and knees, gobbling up the fried bananas which had fallen on the floor. He was stuffing them away like a nannygoat, as fast as he could find them. When the old man saw him there chewing away like a goat he became furious and picking up the strop he went after Willie with a vengeance. Now Willie began to howl—*Bjork! Bjork!*—and suddenly everybody began to laugh. That took the steam out of Mr. Maine and he relented. Finally he sat down and Stanley's aunt brought him a glass of wine. Hearing the racket some of the other neighbors came in and there was more wine and then beer and then schnapps and soon everybody was happy and singing and whistling and even the kids got drunk and then crazy Willie got drunk and again he got down on the floor like a nannygoat and he yelled *Bjork!—Bjork!* and Alfie Betcha, who was very drunk though only eight years old, bit crazy Willie Maine in the backside and then Willie bit him and then we all started biting each other and the parents stood by laughing and screaming with glee and it was very very merry and there were more fried bananas and everybody ate them this time and then there were speeches and more bumpers downed and crazy Willie Maine tried to sing for us but could only sing *Bjork! Bjork!* It was a stupendous success, the birthday party, and for a week or more no one talked of anything but the party and what good Polaks Stanley's people were. The fried bananas, too, were a success and for a time it was hard to get any rotten bananas from Louis Pirossa's old man because they were so much in demand. And then an event occurred which cast a pall over the entire neighborhood—the defeat of Joe Gerhardt at the hands of Joey Silverstein. The latter was the tailor's son; he was a lad of fifteen or sixteen, rather quiet and studious looking, who was shunned by the other older boys because he was a Jew. One day as he was delivering a pair of pants on Fillmore Place he was accosted by Joey Gerhardt who was about the same age and who considered himself a rather superior being. There was an exchange of words and then Joe Gerhardt pulled the pants away from the Silverstein boy and threw them in the gutter. Nobody had ever imagined that young Silverstein would reply to such an insult by recourse to his fists and so when he struck out at Joe Gerhardt and cracked him square in the jaw everybody was taken aback, most of all Joe Gerhardt himself. There was a fight which lasted about twenty minutes and at the end Joe Gerhardt lay on the sidewalk unable to get up. Whereupon the Silverstein boy gathered up the pair of pants and walked quietly and proudly back to his father's shop. Nobody said a word to him. The affair was regarded as a calamity. Who had ever heard of a Jew beating up a Gentile? It was something inconceivable, and yet it had happened, right before every one's eyes. Night after night, sitting on the curb as we used to, the situation was discussed from every angle, but without any solution until . . . well until Joe Gerhardt's younger brother, Johnny, became so wrought up about it that he decided to settle the matter himself. Johnny, though younger and smaller than his brother, was as tough and invincible as a young puma. He was typical of the shanty Irish who made up the neighborhood. His idea of getting even with young Silverstein was to lie in wait for him one evening as the latter was stepping out of the store and trip him up. When he tripped him up that evening he had provided himself in advance with two little rocks which he concealed in his fists and when poor Silverstein went down he pounced on him and then with the two handsome little rocks he pounded poor Silverstein's temples. To his amazement Silverstein offered no resistance; even when he got up and gave him a chance to get to his feet Silverstein never so much as budged. Then Johnny got frightened and ran away. He must have been thoroughly frightened because he never came back again; the next that was heard of him was that he had been picked up out West somewhere and sent to a reformatory. His mother, who was a slatternly, jolly Irish bitch, said that it served him right and she hoped to God she'd never lay eyes on him again. When the boy Silverstein recovered he was not the same any more; people said the beating had affected his brain, that he was a little daffy. Joe Gerhardt, on the other hand, rose to prominence again. It seems that he had gone to see the Silverstein boy while he lay in bed and had made a deep apology to him. This again was something that had never been heard of before. It was something so strange, so unusual, that Joe Gerhardt was looked upon almost as a knight errant. Nobody had approved of the way Johnny behaved, and yet nobody would have thought of going to young Silverstein and apologizing to him. That was an act of such delicacy, such elegance, that Joe Gerhardt was looked upon as a real gentleman—the first and only gentleman in the neighborhood. It was a word that had never been used among us and now it was on everybody's lips and it was considered a distinction to be a gentleman. This sudden transformation of the defeated Joe Gerhardt into a gentleman I remember made a deep impression upon me. A few years later, when I moved into another neighborhood and encountered Claude de Lorraine, a French boy, I was prepared to understand and accept "a gentleman." This Claude was a boy such as I had never laid eyes on before. In the old neighborhood he would have been regarded as a sissy; for one thing he spoke too well, too correctly, too politely, and for another thing he was too considerate, too gentle, too gallant. And then, while playing with him, to hear him suddenly break into French as his mother or father came along, provided us with something like a shock. German we had heard and German was a permissible transgression, but French! why to talk French, or even to understand it, was to be thoroughly alien, thoroughly aristocratic, rotten, distingué. And yet Claude was one of us, as good as us in every way, even a little bit better we had to admit secretly. But there was a blemish—his French! It antagonized us. He had no right to be living in our neighborhood, no right to be as capable and manly as he was. Often, when his mother called him in and we had said good-bye to him, we got together in the lot and we discussed the Lorraine family backwards and forwards. We wondered what they ate, for example, because being French they must have different customs than ours. No one had ever set foot in Claude de Lorraine's home either—that was another suspicious and repugnant fact. Why? What were they concealing? Yet when they passed us in the street they were always very cordial, always smiled, always spoke English and a most excellent English it was. They used to make us feel rather ashamed of ourselves—they were superior, that's what it was. And there was still another baffling thing—with the other boys a direct question brought a direct answer, but with Claude de Lorraine there was never any direct answer. He always smiled very charmingly before replying and he was very cool, collected, employing an irony and a mockery which was beyond us. He was a thorn in our side, Claude de Lorraine, and when finally he moved out of the neighborhood we all breathed a sigh of relief. As for myself, it was only maybe ten or fifteen years later that I thought about this boy and his strange, elegant behavior. And it was then that I felt I had made a bad blunder. For suddenly one day it occurred to me that Claude de Lorraine had come up to me on a certain occasion obviously to win my friendship and I had treated him rather cavalierly. At the time I thought of this incident it suddenly dawned on me that Claude de Lorraine must have seen something different in me and that he had meant to honor me by extending the hand of friendship. But back in those days I had a code of honor, such as it was, and that was to run with the herd. Had I become a bosom friend of Claude de Lorraine I would have been betraying the other boys. No matter what advantages lay in the wake of such a friendship they were not for me; I was one of the gang and it was my duty to remain aloof from such as Claude de Lorraine. I remembered this incident once again, I must say, after a still greater interval—after I had been in France a few months and the word "*raisonnable*" had come to acquire a wholly new significance for me. Suddenly one day, overhearing this word in the midst of an argument, I thought of Claude de Lorraine's overtures on the street in front of his house. I recalled vividly that he had used the word *reasonable*. He had probably asked me to be *reasonable*, a word which then would never have crossed my lips as there was no need for it in my vocabulary. It was a word, like gentleman, which was rarely brought out and then only with great discretion and circumspection. It was a word which might cause others to laugh at you. There were lots of words like that—*really*, for example. No one I knew had ever used the word *really*—until Jack Lawson came along. He used it because his parents were English and, though we made fun of him, we forgave him for it. *Really* was a word which reminded me immediately of little Carl Ragner from the old neighborhood. Carl Ragner was the only son of a politician who lived on the rather distinguished little street called Fillmore Place. He lived near the end of the street in a little red brick house which was always beautifully kept. I remember the house because passing it on my way to school I used to remark how beautifully the brass knobs on the door were polished. In fact, nobody else had brass knobs on their doors. Anyway, little Carl Ragner was one of those boys who was not allowed to associate with other boys. He was rarely seen, as a matter of fact. Usually it was a Sunday that we caught a glimpse of him walking with his father. Had his father not been a powerful figure in the neighborhood Carl would have been stoned to death. He was really impossible, in his Sunday garb. Not only did he wear long pants and patent leather shoes, but he sported a derby and a cane. At six years of age a boy who would allow himself to be dressed up in this fashion must be a ninny—that was the consensus of opinion. Some said he was sickly, as though that were an excuse for his eccentric dress. The strange thing is that I never once heard him speak. He was so elegant, so refined, that perhaps he had imagined it was bad manners to speak in public. At any rate, I used to lie in wait for him Sunday mornings just to see him pass with his old man. I watched him with the same avid curiosity that I would watch the firemen cleaning the engines in the fire house. Sometimes on the way home he would be carrying a little box of ice cream, the smallest size they had, probably just enough for him, for his dessert. Dessert was another word which had somehow become familiar to us and which we used derogatorily when referring to the likes of little Carl Ragner and his family. We could spend hours wondering what these these people ate for *dessert*, our pleasure consisting principally in bandying about this new-found word, *dessert*, which had probably been smuggled out of the Ragner household. It must also have been about this time that Santos Dumont came in to fame. For us there was something grotesque about the name Santos Dumont. About his exploits we were not much concerned—just the name. For most of us it smelled of sugar, of Cuban plantations, of the strange Cuban flag which had a star in the corner and which was always highly regarded by those who saved the little cards which were given away with Sweet Caporal cigarettes and on which there were represented either the flags of the different nations or the leading soubrettes of the stage or the famous pugilists. Santos Dumont, then, was something delightfully foreign, in contradistinction to the usual foreign person or object, such as the Chinese laundry, or Claude de Lorraine's haughty French family. Santos Dumont was a magical word which suggested a beautiful flowing mustache, a sombrero, spurs, something airy, delicate, humorous, quixotic. Sometimes it brought up the aroma of coffee beans and of straw mats, or because it was so thoroughly outlandish and quixotic it would entail a digression concerning the life of the Hottentots. For there were among us older boys who were beginning to read and who would entertain us by the hour with fantastic tales which they had gleaned from boooks such as *Ayesha* or Ouida's *Under Two Flags*. The real flavor of knowledge is most definitely associated in my mind with the vacant lot at the corner of the new neighborhood where I was transplanted at about the age of ten. Here, when the fall days came on and we stood about the bon-fire roasting chippies and raw potatoes in the little cans which we carried, there ensued a new type of discussion which differed from the old discussions I had known in that the origins were always bookish. Some one had just read a book of adventure, or a book of science, and forthwith the whole street became animated by the introduction of a hitherto unknown subject. It might be that one of the boys had just discovered that there was such a thing as the Japanese current and he would try to explain to us how the Japanese current came into existence and what the purpose of it was. This was the only way we learned things—against the fence, as it were, while roasting chippies and raw potatoes. These bits of knowledge sunk deep—so deep, in fact, that later, confronted with a more accurate knowledge it was often difficult to dislodge the older knowledge. In this way it was explained to us one day by an older boy that the Egyptians had known about the circulation of the blood, something which seemed so natural to us that it was hard later to swallow the story of the discovery of the circulation of the blood by an Englishman named Harvey. Nor does it seem strange to me now that in those days most of our conversation was about remote places, such as China, Peru, Egypt, Africa, Iceland, Greenland. We talked about ghosts, about God, about the transmigration of souls, about Hell, about astronomy, about strange birds and fish, about the formation of precious stones, about rubber plantations, about methods of torture, about the Aztecs and the Incas, about marine life, about volcanoes and earthquakes, about burial rites and wedding ceremonies in various parts of the earth, about languages, about the origin of the American Indian, about the buffaloes dying out, about strange diseases, about cannibalism, about wizardry, about trips to the moon and what it was like there, about murderers and highwaymen, about the miracles in the Bible, about the manufacture of pottery, about a thousand and one subjects which were never mentioned at home or in school and which were vital to us because we were starved and the world was full of wonder and mystery and it was only when we stood shivering in the vacant lot that we got to talking seriously and felt a need for communication which was at once pleasurable and terrifying.

From Tropic of Capricorn *by Henry Miller. Reprinted by permission of New Directions, New York, N. Y.*

LUNA

from SODOM BY THE SEA

by OLIVER PILAT *and* JO RANSON

Luna Park grew up at Coney Island around an entertainment formula combining the personal adventures of a Cook's Tour with the noisy glamor of a circus. It was a curious formula, evolved by that most strange of all strange partnerships, Thompson and Dundy. Alone, neither Thompson nor Dundy possessed the stamina to reach the top—Thompson being a sentimental spendthrift and dipsomaniac and Dundy being a stuttering skirt chaser and a gambler—but together they formed an unbeatable team. Picking up the mantle of P. T. Barnum, they set styles year after year that dominated the amusement world.

Thompson and Dundy were competitors before they were partners. Each got a start at a fair in his home town. A native of Ironton, Ohio, Thompson was working as a $15-a-week architect's draftsman in Nashville, Tennessee, in the early '90s, when his uncle, who had done some unpaid-for construction for the Nashville exposition, turned over to him an illusion called the Blue Grotto, saying: "Fred, run this show and see if we can pull our money out." Though exotic, the presentation of a cave in Capri could not claim to be very thrilling or funny. Young Thompson required all his instinctive showmanship to popularize it. Instead of hiring barkers, he recited a spiel of his own into a phonograph, put the machine on a revolving base and let it ride. The novelty and flavor of this ballyhoo saved the Blue Grotto.

Encouraged by this success, Thompson advanced on the Omaha Trans-Mississippi Exposition of 1898 with an illusion of his own called Darkness and Dawn, which the irreverent dubbed Hell and Heaven. His chief rival was Elmer Dundy, an Omaha politician and promoter, who had two rather orthodox illusions known as Havana and the *Maine* and The Mystic Garden. Thompson scored a smash success, but Dundy dropped $46,000 during the unfortunate second-year extension of the fair, known popularly as "the hangover."

The loss only whetted Skip Dundy's desire for another World's Fair whirl. He found show business more to his liking than the "hear ye, hear ye" stuff at the Omaha Federal Court, where he had served as clerk of the court under his father, a Federal judge. William (Buffalo Bill) Cody, Indian fighter and circus campaigner, had been a frequent visitor to the Dundy home when Skip was a boy and had filled the youngster with an abiding fascination for side-show affairs. Moreover, Skip had a financial flair. Hadn't he, as master in chancery, sold the bankrupt Union Pacific Railroad for $90,000,000? Concluding that his trouble had been poor shows rather than management, Skip applied for a concession at the Buffalo exposition of 1901 to exhibit a version of Hell and Heaven, which his more successful but less shrewd rival, Frederic Thompson, had failed to patent. Thompson applied for the concession. That left two men scrambling for the right to stage Thompson's show. The other exhibitors at the fair grew so excited over the competition that books were made on their respective chances, Thompson being a favorite. However, Dundy knew enough inside politics and wire-pulling to win.

Overcome with reluctant admiration for such banditry, Thompson came forward with a proposition: if Dundy would let him in on the concession, Thompson would show him a trick worth ten of Hell and Heaven.

"For years people have been content to sit and watch a cyclorama about a garden or a battle," argued Thompson, "but now they are getting bored. They want something new. They want movement, action. Suppose I show you a cyclorama which will make the audience move at the same time?"

"G-g-g-go ahead," said Dundy. After the exhibition it was his turn to yield to admiration. "Let's be p-p-p-partners," he suggested. When Thompson agreed, an association began that reshaped the whole summer amusement business.

Thompson's new illusion, Trip to the Moon, became the sensation of the Buffalo fair. There was a tremendous subjective thrill in imaginary flight for people accustomed to the stodgy presentation of Caprian caves and historic battles. "You got into a big winged thing that looked like a modern airplane," Joe Laurie, Jr., once recalled for Variety, the theatrical magazine, "and you felt like you were traveling up to the sky, and when you got out you met a lot of midgets dressed up like the people in the moon. The whole thing was mysterious and spooky and made your gal hold onto you."

Besides Trip to the Moon and Hell and Heaven, Thompson and Dundy sponsored the Giant See-saw, the Old Plantation and a dozen more shows at the Buffalo exposition. They collared most of the cash at the fair. During a bank scare Dundy felt affluent enough to post the nonchalant sign in his office:

> The earth may quake
> And banks may break
> But Skip Dundy
> Pays in gold.

He did have a passion for gold. His wife's birthday was due toward the closing of the exposition, and Skip promised to give her all the actual gold taken in on that date. Normally that would have meant a few dollars, but Thompson heard of the promise. On the afternoon of the birthday he hustled from the bank with all the gold he could get and replaced every paper bill taken in at all their shows that afternoon. As a result Skip had to carry $900 in gold coins home to his wife that evening!

The partnership operated on the basis of personal fondness and complete trust. Thompson concentrated on showmanship and Dundy on finances. Of course they talked over all important general matters, such as the invitation from George Tilyou to bring Trip to the Moon to Steeplechase Park on the basis of 60 per cent of the profit to them and 40 per cent to him. Dundy would have preferred waiting for the next World's Fair, but Thompson had his way for once and they went to Coney Island. They packed in the crowds at Steeplechase during the summer of 1902. That fall Tilyou (who rarely gave anything away in a business deal) agreed to a four-year renewal contract previously outlined, but with a slight revision: he would receive the 60-per-cent cut from then on. Dundy was furious. "We're g-g-g-going out of here for g-g-good," he shouted.

But where to go? The only other amusement park at Coney Island was Sea Lion Park, which had been operated for one season by an outstanding professional hero of the day, Captain Paul Boynton. The captain had invented an inflatable rubber swimming suit. After pumping air between its inner and outer layers, he was able to propel himself feet first along the surface of the water, like a personal kayak, and to bring himself erect for a survey of the horizon by dropping his legs and giving an appropriate push with his double-bladed paddle. Snugly enclosed (except for his face) in this fifteen-pound raincoat, Boynton had traveled 2,300 miles down the Mississippi to the Gulf of Mexico, had performed for Queen Victoria in England, and had sunk a Chilean man-of-war during the conflict with Peru by swimming out to the vessel at night and making fast a torpedo with a short fuse. For a while the captain rested from his labors by running the Ship Tavern, on 29th Street near Greeley Square, and telling choice anecdotes to such pacemakers of the '90s as E. Berry Wall, Howell Osborn and Fred May, who gathered to partake of his grilled marrow bones and brown ale. Finally Boynton bought a site at Coney Island about a thousand feet from the ocean for the creation of a water carnival. His chief attraction was shoot-the-chutes, in which a flat-bottomed boat slid down a water incline to a lagoon. At intervals the chutes stopped shooting to permit the captain to paddle about in his famous rubber boat. There was also a sea-lion act, to justify the name of the park.

Since his enterprise had run into financial shoals, Boynton was eager to lease his property to Thompson and Dundy for twenty-five years. Then Thompson humped over his drawing board on plans for a park that would give the proper setting to Trip to the Moon, as well as to an ambitious new illusion in the Trip manner. Twenty Thousand Leagues under the Sea depicting a submarine voyage to the polar regions. Partly to please Dundy, who was circus-crazy, Thompson planned a tremendous program of aerial and animal acts. He filled in the picture with the shoot-the-chutes, which came with Boynton, rides and bands and accommodations for dancing and swimming. Thompson classified attractions into those that furnished thrills and those that drew laughs, those in which the customers could participate and those that they merely observed. By careful spacing of outstanding attractions he sought to keep the crowds moving; by spreading an icing of free acts he schemed to keep them contented.

The architectural scheme of the park had to be oriental, Thompson decided, to lure people by its novelty during the day and to furnish a picturesque profile against the night. What should be the name? Dundy suggested the name of his sister in Des Moines, Luna Dundy. Luna Park? Wonderful, said Thompson, pointing out its aptness in view of the basic Trip to the Moon.

Finally everything was planned except finances. As outlined by Thompson, the park would cost $700,000. Dundy figured he could raise $220,000. "Oh, forget it," said Thompson. "What's $500,000? Let's go ahead with the plans, and when the cash gives out you can run up to Wall Street and corral the other half-million."

Skip did most of his financial work among the Coney Island racing crowd, persuading Bet-a-Million Gates, the steel man, and George Kessler, the champagne salesman, to make heavy initial investments. Then, when the time came to raise more money, Dundy did run to Wall Street and get another half-million. Even so there were times when the till was almost empty. As between Thompson and Dundy, no books were kept. When Thompson wanted some money, he went to Dundy, and if Dundy had enough to spare, Thompson got some, as a rule. Otherwise he waited a while.

"We eat out of the same pot, put our money in the same bag, and never have an accounting of our personal wealth," Dundy explained on one occasion. "We have never had a quarrel. We harmonize just because we are different."

Shortly before the opening day in May, Thompson indicated the threadbare seat of his only pair of pants. "How about some money for a new pair, Skip?" he demanded.

"F-f-f-red," said Dundy, "did you ever think what a lot of lumber seven dollars will buy?"

That settled the pants. When the gates opened at Luna, Thompson and Dundy had only twelve dollars between them and were sleeping together at a house in Coney Island with such a leaky roof that they raised umbrellas when it rained. But what did they care, with the completed Baghdad outline of red-and-white minarets, spires and towers springing upward against the heavy purple sky under the illumination of 250,000 electric lights? The crowds thought Luna stood for light, just as crowds at later Lunas in cities like London and Paris assumed that Luna stood for light. The crowds were entranced by the lighted-Christmas-tree appeal of the new Coney Island park, by its Hans Christian Andersen sort of magic. New York was vanquished even before it got past the bands playing outside as come-ons and the parades of cowboys, clowns, Indians and elephants.

If the original Chicago Midway in 1893 gave country cousins a chance to kick their heels, a park like Luna a decade later gave middle-class city folk a chance to escape from the rut of cautious living. Luna not only had appeal for people with money and leisure, it served as a Caribbean cruise for the stenographer and truck driver who couldn't afford to go to sea.

The impact of Luna's light and beauty even on sophisticates and littérateurs might be gauged by Maxim Gorki's impressions. "With the advent of night a fantastic city all of fire suddenly rises from the ocean into the sky," the Russian author wrote. "Thousands of ruddy sparks glimmer in the darkness, limning in fine, sensitive outline on the black background of the sky shapely towers of miraculous castles, palaces and temples. Golden gossamer threads tremble in the air. They intertwine in transparent flaming patterns, which flutter and melt away, in love with their own beauty mirrored in the waters. Fabulous beyond conceiving, ineffably beautiful, is this fiery scintillation."

By July 4, 1903, Thompson and Dundy had paid every cent they owed, and by the end of the season they were rolling in money. Those who gambled with them were rewarded proportionately. Charles F. Murray, who had linked George Tilyou's Steeplechase Pier at Atlantic City with the boardwalk by the bold device of entertaining city officials in one hotel and police officials in another while his gang of men set secretly to work, broke away from the Steeplechase horses to ride with Thompson and Dundy. He went along on a percentage basis, without salary, and for his courage received $116,000 at the end of the first season, with which he promptly retired from show business.

Thompson and Dundy plowed back their profits. They bought more sand on which to erect new attractions. Thompson pulled a master stroke by getting four elephants to slide down a special shoot-the-chutes. He claimed the largest show herd of elephants in the world, plus forty camels, and he featured them in a dazzling new production, an oriental pageant modeled after the Durbar Procession and called the Streets of Delhi. Thompson became almost foolishly fond of elephants. When Jumbo, one of his favorites, had to be killed, he preserved two of its feet and a piece of its hide for an office chair. His chief desk ornament was a curio modeled in Japan, consisting of an ebony bridge on which stood six elephants led by a great bull.

Another illusion designed and staged by Thompson in 1904 was called Fire and Flames. It had an auditorium so arranged that spectators seemed to be on the other side of a street from a gigantic conflagration that was being fought with all the drama of a fake wrestling match.

The Luna Park program, which drew four million visitors in 1904, read:

THE STREETS OF DELHI

FIRE AND FLAMES

TRIP TO THE MOON

TWENTY THOUSAND

LEAGUES UNDER THE SEA

SHOOT THE CHUTES

THE SCENIC RAILWAY

THE CIRCLE SWING

WHIRL THE WHIRL

THE INFANT INCUBATORS

SEA ON LAND

· THE FATAL WEDDING

THE OLD MILL

THE MINIATURE RAILWAY

AND THE LAUGHING SHOW

This was an era of great shows at Coney Island, such as Mount Pelée, which "by electric appliance, water and pictorial effect" showed the devastation wrought by the eruption in Martinique in 1902; the Johnstown Flood, which depicted the tragic overflow of the Conemaugh and Stonycreek rivers at the foot of the western slope of the Allegheny Mountains in 1889; and the similar Galveston Flood. But none of these could compare with such an illusion as Trip to the Moon, which cost only $72,000 to build and drew $250,000 in receipts at Luna in three years.

Luna's 1904 aerial circus, staged on three circular raised platforms over the lagoon at the foot of the shoot-the-chutes, includes such acts as the Stickneys, bareback, somersault and high-school equestrians; Spessardy's bears; Zolas, globe and spiral tower; Joseph Ashton, bareback rider; the Jennetts, equilibrists; François, Du Crow and Loranz, breakaway ladder; Bonner, the educated horse; and Dracula, the aerial contortionist.

Luna enjoyed such a vogue that John W. (Bet-a-Million) Gates and other financiers persuaded Thompson and Dundy to launch an attack at the very heart of New York. Funds were raised—$2,000,000 for property at 43d Street and Sixth Avenue, and $1,500,000 for the theater itself—and the Hippodrome sprang into being. With 5,200 chairs it had the greatest seating capacity of any theater in Gotham, far outranking the 3,400 and 3,600 seats respectively of the Metropolitan Opera House and the Academy of Music. For his urban debut Thompson merely sharpened the Luna formula. Boldly combining the Cook's Tour and circus elements, he staged a Yankee Circus on Mars as his premier offering in the spring of 1905. This included the quaint Coney Island gesture of elephants sliding down the shoot-the-chutes. Elephants also had been worked into the decoration, on the façade of the building, on either side of the box-office windows, in the corridors and above the proscenium arch. The public loved it. More than six thousand persons jammed the opening performance, and social and political figures like Stanford White, Harry Payne Whitney, O. H. P. Belmont, Gladys Vanderbilt, Robert Goelet, Clarence Mackay and Chauncey Depew (who had ridden Targit Ali, biggest of the Luna elephants on the opening night of Luna the year before) expressed themselves as entranced with the show.

This was the summit for Thompson and Dundy. Including another new venture, the Colonial Music Hall, the partners had

$6,000,000 worth of shows and an army of three thousand employees. However, they were continually warring on themselves. Thompson drank excessively and wasted money. Dundy would gamble on anything, the turn of a card or tomorrow's weather; once he even persuaded straitlaced George Tilyou to toss a coin over an eighty-thousand-dollar wheel that came into dispute between them. Dundy also prided himself on his feminine conquests, not generally arduous in the show business. There were stories current in Coney Island that he had a glass room specially built for the multiple visual enjoyment of amatory antics.

However, the partners served as a check on each other. When Thompson began to shed too many ten-dollar gold pieces—gold-carrying being a habit acquired from Dundy—Skip would invent a sudden financial stringency to serve as check rein. Similarly when Skip became immersed in one of those tremendous *Schlager* games at the Island, when $50,000 would swing on a single hand, and when a urinal was passed around at intervals to avoid the necessity of leaving the table, only Thompson could lure Dundy away to sleep on the pretext of a talk about a future attraction. And when Thompson drank too deeply at one of the Coney Island bars, Dundy would stride in, snatch the glass from his hand and hurl it to pieces on the floor, shouting to the proprietor that if another drink were ever served to Thompson there, he'd ruin the place like "C-c-carrie Nation." And when Dundy slipped into a mess that he fondly imagined was a love affair, Fred Thompson offered quiet, common-sense advice. Theirs was a rare partnership, in which each gave the other strength.

Thompson was only thirty-three in 1905, but Dundy was ten years older and already bald. Vanity required the wearing of a toupee, but business acumen consented to the occasional sacrifice of vanity for financial profit, as when one of the Luna Park customers came in with a complaint—say a tar stain on a dress—after riding through the Old Mill.

"This dress cost me eighteen dollars and was bought only yesterday," the woman would exclaim.

Dundy would inspect the dress carefully. Then, with slowly

growing amazement, he would reach up with his right hand, remove his toupee and stuff it into his right-hand coat pocket. "How m-m-m-m, how much?" he would ask, before the flabbergasted woman could recover.

"I don't remember the exact price, but it was a good dress."

Dundy would pick up the bottom of the dress, noting that it had been to the cleaners several times, so that it couldn't be so new. However, he would offer nine dollars. When the woman accepted, he would say: "T-t-take it off in the other room."

"But I can't take it off, I'd have nothing to wear!"

Stuttering more than ever, and replacing his toupee on his head as a crescendo of drums in the act, Skip Dundy would point out that he couldn't afford to pay for an old, cheap, admittedly damaged dress if he didn't at least get the dress. Invariably this routine proved too much for the woman, who settled for two dollars.

Skip was sufficiently sensitive about his baldness to try endless remedies. Once a woman named Elsie Marosie brought him into court in a suit for $950, claiming that after six months he had paid her only $50 out of a promised $1,000 for thatching his dome with natural hair. She alleged the development of "incipient signs of hair growth" on his head, but Dundy denied any incipient signs and said further that incipient signs were of no value, since he still had to wear a wig.

The winter of 1906-07 proved disastrous for the partnership. The first ominous development was the marriage of Fred Thompson to Mabel Taliaferro on November 29, 1906, after a courtship of only two weeks. Mabel was a former child actress who landed broke and discouraged at Coney Island at the age of nineteen after participating in entertainment tours as far as Australia. She was a pretty girl with a vivacity unhandicapped by excessive thoughtfulness, as was shown by her account of their honeymoon in a magazine known as the *Bohemian*: "My husband and I traveled abroad for four months, through Switzerland, Italy and France in an automobile. It was gloriously exciting. We reached Milan during the riots, the 'general strike' they called it, and the mob scenes we witnessed would have made several theatrical managers turn green with envy. We were obliged to flee the town in a most dramatic manner in order to escape with our lives. Of course we went to Paris and the beautiful Riviera, and altogether it was the most delightful trip I ever had. When we returned, my husband and I did a little traveling with the Ringling Brothers' circus, so that I could get all the tan-bark atmosphere necessary for *Polly of the Circus*."

Out of love for his wife Thompson decided to make her a star and plunged headlong into a new field, that of straight dramatic production, to the neglect of the carnival work at which he was a recognized master. More important, his absorption in Mabel Taliaferro deprived Skip Dundy of his companionship and his tolerant advice in affairs of the heart.

On February 5, 1907, Skip died unexpectedly, at the height of his power. Coney Islanders whispered that he had been killed by a hatpin plunged into his breast by a brunette companion whom he had set up in an establishment for a while, but that could not have been true, because an official family statement gave as cause of death "acute dilatation of the heart, superinduced by pneumonia."

Skip Dundy's death left his partner rudderless. He didn't have to worry about the Hippodrome, for the partnership had been eased out in favor of Lee and J. J. Shubert by Bet-a-Million Gates and other Wall Street financiers after a quarrel over the sale of tickets to speculators, but he did have Luna Park. Instead of devising a worthy successor to Trip to the Moon, which had finally grown stale, he concentrated on pleasing Mabel Taliaferro and having a good time. Entering a bar with three companions, he would throw down a ten-dollar gold piece for four cocktails and tell the waiter to keep the change. He carried as much as $10,000 in gold with him at one time, spending the coins as though they were hot. He had a glass floor in his apartment on 41st Street in New York—not for the purpose alleged in the stories that Skip Dundy used glass in a room, but to help deaden the noise from a restaurant downstairs. However, he had a special dumb-waiter direct from the restaurant to bring up his meals, and two Japanese to serve the food. Thompson was crazy about yachting. He would drive to the Battery in his car, get into his yacht and sail all of three or four miles to Sea Gate and from there drive in another car to his second home in Luna Park. He could have covered the entire distance by car in half the time. In July 1908 Thompson's schooner *Shamrock* won the thousand-dollar Lipton Cup for an ocean race to Cape May, with Thompson on board. To reward his sailing master, Captain Barr, for breaking a record by thirty-eight seconds, Yachtowner Thompson presented him with thirty-eight one-thousand-dollar bills.

That fall, Mabel Taliaferro, still playing the title role in *Polly of the Circus*, interrupted a tour at Baltimore for an appendicitis operation. Thompson rushed to her bedside only to find her leading man, Thomas Carrigan, already there. The Thompsons separated that winter, although Miss Taliaferro did not sue for divorce until 1911, when she charged extreme and repeated cruelty. She got her decree without opposition (and proceeded to marry Carrigan at a ceremony staged in a field of daisies. She divorced Carrigan a few years later on the ground that he had left her to join the Marines. Then she married Captain Joseph O'Brien, whom she divorced on the grounds of cruelty in order to marry Robert Ober, an actor with whom she appeared in vaudeville.)

The break-up of his marriage struck Thompson at the core of his vanity, but for a while he consoled himself with his status as the great American showman. He wrote a revelatory article for *Everybody's Magazine*, giving in detail his theories as an outstanding carnival man.

"The difference between a theater and the big amusement parks is the difference between the Sunday school and the Sunday-school picnic," he said. "The picnic and the open-air park are designed to give the natural bubbling animal spirits of the human being full play. The first step, so far as the public is concerned, is to create an impression that there will be things doing, to get emotional excitement into the very air. When people go to a park or an exposition and admire the buildings, the exhibits and the lights without having laughed about half the time until their sides ached, you can be absolutely sure that the enterprise will fail."

At Luna, Thompson tried to limit the length of all shows to twenty minutes, to keep the crowds continually on the move. As soon as he saw people seated on benches, he would order the bands to march about, playing such lively tunes that rest became impossible. On one occasion this practice had an unexpected result. "It rained hard," Thompson revealed, " but I insisted on the bands playing, all six of them. After a while the big band of sixty pieces began to play:

> "Ain't it a shame, a measly shame,
> To keep me standing out in the rain!

"The other bands took it up, and for an hour they played nothing else. I gave in."

His financial problems were becoming so acute that he was losing hope of making a recovery. In 1912 Thompson acknowledged himself personally bankrupt. He had $665,000 in hard debts and a pitiful few thousands in soft assets. "It's proof I'm no piker, isn't it?" he said, with a laugh at Luna, where he was working as manager, no longer owner. A reporter asked: "Did financing your former wife in her theatrical career get you into financial trouble?"

"Now that is nobody's business," shouted Thompson, suddenly furious.

As a showman he was nearly finished. In 1913 he married Serene Pilcher, a level-headed woman from his home town of Nashville, but even she could not reform him. Casper Balsamo, his personal assistant, had orders to send up two quarts of Scotch whisky and two eggs and a milk shake for Thompson's breakfast. After sipping a glass of whisky and soda, sitting in pajamas on the side of his bed, Thompson was able to plunge into the dictation of letters and to handle a considerable amount of theatrical management for Klaw & Erlanger, but nothing striking or sensational. During prolonged bouts he could sometimes be located in a ten-cent movie house where an old picture showing Mabel Taliaferro was running. He died in 1919 of a complication of causes, including hernia and alcoholism, and the Brooklyn *Eagle* editorial summed up his career in this fashion: "A man who seemingly might have done anything in the field of spectacle and illusion did two notable things and then stopped. The loss from his abandonment of his early ideals was almost as striking as the things he accomplished when he held on to them." Frederic Thompson was buried in Moravian Cemetery, Staten Island, where for years no stone marked his grave until Dr. Martin Couney, the incubator-baby man, and other old cronies at Coney Island chipped in for the purpose.

Barron Collier took over Luna Park after Fred Thompson's eclipse. The streetcar advertising expert and his associates ran the place along familiar lines, drawing millions of visitors each season without making as much money as might have been expected. The development of autos aided Luna, which always played to a slightly more well-to-do crowd than Steeplechase, but autos themselves and then the movies tended to date Thompson's early amusements, and the new owners had no new formula.

Take for example the sinking of the *Titanic*, a graphic and oratorical portrayal of the great marine disaster of 1912 in which 1,513 lives were lost. The Luna Park impresarios didn't even make it mechanically perfect. The curtains failed to close properly at the end of Act I, when the liner was well launched on its voyage. A gap remained through which the audience could see the ship furiously backing into position. The lecturer ignored the guffaws and proceeded through Act II, when again the curtains balked and allowed another glimpse of a giant vessel insanely proceeding in reverse, as though trying to escape fate. The audience laughed all through Act II and was still laughing when the lecturer concluded: "Such was the fate of the *Tyetanic*." However, as the lights went on at the close of that initial performance of the 1914 season, the lecturer had his revenge. Loudly counting the entire nine persons at the show, he pulled out nine tickets, all shot full of holes and clearly marked complimentary. The show didn't last, but the lecturer enjoyed the last laugh.

Into the Moon building, where the Trip once drew capacity crowds, cycloramas like the Battle of the Marne and Little America played during the '20s and '30s, without making any excessive dent in the public imagination.

Luna continued to stage excellent circus acts, including an occasional elephant, but the public didn't enthuse over elephants as it once had. Only slight attention was paid to Mom, the talking elephant, or to Adele Nelson's amazing baby elephants, which performed the Charleston and the shimmy, God save their thick hides. Topsy, the 55-year-old, 7,000-pound pachyderm, took a swim in the surf one day without causing a ripple in the metropolitan press.

Around a circular slatted platform high upon a pole, Robert Cimse scooted on a motorcycle with no walls to hold him, while his sisters, Mary, Emma and Lily, did trapeze stunts overhead and occasionally reached down to pull up the platform holding the speeding cyclist himself. . . . Ben Beno performed a flying somersault on a chair fifty feet up in the sky, losing the chair and catching the bar with his toes. . . . Janette May, an auburn-haired girl in tights and spangles, did giant one-arm kickovers from a loop 150 feet high, undaunted by the death of Lilian Leitzel during a similar act elsewhere. . . . Zacchini, the human projectile, landed improperly enough after being shot from a cannon to fracture a vertebra. . . .

There would be applause from the Coney Island crowd, but listless and preoccupied applause compared to the roar that would have greeted identical hair-raising acts under a circus tent. Invariably, during the climax of some thrilling aerial achievement, a girl with a name something like Sylvia would turn her eyes away from the performer to say angrily to her stout companion: "But why d'ye hafta wear a red dress, Ma, it makes ye look big," and the stout one would reply with a shrug: "Whosa gonna look?"

Roller skating, kiddie rides, marionettes, cockroach racing, even a White Mouse Hotel—a doll's house inhabited by mice—were tried out at Luna during the '30s without conspicuous success, possibly because sooner or later a girl with a name like Sylvia would forget everything else in order to turn angrily on a mother who would shrug and reply: "Whosa gonna look?"

Who, indeed? During some seasons, only a fraction of the lights were lit. During others, painting of attractions was neglected, without arousing public protest. Visitors simply yawned and hurried to their homes or the beach. Perhaps 1935 was a representative recent year—midway between two discouraging Luna Park bankruptcies. There were such orthodox attractions as a rabbit game, a poker game, two guess-your-weight platform scales, two shooting galleries, a sportland or penny arcade, a vaudeville show in the Willow Grove, bars and refreshment stands and a Chinese restaurant named Casino de Marie. Also Law and Outlaw, Hu Gard's Mysteries, the Five Presidents, Coal Mine, Grand Canyon, Ghost Train, Honeymoon Lane, Aero Trainer, Airplanes, Drive-Your-Own Plane, Lindy Loop, Circle Swing, Pop-'em-In, Cross-the-Line, Tilt-a-Whirl, Red Bug and Leaping Lena.

What else? Well, there were new handball and basketball courts, new ping-pong, medicine-ball and punching-bag facilities. The Luna Park ballroom offered not only free dancing to adults but free instruction to children during the afternoons. The Luna Arena was making an attempt to revive the glory of old championship bouts at the Island by staging boxing and wrestling matches, at prices ranging from fifty-five cents general admission to $1.15 ringside.

The Dragon's Gorge, earliest scenic railway at the park, was still furnishing an underground ride. Captain Boynton's shoot-the-chutes were operating as usual but no spectacle of elephants riding down a special chute of their own. Instead the park offered Adele Richman's entertaining but less majestic pig slide. Perhaps the descent from elephants to pigs measured the decline of Luna in the amusement world.

Noel Coward, the English playwright, came nearest to expressing the feeling among sophisticates that Luna Park was playing down too much to public taste. After visiting several side shows, he was hurrying out, when a gateman stopped him, saying: "What's the matter?" "Oh, nothing's the matter," said Coward, "only it's much, much too gay!"

In 1941 a syndicate headed by Milton Sheen and William Miller tried an ambitious revival of Luna on a war-hilarity basis, with attractions ranging from replicas of British Wasp and Hurricane planes to three night clubs.

A BROOKLYN CHILDHOOD

by JOSEPH MULVANEY

Every New Yorker who has never had much to do with Brooklyn is certain that life over there is dreary and uneventful. I was brought up in Brooklyn nearly half a century ago and I felt the same way about it. Only across the river, I thought, were adventure and excitement to be found; in Brooklyn the days were long and the seasons interminable, for nothing of interest ever happened there or, I was confident, ever would. Looking back on it now from the other side of the river, I'm not so sure.

There were a dozen children in my family, which made it no more than a fair-sized one for the robust neighborhood we lived in, and we filled a three-story house on Degraw Street, which is in the section now known as South Brooklyn. All of us started school at the opening of the first term after we became four— a single term's delay would have been taken by the family as a confession of mental weakness—and we could read, write, and figure even before that. My oldest sister, Sadie, was a teacher at sixteen and, for $600 a year, maintained rigid order among a lot of young hoodlums in an old school at York and Adams Streets, in the district under the elevated lines which crossed, and still cross [1943], the Brooklyn Bridge. She had evaded Teachers

Training School and several years of preparation by taking a special course from the nuns of St. James's Pro-Cathedral School, on Jay Street. The rest of us hoped to get jobs like hers when we grew up. Didn't she have a five-hour day, a five-day week, all the legal holidays, and two months' vacation? Wasn't she paid extravagantly for going through the routine which we had to endure for nothing?

It was, of course, a tough school. Alfie Capone, a stocky, swarthy, silent, troublesome boy, was one of the pupils, and there were others more troublesome. It was nowhere near as tough, though, as P. S. 58, which was a block from our house and which I attended, or P. S. 32, over on President Street. Both of these schools had reform classes. Kids from around the Gowanus Canal dominated 58 and 32, and I did my best to make myself worthy of their companionship. They rated me as something of a sissy, though, for while in moments of desperate valor I might defy authority and had once told a teacher to shut up, I had never had the courage to swear at one, or throw a book or a slate at one, or shake a fist in one's face, or kick one in the shins, or butt one in the stomach. Moreover, the worst punishment I had ever suffered was a belting across the skull with a pointer, and that for mere inattention.

Physical violence by pupils and corporal punishment by teachers were daily occurrences in all the Brooklyn public schools. They were a fighting tribe, those teachers, and they needed to be to survive. Often my brothers and I wondered how Sadie kept control of her young charges. One teacher in her school was known to her classes as "The Horse-Killer." Another, a dark wisp of a girl who carried a withered right arm hidden in a black lace sling and so was looked upon as a mystery, had a left like a rifle. With her one good hand she could put down a rebellion. Whirling suddenly from the blackboard, she could groove the skull of a whispering boy with an eraser from a distance of thirty feet. Teachers did not walk alone in the district of Sadie's school. They walked in groups.

Strong-arm methods ruled family life, too. In our house, punishment was dealt out, depending on the seriousness of the offense, with a razor strop (routine misconduct), a sewing-machine belt (spirited transgression), or a whip (high crime). When my father needed the belt to administer discipline, he would take it off Mother's sewing machine, double it up into a big loop, and start flailing. The whip was a five-foot length of cowhide, tapering from two inches in diameter at its handle to a pointed tip. It was painted to match the wallpaper of the room in which it hung. From time to time, the baby of the year would reach for it and chew the paint off the tip. It was always repainted. After years of chewing, it took on the shape of an Indian arrowhead, and it was almost as hard and effective as one. Don't think my parents were cruel, though. Compared to them, Job was an unprovoked hothead.

Baths were required at least twice weekly at our house, usually on Wednesday and Saturday nights. We kids were bathed in washtubs in the kitchen; then, eyes stinging from Babbitt's soap and skins scoured by coarse brushes, we were wrapped in blankets, tucked into the dumbwaiter, hoisted aloft, and dropped into bed, where we swung into the strife that preceded sleep. The strife usually consisted of a pillow fight (we didn't throw pillows; we crammed them into one end of their cases and swung them like clubs), after which we would go to sleep listening to the chugging of the steam locomotives on the Fifth Avenue and Fulton Street elevateds.

We learned to smoke early in primary school—corn silk first, then horse-chestnut leaves, then cinnamon cigarettes, and finally Cycle cigarettes, at four for a cent and no questions asked. There were crap games under the gas lamp on our corner. For the very young, the stakes were cigarette-box pictures and marbles; boys of eight or nine played for pennies. Of sex we knew little until we reached high-school age, which was around twelve. Before achieving that maturity, we thought of girls only as tattling nuisances. One of us boys, having listened to older boys talk, might remark now and then that Bessie or Jessie or Tessie had a good leg, but later I'd ponder secretly over which of her legs was good. Occasionally, catching a glimpse of untrimmed lingerie, we would chant derisively at the wearer, "You'll never go to heaven when you die, because you don't wear ruffles on your drawers!" It was just something we'd heard. Once an older boy whispered that a schoolmate of mine was a "morphodye," which was a new one to me. By discreet questioning I learned that it meant half boy and half girl. I didn't believe it. My schoolmate bore no resemblance to Albert Alberta, the half-man, half-woman in the circus sideshow.

Most of the time, my younger brothers and I were concerned with matters more immediate and more engaging than sex. In the spring it was likely to be kite-flying. A kite cost two cents and a ball of cord to tether it was five. The cord could be length-ened with fishing line filched from Father's drawer. We'd take our kites to the top floor of our house, then up the ladder, through the trap door, and onto the roof, over which cool, fresh breezes always blew. Kite-flying was not simple or es-pecially safe. You had to run to make your kite take off, and it was hard to remember not to run right off the roof, which would have meant a drop of three stories to the flagged yard. Kite strings were likely to wind around neighboring chimneys, which resulted in the loss of a kite, a nickel's worth of cord, and most of Father's fishing line. There was also the chance that someone would close the hatch behind us and leave us marooned and uncertain whether we were on our own roof or the roof of one of the other identical houses that stood close together the whole length of the block. Then, too, nervous neighbors might call the police—and often did—when they heard what they imag-ined were burglars tramping on their roofs and trying their hatches.

Our summer vacations always dragged. Children in our neigh-borhood weren't taken to the country. The cost at places my family might have gone to was prohibitive—as much as five dollars a week for each of us—even though my father, a city detective, owned three big brick houses and was considered pros-perous. Swimming, the favorite summer sport in Brooklyn, was lethal for beginners. You'd go down to Long Dock, on the East River, with older boys who had promised to teach you. You'd strip and then suddenly your tutor would flick you off the stringpiece and you'd drop twenty feet into the water. If you went under twice, he would dive in and rescue you. If you couldn't learn in three lessons, you were given up.

I was given up. My scant swimming ability was acquired in the sissies' course, which I took with other boys who had flunked the hard one. We'd go out to Bay Ridge and hire a rowboat for ten cents an hour. Then, while one of us rowed, the rest would strip and slip overside, hang onto a rope at the stern, and paddle with their feet. The oarsmen on these excursions generally had a weakness for rowing into the wake of ferryboats and liners, which added a fillip to the occasion. Sometimes we'd get caught in an ebbing tide, which might have carried us to Rockaway or, indeed, to Bermuda if some passing barge captain hadn't thrown us a line. With two companions, I was rescued once by a man who rowed out from a barge and towed us back. We had to wait on his barge from dusk to midnight for the tide to turn, but we were fed well and free, and were entertained under the stars by the bargeman's two pretty daughters, who sang and played mandolins.

The big event of any summer, of course, was the Fourth of July. Revolvers were seventy-five cents, single-shot pistols a quarter. For a week after the Fourth, we picked gunpowder from one another's faces with pins or needles. Occasionally our eyes, spattered with explosive, required the attentions of a doctor or druggist, which cost at least a dollar. Gunpowder from blank cartridges was good for tattooing, if you made a thick paste of it with spit and were brave enough to stab it into your arm with a needle. My oldest brother's arm today retains his self-inflicted initials. Some kids preferred coal dust to gunpowder for tattooing. Often, in school, I tried ink and a pen point, but that was no good. Don't waste your time with it. Mineral grains are essential.

During the autumn, from Labor Day on, we prepared for Election Day. We went around to all the saloons and stores in the neighborhood to steal boxes and barrels for the fire. Toward the end, we even carried off billboards and wooden stoops in a desperate attempt to get enough fuel. We stored the loot in the cellar of some friendly merchant or took over an empty house, which we entered through the coalhole in the sidewalk. On Election Day, towers of beer kegs and paint barrels burned until around midnight, when the results usually became known and most of the nearby awnings were charred. No matter who won the election, it was considered a success if the fire was big enough.

Winter brought revenue from snow shovelling—fifteen cents for a householder's sidewalk, ten for his areaway. If a boy's back and arms held out, he might make almost a dollar in a single day in this way, provided he gave up snowballing and sleigh riding, but that took a lot of determination—more than most of us had. Often my parents would make me clear our own walk and areaway first, unremunerated, while my friends were amassing wealth. I wished then that I was an orphan.

We kids read a good deal. Five cents got us "Old Sleuth," "Young Sleuth," "Nick Carter," "Cap Collier," "Wide Awake," "Happy Days," or any one of a number of similar classics. Along with these I read fitfully in "Pickwick Papers" and Dante's Inferno," in the edition with the terrifying Doré illustrations. At least once a week I returned to the big red-and-gold Dante volume to shudder and squirm in torment with the lost souls. As for plays, I was taken to see, and enjoyed, "The Span of Life," "The Still Alarm," and "Yon Yonson." Once I wanted to see Ada Rehan in a French play, but my father wouldn't permit that. He said that she might be Ada Rehan to everybody else but she was still the Crehan girl, daughter of plain Mr. Crehan down the block, to him, and he was damned if he was going to let me waste money to see her now when I could have seen her for nothing on the streets of our neighborhood a few years earlier.

Our next-door neighbors were the McArdles. They were often visited by a placid old lady named Lucy, a relative of theirs, who wore black and had bonnet strings tied in a bow at her throat. She talked a great deal about her son Jim, who, it seemed, was a good lad but too easy-going. He was falling in with bad company—actors and that sort of people. Why, just last week, we would hear, she had gone to his flat and driven out a pack of people who were dancing and drinking wine. She had herded them out of the place with her umbrella, while Jim had just stood there laughing at her. She had nearly forgotten herself and used it on him. Before she left, she had made him get a man to paint over the walls of his bathroom and so get rid of those pictures of hussies without even enough clothes on to save their decency. Off and on for years the neighbors talked of Jim, always speaking of him simply as Lucy McArdle's cousin. When neighborhood girls grew up, they usually went to work for the American Can or the American Steel & Wire Co., and it was invariably Lucy McArdle's Cousin Jim who had spoken for them. He had something to do with railroads, I understood, and for a long time I thought he was probably a trolley conductor—a high position, to my mind. I was nearly grown up before I learned that he and Diamond Jim Brady were the same man.

Mr. and Mrs. Harris, a strange, secretive couple, were also neighbors of ours. They had a son, Carlyle, who was handsome and reckless and had once suffered a broken arm in a fight with my oldest brother. Mrs. Harris wore bloomers and rode a bicycle, which no other woman in Brooklyn dared do. Of course she didn't ride it on our block—we kids would have stoned her—but I used to see her pushing her heavy "safety" off to less circumspect parts of town and, later, back home again. No woman on our block would speak to her.

There came a time when my brothers and I sensed that something mysterious and exciting had happened nearby, but we could not discover what. Our parents would not let us read the newspapers. In a few days we began to hear older boys ask this riddle in stores and on street corners: "When they burn Carlyle Harris, where will they send his ashes?" The answer, which baffled me, was "To hell in pots," and it was considered very funny by those in the know. Years passed before I found out what it meant; I was too ashamed of my ignorance to ask my friends and I couldn't mention the matter at home, because to me "hell" was a curse and "pots" a dirty word. When at last I did learn what all the commotion had been about, I no longer cared much. It seems that, like his mother, Carlyle Harris was a sort of pioneer: he was one of the first persons electrocuted in this state. He had murdered his bride. Her name was Helen Potts.

Another riddle that was current briefly in my youth was this: "Why are two Irishmen going to call on a girl like the East River?" You gave up. "Because they are going to Bridget." The East River had been spanned some ten years before, which made the riddle even flatter. They were still charging tolls on the Brooklyn Bridge in those days; the tariff for walking across was one cent, but it was worth it because you could see the crack in the middle of the vast, suspended structure which drew together under the weight of passing cable cars and then opened again. You could stare back at Columbia Heights, too, and try to see the window from which the crippled Washington Augustus Roebling had fulfilled his greatest contract by watching over the completion of the bridge through a telescope.

South and west of our street stretched an area dominated by Scots and Swedes. Often I explored it and made friends. On First Place lived the Nobles family: Milton and Dolly, both of whom had been on the stage, and their two children, who also eventually became actors. The walls of the Nobles' living room were covered with photographs of Mr. and Mrs. Nobles in the many lovers' rôles they had played together. Mr. Nobles had written "The Phoenix," the play from which came the line "And the villain still pursued her!" I recall how proud he was of Maude Adams' Broadway début, for he had carried her onto the stage long before, when, as a nine-month-old infant, she played her first rôle, in stock in Salt Lake City.

Now and then, listening to the Scots and Swedes talking on their stoops in the evening, I'd be puzzled by guarded remarks about what sort of weather it was for Johnny and speculation as to whether Johnny would go out. Again I pretended to be knowing rather than ask questions, so it was not until a long while later that I learned what those rusty-faced shipmasters and outfitters were talking about. "Johnny" was Dynamite Johnny O'Brien, a smuggler who, on a dark evening, would put out from a Red Hook slip in a lightless launch with explosives, machine guns, and rifles for Gomez and García in Cuba. It was Johnny's problem to avoid the Coast Guard cutters and torpedo boats which lay in wait for him off Atlantic Highlands and to transfer his cargo at sea to blockade-runners, for which Spanish warships were lying in wait off the Cuban coast. I've often suspected that Johnny of Red Hook may have kept the Cuban revolution going until the United States officially went to war with Spain.

Of the opposite sex, the youngster in our neighborhood who made the greatest impression on my gang was neither a beauty nor a tomboy but the little Gallagher girl. She had been crippled, by infantile paralysis, according to the story we all accepted. For a year or so she was bedridden, then she was allowed outdoors in a wheel chair, a big-eyed wraith of a girl with a gentle smile and soft, curling brown hair that framed her face—like a halo, I used to think. She was not strong enough to talk much, and she read a great deal and sometimes sat for hours in the sun with eyes half closed, watching the rest of us roller-skating or playing tag and hopscotch. Physicians told her parents that she was incurably crippled and could not hope ever to walk without crutches again.

Then she read or heard of the old tradition that, on the day of the Feast of the Assumption, water is a cure—not water in a washbasin or bathtub but open water, the opener the better. I believe the tradition also holds that only the pure in spirit as well as in body can benefit. The Gallagher girl told her mother she wanted to go bathing at Coney Island on Assumption Day. Her doctors thought it unwise, the parish priest was startled, her parents were fearful, but none of them felt that such a request could be denied. So they took her to Coney Island on the day of the feast, in August.

The Gallagher girl hobbled on her crutches to a warm, sunny bathhouse, where her mother tremblingly took off the girl's clothes and covered her emaciated figure with a heavy flannel bathing suit that covered her from her neck to her ankles. Her father carried her to the edge of the water. With eyes wide and body shaking, she tucked her crutches under her arms, set their tips in the sand, and swung her feet into the surf. For a moment she stood there, then she turned her head, smiled, dropped the crutches, stood erect, and walked into deeper water.

The Gallagher girl never used crutches or a wheel chair after that and, as far as I know, may be alive today. Naturally, we kids were all very thrilled at first by what had happened, but then we decided that the Gallagher girl had never been like the rest of us and such a thing was almost to be expected in her case. So when, the next time we had composition in school, we were ordered to write about some unusual experience we had had or heard of, I described a purely imaginary mountain-climbing expedition in the Alps. I could think of nothing interesting nearer home.

A BAD DAY IN BROOKLYN

by EDMUND WILSON

On Wednesday, March 25, in Brooklyn, three people tried to kill themselves.

The Bay Ridge section of Brooklyn is inhabited chiefly by Scandinavians. Fifth Avenue near Leiv Eriksson Square is an infinitely continuing suburban business street of drug stores, small department stores, five-and-ten-cent stores and phonograph and radio stores run by people whose names end in -sen: a good many of them have cut-rate prices in the windows. The people on the streets are nothing if not respectable and they are not in too much of a hurry: tall blond Scandinavian men and girls and fat Scandinavian children. The Scandinavians get Americanized with a rapidity that is nobody's business. Around the corner, the side streets have rows of little ugly brownstone houses, each with two stories of polygonal bay-window sticking out, which go down a hill toward the water, all alike like steps.

Otto Reich lives in a four-story building above a Beauty Shoppe, where the bright Scandinavian girl says that he has nothing to do with them and they don't know anything about it. The narrow stairs have green linoleum, a glue-yellow, sticky-looking dado and a dispiriting backhouse smell.

Otto Reich is nineteen years old: he is a blond German boy with blue eyes, light hair smoothly slicked back, bumpkin nose, fleshy red mouth and recessive chin. He was born in Berlin and trained to be a waiter—he used to work in the big Hotel Eden. But he wanted to see other places and he wanted to get away from his family, with whom he had always lived. So a year ago he borrowed money from his brother-in-law and came to the States. He wanted to be alone and independent.

But when he first arrived in New York, the hard times had already set in and he couldn't get a waiter's job. For eight or nine months he worked as a bus-boy in various restaurants, hotels and clubs. A bus-boy works ten or twelve hours with an hour off in the afternoon; his pay is about $40 a month, with practically no tips. Finally, Otto got a job at the St. Martin waiting on the hotel officials. He asked to be put on room service, and when there was a vacancy, they had him fill it. He got $38 a month and about $12 a week in tips. Eating at the hotel, he was able to save almost the whole of his wages and was gradually paying back his brother-in-law in Germany who had lent him the money to come over.

Since the depression the New York hotels have made a wage cut of 10 percent and a general reduction of their staffs. When there is an increase of business over a holiday or week-end, they make the room-service men help out after hours in the restaurant with no extra pay, but only tips. One Saturday night at the St. Martin, when Otto had been there four months, they told him to go to the restaurant. He was already working from seven in the morning till nine o'clock at night, which meant that, living in Bay Ridge, he had to get up at five-thirty in the morning and didn't get home until after ten. If he worked in the restaurant, too, he wouldn't get home till after one and would have only four hours of sleep. In Germany everywhere you worked only eight hours a day: the unions had fought it out with the hotels. At the Eden, he had worked from six to three and then he had had his time to himself.

Besides, he didn't get along with the head waiter in the St. Martin restaurant—he had already worked under him when he was waiting on the officials. The head waiter was an Italian and Otto had a low opinion of Italian waiters. The German and French waiters were the only waiters who understood "service." He had been trained to give service in Germany in one of the best hotels—service means wiping the knives and forks and polishing the plates before they are set down on the table, taking the cover off the dish and showing it to the guest, and a great many other useful acts and ceremonies—he had been thoroughly instructed in all this and knew exactly how these things ought to be done. But Italian waiters are uneducated imbeciles and they are not clean—that is why even smart American hotels like the St. Martin that want to have service can't get it. This particular Italian head waiter used always to be coming up behind him and gabbling at him. He would keep telling Otto to do things differently, but the head waiter was foolish—really he was foolish. He used to bawl Otto out in front of the people he was waiting on and Otto always did what the Italian told him, but the Italian was wrong—always wrong. Tonight he felt he couldn't face it, he was too much nervous already—so he told them he was only hired to work from seven to nine and took the subway home to Bay Ridge. The next morning when he came to work, he found his time-card gone and on inquiry found that he was fired.

That was February 16. Every morning after that, he went to the Geneva Association, the international waiters' organization, and every morning he found the same men there, waiting like him for jobs. There are three or four waiters to every job at the present time in New York, and Otto presently got so discouraged that he began applying at bakeries and factories, but things there were just as bad. The worst of it was that when he had lost his job, he had only half paid his brother-in-law back. He had given him a note to pay him back in a year and now the year was nearly over.

Every night he would go back to his room and brood. He had no friends that he cared about in New York, so he had gone to live in Bay Ridge soon after he had come over, to be near a German couple who were the only people he liked. The wife had been a schoolmate of his sister's and she had sent him her address. He had taken a room on the same floor at $5 a week and had furnished it in such style as he could afford. He bought a lavender sateen spread for the bed and lavender sateen cushions for the sofa and a cheap imitation tapestry for the mantelpiece; and he decorated the wall with pennants of Bear Mountain, Palisade Park, Long Beach and the Statue of Liberty. He kept a bottle of perfume exactly in the center of his dressing-table and on the wall on either side of it hung a pair of boxing-gloves. He had always boxed regularly in Germany, and though he hadn't been able to much since he had come to the States, he did boxing exercises every morning at five-thirty when he first got up. He never turned the heat on in winter and always slept cold with all the windows open, as he believed that cold was good for the health. At the time he was working, he never went out dancing, but went to the movies once a week, on his night off.

The German woman's husband, who was a coppersmith, was out of work, too—he was lucky if he was able to put in a few days occasionally at the dry dock. He had gotten to coming home and brooding, too, and he had finally resorted to buying a radio so as to make things a little bit gay in the evenings. The German couple were very kind to him and he trusted them. He would go in every night and talk to them and play with the kid and listen to the radio. They had told all about themselves to each other by this time and they were pretty well talked out: every time any of them got a letter from Germany, that was an event—it gave them something new to talk about. They didn't know any of the Scandinavians.

But Otto was afraid to write home. He couldn't bear to let his parents know how badly he was doing in America. He was the only son and they counted on him. And they were poor and if they knew he was out of work, they would want to send him money. Also, he couldn't bring himself to tell his brother-in-law that he couldn't pay him back. One day in March he got a letter from his mother saying that his father was seriously sick.

He went on looking for a job—he would have taken any kind of a job—until he had only $4 left. He had been depending lately on the German family for meals. One night he went out for a walk about eight and the next thing he knew he was in his room sitting up on the bed with his clothes off. His German friend was sitting beside him and there was a man who had been working over him with a pulmotor. It seemed that there was an ambulance outside and that he had tried to commit suicide. A man from upstairs had come down and found him lying unconscious in the hall and the hall full of gas. He had evidently turned on the gas and then, when he was nearly asphyxiated, broken out of the room.

He couldn't remember anything about it. He couldn't even remember ever having thought of suicide. He thought he must have gone crazy for a while. And he couldn't sleep all the rest of the night after they left him, blaming himself and worrying over having done such a thing.

II

The Brownsville section of Brooklyn is mostly Jewish. Only fifteen years ago, it was all country and there was nothing but little farms there, but it was built up on a real-estate boom and today it is a paradise of brick—all fairly low buildings and mostly very clean and neat, not an unattractive place to live. There are light-brown brick apartment houses, streets of double brick houses whose monotony has been carefully mitigated by making the brick different tints of orange, yellow and red and the woodwork, say, on one side green and on the other side yellow, apartment houses in red-brick cliffs wired with identical green fire-escapes but with an effect of distinctiveness carefully provided by making the façades rise to slightly unconventional curves at the top, little special gingerbread-brick mansions with little brick and iron-grille walls around their front yards and the signs of Jewish doctors and blue fleurs-de-lys of stained glass in the narrow front windows, shabbier duocellular brick houses all with green woodwork on red brick and each with a clothes-pole mast leaning askew at the summit of its front, and on Livonia Avenue under the El, dingier brick.

Irma Meyer lives under the El in the first of a small solid row of tarnished pink brick houses. Her parents are Polish Jews. When she was sixteen she married a truck driver and she has had two children by him. She is twenty-one now. She has a cunning rather little-girl-like face, with skin extremely dark, slanting eyes and un-Jewish snub nose.

Jake Meyer turned out to be a loafer and his sister, who was well off, had to carry them. Jake's sister was married to a custom tailor who was in business for himself, and she sent her sons to Duke University and had two big white Russian wolf-hounds. She helped Irma out with money regularly—Irma and her husband hadn't spent $10 on the children since they were born— and once Jake's sister had taken the whole family in for two weeks when Jake wasn't working.

But Jake didn't want to work. He had a little dinky $75 truck and he was supposed to deliver orange drink in it and get so much a case on commission, but some days he wouldn't show up and they finally fired him. Irma went to his boss and pled with him and told him about the children and they consented to take him back. But then she found he was going with other women and was driving them around in the truck. The first part of March Jake disappeared and left her without any money. The husband of Jake's sister, in the meantime, had gone bankrupt on account of the depression and now had to work for somebody else: the family had had to sell all the nice things they had bought when they were rich, and they couldn't give Irma any more help. It was all they could do to pay for their sons at Duke. The only things they kept were the Russian wolfhounds. Irma couldn't go to work because she didn't have anybody to take care of the children. She couldn't put them in a nursery because the nurseries were closed on Saturdays, whereas any place you worked always did business on Saturday. She couldn't take them and go to live with her parents either, because her brother wouldn't let her. Her father was a presser and since the slump had been making almost nothing: the pressers had been harder hit than anybody, because the only time people got their clothes pressed now was just before the holidays, and he had only two seasons a year of about two weeks each. Her brother, who was doing better, had come to the rescue of their mother and father, and he said that he hadn't taken his mother out of that cold flat and put her in C and D4 of a fine new apartment house to have her made a housemaid of.

Irma was behind with two months' rent, $32 a month, and she owed all the tradesmen money. She wasn't paid up on the bedroom set and expected to have it taken away any day. For food, she had to go to the police station, where once a week they gave her potatoes and onions and canned goods. The children were too young for this food and needed milk, but they told her at the police station that she could feed them on cabbage. She also appealed to the Jewish Aid Society and they recommended her case to the Mayor's Committee, who gave her $15. Finally, she got a dispossess notice.

After two weeks Jake turned up again. Irma got a warrant against him for abandonment and had him up in court, where the judge sentenced him to pay her $15 a week. Afterwards he followed her home and she got a cop in to kick him out, but the cop said he had a right to stay there. So he came home at night and flopped on the couch. He gave her a little money, but he wasn't doing very well and by the time he'd paid for gas and oil and the garage expenses he only had a few dollars left. The bills kept piling up and the apartment looked more and more of a mess and it was nag-nag every night until finally they got disgusted and wouldn't talk to each other any more. Jake's sister used to come to see Irma and would leave one of the Russian wolfhounds there to amuse the children and cheer her up. But nobody had any idea how low in her mind Irma was, because she kept up a good front and didn't talk about it.

Finally one day she went out to the butcher's and saw Jake with another woman riding around in his truck. When he came home, she wouldn't let him in and slammed the door in his face and locked it.

That night she put the two children to bed in the front room and fastened paper over the place where there was a pane out in the folding glass doors between the bedroom and the sitting-room. Then she closed all the windows and turned on the gas in the kitchen and sat down to wait. But it occurred to her that if the gas was on the whole night, it might eventually leak through into the bedroom, and she decided she had better wait till near morning and arrange so that the milkman would be sure of coming in and turning it off after she had been suffo-cated. So she turned the gas off and wrote the milkman a note and put it outside in a milk bottle. Then she waited a good part of the night, so as not to give the gas many hours, and at last turned all the burners of the stove on and sat down in the kitchen to wait. She read a magazine called Airplane Stories to keep her mind off how long it was going to take. It wasn't bad—she just gradually became unconscious.

But there was no door between the kitchen and the sitting-room, and she hadn't allowed enough time for both of the rooms to get filled. When the milkman came in the morning and broke in, she was still alive and they brought her to.

Irma's attempted suicide had no effect on Jake. He told her she had only done it to make people pity her and came back to flop every night as usual without having anything to say to her.

III

Beaver Street, off Flushing Avenue, is a sort of Sicilian sec-tion. It is an old part of Brooklyn and most of the buildings are old-fashioned frame affairs covered with clapboards, and a faded brownish yellowish, as if they had never been painted any par-ticular color since they were first put up sixty years ago. They run to wooden cornices with little fancy faded friezes and little peaked projecting fancy hoods over the windows. There is also a sprin-kling of new stucco houses in the Mediterranean taste, covered with pink, white and green scales like the jars of peppermint and wintergreen candy tablets in the little corner candy and cigar stores.

The Dimicelis live in one of the faded buildings above a grocery store. They had to move there from a better apartment when Mr. Dimiceli was earning so little. They don't know many of the Italians in the neighborhood—they are not so friendly, because Mr. Dimiceli is a respectable man who speaks not Sicilian dialect but good Italian and used to be in business for himself. The surounding tenements are full of Italians of the class that knife each other and live in squalor. The Dimicelis' flat is absolutely clean and it is furnished with a vivid color which contrasts with the discolored streets of Flushing. The walls of every room are decorated with bright religious prints in green, blue and red—the Bleeding Heart, the Holy Family and the Virgin with flowers in her arms over the bed in the bedroom, the Last Supper over the kitchen table; and the whole place has the brightness and the clear outlines of one of those simple prints: bedroom walls in green, kitchen oilcloth in blue and white squares, kitchen curtains in green and white, sink and kitchen table absolutely white, three yellow canaries in yellow cages in the kitchen.

The Dimicelis themselves are clear, vivid and handsome, too. The mother and daughter have just been out to the hospital, and they are wearing clean dresses in plain colors, the black-eyed daughter, white, and the mother, with her black hair smoked gray, blue—with black stockings and polished shoes. Mrs. Dimiceli is a small woman with a quick attractive, fine-boned face, where irony, sadness, pride and calm succeed each other in responsive flashes.

Mr. Dimiceli is less a Sicilian than a type who has become familiar all over the world with the development of modern engineering. He is tall and thin with strong dark eyes like lenses behind the lenses of rimless spectacles, strong black hair brushed back and parted in the middle and long flexible tool-like fingers. Mr. Dimiceli left Sicily when he was a young man and went to France, where he worked for thirteen years as a skilled machinist in automobile plants. Several years before the War, he came back to Palermo and went into business as an electrical contractor. Electricity was at that time still more or less of a novelty in Sicily and Mr. Dimiceli got a good many commissions wiring Sicilian towns. Then the War broke and he had to serve. He went through the whole four years and a half of it as a sergeant of horse artillery. There is a picture of him in the apartment with his képi, a Caruso mustache and a whole rainbow of campaign ribbons. During the War he had Mrs. Dimiceli sell all his electrical equipment so that the family would have something to live on in case he got killed.

When the War was over and he came home to Palermo, he couldn't get his business back again because it had been captured while he was away by other contractors who had sprung up in the meantime. Finally, he decided that there were better opportunities in America than in Europe, so he brought the family over and got a job with a company on Long Island that made automobile parts. He became shop superintendent and worked there until the fall of '29, when the company sold the patent on a piston it had been making to a firm in Cleveland and sent all its big machines out there. They laid off something like three hundred men and among them Mr. Dimiceli: they gave him a recommendation which said that he was "a very reliable man and only the fact we are reducing our production forces us to part with him." They only kept on the men who had been with them longest. Mr. Dimiceli, however, got a job the next month with the Otis Elevator Company, but as the demand for elevators was declining, the Otis people, also, were obliged to lay off their newest men last spring.

After that, Mr. Dimiceli went out every day looking for work, but all he was able to find was odd jobs at the rate of one or two days a month. Sometimes the best he could do was to make a dollar a day driving a truck. Mrs. Dimiceli had to begin to look for work herself, and she succeeded from time to time in getting from $7 to $12 a week finishing dresses for a Brooklyn dressmaker. The youngest son also turned to, and earned $5 a week as a delivery boy. The eldest son was married and had a child and made only $20 a week as a presser, so that he couldn't help them out. The family had come down in the world and as time went on, they couldn't see how they were going to be able even to stick where they were. They owed three months' rent on their new and inferior apartment, and it was only the fact that the landlord was an Italian and a friend of theirs that made it possible for them to stay on there.

Mr. Dimiceli was a man in his fifties, who had once been a successful contractor in Palermo, whose career had been broken up by the War, and who now spent every day going the rounds of the factories in Brooklyn and Jersey and not being able to get even the lowest paid job. Wednesday night, when he came home he was nervous and gloomy, but the family didn't notice it particularly because he was nervous and gloomy every night. He would come back and read the paper and sometimes just lie down on the bed without talking. Nobody had any suspicion of what he was going to do. The family were down listening to the radio in the apartment of the woman below, when the youngest boy, who was coming upstairs, heard a shot from their apartment. He found his father sitting in the kitchen with his head all covered with blood. He had turned the gas in the stove on, too, but had evidently been afraid that that wouldn't be quick enough. They took him to the hospital, and the doctors couldn't tell Mrs. Dimiceli whether he was going to live or die.

Mrs. Dimiceli says that the Italians who come over and go in for racketeering in America have wonderful opportunities, but that it is no place for a skilled machinist.

New Republic, April 22, 1931. *Reprinted by permission of New Republic, Inc.*

Civic Virtue

BROOKLYN HAS BEEN moralizing itself since the town began. It has done overly much probing of the state of its soul, knowledge, and culture. The temperance movement got some of its strongest support in Brooklyn, and so did women's suffrage and abolition. Brooklyn's Institute of Arts and Science started a hundred and twenty-five years ago as the Apprentice's Library, where boys bound out to learn a trade could congregate. They had been hanging out in grogshops or else buying gin to take out and getting drunk under ropewalks. The library died out, and rose again as the outfit controlling the Brooklyn Museum, the Children's Museum, the Botanic Gardens, and other cultural enterprises.

Prospect Park, a lovely place, is considered to be the work of James S. T. Stranahan, a great water-front builder and a man of public spirit. Years before him, Hezekiah Pierrepont wanted the Heights, the area overlooking Manhattan, to be made into a park, or at least be the site of a promenade, and he failed. Stranahan, a politician as well as a financier, pushed through his plan for a park. In 1869, he said: "At no time in the history of the two cities has the tendency appeared to be so strongly established toward a state of things in which the capitalists have their residence in the city of New York, while their clerks and workmen only have houses in Brooklyn, with the inevitable consequence that the profit of the labor represented by our population should be mainly enjoyed outside our limits, and that our taxable property should be of hopelessly inferior character. The question which was pressed upon us was whether any plant of improvement could be devised and undertaken which would be adequate to attract and hold among us a large share of that class of citizens which it was necessary should be attracted, if we were to avoid throwing upon our people of moderate means, and upon the poor, an excessive and crushing burden of taxation." Quite a statement for two sentences. His park has made a fine playground for Brooklyn people, and it did attract the wealthy kind of people he wanted, and Park Slope to the west of the park became the town's Gold Coast.

James Gibbons Huneker in New Cosmopolis had this to say: "Nor must I miss Prospect Park, Brooklyn, near enough to reach in half an hour [from New York], and from grassy knolls of which the turrets and pinnacles of Manhattan may be seen. It is far more captivating than Central Park, and the Flatbush Avenue entrance reminds me of some vast plaza in a European capital, upper Brussels, for example. It is imposing with its MacMonnies monument, its spaciousness, and general decorative effect—an effect enhanced by the Italianate water-tower and the Museum farther down, whose vast galleries house so little original art, with the exception of the Sargent water-colors and former Chapman pictures. It is only fair to add that Prospect Park began with natural advantages made the most of. This park really makes Brooklyn habitable and not merely an interlude of bricks and mortar before achieving the seashore."

Then there is Greenwood Cemetery, a place of rather odd beauty. There are trees, fanciful crypts, and a fine view across the water to Manhattan. It was started early in the nineteenth century as a rural burial ground, a rather startling idea to people who had buried their families and wanted themselves buried in churchyards. It was years before the old custom was broken down, but eventually Greenwood became quite fashionable as what they call a resting place.

We have mentioned the park and cemetery in a collection touching upon the town's thought because, although certainly palpable, they represent in an undefinable way much that is Brooklyn.

The Central Brooklyn Public Library was started in 1897 and completed in 1940. It's no cathedral; it was just that money would run out. The legendary acumen of Brooklyn's politicians at getting appropriations would fail when the matter of the library would come up. Until 1935, it resembled an unrepaired battlefield. That year, the late Borough President Raymond V. Ingersoll, a Fusion product and a good citizen of the town, pushed it through. While the library had been a-building, Brooklyn, always a bookish community, was served by many branch libraries and the ramshackle, pleasant old library on Montague Street.

LIVELY TIMES

TEMPERANCE AGITATORS BEFORE THE EXCISE COMMISSONERS

Complaining Against Liquor Dealers for Selling to Minors

Intemperate Language Used on Both Sides—Mr. Ide's Warmth of Temper.

Mr. Edwin P. Ide, the Temperance man, and Louis Froelich, the President of the Liquor Dealers' Protective Union, had several tilts before the Excise Commissioners this morning. Mr. Ide became excited while Froelich grinned, and General Jourdan had to call them both to order. Commissioners Jourdan and Lauer heard the complaints against liquor dealers detected in violations of the Excise Law. Mr. Ide had three cases to bring before the Commissioners of selling beer to minors. His language on the stand was not at all times temperate and once he had to be rebuked by General Jourdan.

The first complaint was against Rudolf Kunzer, of No. 38 Humboldt Street. Mr. Ide said of this:

"I was sitting in Captain Worth's station-house on the evening of June 28, Thursday, when a man came in apparently very much aggrieved [sic] because his wife had received nineteen trade dollars in exchange for a $20 bill when she bought some beer from a liquor dealer. I went to the dealer's place with Mr. Wassmer and was speaking to him about it when a little girl came in with a pail and asked for some beer. The beer was given to her and she paid for it, then I asked the girl if I might taste it, and she said 'yes,' and I tasted it and I saw it was beer. Then I went to her house and saw her mother."

Minnie Bovee, the 12-year old girl whom Mr. Ide had intercepted, said that she had gone for the beer for a friend of her mother's, who was visiting the house. Mr. Ide followed her back to the house and frightened her mother so that she fainted, and the beer was then so stale that after taking a sip of it, the gentleman who sent her for it threw it into the water sink.

Louis Froelich moved to dismiss the complaint on the ground that the defendant acted under the law in selling beer to the girl, as she had her mother's consent to the purchase.

The matter was referred to the council of the board for an opinion.

Mr. Ide also complained of Martin Meyer, of 13 Graham avenue, for selling beer to a minor. He said that Mr. Scofield and himself were taking a quiet stroll, on a Wednesday, in that neighborhood, when they noticed children, from 3 years old upward, going for beer with pails and pitchers. It saddened him very much to see the sight.

"Keep down to the facts," said General Jourdan. "This is no time for speech making."

Mr. Ide looked aggrieved as he went on to say that he saw a girl go into Meyer's place with a pail, put it on the bar, and have it filled with beer. When the girl came out he asked her what she had in the pail and she said beer. He asked her if he might taste it and she said he might, and he took a swallow of it. She said her name was Mary Hartman, and she lived at 23 Graham avenue.

"You drank the beer, did you?" asked Louis Froelich.

"I tasted it," said Mr. Ide.

"You sneaked into the hallway to taste the beer which this little girl had?"

"I went into the hallway," answered the witness, with rising temper.

"Nice way to get free beer," sneered Froelich.

"Oh say some more, say some more, Froelich," said Mr. Ide, now in a white heat. "I want you to get at me once, only just once, that is all I ask."

"You ain't my equal," retorted Froelich, and then *sotto voce*, "or the equal of any decent man."

Martin Meyer, the defendant, admitted that his wife had sold the girl beer, and said that shortly afterward the girl's mother came to him and said that he had only sent half a pint of beer instead of a pint. His wife had sent a full pint.

"Our friend, Mr. Ide, swallowed half of it in the hallway," said Froelich.

Mr. Ide rose to his feet and fairly shouted: "I swear that I only took a small swallow of that beer. I wish to say right here that I only sip the beer just to get legal evidence. I don't drink it."

"Oh-h-h," drawled Froelich, and the liquor men all laughed. This case was also referred to the Board for an opinion.

The next complaint for selling beer to minors was made against Charles Schnell, of 664 Flushing avenue. Mr. Ide had Officer Travis to go with him to that place, where he tasted a beer that a 12-year old boy was getting in a kettle. It was on a Sunday, after Mr. Ide had been to church. The officer did not sustain Mr. Ide in every particular, and this provoked that gentleman in saying:

"Oh, oh! this is the kind of officer I have to deal with. I am glad I found it out."

As the case progressed he made some further reflections upon the officer, who was his own witness, when Counselor Baker, who appeared for the defendent, said:

"The Commissioners are competent to deal with the officer."

"And the public will deal with them," retorted Mr. Ide.

A tilt ensued between counsel and witness, the latter of whom began to orate when General Jourdan said:

"No debate here. I preside, and you must keep order."

"Very well, sir," said Mr. Ide, as he sank back into his chair and submitted to Mr. Baker's cross-examination. Mr. Baker was going into Mr. Ide's present employment and antecedents when he was stopped by General Jourdan, who told him to confine himself to the case.

As a clear case of selling on Sunday was proved the Commissioners voted to revoke Meyer's license. Subsequently the license of Christian Goetz, proprietor of the Bedford Brewery, was revoked, and several saloons were placed under police surveillance.

Brooklyn Union, *July 13, 1883*

Brooklyn had great churches and great ministers—it has some yet—and considerable of the intellectual life of the nation about the time of the Civil War was spent here. The moderate abolition movement, temperance, and women's suffrage all got either their start or a great push in Brooklyn. And it was a frightening combination of Victoria Woodhull, Tennessee Claflin, and Susan B. Anthony that finally brought the Tilton-Beecher case to the attention and scandal of the nation.

When Henry Ward Beecher died on March 8, 1887, there was brought to a close a triumphant and uncomfortable period of quasi-religious, quasi-liberal, quasi-political thought in America, and it was all Beecher's. There were many men, such as Dr. Richard S. Storrs, of greater intellectual capacity than Beecher, and thousands of men, in and out of the clergy, of stronger moral fiber, but Beecher was the man the country looked to. He was even more of a national figure than a local one, and his own thoughts were more on the national than on the local scene. Although his work doesn't read particularly well after seventy years, he must have been a great speaker. Some enthusiasts said he was the greatest orator since St. Paul, and that was in a day of "tasting" ministers; people shopped congregations until they got a preacher they liked. Beecher had to turn them away.

His trial for adultery, a not unusual crime, had an enormous impact on the country. A critic for the Nation, reviewing in 1903 Lyman Abbott's biography of Beecher, wrote: "In one respect Dr. Abbott's statement [in a chapter called "Under Accusation"], however wise and just, must prove misleading to the reader who is under middle age. Dry, hard, and cold, it gives no sign of the social demoralization that overwhelmed the local community for a succession of years, during which one sordid theme engrossed the general mind, and with its terrible insistence broke up the peace of families and alienated friend from friend."

Beecher was, to the public at least, one of the most important men in America at the time of the trial in 1874. He not only was the Great Preacher, he was a powerful political figure and American symbol. Sex in the clergy has always been a titillating subject when exposed to the public, and from the contemporary newspapers and journals it is hard to judge now whether people read about anything else during the months the case dragged along. There were columns in the newspapers, articles in learned journals, and scurrilous doggerel and cartoons in broadsheets. It was Theodore Tilton vs. Henry Ward Beecher for alienation of the affections of Elizabeth Tilton, and Beecher was acquitted by a vote of 9 to 3, a probably higher expression of faith in his his virtue than he would have received in a nation-wide poll. Beecher, although he appeared even to his friends to be both a jackass and a sniveler, survived with some glory. Tilton was ruined and left the country. Beecher showed some courage thereafter in embracing a loose form of Darwinism, recanting the doctrine of hell, and especially in breaking with the Republican Party, which he had helped to build, and supporting Cleveland against Blaine. Cleveland had admitted an illegitimate daughter, and Beecher's past too was brought up again.

There were other flashy preachers in Brooklyn, but none with Beecher's hold on the country. Dr. T. DeWitt Talmadge showed up in the later years of Beecher's career. He attracted huge audiences with his Fundamentalist approach to sin, and, with at least three police officers, he would visit the dens and dives of New York during the week and hold his audience horror-bound on Sundays. After him came S. Parkes Cadman, who would answer questions on the radio. Talmadge was the first man to syndicate his sermons, a practice that others too, especially Cadman, found profitable.

In the main, though, the clergy of Brooklyn has been sober, intelligent, and devoted to the people it serves. Some of them were on the picket lines in the bloody strikes of a decade or so ago, and in one case the president of a corporation left Trinity Church when he found the assistant rector aiding some men striking at his plant The Christian Century congratulated Trinity, remarking that often in similar cases the member of the congregation remains and the clergyman goes.

A verse keeps recurring to us:

> Beecher, Beecher is my name—
> Beecher till I die!
> I never kissed Mis' Tilton—
> I never told a lie.

FOREWORD TO HENRY WARD BEECHER
by PAXTON HIBBEN

by SINCLAIR LEWIS

When the Reverend Henry Ward Beecher was sued on a charge of adultery with the wife of his friend Theodore Tilton, the America of 1871 was ecstatically shocked.

For Mr. Beecher was, till his death in 1887, the archbishop of American liberal Protestantism. He came out for the right side of every question—always a little too late. John Brown's rifles were called "Beecher Bibles," and from the pulpit Beecher sold female slaves, to gain their freedom. He was referred to as "the greatest preacher since St. Paul," he was mentioned for the presidency, he was a powerful writer of trash, and all over the land, families got out the carry-all to drive into town and hear him lecture on everything from "The Strange Woman" to the cozy theory that a worker who didn't rejoice in bringing up five children on a wage of a dollar a day was a drunken gunnysack.

Plymouth Church, in Brooklyn, paid him $20,000 a year, and in his pocket he liked to carry uncut gems. He would have been an intimate friend of Lincoln except for the detail that Lincoln despised him. He confided to many visitors that he was always glad to pray with Lincoln and to give him advice whenever the president sneaked over to Brooklyn in the dark, and the only flaw is that nobody except Beecher ever saw him sneak.

During the Civil War, Beecher went to England and helped out the American Minister by converting to the cause of the North some tens of thousands of Midlanders who were already converted.

He was a combination of St. Augustine, Barnum, and John Barrymore. He differed from the Reverend Elmer Gantry chiefly in having once, pretty well along in young manhood, read a book, and in being a Beecher, which was a special state of grace. His father, Lyman Beecher of Litchfield and Cincinnati, was a powerful hellfire preacher and progenitor, and his sister was Harriet Beecher Stowe, whose *Uncle Tom's Cabin* was the first evidence to America that no hurricane can be so disastrous to a country as a ruthlessly humanitarian woman.

At the sunlit height of Beecher's career came Tilton's suit for alienation of affection, and in Brooklyn and Litchfield they are still arguing about it. But its effect upon the protestant church, which might otherwise have taken over the whole government, is only beginning to be seen.

This book, the late Paxton Hibben's story of Beecher, was published in 1927. It had great praise, but it also met with a hush-hush campaign on the part of certain pious writers and editors and librarians that amounted to violent suppression. The

Committee of The Readers Club believes that it is reviving a book which is more stimulating now than when it was first published, fourteen years ago.

Nothing could finally suppress and silence so courageous and intelligent a man as Paxton Hibben, not even his death, in 1928 when he was forty-eight years old. He had been a member of the American diplomatic corps in Europe and Latin America, well trained in the service correctitudes of that caste, and he was a foreign correspondent of standing, yet he had taken the risk of vastly displeasing his superiors by his reports on Greece and the new Russia.

When he turned to biography, in this book, the exactness of his scholarship would suggest that he had all his life never strayed farther from a library than to the University Co-op, though actually it was his foreign training which enabled him to see the contrasts which make this portrait so human.

Beecher is here entire, from his boyhood, blundering, lonely, almost abnormal in the longing for friendly sympathy, through his frantic and fairly phony days as an ambitious young preacher on the Indiana frontier in 1837, up to his antimacassar splendor as a metropolitan pastor filled with pomposity and metaphors and the best oyster stew. He slapped the backs of all men, he tickled the ribs of almost all the current ideas, and he kissed a surprising proportion of the women.

The subtitle of the book is *An American Portrait*, and indeed here is the portrait of that blowsy hoyden of an America that existed when Grant was accounted a statesman and Longfellow an epic poet. Although Hibben never wanders from his scrupulous portraiture to give highfalutin panshots of the whole country, yet in understanding Beecher we understand everything that was boisterously immature in American religion, American literature, American manners, and the American relationship, ardent but sneaking, between men and women. We understand all the spirited spinsters who wanted to paint water lilies on the backs of the herded buffalos. We understand what we are still living down. Here is the story of our own grandfathers, which is one-quarter of our own stories. Though we speak with the brisk quack of the radio, our words are still too often the lordly lard of Henry Ward Beecher.

In discovering his emptiness, the country discovered its own emptiness and, as Captain Hibben says, "When the social history of the last quarter of the nineteenth century comes to be written, the Beecher case may be found to have had more to do with clearing the intellectual ground and freeing the minds of men from the clutter of the past than any other one episode."

Hibben does not spare his patient. The horsechair hypocrisies of Beecher are set down like fever symptoms on a chart. He does not flinch from the charming melodrama of Beecher's association with the wives of all the backers of his one-man show. Yet the book is never lip-licking and never a tirade. You see that, given the glacial hellfire of old Lyman Beecher, his son Henry would have to be a hypocrite, exactly in ratio to his own energy and imagination and desire for affection.

When it was published, this book was a little ahead of its time. The Committee believes that now it is just at its time.

From The Readers Club edition, 1942. Reprinted with permission of the author.

from . . .

HENRY WARD BEECHER: AN AMERICAN PORTRAIT

by PAXTON HIBBEN

It was a great pity that there was no telephone service in 1870. Everybody connected with what came to be known as the Beecher Scandal wrote a vast deal too freely. "In the peculiar atmosphere of this case, where people shriek in stilted English, instead of talking quietly, and where the most hideous offenses do not seem incompatible with perfect sainthood, even Mr. Beecher seems to lose his power of lucid expression," complained the New York *Times*. It would have been far better for Henry Ward if he had lost his power of any kind of expression. As

Thurlow Weed's old Albany *Journal* put it, "It is Mr. Beecher's own hand which furnishes the only evidence that seriously inculpates him. He is his own accuser, and he must defend his name against himself."

A judgment natural enough when the flood of letters which distinguished the Beecher case was first released. But it fails to include a number of elements in the situation in which Henry Ward Beecher found himself in the opening days of 1871. The immediate and pressing problem was how to handle Theodore Tilton; but it was by no means the only problem. Brother Bowen of Plymouth Church was, and had been all along, Beecher's most dangerous enemy—the more dangerous as he remained in the background, outwardly friendly. And while Henry Ward was afraid of Theodore's impulsiveness, he was twice as fearful of Bowen's cold-blooded animosity.

For Henry Ward Beecher was confronted not just with the peril of his relations with Lib Tilton—that alone he might face down. Indeed, when he came at last to tell his story to a jury, he did stoutly maintain that from that fateful night in the upper room of Frank Moulton's house until Theodore Tilton appeared like an avenging angel before Plymouth Church in July 1874, not the slightest suspicion ever crossed his mind that Tilton thought him guilty of adultery with his wife. It was his story, and he stuck to it. He insisted, on oath, that what he thought Theodore Tilton and Frank Moulton and Mrs. Moulton and Mrs. Bradshaw and Tilton's mother-in-law and half of Brooklyn were talking about for three years was just that Lib Tilton had confessed to her husband that her Pastor had made "improper solicitations" of her—which, of course, was quite all right. Henry Ward admitted that Tilton had every ground for thinking this, and that he was convinced that Tilton was sincere in believing it. But adultery—no. And what he then swore he had been so contrite over that he had prayed to God to put it into the heart of the lady's husband to forgive him for was, he said, that he had advised Mrs. Tilton to leave her husband (which she had not done), that he had repeated unfounded and damaging stories about Tilton to Bowen (which he took back in a letter to Bowen on January 2, 1871), and finally that he had counseled Bowen to discharge Tilton from *The Independent* and the Brooklyn *Union* (which Bowen told Henry Ward he was going to do, anyhow).

All of this was all very well, and plainly necessary if Henry Ward were to defend Theodore Tilton's suit in which adultery was specifically set forth. But unfortunately it did not account for the fact that there was an adultery charge afloat against Henry Ward Beecher, the existence of which Beecher himself admitted in writing early in 1871. If it was not Tilton's charge, whose was it? And in heaven's name, just how many adulteries was the pastor of Plymouth Church chargeable with, anyhow? Poor Henry Ward dared not plead knowledge of Tilton's charge, because he was being sued by Tilton, and he would unquestionably lose his case if he admitted that for three years and a half he had been making stupendous efforts to keep Tilton quiet. But he was not being sued by Bowen. And so:

"Mr. Evarts: *'Well, did Mr. Moulton say that Mr. Bowen charged that you had confessed adultery to him?'*

"Mr. Beecher: *'I—he did—yes, he said so.'*"

Unhappily for Henry Ward, however, Bowen did not confine himself to simple adultery. In the letter he had written Tilton from Woodstock just after the first Mrs. Bowen's death, and in statements he had made since, he preferred far more terrible charges against the pastor of Plymouth Church. And Henry Ward's mental anguish was in no wise affected by the truth or falsity of these accusations—or Tilton's accusations, either, whatever they might be. As a minister of the Gospel and the Great Preacher he was just as surely ruined if they became public, whether any or all of them were true or not. So that if Henry Ward Beecher expressed his worry and despair during those black years in extravagant language (and he did), it must be admitted he had some reason so to do. The character of his language alone cannot fairly be cited as indicating a guilt which, after all, is of no consequence now. Its significance in this study is that it reveals a terrific and long-sustained emotional ordeal, out of which Henry Ward Beecher was to emerge a very different man. It is for this reason that documentary evidence is now here assembled.

When Frank Moulton undertook to do what a heathen could, as he expressed it, to aid Henry Ward Beecher and Theodore Tilton to settle their griefs in a Christian spirit, he had not the slightest idea what he was in for. The whole Bowen ramification to the affair came to him as a terrible shock, and he went straight to Beecher for an explanation, before he would go a step farther. According to Moulton, Henry Ward assured him that the facts were not as Bowen pictured them. He admitted, Moulton said, a little matter of what he called a "paroxysmal kiss," but insisted that Bowen could prove nothing against him. The expression "paroxysmal kiss" achieved a wide currency in the seventies. "Words are things," declared that astute old trial lawyer, William A. Beach. And from the voluminous pages of Henry Ward Beecher's writings he marshaled dozens of examples of the use of a word as rare as "paroxysmal" to annihilate Henry Ward's denial that he ever said anything of the sort.

Francis Moulton had hardly bargained for anything like this. He had conceived the affair with Lib Tilton the great weakness of a great man—deplorable, of course, but romantic at that. That there had been more than one such incident in the life of Henry Ward Beecher had never occurred to Francis Moulton. It was a day when people believed in things happening out of a clear sky.

Moulton had put his hand to the business, however; so he went on with it. His troubles were only just beginning. Promptly he squelched Theodore's inclination to publish a garrulous letter to Bowen, reviewing all the shocking details of Bowen's charges against Beecher. He set the machinery in motion to finance a literary journal, *The Golden Age*, to keep Theodore Tilton busy editing a paper of his own—what Theodore had really wanted to do for the past four years; and he arranged for arbitration of Tilton's claims against Bowen for breach of contract. He told Beecher to go on with the auctioning of the pews of Plymouth Church, and though the receipts fell below the previous year for the first time since 1862, they still came to the respectable sum of $47,309—Henry C. Bowen paying the highest figure. In short, as Henry Ward put it, "The friend whom God has sent to me (Mr. Moulton) has proved, above all friends that ever I had, able and willing to help me in this terrible emergency of my life. His hand it was that tied up the storm that was ready to burst upon our heads."

But Brooklyn folk appear to have suffered from peculiarly ostrich-like habits. It never seemed to occur to the quartet so busily engaged in keeping dark the secret—whatever it was—of Henry Ward Beecher's relations to the Tilton family that there was danger from any other source than one of their number. Yet since the fatal hour three months before when Lib Tilton sobbed out her story on Susan Anthony's bosom, it had spread like wildfire in the radical suffrage group. After all, Henry Ward and Theodore and Lib Tilton had all belonged to that little circle. Only a year before Beecher as president of the conservative and Tilton as president of the radical wing of the suffrage movement had been exchanging public messages. Even Frank Moulton was mildly identified with suffrage activities. On the whole, the suffragists had quite as good a right as any one to gossip about Henry Ward Beecher and Lib Tilton—and without having Beecher call them "human hyenas" for it either.

What was particularly dangerous in the knowledge of the Beecher Scandal possessed by the suffrage group was that it was both first hand and complete. Henry Ward might take his solemn oath to his wife, to Plymouth Church, to a jury of twelve good men and true, or "challenge man, angels and God"—as he did on occasion—to prove him guilty of anything worse than kissing and fondling Lib Tilton during the absence of her husband. All of this was without effect on Mrs. Stanton and Miss Anthony. Both knew the whole truth. And while in general they were remarkably discreet about it, they did discuss it in their own group—and their discussion brought the horrid business right back to Henry Ward Beecher's own doorstep. For not only was his sister, Isabella Beecher Hooker, a leading member of the group, but his intimate friend and business associate, Samuel Wilkeson, Jay Cooke's publicity man, was Mrs. Stanton's brother-in-law.

"At the time of our first knowledge of the affair, Mr. Wilkeson heard of it," says Mrs. Stanton. "He besought the ladies not to make it public. To him it was a matter of money. He was stockholder in Plymouth Church, in the *Christian Union* and in 'The Life of Christ.' Now the destruction of Mr. Beecher would be the destruction of all of these. As Mr. Wilkeson expressed it, 'It would knock the "Life of Christ" higher than a kite.' Hence his concern in keeping the matter secret."

To Sam Wilkeson everything was a matter of money. He was certain he knew just how to conjure the danger to his friend Beecher, and save his own investments in the Beecher enterprises from being knocked higher than a kite, at one and the same time. He would buy Theodore Tilton with Jay Cooke's purse, as he had secured the services of Beecher's editorial pen for $15,000 worth of Northern Pacific stock. He had a free-handed way of doing one man's business with another man's money, had Sam Wilkeson—to every man his price, he figured. "Keep quiet. Don't talk. DON'T PUBLISH," he wrote Theodore—and offered him a job with Jay Cooke & Co. Tilton was hard up. But he was not for sale. He did not even reply to Sam Wilkeson.

Henry Ward, too, was climbing his Golgotha. Mrs. Morse wrote warning him of the rapidity with which knowledge of his secret was spreading. "Do you know when I hear of you cracking your jokes from Sunday to Sunday, and think of the misery you have brought upon us, I think with the Psalmist: 'There is no God.'" There was a sinister note in her letter, also: "I thought the least you could do was to put your name to a paper to help reinstate my brother (in the Custom House). Elizabeth was as disappointed as myself." As Henry Ward read it, he could see unfold before him long years filled with the increasing demands of this half-crazy woman, as he called her—now a job for her brother—later money—and more money . . .

Nor was Lib Tilton any happier. "I have had sorrow almost beyond human capacity," she wrote a friend at this time. "We have weathered the storm, and I believe, without harm to our *Best.*" Our *Best* was Beecher. And she speaks pathetically of the child she had miscarried that fateful Christmas —"a *love babe* it promised, you know," she says.

"Does God look down from Heaven on three unhappy creatures that more need a friend than these?" wrote Henry Ward of Lib, Theodore and himself.

But even in his moments of profoundest grief, Henry Ward Beecher never quite lost his shrewdness. Thanks to Frank Moulton, the danger that Theodore Tilton's accusation "was to be at once publicly pressed against me," as Beecher put it, had been dissipated. But it had all been verbal, and Henry Ward had an almost childish confidence in the efficacy of documents. He would like to have something from Theodore in writing with which he could defend himself against Mrs. Morse's future importunities, and also, perhaps, tranquilize such of his business associates as, like Wilkeson, might come into possession of the facts and be worried about their investments in him. Henry Ward went to Moulton about it, and Frank got Theodore to write, "that notwithstanding the great suffering which he [Beecher] has caused to Elizabeth and myself, I bear him no malice, shall do him no wrong, shall discountenance every project by whomsoever proposed for any exposure of his secret to the public"—which was not exactly what Henry Ward had hoped for.

Beecher's greatest worry, however, was Lib Tilton. She loved him, he knew—in fact, that was just the trouble. "Would to God, who orders all hearts, that by your kind mediation, Theodore, Elizabeth and I could be made friends again," he wrote Moulton. "Theodore will have the hardest task in such a case; but has he not proved himself capable of the noblest things? . . . Of course, I can never speak with her again, except with his permission, and I do not know that even then it would be best. My earnest longing is to see her in the full sympathy of her nature at rest in him." And having arranged with Frank Moulton to advise Elizabeth to turn her affections back upon her husband, with Theodore's permission Henry Ward wrote Lib herself, urging her to do just as Frank Moulton should counsel her:

"I beseech of you, if my wishes have yet any influence, let my deliberate judgment in this matter weigh with you. It does my

sore heart good to see in Mr. Moulton an unfeigned respect and honor for you. It would kill me if he thought otherwise. . . . You and I may meet in him. The past is ended. But is there no future?—no wiser, higher, holier future? May not this friend stand as a priest in the new sanctuary of reconciliation, and mediate, and bless you, Theodore, and my most unhappy self?"

It is hard to see how Henry Ward Beecher could have done any more than this to liquidate the whole affair. If he had only stuck to it! But nowhere in his long life had Henry Ward Beecher learned the discipline of self-denial. After all, why should he give up what he called the "inspirational" quality he found in Lib Tilton now that everything was so nicely settled? For four years she had exercised "the most calming and peaceful influence over him, more so than any one he ever knew." To her he opened his heart as to no one. Once Lib had written Theodore: "Do not think it audacious in me to say I am to him a good deal, a rest, and, can you understand it, I appear even cheerful and helpful to him . . . I strive in my poor word-painting to give you the *spirit* and impression which I give him, and he to me. . . . The trinity of friendship I pray for always." Well, why not? thought Henry Ward.

It was partly Theodore's fault. Toward the end of February, and just before Frank Moulton was leaving for Florida, he sent for Beecher to come to the little house in Livingston street. Henry Ward was so eager that he got there before they had finished breakfast. Tilton swore he summoned Beecher to question him as to the paternity of little Ralph Tilton, who had been born on June 20, 1869. "I want if possible to shield him [Ralph], but I want more than that to know the truth," Theodore said. Beecher, of course, swore that what they talked about was not his, but Theodore's, sins. One can take one's choice. But both are agreed that, as they were talking, Lib Tilton came in; and thus these two met again for the first time since that night two months before, when Henry Ward had left her lying "white as marble, with closed eyes, as in a trance, and with her hands upon her bosom, palm to palm, like one in prayer."

And straightway Lib Tilton wrote her Pastor secretly—and secretly he replied. Strange, cryptic little notes, mostly without date or signature, a fragment only of what passed between these two—she thirty-seven, he fifty-eight—and both with all the world to lose by folly.

"My Dear Friend," wrote Lib. *"Does your heart bound towards all as it used? So does mine! I am myself again. I did not dare to tell you till I was sure; but the bird has sung in my heart these four weeks, and he has covenanted with me never again to leave. 'Spring has come.' . . ."*

And a little later there was another letter:

". . . In all the sad complications of the past years, my endeavor was entirely to keep from you all suffering, to bear myself alone, leaving you forever ignorant of it. My weapons were love, a larger untiring generosity and nest-hiding! . . ."

So "nest-hiding" came to be a popular and somewhat ribald term in those days.

Henry Ward's answer to the first of these pathetic notes—and other secret notes of his besides—Theodore found when Lib had left his house forever—hidden away in the little closet where she kept the death-mask of her baby Paul.

"No one can ever know, none but God, through what a dreary wilderness I have wandered, . . ." wrote Henry Ward in one of them. "Should God inspire you to restore and rebuild at home, and while doing it to cheer and sustain outside of it another who sorely needs your help in heart and spirit, it will prove a life so noble as few are able to live . . . If it would be a comfort to you, now and then, to send me a letter of true *in-wardness*—the outcome of your inner life—it would be safe, for I am now at home here with my sister, and it is *permitted to you*."

"Judge Fullerton: 'Your wife was away, was she not?'

"Mr. Beecher: 'She was.'. . . .

"Judge Fullerton: 'Do you recollect where your wife was at this time?' . . .
"Mr. Beecher: 'I presume she was in Florida, Sir.'"

* * *

The peculiarly friendly competition of the religious in Brooklyn shows itself each year in the rather sweet parade of the Sunday-school children on Anniversary Day. It is reported thoroughly in the Eagle and in church and neighborhood papers. We like the reminiscent description that follows:

ANNIVERSARY DAY

by HENRY COLLINS BROWN

But the day of days, red-letter included, was unquestionably Anniversary Day. I do not think its counterpart exists anywhere else in the world. It is the day when all the churches bury their theological hatchets and unite in one grand demonstration of fraternal amity. It is practically a holiday in Brooklyn and more than two hundred thousand children are in line. It is an imposing spectacle. A smile was occasionally furnished by some of the prize banners carried aloft in honor of some outstanding achievement, such as "Largest Monthly Contributors," "Workers in the Vineyards," with an unusual proportion of sour-faced mugs; "Cheerful Givers" always smiling, because they never gave enough to hurt themselves or any one else; the "Sowers," the "Reapers," "Lambs of the Upper Fold," etc. The reviewing stand was always graced by the presence of the Honorable Seth Low, J. S. T. Stranahan, Henry C. Murphy, and "Al" Daggett. Mr. Low always made a speech which was in effect that if you wanted to grow up to be a great and good man like him, there was just one rule—"Go to Sunday School." We children looked forward to this celebration with an interest that I cannot possibly describe. Nothing in my life that I can recall, before or since, ever equalled the anticipation with which I looked forward to the Anniversary parade. I belonged to Doctor Edward Eggleston's Church on Lee Avenue, corner of Hewes Street,[1] and I was a member of a small military organization which was attached to the Sunday School, and was known as the "Christian Endeavor Zouaves." We were gorgeously arrayed in red shirts and blue trousers, with a red stripe down the sides. We wore the regulation Grand Army cap, trimmed with gold braid, and carried a wooden gun. For months before the parade we were drilled in the manual of arms and on this day of days a space was cleared for us in front of the Bedford Avenue fountain and there we went through our evolutions to the delight and amazement of our friends and relatives.

Exactly why we should have had a military organization attached to a church I have never been able to ascertain, especially to the Church of Christian Endeavor, which Doctor Eggleston always wished to have called the Church of "Christ the Carpenter." My own theory was that it was due to the fact that our captain, A. G. Brown, who kept a shoe store on Fourth Street, was an ex-army officer of the Civil War and felt impelled to keep up the military spirit and to keep alive the patriotism inculcated by his strenuous experience with the Boys in Blue. The gallant captain has long since gone to his last reward, but I always look back on his efforts with kindly recollection. He certainly cured me of stoop shoulders and a tendency to smoke cigarettes and imparted to our particular set a truly military air, which was of vast benefit to us in promenading Bedford Avenue Sunday afternoons.

I cannot close these recollections of Anniversary Day without trying in some way to express, however feeble, the anguish and the unmitigated grief which was our state when Anniversary Day turned out to be a stormy one. No doubt many of the girls and boys of that day have since then passed through many of

[1] Dr. Eggleston was author of *The Hoosier Schoolmaster*, a number of other popular novels, and some scholarly treatises on the American language.

life's disappointments and perhaps the cup of sorrow has been pressed to their lips more than once. I hope not, and yet I make bold to say that I doubt if ever any sorrow or any disappointment in a sense was keener or more deeply felt than a rainy morning on Anniversary Day. We were a tired, foot-sore and weary lot of children when the parade was over, but the ice cream and cake served out to us in our Sunday Schools was a rich reward for all our exertions. As we were all decked out in our most expensive finery, and looked very pretty, I think our parents felt fully recompensed for the trouble that they took as their share of the holiday. The stomach aches, cramps, sniffles, etc., that developed during the night were philosophically accepted by our Spartan mothers as part and parcel of the day's festivities.

THE BROOKLYN LIBRARY

by LEWIS MUMFORD

Toward the beginning of the last decade, a lonely horseman, reining his steed at the main entrance of Prospect Park in Brooklyn, would have beheld on his left a melancholy ruin. It was a gray building, four stories high, with classic lintels and cornice, its windows gaping, apparently abandoned about the time the Romans left Britain. It looked like something that had been consigned to the dump, only to be dropped by someone at the thither end of Grand Army Plaza in a fit of discouragement.

Ten years have passed and the ruin is gone. Or, rather, it has been incorporated into the handsome new Public Library that now spreads beneath the hill at the corner of the Botanical Garden. It turns out that the original building was to have been part of an imposing structure, designed a generation ago in the worst manner of that imperial age but never finished. Most of the money needed for it would have been used to construct an imposing dome, a weird inspiration due in perhaps equal measure to Raymond Almirall, the original architect, and Kubla Khan.

As, facing a group of pines on a mound in the foreground, one approaches the new building from the subway station, the effect is unexpectedly exhilarating. The bright limestone walls, the handsome, bowed-in front of the central mass glittering with gold, the good proportions, the absence of dreary columns, all create a sense of happy expectation. The underlying conception of this building is classic, and vertical window panels regularly punctuate the façades of the two wings. This means the internal functions must fit the plan and elevation instead of having the plan and elevation draped closely around them. Still, when one has said this, one has admitted the worst. Comparing this library with the Bronx County Courthouse or the State Capitol at Salem, Oregon—the two buildings that are its closest stylistic rivals—the new library wins hands down. The architects are Githens & Keally.

There are three ways of approaching the interior. If you can't climb steps, you enter on the side, at ground level, and are taken up in an elevator—a thoughtful provision for the aged and the crippled. If you are a book from a branch library, you enter by way of the handsome delivery quarters in the rear—looking on the outside like a small concert hall—and are taken by an elevator directly to your appropriate department. Otherwise, you come in at the front entrance, with its playfully sculptured bronze-and-gold doors. The wings of the building, three stories high, converge on the central mass. Thanks to the elemental cubic forms and the clean outlines, the building from a distance has a powerful aesthetic effect. Nor is the effect spoiled when one gets nearer, for the golden lettering, apart from the Carolingian incisions on the plaques between the windows of the wings, is good. The inscriptions, too, around the entrance are what good lettering should be—intelligible and decorative.

The general exterior form of the building is repeated in wood in the interior entrance to the circulation room, which, with its bank of lofty windows and its serene sense of space, is perhaps the most vital point of the whole design. Such interiors have the power to take the kinks out of one's backbone. Although the functions performed here could be carried on in a room only a third as high, I am all for this kind of lavishness. Like the rest of us, Brooklynites spend most of their days in subways, cramped offices, and skimpy flats or houses, and the chance to expand their lungs once more amid great architectural space can hardly be classed as a luxury.

The two long wings are equally spacious, but their form is more conventional. The wing on the right was the original structure. On the ground floor it forms the main reference room, lined with bookshelves, always flooded with light—from the windows by day and from the ceiling at night. The other wing is devoted chiefly to children's books—there are a lot of children in Brooklyn from infancy through high-school age—and at the far end of the main juveniles' room is a glassed-in-balcony where the younger children can assemble in more intimate quarters for their oral story hour. Up to this point the plan is simple, spacious, direct, and elegant, and the interior decoration matches it. Probably the chief weakness of this formal kind of elevation will come out on the second floor, as yet unfinished, where the special rooms of the library will be located. The tall windows and regularly spaced bays are going to make it difficult to carve this floor into intimate quarters, except at an excessive waste of space.

The building is not yet open to the public, and it is hard to give any final verdict on such a structure before it has been subjected to the test of daily use. (The completion of this part of the building awaits the appropriation of funds.) A few years ago, for example, one might have objected to the fact that the book stacks were not to be placed above ground in one of the wings of the building, so that they would be available for use by responsible scholars. Today, by contrast, it is reassuring to realize that the books are safely tucked away in a vast, air-conditioned crypt, which can easily be deepened.

A few weaknesses, however, might be noted here and now, in case anybody should ever build a library again. Though excellent provision has been made for rest rooms for the staff, there is no place for meeting and relaxation by the students, scholars, and writers who will use the building. There should be a special corridor for walking up and down, for conversing, for smoking a cigarette. Most of the big new libraries have been designed apparently only for deaf-mutes and paralytics; there is seemingly no recognition of the fact that scholars need a place to stretch their legs in or that a library is one of the most natural places in the world in which to exchange thoughts with one's colleagues.

As for the long main reference room, its only advantage is its simplicity in form and function. I believe that there are better architectural solutions for this problem than the precedents of either the circular room of the British Museum or the long room of the Bibliothèque Nationale. A series of semi-enclosed bays around a soundproofed central unit for the delivery department would make a much less restless place than any of these, with their unavoidable foot traffic and noise. It is on such points that one's principal doubts arise. As a matter of fact, the rear part of the central mass has been conceived more organically, and from the courtyard one can see how handsome the whole structure might have been had the architects dared to depart from the monumental formalism of the main façades.

But, after all, library-building is still the most backward realm of American architecture, and this new edifice is the first attempt in this country, to my knowledge, to push even in part beyond inept tradition. Put alongside the Widener Library at Harvard, the Yale Library, the Harkness at Columbia, the Congressional, or the New York Public Library, Brooklyn's new one is tops.

from . . .

A TREE GROWS IN BROOKLYN

by BETTY SMITH

The library was a little old shabby place. Francie thought it was beautiful. The feeling she had about it was as good as the feeling she had about church. She pushed open the door and went in. She liked the combined smell of worn leather bindings, library paste and freshly-inked stamping pads better than she liked the smell of burning incense at high mass.

Francie thought that all the books in the world were in that library and she had a plan about reading all the books in the world. She was reading a book a day in alphabetical order and not skipping the dry ones. She remembered that the first author had been Abbott. She had been reading a book a day for a long time now and she was still in the B's. Already she had read about bees and buffaloes, Bermuda vacations and Byzantine architecture. For all of her enthusiasm, she had to admit that some of the B's had been hard going. But Francie was a reader. She read everything she could find: trash, classics, time tables and the grocer's price list. Some of the reading had been wonderful; the Louisa Alcott books for example. She planned to read all the books over again when she had finished with the Z's.

Saturdays were different. She treated herself by reading a book not in the alphabetical sequence. On that day she asked the librarian to recommend a book.

After Francie had come in and closed the door quietly behind her—the way you were supposed to do in the library—she looked quickly at the little golden-brown pottery jug which stood at the end of the librarian's desk. It was a season indicator. In the fall it held a few sprigs of bittersweet and at Christmas time it held holly. She knew spring was coming, even if there was snow on the ground, when she saw pussy willow in the bowl. And today, on this summer Saturday of 1912, what was the bowl holding? She moved her eyes slowly up the jug past the thin green stems and little round leaves and saw . . . nasturtiums! Red, yellow, gold and ivory-white. A head pain caught her between the eyes at the taking in of such a wonderful sight. It was something to be remembered all her life.

"When I get big," she thought, "I will have such a brown bowl and in hot August there will be nasturtiums in it."

She put her head on the edge of the polished desk liking the way it felt. She looked at the neat row of freshly-sharpened pencils, the clean green square of blotter, the fat white jar of creamy paste, the precise stack of cards and the returned books waiting to be put back on the shelves. The remarkable pencil with the date slug above its point was by itself near the blotter's edge.

"Yes, when I get big and have my own home, no plush chairs and lace curtains for me. And no rubber plants. I'll have a desk like this in my parlor and white walls and a clean green blotter every Saturday night and a row of shining yellow pencils always sharpened for writing and a golden-brown bowl with a flower or some leaves or berries always in it and books . . . books . . . books. . . ."

She chose her book for Sunday; something by an author named Brown. Francie figured she had been reading on the Brown's for months. When she thought she was nearly finished, she noticed that the next shelf started up again with Browne. After that came Browning. She groaned, anxious to get into the C's where there was a book by Marie Corelli that she had peeped into and found thrilling. Would she ever get to that? Maybe she ought to read two books a day. Maybe. . . .

She stood at the desk a long time before the librarian deigned to attend to her.

"Yes?" inquired that lady pettishly.

"This book. I want it." Francie pushed the book forward, opened at the back with the little card pushed out of the envelope. The librarians had trained the children to present the books that way. It saved them the trouble of opening several hundred books a day and pulling several hundred cards from as many envelopes.

She took the card, stamped it, pushed it down a slot in the desk. She stamped Francie's card and pushed it at her. Francie picked it up but she did not go away.

"Yes?" The librarian did not bother to look up.

"Could you recommend a good book for a girl?"

"How old?"

"She is eleven."

Each week Francie made the same request and each week the

librarian asked the same question. A name on a card meant nothing to her and since she never looked up into a child's face, she never did get to know the little girl who took a book out every day and two on Saturday. A smile would have meant a lot to Francie and a friendly comment would have made her so happy. She loved the library and was anxious to worship the lady in charge. But the librarian had other things on her mind. She hated children anyhow.

Francie trembled in anticipation as the woman reached under the desk. She saw the title as the book came up: *If I Were King* by McCarthy. Wonderful! Last week it had been *Beverly of Graustark* and the same two weeks before that. She had had the McCarthy book only twice. The librarian recommended these two books over and over again. Maybe they were the only ones she herself had read; maybe they were on a recommended list; maybe she had discovered that they were sure fire as far as eleven-year-old girls were concerned.

Francie held the book close and hurried home, resisting the temptation to sit on the first stoop she came to, to start reading.

Home at last and now it was the time she had been looking forward to all week: fire-escape-sitting time. She put a small rug on the fire-escape and got the pillow from her bed and propped it against the bars. Luckily there was ice in the icebox. She chipped off a small piece and put it in a glass of water. The pink-and-white peppermint wafers bought that morning were arranged in a little bowl, cracked, but of a pretty blue color. She arranged glass, bowl and book on the window sill and climbed out on the fire-escape. Once out there, she was living in a tree. No one upstairs, downstairs or across the way could see her. But she could look out through the leaves and see everything. . . .

Francie breathed the warm air, watched the dancing leaf shadows, ate the candy and took sips of the cooled water between reading the book.

Politics

MILTON MACKAYE in his book The Tin Box Parade described James A. McQuade as "a short, stocky Irishman with a lugubrious, oily manner, and a slightly musty smell." Mackaye then recounted one of the great episodes of the Seabury Investigation of 1931. McQuade was Register of Kings County (Brooklyn) at the time, and it had been found out that in six years, with no source of income other than his salary, which totaled less than $50,000 in that time, he had banked some $520,000. He told Seabury he had borrowed the money.

"Yes, money that I borrowed," McQuade said. All the reporters that had covered the investigation harped on the Register's sadness. More from the transcript:

"If you want me to get to the start of it, I will have to take and go over the family in the entirety, without feeling that I am humiliated in the least or am not humiliating the other thirty-three McQuades. If this committee can take the time, if it can take the time to listen, and you can, and the public in general, I will go over it from the start.

"I unfortunately went into politics. I say that cautiously."

Seabury: "You don't base that on this deposit, do you?"

McQuade: "I am going to get to that deposit if you will let me—if you will let me. I bailed out a man who stole off McQuade Brothers $260,000, which necessitated the folding up of the McQuade Brothers firm, selling eight seats they had on the Curb Exchange for $6,000 a piece, that afterward brought $225,000. [One of the McQuade brothers was sentenced to the Federal penitentiary for running a bucket shop.] After they liquidated, the thirty-four McQuades were placed on my back, I being the only breadwinner, so to speak, and after that it was necessary, to keep life in their body, sustenance, to go out and borrow money.

"After they paid up all they could I took over their responsibilities. It was not necessary. I felt it my duty, being that they were flesh and blood, part and parcel of me, to help them. I am getting along in fairly good shape, when my mother, Lord have mercy on her, in 1925 dropped dead. I am going along nicely when my brother, Lord have mercy on him, in 1926 or 1927 dropped dead. But doing nicely when I have two other brothers, and when my brother died he willed me his family, which I am still taking care of, thank God. Two other brothers, who have been sick and are sick, so much so that when your Committee notified me, I was waiting for one of them to die . . ."

On it went like that. To save the other McQuades, James A., whom Pete McGuinness once called "Pay Roll Jim, the Jesse James of Greenpoint," had borrowed $1000 here, paid it back with a $1000 borrowed there. He destroyed any accounts, he said, once a debt was paid because, "it was off my mind and I thanked God for it and destroyed anything I might have."

He showed a strong spirit, too. "With all my troubles," he told Seabury, "and I had plenty of them, I never cried. My name is McQuade."

"That's what I thought it was," Seabury said.

These disclosures evidently did not harm Mr. McQuade, as he was elected sheriff of Kings County a month later. Observers attributed Mr. McQuade's election to his name's remaining on the Democratic ballot. And with a few minor exceptions—certain reform years—this has been true of Brooklyn since the Civil War: Get your name on the Democratic ballot, and you're elected. We won't go into the ramifications of the labor and racial votes; American Labor Party, Liberal Party, and backroom agreements with the Republicans that make up the strength of the Democrats. All we want to say is that while great machines have collapsed in other cities, the one in Brooklyn apparently is still going on.

Tammany, in many ways, was never quite in it with the Brooklyn crowd, especially in efficiency. And only in the McCooey days would Brooklyn have much to do with Tammany. There have been only five leaders of the party in Brooklyn since the Civil War—McLaughlin, McCarren, McCooey, Kelly, and Cashmore. The first four were bosses, and the last—well, it's hard to tell. He's only been in a few years at this writing, and he runs around a lot.

And yet, while Brooklyn can be classified as almost an epitome of the machine politics that has dominated this country's cities for the last eighty years, it had four years in which its administration was considered to be the apotheosis of good municipal government. One lyric citizen said during this period: "To draw a parallel between modern Brooklyn and ancient Athens is, of course, of all things the most easy. Their graceful culture, their love of art, their intense local feeling—which outer barbarians are apt to term pragmatical self-complacency—their acknowledged supremacy as centers of learning and governmental wisdom and so on place them in a relation which it would be a little short of blasphemy to question." The man was serious.

This was during the time of "the Brooklyn idea" and the Seth Low administration, 1881-85. For a long time, authority had been diffused in the city charter, and responsibility had been juggled by aldermen, mayors, and commissioners about the way the present Brooklyn College basketball teams handle a ball. Finally, when Frederick Schroeder was mayor, he obtained from the legislature a "single-head" charter, centering the government in the mayor, and Low was the first mayor under it. He gave the town an honest, nonpartisan administration, and was wonderfully high-minded about it. He was only thirty-two, was of the brilliant, wealthy Low family, and remarkably handsome in a well-bred sort of way. At the ceremonies for the opening of the Brooklyn Bridge, someone described him as looking like the valedictorian at some exclusive college graduation, which seems, from the view one gets of him now from his writings and speeches, a remarkably apt simile. He was righteous and serious, and one wonders what, could they have occurred at the same time, Wolcott Gibbs would have done with him. He wrote many articles, and even contributed a chapter to Lord Bryce's American Commonwealth. Reformers from other cities in America consulted him; editorial writers about the country praised him; and Brooklyn, for a while, had a high pride in its city, its government, and its culture.

Within three or four years after Low left the mayoralty, though, the Brooklyn idea wasn't doing so good. All that control vested in one man merely meant that Boss Hugh McLaughlin had to send orders to only one of his boys instead of wasting time in communicating with several. Low became president of Columbia University after his work in Brooklyn, and the second mayor of Greater New York in 1901-03. William Travers Jerome laughed obscenely at the idea of anyone voting for Low for a second term, yet he supported him as one of the best men available. Low was defeated in an unduly complicated election, and the Who's Who items about him stop right there. He died in 1915.

Another man who figures in Brooklyn history was William J. Gaynor, who introduced a curious form of government to American municipalities—government by lawsuit. He liked to fight, and William Ziegler, a courageous and wealthy man, backed him with money and influence. Whenever Gaynor got wind of a municipal steal, he would sue the administration, usually representing the taxpayer Ziegler. They kept the city from being sold entirely to some transit and other public-utility highbinders. Gaynor's persistence helped send John Y. McKane to jail, and commissioners of public works, and similar officers, began watching what both their right and left hands were doing.

After serving as a judge, Gaynor was elected mayor of Greater New York in 1909, with Tammany support, oddly enough. During the campaign, he visited his new friends for the first time, and made the statement: "So this is Tammany hall." It endeared him to the World. Gaynor was shot one day by a man who'd gone crazy after getting fired from a city job. Gaynor recovered, but he was completely furious about a photograph taken of him when staggering from the wound. This picture still turns up occasionally in collections of great photographs. He also is remembered for making a deal which allowed some private corporation to horn in on the city's subway system. The subways were recaptured only a few years ago after years of mismanagement and no return to the city, which had paid for well more than half their cost. The private holders had always got theirs, though. Gaynor was not quite at fault in this; he seems to have thought he was making an advantageous bargain, and, too, he was stymied by a debt limitation, imposed by the state, which would not allow him to issue municipal bonds to get money to complete the system. We are printing a few of Gaynor's letters which indicate the man's sharp, aggressive humor, and his showy erudition. We have a hunch La Guardia, at least, had read them.

One of the odd things about political writing is that it is usually best when about dead men. A live politician, active and out of jail, seldom is treated dispassionately by an author. A boss sometimes will appear as a kind, honest old soul, who never got any money "personally," but is surrounded by rapscallions, or else as an evil, black scoundrel living off whores, murderers, and Standard Oil. For this reason, we have used "Orders from Willoughby Street" from Harold Coffin Syrett's, The City of Brooklyn, 1865-1898: A Political History, an interesting period which takes Brooklyn through its fantastic expansion after the Civil War to the time it ceased to be a city. Dr. Syrett's writings on Gaynor, McLaughlin, McKane, Kinsella, and others of the period, make excellent reading, and we wish we could print more of him.

ORDERS FROM WILLOUGHBY STREET

from THE CITY OF BROOKLYN, 1865-1898

by HAROLD COFFIN SYRETT

Despite charter differences, American cities had one feature in common. Each had its boss. Supported by the taxpayers, but rarely holding office, the machine leader was as much a part of the municipal scene as the city hall or the Civil War monument. No American city escaped his influence. With much justification, New York thought that the endless succession of Tammany rulers had earned it the right to be called the most corruptly governed city in the nation. Cincinnati was convinced that Boss Cox was as obnoxious as any Tammany overlord. In New Haven, there were complaints against "the machine of the corrupt, selfish and irresponsible 'Boss'." Boston's ward leaders were so powerful that the taxpayers had to forego the luxury of a single boss. Philadelphia was run by "King" James McMannes and "Judge" Israel Durham. The administration of Pittsburgh was shared by William Flinn and Christopher Magee. Edward Butler headed the St. Louis machine; Albert Ames controlled Minneapolis; and Blind Boss Buckley ruled San Francisco.

Brooklyn, too, knew what it meant to take orders from a boss. When the city was incorporated in 1834, Hugh McLaughlin was a school boy, living at the foot of Columbia Heights in the same house in which he had been born seven or eight years earlier. His parents, migrating from Ireland in the first years of the nineteenth century, had ten children, of whom Hugh was the youngest. At the time of his father's death, Hugh, though only thirteen, left school to become a "whip boy" on a rope walk. Later he ran a fish market with his brother Luke. When the latter died, he carried on the business alone until 1855, when he went to work in the Navy Yard.

Like many another vigorous young Irishman, he took an early interest in politics. Because of his reputation as a fighter and the gang of tough young men of which he was the acknowledged leader, his value to the party was soon recognized. Henry C. Murphy, the Democratic leader, more than once watched "this active, broad-shouldered, square-fisted, young fish merchant in many a rough and tumble fight, and had noted his control over the laboring element in the party." By 1850, McLaughlin was a Murphy lieutenant, and had joined the volunteer fire force, "spending much of his time in the political atmosphere of fireman's hall in the basement of the City Hall." The party in the mid-'fifties was dominated by a group of older men, who were working for Buchanan's election. When McLaughlin demanded representation in their councils, he was at first refused; but, as he came from the most populous ward in the city and controlled a large number of the younger members of the party and a considerable share of the labor vote, he was soon admitted to the Democratic General Committee.

As a reward for his activity in the campaign of 1856, he was appointed Boss Laborer of the Navy Yard. Here he gained a local following and the dubious distinction of being the first political manipulator called boss. He never liked the name and was always at considerable pains to explain why it was not appropriate.

They call me Boss as a term of opprobrium, because they cannot call me a thief, or worse. Now, I understand a boss to be a man who dictates or threatens. I would be ashamed to threaten any man. You see that old fellow there (pointing at a poorly clad old man in the corridor). He calls me Boss because he worked in the Navy Yard when I was Boss there. So do hundreds of others. For years after I left the yard I would allow no man to call me Boss. My office is here today (pointing at iron stairs on the top steps of which he stood) and it is out there to-morrow (pointing at the sidewalk) Does that look as if I was one of those high-toned fellows, with wings, you know, and luxurious quarters, who boss political parties, and whom I despise? I do my best to persuade men to my way of thinking when I can and if I succeed, am I to be called "Boss" for it?

Because of McLaughlin's steady adherence to Democratic principles and the decisive part he played in the municipal campaign of 1857, the party chiefs thought that he deserved some recognition. Moreover, he was now in a position to make demands rather than receive favors. In 1860, he was the Democratic candidate for sheriff of Kings County; but the Democrats were split, and the Republicans captured the major offices. In the same year he was a delegate to Charleston, where he cast his vote for Stephen A. Douglas. With the declaration of war, he placed himself at the head of the War Democrats. Representing a bi-partisan ticket known as the Fort Greene Movement, he was elected register in 1861. He was re-elected in 1864, defeated in 1867, and victorious for the last time in 1870. Aside from three terms as register, Hugh McLaughlin never held any other office.

When McLaughlin retired from the register's office in 1873, he was undisputed leader of Brooklyn's Democrats. In the future he would occasionally lose the patronage to the opposition, but not until the formation of Greater New York was his grip on the party shaken. His ability to rebound from apparently overwhelming defeats gave him a longer tenure than any other city boss. While he was consolidating his control over the party in the late 'sixties, Tweed was in a similar position in New York, When he finally stepped down in 1903, Tweed had been followed by Kelly, Croker, and Murphy. During this period in which McLaughlin ruled Brooklyn, bosses in other cities seized power, made vast sums of money, and disappeared "into jails, or foreign lands or remote ranches of the Southwest." His long reign was the more remarkable, because he managed to maintain his leadership at a time when the character of the American city was undergoing its greatest change. Republicans and reformers frequently predicted his downfall. As early as 1872, the *Union* wrote: "His good old Ring days are rapidly disappearing, and his power is correspondingly waning. He already has no party and his friends are rapidly withdrawing from him." But wishful thinking never affected his long career.

McLaughlin's system was as simple as it was effective. A semblance of popular control within the Democratic party was maintained by the general committee which was composed of one delegate from each election district in Kings County. Although it theoretically ran the party, its decisions were usually determined by an executive committee made up of the leaders of the assembly districts. Through his ability to ostracize any member of the executive committee, McLaughlin ran the party, and more often than not the party ran the city. Like every boss, McLaughlin was tolerated by the voters because his organization had something to give. In return for a job, a contract, or the charity dispensed by the county officials, the machine asked only for a man's vote.

A large share of McLaughlin's power could be traced to his ability to select his party's candidates. A plausible explanation of how this was accomplished was provided by the *Eagle*, when it put these words in his mouth: "Give me the three inspectors of a Democratic primary, and it is immaterial to me how many votes are polled and for whom they are cast." After he had been "given" the inspectors, it was a simple matter to select the Democratic General Committee and the nominating conventions. The power to make or break any Democratic candidate for office meant that McLaughlin's authority was almost limitless. A Democratic district attorney was not inclined to prosecute a loyal party follower. If he was forced by public opinion to take such a step, the machine could arrange to have a reliable judge try the case. After 1882, McLaughlin's opportunity for dispensing patronage was enlarged, for in that year the aldermen were deprived of the right to confirm the mayor's appointments. If McLaughlin's choice happened to be elected mayor, the Boss' task was relatively easy.

McLaughlin names the Mayor [wrote the New York Tribune]; the Mayor reappoints the Boss's men as heads of departments; the Boss's men fill the departments with Democratic place-hunters; the office-holders raise a boodle for the re-election of the Boss's candidate for Mayor; and the boodle is used in hiring the naturalized citizens ground out in Judge Moore's court to vote for the Boss's ticket, and in employing McKane's swarms of repeaters to violate the election laws. So is the circle of Ring iniquity in Brooklyn squared.

To run such a machine required the strictest discipline. McLaughlin never forgot an offense, and, while he might postpone punishment, he inevitably meted it out. To him an offense was any departure from regularity. According to Republicans, he hated "independence in politics as thoroughly as the Pope of Rome does the exercise of private judgment in matters of religion." To enforce his dictates, he was aided by the knowledge of his followers that his power was supreme. Democratic office holders knew that if they disobeyed the Boss, they would no longer have a political future. Because they owed their nominations to McLaughlin and his lieutenants, they recognized that they were responsible to them rather than to their immediate superior or the voters. Moreover, there was a moral element which made them feel "that it would be some sort of ingratitude on their part if they failed to carry out the wishes of the men who made their appearance in public life possible."

To maintain the supremacy of the machine, McLaughlin had to exercise care in the selection of his subordinates. It was his practice to pick young men and start them at some routine job. Any Democrat with a following in his ward could count on a clerkship or some minor office. If he remained loyal, he was promoted to a higher position or a place of some responsibility in the party. Watching over these officials and party hacks to see that the Boss' orders were followed was a small clique of politicians who were responsible only to McLaughlin. At the outset of his reign, McLaughlin's principal adviser was William C. Kingsley, who had moved to Brooklyn when the machine was in its formative stage. The Boss had picked him as a coming man, and seen that he was awarded lucrative paving contracts and the construction of the Hempstead Reservoir. In return, he was credited with being the brains of the organization and the party's money raiser. Because he preferred to remain in the background, any estimate of his influence is largely speculative. A man of "culture, taste, and tone," Kingsley was apparently never repulsed by the absence of these traits in Hugh McLaughlin.

Much more in the public eye than Kingsley were Robert Furey and William A. Fowler, McLaughlin's lieutenants in the 'seventies. Furey ran the common council; Fowler handled the board of city works; while the Boss tended to the supervisors. Bob Furey was "a smooth, sleek, sharp young contractor," who had served as street commissioner, knew all the intricacies of Kings County politics, and in his own words was, "a believer in the time honored doctrine, that to the victor belongs the spoils." No job was too important or too trivial for him to undertake. "Whenever ward leaders were to be instructed, Furey carried the instructions; whenever a party policy was to be promulgated, Furey was the messenger that bore the tidings."

Billy Fowler was the party's back slapper. He had served on the old water and sewerage board and was the central figure around whom the appointment squabbles of the 'seventies were to center. Externally he appeared to be a jovial, good natured friend of the most powerful man in Brooklyn. But behind this façade of good fellowship was "a keen, eager, speculating politician, a professional in that line, and not possessed of any very great capacity in public affairs, other than intrigue." The Republicans justly called him, "this good-natured, round-cheeked, jolliest of robbers, whose rollicking way of making his steals have cost this public millions that have gone into the pockets of the Ring.

As McLaughlin grew older, he tended to dispense with subordinates. Because the charter after 1882 entrusted the mayor with such extensive authority, the Boss no longer needed assistants, but only a messenger to carry his wishes to the city hall. This position was entrusted to James Shevlin, one of the Boss' numerous in-laws, and usually known to the boys as Shev. Born in Ireland, he fought for a short time as a sailor in the Civil War and returned to Brooklyn to work in the boiler shop of the Navy Yard. After the war he made a small fortune carting illegal whiskey in the fifth ward, a part of Brooklyn then referred to as Irishtown. In 1872, he was made a keeper at the penitentiary. Retiring ten years later, he became the Boss' errand boy. His proximity to the throne enabled him to form profitable alliances with many corporations and contractors dealing with the city.

The countless members of the McLaughlin family also shared in running the Democratic machine. The most prominent representative of the clan was the Boss' namesake, Bub, who frequently acted as a lieutenant for his uncle. Besides a short term in the common council, he served as fire commissioner and under-sheriff of Kings County. If he had any special function in the organization, it was to handle his uncle's affairs in state conventions. While Bub was the most successful member of the family aside from the Boss, many others worked in the city and county governments. In the 'seventies, relatives of McLaughlin included a doorkeeper at the city court, a laborer in the repair yard of the department of city works, a fire commissioner, an inspector in the fire department, the county auditor, a police captain, the keeper of the penitentiary, and an officer on the water board. With justification the Republicans complained, "Talk of nepotism, we are run by the McLaughlin family. . . ."

Certain other members of the family, though holding no official position, were credited with exerting considerable influence over McLaughlin. His daughter, Laura, was said to be "her father's special pet and adviser." Of even greater importance was the Boss' sister, who was known to every party worker as "Aunt Nancy." Keeping well out of the limelight, she was nevertheless respected by the politicians, who had seen more than one ambitious man forced out of public life by incurring her displeasure. The Boss' wife was never a factor in Brooklyn politics. Brought up in the Dutch Reformed Church, she became a devoted and active member of the Catholic Church after her marriage. Following her husband's death, she received the title of Marchioness from the Pope and provided the funds for the construction of the Church of St. Hugh at Huntington, Long Island.

Hugh McLaughlin was not an ambitious man—not that he was lazy, for he was a hard worker; but he set definite limits to his horizon. His sole aim was to maintain his ascendency over the Kings County Democracy. Influence beyond Brooklyn was always secondary. State and national tickets had little significance aside from the assistance they might give to his local candidates. Moreover, he never permitted himself to become involved in party doctrine. There is no record of McLaughlin ever having offered an opinion on states' rights, the tariff, or the currency.

Because the Boss placed the Brooklyn branch of the party above every other consideration did not mean that he was of no political significance beyond his native city. The fact that he controlled a powerful bloc of Democratic votes outside of Tammany often gave him the balance of power in New York State. In the contest for the gubernatorial nomination in 1879, McLaughlin was credited with turning the tide from Slocum to Robinson. He was always on intimate terms with Samuel Tilden. In the state convention of 1874, he swung the Kings County delegation from Church to Tilden. In 1875, he entertained Governor Tilden in his own home, and "afterwards, during the day, Mr. Tilden expressed himself delighted with Mr. McLaughlin's strong sense, simple and clear statement, robust frankness, and entire self-possession." When the Governor visited the city to review the National Guard, a reporter noted that "his meeting with Hugh McLaughlin was very cordial, and his conversation with him, which was quite long, was the only noticeable confab he indulged."

He was likewise a close associate of David B. Hill and exerted a greater influence over him than over any other occupant of the Albany State House. At the same time, he managed to maintain close connections with President Cleveland. In 1888, the Brooklyn press reported:

In these days exceeding honor is paid to Brooklyn's mighty ruler. The Governor of the State leaves the Capitol and comes to the City of Churches at midnight to hold secret converse with the gifted being who holds the political destinies of this great community in the hollow of his hand, and the President sends him by a special envoy of high official station an invitation which is an entreaty to visit the White House, and when it is accepted puts aside for the time the cares incident to the government of the greatest nation on earth in order that he may take his distinguished visitor out to Red Top—the private residence of America's first citizen—there to gather, undisturbed by the outside world, wisdom and a deeper knowledge of state-craft from the Sage of Willoughby Street.

One of Hugh McLaughlin's more useful political assets was his apparent pliability. He soon learned that it was easier to make a show of giving in to public opinion, while he quietly assumed an opposite course. With the exception of Kalbfleisch, he always chose an eminently respectable candidate for mayor. After the election, the mayor continued to be respectable, but McLaughlin either ruled or discarded him. A similar technique was employed by McLaughlin in his external relations with the Democratic General Committee. On numerous occasions, when the Democrats were accused of being dominated by the Boss, he would withdraw from the committee, or permit an ostensible reform. When he resigned in 1873, he was given "a magnificent testimonial framed in a carved mahogany frame ten feet high." At the same time, he permitted a group of independent Democrats to be appointed to the committee. The reformers were overjoyed, but they soon realized that they had been hood-winked:

They found that Mr. Hugh McLaughlin's nominal retirement was practically a continuance of his dictatorship, that his control of the organization and of the party conventions was as complete and thorough as before; that he, not the party, named the nominees; that the party patronage upon which depends his power was still in his hands; that every effort in the direction of reform was throttled by him; that the expression of honest conviction was met by menace; that independent action was severely punished; that the exercise of individual judgment meant to him treason; that the new element in the committee was simply utilized as a veneering to screen these facts from the people, and that instead of accomplishing reform they were really strengthening and perpetuating the power which the people desired to destroy.

McLaughlin's trick of appearing to accede to the public will elicited considerable discussion as to how much he heeded the wishes of the voters. The *Herald* flatly asserted: "No suggestion could be more ludicrous to a Brooklyn politician than one to the effect that 'Boss' McLaughlin might be persuaded to fear public opinion." The *Union* said: "He does not seek conflict with public opinion; far from it; but he moves large bodies of men through self-interest and through influences which set them to manufacturing what opinion is necessary to make the results which he secures at the ballot box and elsewhere appear as if they might be the legitimate outcome of nothing more harmful than well-disciplined machine government." To the *Tribune*, he was a product of public opinion; and Brooklyn received no better than it deserved: "McLaughlin is 'Boss' because there has been no health or purity or wholesomeness in the public opinion, no standards of morals in the politics, no sense of pride and self respect in the masses, no regard for common honesty and the common weal in the community which he dominates."

McLaughlin was never a fighter. He had a natural abhorrence for open conflict within the organization and was happiest when the wheels of the machine were moving smoothly. There is reason to believe that he was genuinely sensitive about the names he was called. Because he was a poor speaker he seldom permitted himself to be drawn into any dispute. A few times he was so goaded by accusations that he attempted to strike back. Such an occasion was his dispute with Dr. Porter, a Protestant minister. When the clergyman supported in and out of the pulpit a candidate for surrogate, McLaughlin declared that it was part of a deal by which the cleric's son was to receive an appointment. There was no malice in this charge. Why else would a man support a candidate? Porter wrote an open letter in which denunciatory remarks were mixed with literary allusions. McLaughlin's reply was illustrative of why he usually refused to become embroiled in such disputes.

I don't know anything about the pagan gods, nor about Lord Bacon, nor The Sorrows of Werther, nor Harvey's Meditations, nor about Gray sitting in a graveyard. . . . There is one thing in the letter than I can understand; that is the quotation from this man Bacon: "*That adversity instructs the wise, but makes the foolish weak or mad.*" I suppose that he means me, by the "foolish. . . ."

I don't know why Gray, whoever he was, sat in a graveyard or what that has to do with the bargain between Dr. Porter and Mr. Livingston. So all this stuff about being wounded—I am not aware that I was wounded—I don't see any wounds—and Rachel weeping and refusing to be comforted—I don't know anything about that—there don't seem to be any connection between Livingston's running with Dr. Porter to help him and the wailing of a woman.

McLaughlin's aversion to public discussion was carried over to private conversation. He was by nature a retiring man and the fact that he had many favors to give and few to ask made him a better listener than talker. An acquaintance once remarked: "Conversations are like boxing bouts—one has to do all the leading." His answers to direct questions were usually a simple negative or affirmative, or "I wouldn't if I were you," "I don't think so," "All right," "Go ahead."

In some ways Hugh McLaughlin was vastly superior to other machine leaders. As long as he was boss, the Brooklyn organization never exacted any tribute from prostitution. When corrupt alliances between the municipal government and private corporations were discovered, McLaughlin was never involved. Although his henchmen often were the authors of fraudulent deals, there was no indication that they had acted on the Boss' orders. While he believed that the city should support a large segment of the party, he insisted that the government deserved an adequate return from the Democratic officials, clerks, and laborers.

Nor was he ever accused of either public or personal dishonesty. The *Union* once said: "We do not charge that the head of the McLaughlin family ever appropriated one dollar of the public money to his own use." At another time the same paper wrote: ". . . whatever faults he may have, he possesses one strong Republican virtue—that of telling the truth and keeping his word." McLaughlin, who was often cynical, did not place such a high estimate on his own integrity:

A man once asked me if I thought the majority of men were honest, and I told him that in a civil service examination for honesty only a very few men would get a rating of 70 per cent.
"What rating would you get?" and I told him I would consider myself lucky if they gave me over 50!

The assertion that McLaughlin was an honest boss was remarkable in view of his wealth. In 1892 his name appeared in a list of Americans worth more than one million dollars. The same source gave the origin of his wealth as "politics and real estate." It was estimated that his three terms in the register's office netted him $100,000 in fees. Using the profits from this position, he invested heavily in real estate. His influential, but extra-legal, position enabled him to know which section of the city would receive public improvements and offer a favorable opportunity for speculation. An example of this was his purchase in 1868 of land which later became part of the entrance to Prospect Park. This was obviously a form of graft, but one student of municipal government has called it "honest graft."

But if McLaughlin was rich, he was also unassuming. A visitor from New York wrote: "He keeps no horses, wears no diamonds, travels about the city on passes and in vehicles of his friends, dresses like a Canarsie clam baker, and smokes the cigars that are sent to him." He never permitted himself the luxury of an office. For some years after his last term as register, he could usually be found at the coroner's office; but in the late 'seventies he moved his headquarters to Kerrigan's auction rooms on Willoughby Street. He would arrive there in midmorning, return home for lunch, and be back at his old stand until nightfall. It was there that he held court, issued orders, and listened to complaints. If he wished to confer with anyone, he would dispatch the first person he saw as a messenger. More than once such an errand was run by a judge or commissioner. When he gave his commands, the politicians invariably referred to them as "orders from Willoughby Street." No matter how important the personage, he had to go to Kerrigan's if he wanted a favor from the Boss. At one time or another his visitors included "judges, merchants, doctors, millionaires, men in all the walks of life, the rich and the poor, the exalted and the lowly."

He was in many ways a simple and moderate man. He drank so infrequently that it was "almost the truth to say that he is strictly temperate." He was a devoted Catholic, attending church regularly and making numerous contributions to the church. In the midst of his bitterest political struggle, he told the Democratic General Committee: "If more people would go to church with their wives, there would be less divorce, and fewer adulteries." He was always generous, but never ostentatiously so. It was estimated that "he paid for burying most of the poor Irish in Brooklyn, although so tactfully and quietly that few realized the generosity involved."

His recreation was characteristic of the simplicity which marked his life. He is reported to have said that he never read a novel, and there is nothing to indicate that he was addicted to non-fiction. He liked to watch prize-fights, other athletic contests and vaudeville. The only game which he was known to enjoy was dominoes, which he played night after night in the basement of the city hall. But his most abiding passion was his garden. Frequently politicians paying a Sunday visit found him at work among his flowers. Forty-two years after the Democratic convention of 1860, he recalled that, as he sailed down the bay on his way to Charleston, his thoughts were not on platforms and candidates, but, "on some verbena vines which I had planted that sunny morning in my mother's garden."

In the summer McLaughlin always retired to Lake George where he could indulge in his favorite sport of fishing. Even there, however, he was not free from political worries, for the place hunters followed him to this temporary "Mecca of aspiring Democratic statesmen." As the leaves began to turn, the Trout Pavillon, where the Boss maintained his summer headquarters, was filled with candidates who were, "aching to serve the people in one capacity or another."

In appearance, Hugh McLaughlin afforded little indication that he was one of the country's most successful bosses. He looked like neither a reformed thug nor an overdressed dandy. Instead, he resembled the petty politicians who whiled away the hours whittling on the court house steps. One observer remarked that, as the Boss strolled along "with an easy gait, his hands in his pockets," he could have been mistaken for a "well-to-do . . . farmer." The best description of Hugh McLaughlin was recorded by a New York Sun reporter in 1875.

He is six feet and over, his corpulent body representing good living. His shoulders are thrown back as his stomach is thrown forward. His hat is always last year's, with the silk brushed the wrong way. His suit, which is all from the same piece of cloth, is always dingy and unbrushed. The coat is cut away so the pantaloons pockets can be reached and the tinsel covered package of Mayflower drawn forth for use. His boots are sometimes blacked, but the polish is that of some time before. As seen a block away there is nothing attractive in Mr. McLaughlin's appearance more than in that of any portly six footer. But as he steps among the politicians and finds a pathway ready for him in their midst there is that about the bearing of his round head, and the quiet keen look of his small blue eyes that betrays the leader. As soon as he is within the rotunda he is encompassed by politicians. He stands above them all, erect, uncompromising in his bearing and with a mild yet powerful dignity. His face is good natured, and bears the imprint of his Irish birth: his cheeks are full, fat, and smooth, but not puffy; his forehead slopes back gradually until it goes beyond a peninsula of hair which in boyhood was twisted into curly forelocks. His chin is doubled and clean shaven, but there are little tufts of gray sprinkled whiskers in front of each ear. The upper lip is covered by a short stiff mustache which is growing gray, and which would be long but for the frequent singes that it gets from the cigars that burn to stubs beneath it.
Perhaps, the eye alone, of all the man, by whom so many are controlled, is the only feature that indicates his possession of a leader's power. It is of true Irish blue, but gives forth a

clearer, more definite and positive expression than is usual in a genial Irish look. It never betrays itself. The expressions that pass over it are worth observing, for they reflect apparently not what the man thinks, but what he wishes his companions to believe he thinks. The prevailing look is that of a mild, well-poised man. As the politicians buzz about him the eyes look far, very far away, but the ears drink in everything. If in the flow of talk there is any humor, the Boss gives a low, Jay Gouldish, simpering chuckle, the only unmanly characteristic he has.

After 1893, Hugh McLaughlin was a pathetic figure. In that year the Republicans took over the city government and did not relinquish it until the formation of Greater New York in 1898. The Boss still ran the party, but he was an old man and had little patronage with which to appease his followers. For the third and last time he resigned from the Democratic General Committee.

When Brooklyn became a borough, open conflict between McLaughlin and Tammany could no longer be avoided. Charles F. Murphy, determined to make Brooklyn a part of the Manhattan machine, employed Patrick McCarren to lead a revolt against the aged Boss. In 1903, when McLaughlin refused to support the Tammany candidates, the executive committee overruled him. While the vote was being taken, McLaughlin was playing dominoes in the basement of Borough Hall.

A year later he died.

Reprinted from The City of Brooklyn, 1865-1898: A Political History, by Harold Coffin Syrett. Number 512 in the series, Studies in History, Economics and Public Law. Copyright, 1944, by Columbia University Press.

from . . .

MAYOR GAYNOR'S LETTERS AND SPEECHES

June 10, 1912.

The National Publicity Bureau: You ask me to give an interview saying "What I would say to the readers of 3,000 newspapers." I would say to them to be very careful about believing all they see in the newspapers.

C. E. Baird, Esq.
Scranton, Penna.

"THE VESTIBULE OF HELL" AND "SCAMPS"

December 16, 1912.

Reverend and Dear Sir: I thank you for sending me the address to your congregation regarding conditions in Greenpoint, Brooklyn. I am aware that your congregation is very large, and it is due to you that I take notice of what you say. I agree with you that the people of Greenpoint are not given over to vice and crime and disorder. The very few preachers who are saying that are mere notoriety seekers, and, as a rule, minister to empty benches, as might be expected. People go willingly to hear those who have the great charity and love of Jesus in their hearts. There are bad people in Greenpoint, the same as everywhere else, and we must do the best we can to turn them from their evil ways. I see one clergyman over in your immediate neighborhood says that Brooklyn is the "vestibule of hell." These are his words. What a charitable soul he must be. And yet the truth is, shown by the records, that Brooklyn is freer from crime and vice than any other equal population in the world. Its entire criminal business above the grade of petty offences is disposed of by one criminal court. Just think of that being true of 1,750,000 people. And yet there are some scamps who call Brooklyn the "vestibule of hell." But we must be charitable and kind to them, and try to reclaim them from their uncharity, and their propensity to bear false witness.

Rt. Rev. P. F. O'Hare
Brooklyn, N. Y.

SUNDAY GAMES

June 11, 1912.

Dear Dr. Bailey: Your letter communicating to me the resolution passed by the Prospect Heights Presbyterian Church with regard to playing games in the parks on Sunday is at hand. A great majority of the people of the city, and I think of the clergymen of the city, would be opposed to stopping them. I was myself brought up to the observance of a still Sabbath. But as we had to work hard in the fields and woods on week days we were willing to keep still on Sunday. Of course you know that is not the case with our city men and boys. Many of them have no day of recreation except Sunday. What would you do with them? If they do not play in the fields they will go somewhere else, as you know. Where would you have them go? No doubt your church has solved that problem, and I should be very glad to have you let me know how it has been solved. Some of our clergymen who have not been able to solve it are offering to go into the fields and play with the boys of their congregation on Sunday afternoons. They dread to have the boys driven to the saloons, or to worse places. The conditions in cities and in the country with regard to Sunday are very different. Please remember also that people have a right to indulge in any game or recreation on Sunday which is not prohibited by law.

Rev. Edwin D. Bailey
Brooklyn, N. Y.

April 12, 1911.

Reverend and Dear Sir: Your letter informing me that as you walk about the city visiting the homes of your parishioners people apply opprobrious names to you, and throw empty cans and rubbish at you, and otherwise assault you, on account of your beard, is at hand. You ask me, "Is it a crime in the City of New York to wear a beard"? No, it is not. I wear one myself and nobody ever takes any notice of it. How is it they take notice of your beard? Have you trimmed it in some peculiar way, contrary to the Scriptures? For you know the Scriptures say, "Ye shall not round the corners of your heads, neither shalt thou mar the corners of thy beard."

Yes, if they assault you, and throw cans at you, you have a right to defend yourself to the last extremity; but if you find it necessary I will have a detective go around with you for a few days until we arrest some of those who are wronging you. Are you certain that it is your beard which is the cause of the trouble?

Rev. Basil M. Kerbawy
Brooklyn, N. Y.

ARGUE LIKE FRANKLIN

March 8, 1911.

Dear Sir: Your letter challenging me to a debate with you on Socialism is at hand. The mere fact that you make the challenge is probably proof positive that you are not fit for such a debate. People who want to force things down the mental throats of others do their own cause more harm than good. Did you ever read that part of Benjamin Franklin's autobiography in which he says that experience had taught him that the way to convince another is to state your case moderately and accurately, and then scratch your head, or shake it a little, and say that that is the way it seems to you, but that of course you may be mistaken about it; which causes your listener to receive what you say, and as like as not, turn about and try to convince you of it, since you are in doubt; but if you go at him with a tone of positiveness and arrogance you only make an opponent of him. I write this to you in the hope that it may make you stop long enough to think that possibly you are not so infallible as you think you are. You compliment me because I know the meaning of the red flag of the Socialists, and stated it in my message to the Board of Aldermen. It is just possible that I have done more to make the people of New York understand the meaning of your flag and of Socialism than all that you have ever said with stridulent voice. If you wish to be a teacher, just read the passage I have mentioned from Franklin, and cool off a whole lot.

T. N. Fall, Esq.
Brooklyn, N. Y.

CONVERTING THE JEWS

April 21, 1910.

Reverend and Dear Sir: It seems to me that this work of proselyting from other religions and sects is very often carried too far. Do you not think the Jews have a good religion? Have not the Christians appropriated the entire Jewish sacred scriptures? Was not the New Testament also written entirely by Jews? Was not Jesus also born of the Jewish race, if I may speak of it with due reverence? Did not we Christians get much or the most of what we have from the Jews? Why should any one work so hard to proselytize the Jew? His pure belief in the one true living God comes down to us even from the twilight of fable, and is the one great unbroken lineage and tradition of the world. I do not think I should give you a license to preach for the conversion of the Jews in the streets of the thickly settled Jewish neighborhoods which you designate. Would you not annoy them and do more harm than good? How many Jews have you converted so far?

Rev. Thomas M. Chalmers
Brooklyn, N. Y.

The Greaves Publishing Co., London 1913

BROOKLYN'S FOXY GRANDPA

from THE TIN BOX PARADE

by MILTON MACKAYE

In these decadent days two things save the once haughty and independent city of Brooklyn from complete anonymity in its native land—a goofy baseball team in the steerage of the National League and a persisting belief among Americans that the Brooklyn Bridge is the acknowledged Eighth Wonder of the World. Otherwise Brooklyn is, to the country at large, a mere section of New York with no identity of its own; a necessary tail to Broadway's kite, a place where people live, and what of it? This attitude, of course, affronts the community's dignity and is very painful to local citizens; furthermore, it is decidedly unjust. Brooklyn, in population and politics, is the most important borough of New York. Some two million five hundred thousand human souls reside there, and by the simple examination of census figures it will be seen that it is the third largest city in the nation, outdistanced by Chicago but larger than Philadelphia.

Despite the general indifference to its distinctions, Brooklyn manages to hold its head up and maintain a considerable isolation. It has its own department stores and shopping centers, symphony and operatic seasons, its own Art Museum, educational institutions, and daily newspapers. Also it has the Brooklyn Paramount Theatre which, as any curator of movie lore will tell you, is every whit as garish and gorgeous, polished and stalactited, as the sister Paramount in old Times Square. In other words, Brooklyn is an entirely self-sufficient city within its own boundaries and growing by the minute, while the population of Manhattan subsides. It boasts thirty miles of water-front and thousands of docks (surpassing Manhattan as a shipping center), and the output of it factories was valued at a billion dollars a year when factories still had an output and the buying public still had a billion dollars.

This rich and imposing domain was ruled over for twenty-four years by a small, round, professional politician who started life as a shipyards worker and bowed out of life full of honors and extremely wealthy. John H. McCooey, known deceptively in his later years as "Uncle John," wielded more local power in the nineteen-twenties than any other man in the United States. He was not only Democratic boss of the county, he was boss of everything else; dictator to business, dictator to the professions, moral and ethical preceptor. He and he alone decided who would man the public offices, preside in the courts, staff the hospitals, run the schools; and in banking, brokering, and shopkeeping it was important also to have his good will. Only the churches were exempt from his benevolent dominion (Uncle John early decided, rightly or wrongly, that God could manage his own affairs), and even there a little crusading fervor was to be found. McCooey owned the borough outright, and there were no mortgage payments to meet.

Uncle John found Brooklyn's comparative anonymity a valuable asset in politics. The great daily papers on the other side of the bridge years before had chosen Tammany Hall as the villain of the piece, and they were only mildly interested in what occurred in Kings County. The recurring investigations invariably concerned themselves with Manhattan, and McCooey was content to let things stand that way. "I don't bother with New York County," he said. "I just mind my own business. I find I get along better when I do." And so he did. Public scandals in Brooklyn were few because nobody bothered to dig them up. Tammany got the bad name, and John McCooey continued to rule without opposition.

The fact is that Brooklyn was infinitely corrupt, and its officialdom not only corrupt but second-rate. In Manhattan there were nominal Tammany men of intellectual attainments; it was necessary, in view of public opinion, to elect or to appoint them now and then. Joseph E. Corrigan, for example, became Chief Magistrate when the lower courts were under fire, and his excellent reputation has never been questioned; Dick Patterson was an honest Commissioner of Corrections; John H. Delaney, head of the Board of Transportation, was energetic and knew his job; Jim Foley, Murphy's son-in-law, proved to be a great Surrogate; the Appellate Division ranked at one time as a court of real distinction. But there was no public opinion in Brooklyn and no need for window dressing; the result was that McCooey's office-holders, almost without exception, were colorless mediocrities, insipid when upright and hard to take at any time.

In Manhattan, however weak and meaningless the Republican organization itself, there is always an opposition of sorts. It may not be an opposition on election day (and, indeed, usually isn't), but between times it keeps Tammany watching how the corners are cut. For the most part, this opposition, inasmuch as it is effective, is made up of outstanding citizens who do not dabble in local politics to any great extent but try to keep outward decency up to a standard that can at least be stomached. The Association of the Bar of the City of New York has its weaknesses, but it *will* prosecute an errant judge to the limit when a case is made out against him. The Merchants' Association occasionally takes a stand on a question in which the pecuniary rewards of its own members are not concerned. The New York County Grand Jury, even though afflicted with clothes-horse district attorneys for almost twenty years, does indict political offenders when the provocation is great.

In Brooklyn during the prosperous years of McCooey's reign there was no opposition. On a number of election days his borough gave a large plurality for every Democratic candidate except one assemblyman in the Republican section of Flatbush. Finally even this troublesome fellow was eliminated, and Uncle John had all city, all county, all borough, and all State patronage. Apparently there were no independent right-thinkers to give trouble; certainly there was none to whom the newspapers would listen. McCooey owned not only the politicians but the grand jury, and owning a grand jury is a sizable asset for any Boss. It makes the prosecution of political knaves a possibility only if they are discovered stealing nickels from the poor box or firing Roman candles into the rheumy old eyes of apple-women —and even then only if they are not found, by competent medical men, to be suffering from nervous collapse. McCooey had another asset; he owned the Brooklyn Bar Association. So far as is known, this group never did anything to improve the courts of the county, and more, when certain judges were under public attack, the Association either failed to investigate them or decided they were fit to serve.

County Judge George W. Martin was accused of being an officer in a company which sold bad stock. Kenneth Spence, well-known New York lawyer, was special Federal Attorney in the case, and Martin for the time being retired from the bench. The Federal Grand Jury decided that Martin had committed no crime and left the matter there. "The question of judicial ethics," Spence said, "is not a matter within the province of the United States District Attorney to pass upon." Testimony bearing upon the charge that Martin had violated the judicial code of ethics was relayed to the Brooklyn Bar Association. Nothing came of it. Martin went back on the bench.

Statements that Brooklyn had a weak bench always annoyed McCooey. "We have an excellent bench," he said at one time. "There is no reason that good Democrats don't make as good judges as good Republicans." County Judge W. Bernard Vause was one of his favorites, a jurist who excited jealousy among his colleagues because they knew he was the Old Man's fair-haired boy. The Vauses and the McCooeys went abroad together; the two men were close, and they both hunted in Paris, like good Americans, for a place where they could find ham and eggs.

Vause lent his judicial gown to an investment scheme which bankrupted hundreds of small investors—the Columbia Finance Corporation. During the Federal investigation it was discovered also that he had taken part in negotiations, while on the bench, leading up to the awarding of three pier leases to the United American Lines. These leases were granted by the Sinking Fund Commission, a New York City department with which Vause, as an individual, had no influence whatever. A fee of $250,000 was paid by the shipping line, and the share of that which found its way into Vause's pocket temporarily (he undoubtedly had to split with others) is variously estimated at from $60,000 to $190,000. In May of 1930 Vause was indicted for using the mails to defraud in the Columbia Finance case. He resigned his job. Two months later he was convicted and, despite his enlistment of Max D. Steuer as an appeals attorney, went to Atlanta to serve a six-year term. The pier lease matter was never cleared up. McCooey was loyal to his friends *in extremis;* "They have never proved," said Uncle John, "that he was dishonest as a judge."

In the old days before consolidation with New York (1898), Brooklyn was known as the City of Churches. On Brooklyn Heights, where a hauntingly beautiful picture of New York Harbor is had, lived the old powerful families. Mostly they were Dutch or emigrants from Puritan New England. In the eighteen-seventies and -eighties the city was second only to Boston itself as an intellectual center. It was there in Plymouth Church that Henry Ward Beecher preached and drew thousands to hear him, and it was there that the scandal about Beecher arose. There were great preachers after him, but Brooklyn was never quite the same. As the greatness faded out of it the ward politicians came in, and what (because of the Abolitionists) had been a great Republican stronghold was gradually transformed into a Democratic county. Year by year the emigration from Manhattan grew, and gradually the Roman Catholics and the Jews supplanted the Congregationalists and the Unitarians, the Lutherans, the Presbyterians, the Methodists, and the Episcopalians. Brooklyn, the Puritan city, became something else entirely. Its legend still persisted.

John McCooey was born in Manhattan in 1864, and moved first to the Williamsburg section of Brooklyn and then to Chester, Pennsylvania, where his father was foreman of the shipyard. The father died when the son was thirteen; the boy went to work the next day. He was a shipyards worker for some time, first in Manhattan and then in Brooklyn. He helped to build (and he always remembered it) the battleship *Maine* which sank in Havana Harbor, and shortly afterward he was appointed secretary of the Pattern and Moulder Makers' Union. That ended his manual labor, but many years later the gifted Mayor

Hylan remembered McCooey's maritime beginnings and launched the municipal ferryboat *John H. McCooey*. Uncle John liked the idea and wore a yachting cap on deck during the dedication and trial cruise. He was a little ill when the boat struck rough water.

At the age of twenty-four, having shown promise, McCooey was appointed superintendent of a branch post-office. He never worked again. He became in turn Deputy Treasurer of Kings County, secretary of the Municipal Civil Service Commission, Deputy City Comptroller, and finally Clerk of the Surrogate's Court of Kings County, from which he eventually retired with forty-odd years of city service and an annual pension of $7,500.

Henry Hesterberg, father of the dapper Henry Hesterberg who later grew out of knickerbockers and into the Borough Presidency, was the man who recognized McCooey's political talents. He made him assistant leader, and when, because of the growing population, the Hesterberg district was split, McCooey became a district leader in his own right. Also he became the right-hand man of Senator Pat McCarren, then the Boss of Brooklyn. McCarren and McCooey were diametrically opposed in everything except ambition. McCarren was a swaggerer and a roisterer; he loved loud checked suits, the race-track, and a good fight. McCooey was quiet, a moderate drinker though a great eater, and he hated a fight and loved a compromise. An instance of this is found in his relations with Charlie Murphy. As a boy and a shipyards worker he had eaten and drunk at Murphy's saloon in Manhattan. McCarren and Murphy were often at war; McCooey went over one day and had a canny talk with his old friend. He wanted no hard feelings between them; but if matters came to a showdown, he would have to stand with the McCarren organization. Murphy, who believed in loyalty, understood, and it was Murphy eventually who made McCooey's dominance possible.

McCooey ran for Borough President of Brooklyn in 1909 (his only attempt to gain office at the polls) and was defeated. That same year McCarren died, and McCooey became the Democratic leader of Brooklyn. He was no dictator then; he sat very uncomfortably in the saddle. But Murphy was for him. Fourteen district leaders pledged McCooey their support, and there were nine who opposed him. In a very short time twelve of the fourteen McCooey leaders were on the city payroll through Murphy's efforts; the other nine were starved out of politics. McCooey became not only a leader but a boss.

Uncle John (his long mustachios were even then turning white) reversed the current of Brooklyn politics. After the consolidation in 1898 all Brooklyn politicians made a cause out of their hatred of Tammany Hall. "The Tiger Shall Not Cross the Bridge" was a slogan which won votes for Hugh McLaughlin and Pat McCarren alike. They made their alliances with the upstate Democrats and fought Tammany Hall because they feared it. McCooey had obligations to Murphy, and he also saw that the old slogan hadn't taken McLaughlin and McCarren any place in particular. He was the first Brooklyn leader to make his peace with Tammany. He kept his peace with Tammany, and he made Tammany pay for it.

McCooey's rise to power is no story for Horatio Alger. Paul A. Tierney, the newspaperman, described it accurately as the "triumphal progress of a jelly-fish." McCooey won by giving in. As Brooklyn's population increased and Manhattan's decreased, Tammany needed McCooey more and more to control the town. It finally reached the point that McCooey in Brooklyn had a hundred and twenty-five thousand more enrolled Democrats than Tammany. McCooey was a Yankee trader. With him Tammany could win; without him the control of the town was lost. He could set his own price and did. Brooklyn got more jobs than Manhattan. In 1931 every Brooklyn Democratic district leader save one was on the city payroll. That one leader didn't want a job.

McCooey gave in all his life and, by reasons of giving in, created a county machine of vast power. He did not care about the city at large so long as his own feudal strength was increased. And always Tammany needed Brooklyn's votes to put over its projects, and always there was a price to pay. Jobs, jobs, jobs. After Murphy died McCooey was the strongest leader in the five boroughs. By combining with Bronx County he could have taken control of the party away from Tammany Hall and made himself the boss of the city. That, however, would have meant a fight, and McCooey was a man of peace. McCooey preferred to have Tammany the dominant group and to hold over Tammany's head the worrisome prospect of disaster if he should join a general revolt. He preferred rich blackmail to troublesome glory. The city paid as much as $2,000,000 a year in salaries to Brooklyn wardheelers and their relatives.

The McCooey machine was strictly a one-man organization. In 1914 a group of independent Democrats threatened to take his own district away from him, and he won out by a scant seven hundred and fifty votes. That was the last whisper of revolt for many years. For one thing, McCooey had few of those demanding, individualistic district leaders who made life miserable for Olvany and Curry; the Brooklyn leaders were a spiritless lot content to stand under the drippings and utterly convinced of McCooey's invincibility. The old man had a sharp eye for incipient troublemakers and an efficient way of dealing with them —he gave them lucrative jobs before they had quite settled into troublesome ways and made them forever beholden to him. He drowned mutiny with maple syrup. On the rare occasions when these tactics were not successful, he could be utterly ruthless, and his power was far-reaching. The rebel not only found himself out of politics but headed somewhere out of Brooklyn where he might make enough money to support his family again.

As the years piled up on him McCooey gradually took shape in the mind of the New York public as a kind, jovial old gentleman in whom, despite his political status, there was no harm. It is hard to make a white-haired fat man into a sinister figure, although, if memory serves, there have been jolly fat men who were cold and cruel indeed. Uncle John looked a little like an unbearded Santa Claus. His plump rosy cheeks were cherubic; his eyes were round and blue and disarming. On occasions when the mask dropped, his round little eyes could become a predatory and gun-barrel blue, and the startled spectator realized with a mental shiver that everything was not honey and holy-water behind that dimpled smile.

As a matter of fact McCooey became so devious, by long discipline in concealment, that he sometimes must have almost confused himself. He was given to occasional fits of rage when he met with a political set-back, and he enjoyed his rages thoroughly despite the imminent peril of a heart attack. Invariably, however, and with automatic caution, his anger concerned itself with an entirely extraneous matter; his wrath was a thing of variety and resource. During Roosevelt's time as Governor, McCooey advanced as his candidate for State Superintendent of Insurance Arthur L. Somers, a gentleman who was the perennial and decorative Leading Citizen of McCooey's own club. McCooey had been given to understand that Somers was as good as appointed, and when he received the news that Roosevelt, instead, had appointed Deputy Superintendent Behan, he promptly went into a temper. For a solid ten minutes he let fly with profanity and invective—and the subject of all this abuse was Samuel Seabury, who up until that moment had not figured in the conversation at all.

Uncle John went to his office every day. It was located up a creaky flight of stairs at 4 Court Square, and there were no secretaries or receptionists to keep the public out; he believed in accessibility. A single attendant, the faithful Jake Kory, presided in the outer room, but Kory asked no questions about the visitor's mission and merely saw that petitioners kept in line. Sometimes two thousand people a week sat there with their hats in their hands. McCooey did the work of an ordinary district leader; he found a job for this one, gave advice to another, put off a third with promises. Or perhaps he provided the applicant with a glowing letter to the Corporation Counsel, patted his shoulder, and then, when the applicant departed, calmly advised the Corporation Counsel by telephone that he might disregard the letter. McCooey decorated the picture of his frankness and accessibility with certain artistic details of his own. The door between the outer and inner offices was always open, and McCooey and his visitor were in plain view of those awaiting audience.

The Boss faced the door. The room, however, had peculiar acoustical properties. If McCooey turned in his swivel chair his voice was lost to those outside. There was also, it may be interesting to add, a muffler device on his telephone.

In searching through the long newspaper records of his activities it is almost impossible to find any public statement of Uncle John's which was either informative or bright. He talked to reporters at length and said little. On one or two occations, however, he opened up. He spoke of his indifference to editorial criticism. "How much can you sell a column of yesterday's newspaper for?" he demanded. "Who'd buy it? What is it worth? Why, you wouldn't even print it again yourself." On another occasion he called a Brooklyn reporter to his home, and therein lies a story. One important job on the Democratic state ticket inevitably goes to Brooklyn. Uncle John was roused from his bed one night (so the story goes) by a call from Albany. Governor Roosevelt on the wire. Had Mr. McCooey any suggestions for the nomination of an Attorney-General? Mr. McCooey had; he offered three or four names. Had Mr. McCooey ever thought of John J. Bennett? Uncle John stalled for a moment—Bennett, Bennett, who was Bennett?—and then said heartily that Bennett was a very estimable man, but that he hadn't been, of course, very active. He had been, the Governor persisted, State Commander of the American Legion. McCooey, even in a night cap, understood how things were going; he told the Governor that Bennett would be an excellent choice. "I had been thinking about recommending him to you all along. Good night, Governor." "Good night, Mr. McCooey." Uncle John, suspicious of the late hours of the Albany correspondents, promptly called the Brooklyn reporter with the astonishing news that he had a good exclusive story. The reporter arrived. "Brooklyn's choice for the nomination for Attorney-General," said McCooey, "is the Honorable John J. Bennett. I have reason to believe that the Governor will accede to our wishes."

McCooey could never have been a king-maker—he did not have the breadth of viewpoint necessary for the big-time game nor the courage to gamble on long-shots—but as a local boss he was tops. He seldom meant what he said or said what he meant, and he was as foxy as they come. He always had an out for himself on any deal. In 1932 he gave his solemn promise to stick with Curry to defeat the nomination of Governor Lehman, but when the pressure got heavy at the State convention it suddenly developed that "mutiny" had broken out in the McCooey delegation. Hyman Schorenstein and several other district chiefs announced that they were bolting to Lehman. Uncle John went sadly to Curry. "I'm afraid I can't hold my leaders in line," he said. That mutiny allowed Brooklyn to climb on the band wagon very handily indeed, but it had all the appearance of a grease-paint rebellion. Uncle John had never failed before to hold his leaders in line.

On one occasion McCooey's blandness and suavity were of no avail. At the Democratic National Convention in 1932 he erred; he stood out against Roosevelt until the end. Immediately upon returning home he moved, bag and baggage, into the Roosevelt headquarters and began shouting, loudest of all, for "our next President." Brooklyn gave Roosevelt a plurality of three hundred and twenty thousand, but the President had a long memory. McCooey never got a nickel's worth of Federal patronage and was fast losing control of his borough at the time of his death.

The Brooklyn boss was fast on his feet even after the rigor of advancing age slowed down his general activities. Several years before his demise a Brooklyn newspaper which had not been particularly friendly to his dictatorship found itself in financial difficulties. An absentee owner stepped out and turned over control to a corporation of employees. They needed ready money for operating expenses, and some of the agile minds in the business department decided that John McCooey might be persuaded, in the interest of civic pride, to buy a block of stock. They went at the problem handsomely; the employees gave a dinner for Uncle John as a testimonial of their love and esteem. The seating arrangements were sly and premeditated. On either side of the guest of honor the committee placed a golden-voiced persuader, whose job it was, during the course of the dinner, to broach the subject of stock sale. McCooey was delighted at the newspaper's gesture. He said so immediately he entered the banquet room and described in a moving voice how much this honor had touched his heart. "It reminds me," he said as he sat down to the first course, "of a little incident which occurred in the days of Pat McCarren." Uncle John told his story, and that reminded him (as the second course appeared) of an odd situation which had once confronted Mayor Gaynor. McCooey talked, reminiscently and unflaggingly, throughout an eight-course dinner—permitting never an opportunity for the salesman on his right or the salesman on his left to interrupt. He told his last anecdote as the coffee was finished. Then he rose. "Boys," he said happily, "this has been one of the pleasantest evenings of my life. I cannot thank you enough. I have an engagement at the Madison Club within ten minutes, and now I'm sure you'll excuse me. Thank you and good night."

One of the old boss's most valuable assets in public life was his great reputation as a family man. He had no affection for night life or racy companions and liked nothing better than (when political engagements permitted it) a quiet evening at home. He lived quietly and unostentatiously and was often photographed amid a cluster of his kin. He saw to it that they were insulated against poverty and want. His brother-in-law, John H. Byrne, served as Borough President until his death. Margaret J. McCooey, a sister, was advanced in the city educational system from principal to Associate Superintendent of Schools at a salary of $12,500 a year. Adele, a daughter, married the wealthy George Tilyou, Jr., owner of amusement concessions at Coney Island, and Tilyou became an unsalaried member of the Library Board. The McCooey boys all prospered. Everett's gifts for high finance were recognized when he was only twenty-three; J. S. Bache & Co., the brokers, made him their general manager for Brooklyn and he was able to drum up some tidy accounts. Everett was the artistic member of the family; his sweet-throated Irish tenor occasionally gave the radio audience a treat, and he was once offered the presidency of the short-lived New York Civic Opera Association, an honor he declined. Herbert

McCooey and John H. McCooey, Jr., became lawyers, and the latter eventually was elected a Supreme Court Justice.

John H. (Jack) McCooey formed with Gardner Conroy the law firm of McCooey and Conroy. Herbert was also a member, but he specialized in insurance and bonds. His abilities, too, were recognized, and at a comparatively tender age he became vice-president both of the Fidelity and Deposit Company and the American Bonding Company, in charge of the Brooklyn and Long Island business of these concerns. He also formed the insurance firm of McCooey and Schmitz. In these lines he did well. It was pointed out in the spring of 1933 that his company, within a short time, had placed eight hundred and sixty-eight bonds for public works contractors, more than twice as many bonds as had been placed, within the same period, by any of the thirty-four competing firms. The Brooklyn insurance came his way also. There were reasons why it should.

The law firm of McCooey and Conroy had singularly good luck. First of all, they were successful practitioners before the Board of Standards and Appeals, second in success only to the immortal Dr. Doyle. The case of Joseph Zorn, a client, is a notorious one. Zorn received a permit for a gasoline station. The charge was made that the permit had been obtained by fraud, and it was declared illegal by Supreme Court Justice Cropsey in Brooklyn in 1930. Cropsey's decision was upheld in the Appellate Division and the Court of Appeals. As a result, the Board of Standards and Appeals revoked the permit. Zorn already (in 1929) had pleaded guilty to violating building regulations by attempting to install a gasoline tank without permission. In 1931 Zorn engaged McCooey and Conroy to seek a new permit for him. These gentlemen were able to present his case in a more appealing light. Ignoring the decisions of the high courts, the Board of Standards and Appeals discovered that a great injustice had been done. Zorn was granted an exemption from the zoning laws and a permit.

The firm was taken care of in other ways. In Surrogate's Court (where Papa McCooey had been Chief Clerk) Gardner Conroy received forty-eight appointments in two and a half years. Also he was given sixty-three refereeships in three selected months and Jack McCooey seventy-three. The Brooklyn courts generally seemed to realize that there was merit in the law firm. Supreme Court Justice Druhan gave Jack McCooey fifty-two refereeships in one month. "Why not?" demanded Justice Druhan when questioned. "He's a reliable man."

Uncle John amassed himself a sizable fortune. Things kept coming his way. There was for example the $69,000 profit on a Brooklyn school site which went into his pocket. An associate by the name of Charles D. Cords bought a piece of property in Bay Ridge for $57,000 with the aid of a $15,000 loan from the Boss himself; McCooey's name did not appear. The land was located in the middle of a group of gas tanks and incinerators; there was heavy industrial traffic nearby; the neighborhood was not a residence section. A committee from the Board of Education investigated it as a school site and reported: "Too near gas tanks—out." No one knew that McCooey was financially interested. A second trip of inspection was made, and this time Miss Margaret J. McCooey was along. The Board of Superintendents finally decided that the Bay Ridge property, situated as it was, was "especially adaptable to school purposes." The local school board in that district protested. McCooey (and this is based on his own frank testimony before Leonard Wallstein in the condemnation investigation) called in the chairman of the local board, who was also an official of the Democratic organization in the 9th Assembly District. The chairman, when he learned Uncle John was interested, became convinced it was a good site. Next McCooey talked to May Golden, secretary of the local board. Miss Golden's brother was a Democratic magistrate, and she too saw the glories of the school property. "I would start off with this premise," McCooey told Wallstein, "that inasmuch as I had a great deal to do with the appointment of her brother as a magistrate, that she would naturally be friendly to me if I wanted her friendship for this site."

The Board of Education approved the land. Dr. William A. Boylan, who became president of Brooklyn College, backed the property before the Board of Estimate and said it had a "delightful outlook." The question of price, once the city had begun condemnation, went to the courts. Here was the set-up there: Justice Mitchell May, who presided, was an old friend of McCooey's; the city's land expert had obtained his job through McCooey's recommendation; the assistant Corporation Counsel presenting the city's case had been approved for his appointment by McCooey. Here is what happened: The city's land expert valued the land at $253,000, more than three times the assessed valuation; the McCooey experts placed the worth of the property at $353,000; Justice May split the estimates evenly and awarded a price of $303,000. It is interesting to add that the property amid the gas tanks still stands vacant; no one will build a school there while still in his right mind. Mr. McCooey agreed at the end of the condemnation investigation that there were certain unhealthy factors involved in the existing system and that they should be corrected.

Uncle John had few personal weaknesses. He did not drink to excess, he did not care for showy tailoring—but he did like to eat. His paunch was built up in a workman-like way. On many evenings he was required to go from one banquet to another and then to another. Sometimes he resisted the temptation to toy with a little more food, and sometimes he didn't. A friend has recalled an Albany incident. McCooey reached there on an evening train and after a full meal on the diner. An hour later he attended a banquet at the Ten Eyck Hotel (where all politicians gather when the New York legislature is in session) and refused food. In busy conversation with his important neighbor, his eyes strayed to the plate. "That *does* look like good melon," he said, twiddling his thumbs over his round belly. "I think I'll have that and nothing more." He had the melon and the rest of the dinner.

In his later days, when he approached seventy, such a regimen was too much; a heart attack (or it may have been indigestion) often followed his gormandizing. One of his favorite resorts in Brooklyn was Joe Sartori's restaurant. He ate at his own special table there, and once a year he went up-state to Joe Sartori's hunting lodge. There was good hearty food at the lodge, the photographers were there to take his picture, and as a political correspondent phrased it, "now and then a deer was led across the yard for Uncle John to shoot at." This last statement, I am sure, is unreliable because Uncle John's hunting costumes clearly proved that he was not a man to draw a bead from an armchair on the verandah. Abercrombie & Fitch would have disapproved.

McCooey and his son Jack had a great deal in common. Jack, although tall, commenced to put on embonpoint in his twenties and exhibited an extraordinary and heroic affection for food. This fixation began innocently enough, but it often alarmed his friends when they found him anchored in a Childs restaurant late at night devouring half a dozen apple dumplings garnished with whipped cream. Jack and his father were close for years. The son began attending political conventions with his father when he was only twelve and never missed one thereafter. The day he was graduated from college he left for the Democratic National Convention at San Francisco, and the train was held an hour so that he might get his diploma. That was in 1920. He attended Cornell Law School and was admitted to the bar in 1922. After an apprenticeship with Judge Almet F. Jenks, he hung out his shingle and opened an office full of red-leather furnishings and handsome etchings. He was busy, but he found time to have a lot of fun and to become an expert contract bridge player. What system? Tch, tch, Culbertson.

Up until 1932 few of Jack McCooey's friends thought of him as precisely a titan of the law. He was a merry fellow, a good companion, but his performances at the bar had not been impressive. He made a few court appearances, rarely tried a case, and it was common knowledge that his firm's income depended largely on political favors and political sinecures. As a result, there was something of a minor explosion in the town when the news was broadcast that Papa McCooey had nominated his thirty-one-year-old son for a $25,000 job as Justice of the Supreme Court. It was such an audacious and bald transaction that even hardened clubhouse loafers gasped a little over their pinochle games. In other quarters there was raucous laughter; with one move the whole governmental system in New York had been transformed into pure and undiluted burlesque. Uncle John went about his business not giving a damn what anyone thought. He knew Jack would be elected. He knew that the sands of his own life were running out and that, a good family man, he had set his son in a shelter where he could not be disturbed for fourteen years.

"I'm not like some fathers who don't want their sons to go into their own profession," he said. "I like politics, and when my son came to me and said, 'Pop, I want to go on the Supreme Court,' why I said, 'Amen, boy I'll help you.' Some people thought I had a nerve. But that's what you need in politics—guts."

Uncle John had them. The decking out of the immature Jack in a judicial gown was part of a fancy trade which created a surprising lot of pother and protest—surprising because New Yorkers suddenly grew indignant about the kind of barter which had been going on for years. The Second District of the Supreme Court takes in five counties—Kings (Brooklyn), Queens, Richmond, and the Long Island counties of Nassau and Suffolk. There was, along about 1930, a need for additional justices on the bench; it was estimated by various authorities that six members of the court would suffice to catch up on litigation. Unfortunately, only the Legislature could create these new positions, and the Legislature was Republican-controlled. The Republicans, naturally, had no intention of making new jobs for Democrats. Finally an agreement was arrived at; the Legislature agreed to create not six but twelve new judgeships. The Democrats were to get seven and the Republicans five, and each party pledged itself to endorse, sight unseen, the other party's nominees. Thus the slate of twelve candidates was carried on both tickets, and election was assured. It was, if one is not choosey about his phrase, a gentleman's agreement. The result, of course, was to deny to the voters of the five counties any freedom of choice in the selection of their judges. McCooey seized this opportunity to nominate his son.

The New York County Lawyers' Association denounced the deal as a "direct and dangerous assault upon the honor of the

Supreme Court of the State of New York," and the City Bar expressed itself in language equally melodramatic. The Judiciary Committee of the Brooklyn Bar Association handed up a disapproving report, but the Association as a whole, maintaining its long-time record for subserviency to Uncle John, rejected the report, and endorsed the charming Jack. A "No Deal" ticket of judiciary candidates was put in the field, and it managed to poll one hundred thousand protest votes, but the Republican-Democratic judges were elected as everyone had known they would be all along.

Uncle John was called before Seabury to testify concerning his colonizing of the courts. On the witness stand he discussed the inter-party deal and how four of the Brooklyn judgeships had been awarded.

"Now, the other place," he said as he concluded his testimony, "my own son was nominated for that. Do you want any discussion of his availability or anything?"

"There was or there wasn't discussion, you say?" inquired Seabury.

"Oh, there was. Nearly every leader in the party urged me very strongly to nominate Jack. I had no idea there was such unanimity of opinion. I might say, of course, that he has been at the bar for ten years, is generally regarded as capable and efficient, has the poise and the character and the industry, and so long as he was in a receptive mood, I was very glad to recommend him."

Uncle John was at the peak of his power when the judicial deal was put through. Even then, however, a few fine cracks were beginning to show in his tremendously effective one-man machine. Most of the old-line district leaders were as spineless as ever; they were yes-men and never presumptuous enough to offer advice. A few of them were worth mention. There was the debonair Hesterberg, sagacious son of a sagacious father. There was William J. Heffernan, boss of the polyglot district where Al Capone was spawned; Heffernan's badges of office (he was Commissioner of Elections) were a diamond stickpin and a derby hat, and, the owner of three saloons, he won himself a certain small immortality in New York by closing them down when prohibition became the law. There were also Kenneth Sutherland and Hymie Schorenstein.

Sutherland, boss of the big Jewish Coney Island section, was likeable, energetic, and independent. He wore blue serge, pressed to knife edges, and he was one of the leaders of revolt when revolt came. His methods of controlling the vote in his district were neither friendly, admirable, nor refined.

Schorenstein was a veteran Jewish leader, well into his sixties, who always referred to his political protégés as "mine boys." Schorenstein took his Brownsville district away from the Socialists who, in post-war days, had considerable strength in isolated areas and among Jewish laboring people. Like Tom Farley, Hymie was a kindly leader; he sent food baskets to the Christians at Christmas and food baskets to the Jews at Passover. Hymie talked in a Weber & Fields dialect and was the butt of many jokes. Like Sam Goldwyn, the movie producer, he encouraged this humor as good publicity. Hymie had the responsible, $7,500 job of Commissioner of Records for Kings County, and he could neither read nor write. Malicious friends attempted often to trap him into a confession of his inadequacies, but Hymie was equal to the situation; he had always forgotten his glasses when called upon to read. A group of hypercritical citizens who believed that a public official, particularly a Commissioner of Records, should know how to read and write, made charges against Schorenstein to the Governor. The Governor said he had no jurisdiction.

The revolt against McCooey had its genesis in racial fights and enmities in Brooklyn. Districts changed character, and the Old Man, bored by petty factionalism, often failed to recognize the importance of the change. The Ridgewood section, bordering on Queens County, was the first to put a tack on Uncle John's chair. That section, once German, had been controlled by the silent and phlegmatic Hasenflug brothers, Conrad and Henry. The Italians started moving in, and eventually Assemblyman Jerome G. Ambro, a dark and unwholesome Latin, won the leadership. He did not stop there; he proceeded to make himself boss of the one hundred thousand Italian votes in the borough, stealing the crown from Mike Laura, McCooey's friend and Deputy Commissioner of Sanitation. Ambro (that hot Mediterranean blood!) went to the extreme of ordering Laura kicked out of the Michael F. Laura Club, which he was. McCooey did not like Ambro and tried to destroy him. Ambro served as attorney for the shot-riddled gangster "Legs" Diamond in Diamond's trial at Troy, New York, on charges of kidnapping and torturing. Attorney-General Bennett, a Brooklyn boy, denounced Ambro roundly, described him as consorting with sinister characters, and said that he had occupied a room in Diamond's hotel suite in Albany. Ambro, realizing the unpopularity of Diamond as a political issue, maintained he had been Mrs. Diamond's attorney. He was not returned to the Assembly, but much to McCooey's surprise, he retained the leadership of his district and continued on the warpath. The Italians of Brooklyn—the Old Man could hardly believe the election returns—voted solidly for Fusion in 1933.

Uncle John blundered in 1932 and 1933. The feel of the town was getting away from him. He was tired and not too well. He had always gone along with Tammany, and it was a little late to change. He stood with the stupid Curry against Roosevelt in the Democratic National Convention, and he permitted Curry to renominate John P. O'Brien for Mayor. Uncle John, for so many years a dictator, refused to believe there was a general insurrection under way. In the election of 1933 he could not carry his borough for the Democratic mayoralty candidate, and for the first time in twenty years he could not elect his own candidate for Borough President. After the votes had been cast and his defeat was a matter of history, the yes-men district leaders began to lose their superstitious awe of the McCooey command. It was then that Postmaster-General Farley, who had not forgotten the Chicago convention, began putting on the pressure. He had jobs to give, and Uncle John had none. The great one-man machine fell apart like a straw house in a high wind.

John H. McCooey was always lucky. He became ill in the

middle of the free-for-all. He died on January 21, 1934, still, at seventy years of age, the master of Brooklyn.

From The Tin Box Parade *by Milton Mackaye, copyright, 1934, by Milton Mackaye, published by Robert McBride and Company.*

This exchange of letters which Robert Moses had printed in the New York Times explains a lot of Greenpoint's—and Brooklyn's —affection for the late Peter J. McGuinness.

MOSES SURVEYS THE CITY'S STATUES

While we are talking about war memorials, there is the story of the Monitor Monument at Greenpoint, the "Garden Spot of America," which is summed up in what I must admit was a somewhat self-serving letter to my old and esteemed friend, Sheriff Peter McGuinness, Boss of Greenpoint. My letter to Peter, dated Oct. 14, 1936, read, in part, as follows:

Dear Peter: I have made every possible effort to cooperate with Assemblyman Doyle on the Monitor matter but without success. You will recall that he first presented a sketch for a monument which we could not possibly approve and which would have been laughed out of the Municipal Art Commission. I then offered to cooperate with him by having a proper design made, and this was done in the Park Department. He then informed us that he wanted the work done by an ordinary stone-cutter in the district. I even went along with this, although it was against all precedent, but insisted that if the man in question was to do this work he must have a model to work from. We then arranged to have the model made by a relief sculptor of first-rate ability. This man was to get off the relief rolls and do some of this work for the commission at the commission's expense. All sorts of trouble developed in getting the man paid.

At one stage of the game Assemblyman Doyle presented to

me a revised inscription for the monument from which the name of John Ericsson, the inventor and builder of the Monitor, was omitted so as to make room for an elaborate reference to Assemblyman Edward P. Doyle of Greenpoint. I told the Assemblyman that we could not approve this revision.

Apparently the Assemblyman has now gone ahead with a totally different design than the one arranged for, and we shall not approve this design.

I want to go along with you in every possible and reasonable way because you have always been most friendly, helpful and cooperative, but this thing is too raw, and I suggest that you call off the Assemblyman before he gets himself into real trouble.

Peter replied promptly and without equivocation as follows:

Dear Bob: I will take up the matter mentioned in your letter with Assemblyman Doyle and will tell him again what I have always told him, that he is to go along with you, and the same goes for Senator Twomey. They are not going outside of the line.

You have been so kind at all times that I feel that this should never have occurred. I never wanted my name on any of the many monuments that I have had placed in Greenpoint, so why should the Assemblyman have his put on?

You may be assured that I will take care of this matter without delay.

The result was that we got a pretty good monument out of it, very different from what the Assemblyman had planned and better than the public had any right to expect—with the figure of a sailor straining at a rope thrown around a capstan. It is true that we had quite an argument about the nudity of the sailor, which was compromised to the satisfaction of local sentiment by dressing him up in an almost invisible pair of trunks.

By Robert Moses, from the New York Times Magazine, November 14, 1943, reprinted with permission from the New York Times.

... and Crime

Most of the things we are printing about crime in Brooklyn don't need much explaining. Many of the final decisions of the Unione Siciliane, such as the killing of Joe the Boss Masseria, have occurred here, and Murder, Inc. is a Brooklyn product. That superb title, by the way, was hit upon by a World-Telegram rewrite man, and finally had to be adopted by other papers.

We are again quoting quite extensively from Sodom by the Sea, the excellent book on Coney Island by Oliver Pilat and Jo Ranson. They imply, and we think, accurately, that Coney Island is only Brooklyn's by accident of location and finally of political aggrandizement. The Island, a playground and a hideout, is the island of all New York. Most of the prominent thugs and gang leaders of the last century and a half have at one time or another made the place their headquarters.

Another book we are using here is Gang Rule in New York by Craig Thompson and Allen Raymond, an authoritative and popularly written study. The war, except for the chronicling of the Murder, Inc.'s dreary icepick jobs, seems to have interfered with the intensive study that usually goes on about gang machinations, political combines, and plain old murder.

COLONY OF UNFORTUNATES

from SODOM BY THE SEA

by OLIVER PILAT *and* JO RANSON

Coney Island could boast of a surprising quota of criminals long before the New York slums emptied gangsters on the beach in Kenny Sutherland's time. The earlier lawless contributed more to the resort; no other group, except possibly the sports, had a deeper fertilizing effect on the sand. The outlaws usually possessed too little money and the sports too much; otherwise they were not essentially dissimilar. They shared a spirit of unconventionality and cynicism and revealed a common capacity for adventure.

As early as the Civil War a year-round colony of crooks and unfortunates assembled back on the dunes where the grass grew thick and coarse and the few surviving trees were short and stubby. The colony grew from year to year until it included chiselers and murderers, broken-down confidence men and cutpurses, punch-drunk pugilists and even a few horse thieves. The sorriest recruit probably was a woman known only as Diamond Maggie, who had enjoyed a brief day of glory as courtesan at Harry Hill's and the Cremorne in New York before she wasted her chances and health on a criminal who died in jail. She wandered haglike about the Island, accepting scraps of charity and occasionally turning an honest penny by beachcombing. Equally pathetic was one of the three Worrell sisters who had staged opera bouffe in English on Broadway. She joined the colony after an uncongenial marriage and during a spree staggered at night into the marsh back of the resort. While trying to light a consoling cigarette, she set fire to the dry sea grass and burned to death.

Most members of the colony worked when they had to or felt like it. Not infrequently they found congenial tasks, such as tending bar or running games of chance. Whitey Wilson, a former pirate and slave trader, continued a sort of land piracy by operating a cane board whose canes stood at such a great angle that customers had no chance to ring them. Jim Donovan, after giving up dealing faro at Mike Murray's joint in New York because of a nervous condition, thrived on a lung-testing machine that tested chiefly the victim's gullibility and exhibitionism. A woman who ran one of the Island's earliest houses of ill fame married a local painter, gave up her old life and raised a son who turned out to be one of the resort's more decent policemen.

On the whole the colonists were sociable, easygoing and tolerant, with a queer loyalty for the beach. They enjoyed the calm mornings, and ebb and flow of the crowds, the music of the carrousels from noon till midnight, the evening's lights and clamor. They hung on year after year. "Once a man gets sand in his shoes, it's hard to get out," they used to say, or: "No oldtimer leaves except feet first and wearing a pine overcoat."

The central shack of the colony during the '80s was the Hermitage on Coney Island Creek, occupied by Joe Gorman and his wife Mollie. Joe liked to tell how at the age of seven he awoke one night to see his father remove a brick from the chimney, stuff several stolen watches into the opening and then replace the brick. With such inspiration at home, Joe learned to pick pockets as soon as he was tall enough to reach them, but all his skill could not prevent occasional brushes with the law. He had served three terms in prison before he and his wife Mollie, a shoplifter, came to Coney Island to stay.

The piazza of the Hermitage faced west, and from it a series of wooden steps led down to a float where flat-bottomed boats could be hired by excursionists. The only land approach to the Hermitage was by way of a plank walk stretching east, and anybody coming that way could be seen in plenty of time. Joe and Mollie always had plenty of money, though the bar they operated seemed chiefly an accommodation for their friends, who included occasional visitors from the Sixth Avenue sin section of New York. Rumors connected the income of the Gormans with surreptitious night landings of harbor pirates from New York, but such stories were never proved and were generally considered nobody's business.

Joe had another source of income that he never mentioned. He worked as an occasional confidential detective for John Y. McKane. This fact was confirmed decades later by Thomas Byrnes in his *Professional Criminals of America*, which stated: "Joe Gorman is a very clever pickpocket . . . well known in all the large cities of the Union. He comes of a family criminally inclined, as he has two brothers: Tom, a sneak and till tapper, and John, a clever general thief. . . . He was employed as a special officer at Coney Island for a number of years. Since the annexation of the place to Brooklyn he has taken to the turf again."

During the McKane regime Joe Gorman picked no pockets. The Chief would have tolerated anything but that. People who entered a crooked cabaret or engaged in a fake game at the Island did so of their own free will, but there was no choice involved in getting your pockets picked. Besides, the Chief had a queasy feeling at the thought of a stranger's fingers roaming secretly about his body. One of his detectives, George Norton, picked McKane's pocket as a joke. When he learned about it, the Chief knocked Norton down at police headquarters, then fired him.

Next in importance to the Hermitage of Joe and Mollie Gorman as a landmark in the colony of unfortunates was a hotel on the beach side of the Island run by Mike and Minnie Moran. This was a small two-story structure with a few rooms upstairs for rent to week-enders with or without baggage. The lower floors had chairs, tables and a bar. Mike and Minnie had wandered over half the United States. He had dealt poker on Mississippi steamboats and faro in Western mining camps. When police closed his gambling joint on Ann Street, New York, one day in the '70s because he failed to produce the regular weekly protection money, Mike moved to the beach. There he served as a genial host, while Minnie, who had learned shrewdness as a Grand Street belle, attended to business details.

Halfway between the Hermitage and Moran's stood a modest inn operated by Kate Leary, the Joan of Arc of the colony. Kate was the wife of John (Red) Leary, chief lieutenant of Shang

Draper, who was probably the most successful American gang leader in the nineteenth century. Draper and his friend, Alex McCoy, were among the first New York criminals to establish joints specializing in liquor and prostitution at Norton's Point, but Draper soon put his obvious talents to wider use.

Neighborhood gangs had flourished in New York slums as early as the Civil War, but none like Shang Draper's group, which specialized in bank robbery. They were the aristocrats of the underworld. According to the reliable estimate of George W. Walling, one-time New York police commissioner, they committed 80 per cent of all bank robberies between 1860 and 1884 in the United States, getting away with fully $7,000,000. Much of the loot proved unnegotiable, some was kicked back in the form of bribes or recovered by the authorities, but enough stuck to the fingers of the gang to establish as high spenders those members who from time to time hid out at Coney Island.

Red Leary participated in the Northampton (Mass.) bank robbery of January 1876. Members of the Draper gang, including Shang himself, woke up the cashier at his home, marched him to his own institution to open up the vaults, and escaped with $1,500,000 in securities and cash. So tremendous did the hue and cry become that Red decided on a jaunt to Europe and Kate Leary left her Coney Island establishment in the care of Shang Draper's mistress. While Red and Kate Leary were looking at French cathedrals, the identity of all the robbers became known to police through the confession of a minor member of the gang. Much of the missing money was recovered, two of the thieves got twenty-year jail sentences, and even Shang Draper was under arrest briefly until he exerted his political influence.

Red and Kate Leary returned to Coney Island in 1877 and lived quietly in the colony of unfortunates for two years, until Red got careless and went to New York and was picked up by the police.

Kate was a bold girl with hair as red as that of her husband. When political efforts and bribery failed to win his release, she decided on direct action. Posing as the wife of a longshoreman, she leased a fifth-floor room in a tenement at 76 Ludlow Street,

New York, adjoining the Ludlow Street Jail, where Red was being kept pending extradition to Northampton, Mass. Then she brought in Shang Draper and Fatty Dolan with a hydraulic jimmy to challenge brick walls totaling five feet in thickness. Kate shopped and cooked meals and piled brick in the room, while the men worked almost continuously in their tunnel, struggling against time and the threat of noise or an error in calculation.

On May 7, 1879, Kate visited her husband at the prison until 8 p.m. This was a formal visit, full of whispered last-minute instructions. An hour later she saw him again, informally, as Shang Draper holed through the tunnel to the third-tier toilet where Red was sitting.

No alarm was raised, nor was the tunnel leading to the room with its neatly piled ton of excavated brick discovered until 10:30. By that time the fugitive was on his way to Coney Island in a light truck owned by Ed (Goodie) Gearing, a thief who co-operated with the gang. Leary didn't arrive until next day, according to Charlie Kaiser. Kaiser had a variety of jobs in later years and in 1941 was serving at Steeplechase Park in Coney Island as a watchman, but on May 8, 1879, he was just a carefree kid driving a meat truck. At Neptune Avenue and Ocean Parkway he was hailed by Shang Draper, who said his sorrel horses were almost exhausted by the trip from New York. With a gesture of his thumb Draper indicated two packages in the rear of the truck, which he said were very heavy, but Kaiser didn't bother to look. He was content to give the other man a tow up the hill into Coney Island with his powerful team and to accept a cigar as a reward. Later, when he learned that he'd been involved in an escape discussed from coast to coast and that the supposed packages had been Kate and Red Leary, he merely shrugged, more proud than displeased.

So celebrated did the exploit become that it passed into baseball slang. A coach who wanted to instruct a player to break loose and steal a base simply yelled: "Red Leary!"

Coney Island had an inside tip on an equally great sensation, the murder of George Leonidas Leslie, an amazing intellectual who served as technical adviser in safe-cracking to the Draper gang. During the time that Shang Draper's mistress ran the inn at Coney Island for Kate Leary, Leslie became a frequent and warmly received visitor. He also carried on an amour with Babe Irving, sister of Johnny Irving, one of the Draper gang's bank robbers.

The question as to how long such things could continue was answered with the finding of Leslie's bullet-riddled body on the northerly outskirts of New York City. Police learned that the body had been carted from Brooklyn in a light truck owned by Goodie Gearing and pulled by a sorrel horse, and they blamed the murder openly on Shang Draper, Red Leary and Johnny Irving, but had no proof.

Johnny Irving and his chum, Billy Porter, got into Raymond Street Jail for stealing, but they escaped and summered comfortably at Coney Island. A reward of $2,500 for their capture, posted by Sheriff Riley of Brooklyn, was never claimed. However, Irving's career ended in Draper's saloon on Sixth Avenue, New York. A bank robber named Johnny the Mick Walsh put a bullet in Irving's heart, and Billy Porter promptly avenged his chum by shooting the Mick's brains out. When police arrived, Irving and Walsh lay lifeless on the floor, while Shang Draper and Red Leary, who had been interrupted during a meal by the gun play, were sitting down again to their oysters on the half shell.

Red Leary died in 1888 in the prison ward at Bellevue Hospital, and with his death Kate lost her gaiety. To complete strangers at her Coney Island inn she would complain that there was a percentage due her on a lot of bank bonds that had been placed by a fence.

"Money stolen never sticks," she would moralize. "We divide the world into smart people and suckers, but are we the smart people because we break a safe or pinch a watch now and then again? It's the suckers that own the railroad stock and the horses at the track. We're the smart people that don't have a dime in the bank and can't even bet on the races!"

Deficits increased at Kate's inn until she was penniless. Finally it became apparent that her mind was weakening. The authorities would have removed her to Bellevue Hospital had not Joe and Millie Gorman taken her in with them. When Kate died soon afterward at the Hermitage, all the old-timers came by to look at her suddenly peaceful old face. Joe Gorman paid the supreme tribute to the dead by refusing money for drinks that passed over his bar, but there was a hat placed conveniently so that everybody could drop in some coins to back up the boast: "The Island takes care of its own." Members of the colony walked in a snowstorm behind the hearse at the burial in the old Gravesend cemetery.

A patrolman on his way home one Sunday night in 1878 glanced through the front window of the Manhattan Bank in New York and noticed a huge screen in front of a vault. His suspicions were allayed when a middle-aged man in shirt sleeves, impersonating a trussed-up janitor, gave him a casual wave of the hand and resumed dusting off some desks. The man in shirt sleeves undoubtedly was Abe Coakley, though he was subsequently acquitted of any part in the robbery, which netted $2,500,000 mostly in bonds that were recovered.

Abe Coakley had a longer record of residence at Coney Island than any other member of the Shang Draper gang. For decades he ran a bar, and when he gave that up he managed to utilize his long white beard and shaky appearance for purposes of revenue. A confidence man with a prospect ripe for his plucking would approach Abe at Coney Island, saying: "Before we go any further in this deal I want you to meet my dear old father, as fine an old gentleman as ever walked the streets."

Abe would place a skeleton hand on the stranger's shoulder and quaver: "Glad to meet you, my boy. Glad to meet any friend of my son's. New York is an awful wicked city, but my son Joe will take good care of you. God bless you, my boy."

After Joe took good care of his prospect, Abe got his share of the proceeds.

Adaptability to changing conditions was one of the chief characteristics of the old-timers at Coney Island. When horse racing began at the beach, betting centered around a pool at the

Providence Parkway Hotel. This pool was so anxious to have every available dollar that it would continue to accept bets for a minute or even two minutes after the results came by wire from the near-by Brighton track.

One of the colony veterans realized that by using field glasses from the summit of the famous 300-foot-high Iron Tower he could recognize the colors of the winning jockeys at the track. Looking down from the tower, he could see bets being accepted after the race finished. A great idea was born. The old-timer acquired several bright handkerchiefs of different colors and enlisted two friends who had some money. When the racing began, the originator of the scheme caught the result of the first race by glass from the top of the Iron Tower, waved the appropriately colored handkerchief as signal to one friend on the ground, who rushed into the hotel to the other friend, who stood in a last-minute line shuffling toward the betting window. There was time for a whispered name and the placing of a bet before the window closed.

The conspirators had won! Counting their profits, they decided to try the following day. Then also they caught a result in time to wring some sure profits from the pool.

Realizing shrewdly that the changes of detection increased with each success, the three conspirators agreed to pyramid their winnings, to shoot the works on the third try. This time, however, the horse that came in first was disqualified a minute later as a result of a protest by a jockey, and they lost everything. When they tried to corral more money, the secret leaked.

As a result the tract erected a screen between itself and the Iron Tower, the hotel pool stopped selling tickets on the races after the horses went to the post, and three well-established members of the year-round colony of unfortunates remained that way, despite an idea far more impressive than others that achieved fortunes and respectable niches in society for their originators.

From Sodom by the Sea *by Oliver Pilat and Jo Ranson, copyright,* 1941, *by Oliver Pilat and Jo Ranson, reprinted by permission of Doubleday & Company, Inc.*

THE KIDNAPERS OF CHARLEY ROSS

by ROBERT RYDER

It happened on a dark and blustery winter night—December 14, 1874—just about five months after the famous Charley Ross kidnaping at Germantown, Pennsylvania. Down at the foot of the embankment of New York Bay, the water dashed with a rumble up against the rock jetties. Most of the residents in the sparsely located homesteads of Bay Ridge took care in fastening their shutters before retiring for the night.

At the Van Brunt home on what is now 84th Street and Shore Road, Albert Van Brunt, a Flatbush farmer, was on a visit to see his father Holmes who was ill in bed. Albert and some hired men and a few relatives had been sleeping when, about midnight, they were roused by the slam of a loose shutter in the house they owned next door. According to the story a burglar alarm also sounded. Albert got a lantern out and crossed the courtyard to survey matters. Upon entering the house he saw a light upstairs and heard sounds coming from a bedroom. He hid while two men walked past. Stealing back to his father's home next door, he told them all that the house was being robbed. Then he got a shotgun and, at his aunt's insistence, a pistol. His father climbed out of bed to help if possible and the hired men surrounded the other house.

Things happened quickly. Just after midnight the two men came out the rear door. Albert's father gave the command, "Halt, who goes there?" The two robbers fired a shot and then ran back to the house. The shot was returned. Then, after a silence of about ten minutes, out they came again, making a dash across the back yard toward the hedge. Albert and the group fired: one man fell. Albert then drew his pistol and fired at the other fleeing man. The second thief fell but got up again and drew his gun. He was about to fire when a hired man, believed to be named Franks, struck his arm with a rifle butt. The first man was dead; the other was on the verge of death. Holmes Van Brunt asked the dying man, "Who are you?"

"My name is Joe Douglas; my pal is William Mosher. We kidnaped Charley Ross."

"Where is he?" Van Brunt asked.

"The boy is safe on a sloop," came the answer. "Mosher will tell you."

But on being told that Mosher was dead, he dropped off into unconsciousness and died a short time later. The confession was never completed.

Some authorities brought Charley's frantic father to Brooklyn with his other son, Walter, to view the dead men. The son, although young, identified them as the ones who had driven up with horse and buggy that summer morning in July in Germantown, inducing Charley to come along with them for a ride.

Reprinted from New York Folklore Quarterly, *November, 1946, reprinted with permission of New York Folklore Society.*

THE BAD DIED YOUNG

from GANG RULE IN NEW YORK

by CRAIG THOMPSON and ALLEN RAYMOND

Diamond, slain by a gunman who himself was later murdered, was thirty-three years old when they got him. Vannie Higgins, rum runner and all-around plug-ugly in Brooklyn, was thirty-five years old when the gunmen got him. Vincent Coll, the Mad Mick, was only twenty-three. Larry Fay, a smarter business man, who pulled out early from the more dangerous phases of his illicit enterprises, lived to be forty-four before he was murdered. But Frankie Uale was only thirty-five when he died, and the two Amberg brothers, Joe and Louis, or Pretty Amberg, were forty-three and thirty-six respectively.

It is not only the good who die young. Joe Amberg was a small time extortioner and narcotics peddler. He was one of the "six-for-five" loan sharks of Brownsville, which meant that he would lend small sums to the poor at the rate of twenty per cent interest weekly, lending five dollars on any Monday and collecting six dollars at the end of exactly seven days. Borrowers who failed to pay on time were beaten up. That racket still goes on in Brownsville, but Joe, in his conduct of it proved just too cussed to live. He and his chauffeur were lined up in front of the wall of a warehouse in Brooklyn one night and shot down by an execution squad—an end which he met because of his deals with higher-ups in the narcotics trade. Amberg was giving drug peddling a bad name.

Pretty Amberg was a helper for his brother. He was found hacked to bits with a hatchet, in a blazing automobile in the Navy Yard section of Brooklyn. Neither has ever been missed.

Vannie Higgins though never truly a big shot was a cut above the average gangster, partly in the scope of his operations and partly because of a lively sense of humor. He flourished and waxed fat in the Bay Ridge section of Brooklyn, where he was a devoted family man, from the mid-1920's until 1932. He was a lieutenant at times, of Big Bill Dwyer in rum running operations along the Long Island shore and owned some of the fastest rum boats in the harbor.

Vannie was an ardent sportsman pilot and owned several planes. His political connections were among the best. On one of his flights, however, he shocked Governor Franklin D. Roosevelt by landing in a field that had been prepared for him just outside the prison walls at Comstock, New York, and dining within the prison with the warden, Joseph H. Wilson, former owner of a brewery. The Governor informed the Warden that he felt there was some impropriety in his entertaining a character as notorious as Vannie in the prison, since he was not an inmate, but Warden Wilson replied that he had known the rum runner for many years and saw nothing improper whatever in the dinner. That was that.

Vannie always took the risks of his calling along with the profits. He took part in a shooting affray in the Owl's Head Cafe, at Sixty-ninth Street and Third Avenue, in Brooklyn, in 1928, during which a Patrolman Daniel Maloney was killed by another policeman. During the same year he and two of his gunmen were arrested for the murder of another Brooklyn boot-legger, one Samuel Orlando, but there was not enough evidence against them to hold them.

Higgins and one of his shooters, a Bad Bill Bailey, were the targets for the guns of another mob one night in the downtown section of Brooklyn. An automobile laden with poor marksmen sped past the one in which they were riding and poured a volley of shotgun fire into it. Neither was hurt. Bailey, in fact, in-volved during prohibition in plenty of shooting affrays, lived well into the era of legalized liquor in the 1930's, without a knife scratch or bullet scar upon him, and died peacefully in his bed of pneumonia.

Higgins got himself both knifed and shot before he met the usual gangster's end. He flew to Baltimore, Maryland, one day in his plane, on a business errand, and was shot there by a local policeman but not seriously wounded.

In 1931, Higgins was taken to Polyclinic Hospital with several knife wounds which the police said that he received during a business quarrel in the Blossom Heath Inn, a widely known speakeasy, operated at 50 West Seventy-seventh Street by Frank McManus, a brother of George, the gambler. In the same year he was arrested on suspicion of having slain one of his gunmen, a Robert Benson. Bad Bill was arrested with him. Both men were taken to the offices of District Attorney Thomas C. T. Crain in Manhattan for questioning and with them went their lawyers, Ralph Delli Paoli and Abraham H. Kesselman.

Judge Crain had hardly opened his mouth to ask them the first of a series of questions when the two men chorused in per-fect unison, "On advice of our lawyers we refuse to make any further statement."

They hadn't made any statement before, and they declined to make any statement thereafter. Both were released.

Fate caught up with Vannie Higgins in one of his most do-mestic moments. On the night of June 18, 1932, Higgins, with his wife and her mother and their daughter, Jean, went to the Knights of Columbus clubhouse in Prospect Park to the recital of a dancing class, of which Jean Higgins was a pupil. With them in the party were Salvatore Spitale and Irving Bitz, and two of the daughters of Bitz were on the program. It was a pleasant affair, with souvenir programs the cost of which was paid in part by advertisements from Stitch McCarthy, the Manhattan bail bondsman, and Bitz, whose professional card on the program read "Compliments of Uncle Irving."

Spitale and Bitz left early. As Higgins came out with his family, two automobiles of gunmen came rolling by. The first volley of their guns sent bullets whistling past the ears of the family group. The little girl, Jean, was pinked in one ear and dived for the shelter of the family automobile. Higgins' wife and mother-in-law fled screaming back toward the clubhouse. Higgins ran up the street but was slain as he ran. He lived to be carried to the Methodist Episcopal Hospital where he snarled, "The rats! They tried to wipe out my family."

Asked who shot him, however, he fell back on the gangsters' traditional code and said that he did not know.

Reprinted from Gang Rule in New York *by Graig Thompson and Allen Raymond by permission of the Dial Press, Inc., copyright, 1940 by Craig Thompson and Allen Raymond.*

MURDER MONOPOLY

by JOSEPH FREEMAN

Against a background of violence, sensation, and sadism—all tending to obscure its real import—Brooklyn's District Attorney, William O'Dwyer, has run to earth a criminal network which puts in the shade the great racketeering organizations of a generation ago. "Murder, Inc.," is journalese for the ring, and the name is an inspiration; it shows that to some extent at least the press has caught the meaning of Mr. O'Dwyer's discovery: that crime, like business, has outgrown the forms of rugged individualism and moved on to the greater glories of monopoly. Confessions by leaders of Murder, Inc.—its own name for itself is "the Combination"—show that it is a nation-wide, highly organized business which operates major rackets from coast to coast, trains its personnel, has its own code of conduct, and kills on contract. It is a grotesque caricature of American big business, and its ramifications are almost as manifold: labor unions, politics, and industry all covertly recognize the racketeer as a functionary of American society—though they may not be aware of the extent to which his activities center in Murder, Inc.

Today it is almost impossible for a gangster, big or small, to conduct an independent racket. Whether he runs a policy game which nets him millions or a peanut machine which brings him in $30 a week, he can work his racket only with the permission of the Combination. The leaders grant each racketeer his territory, just as an automobile manufacturer grants a dealer his territory. If a racketeer leaves New York for Chicago, he can set up in business only with the consent of the Chicago leader of Murder, Inc. Similarly, no murder can be committed without the okay of the boss of the zone. The boss even reserves the right to choose the killers.

The killings—and they are numbered by the score—are by-products of widespread business operations involving millions of dollars. The Combination exercises control over gambling, prostitution, the illicit traffic in narcotics, the policy game, bootlegging, and the loan-shark racket, to cite its outstanding spheres of influence. By sheer force it also dominates certain trade-union locals, and has a financial stake in various night clubs and cabarets. It operates certain legitimate enterprises and muscles in on others, where it exacts tribute from business men by threats or use of violence. Through its control of slot machines it collects pennies and nickels even from the schoolchildren of the nation. And not least, through its connection with corrupt political machines, it plays an important and sinister role in urban politics. The Combination even has its own banking and credit system designed to lend racketeers money—at an exorbitant rate—with which to start in business. It protects the member racketeer against unauthorized rivals and punishes him when he violates the laws of Murder, Inc. The punishment is usually a violent and horrible death.

At the moment public attention is centered on the first trial which has come out of O'Dwyer's investigations. The defendants, Harry (Happy) Maione and Frank (the Dasher) Abbandando, are charged with killing a fellow-gangster named George Rudnick in 1937. The victim was wiped out because he had turned police informer. According to the prosecution, the defendants strangled Rudnick with a rope, perforated his head and other parts of his body with sixty-three jabs of an icepick, and, to make sure, bashed in his skull with a meat-chopper. Technically the trial is concerned with only one killing, but it is merely the opening gun against Murder, Inc. So far the prosecutor's investigations have shed light on fifty-six hitherto unsolved murders in New York, and he has leads, he told me, which will uncover the bodies of scores of men whose murders were not even recorded on the police blotters. He believes Murder, Inc., can explain the mysterious disappearance of Peter Panto, progressive waterfront union organizer, and of many other members of the waterfront union.

Although his work has just got under way, O'Dwyer has already forged links between various branches of Murder, Inc., in New York. He has related the Combination to Lepke and Gurrah's racketeering in the garment and fur industries, flour trucking, the bakery trade, and narcotics; to the gambling, bootlegging, extortion, and trucking rackets headed by Charles (Bug) Siegel and Meyer Lansky; to the prostitution, policy, loan-shark, and narcotic rackets of the Bronx heirs of Dutch Schultz, whose mob continues to do business as part of Murder, Inc; and to the various criminal and political activities of the Brooklyn underworld headed by Albert Anastasia and Joe Adonis. From New York the lines lead to other cities and other big shots: to the Purple Gang of Detroit; to Frank Nitti, former aide of Al Capone, who now runs the rackets in Chicago and Miami; to Frank Costello, boss of the New Orleans underworld; and finally to Dutch Goldberg of California, who is believed to be the biggest shot of them all.

Much of the information which enabled O'Dwyer to piece

together the pattern of social decay that is Murder, Inc., has come from Abe (Kid Twist) Reles, now state's witness in the case against Maione and Abbandando. This slight, kinky-haired, brown-eyed gangster, with the flat nose, low wrinkled forehead, and heavy lips, began his criminal career in 1920, at the age of thirteen, as a professional racketeer of the prohibition era. He has been arrested forty-three times on every charge ranging from juvenile delinquency and disorderly conduct to murder (no less than five times), and in the course of the present trial has confessed to eighteen murders, six of which he calmly described on the witness stand. In all but five arrests Reles went scot free.

He is known in Brownsville as a cruel, sadistic slugger. His voice is harsh; the words come rapidly; the language is clipped, full of that underworld argot in which money is "sugar," confessing is "singing," and lending at high rates of interest is "shylocking." Behind this lingo are a shrewd, predatory mind and a strange rationale. Reles considers himself and his associates cool, calculating business men operating a vast enterprise.

"The Combination," he boasted to O'Dwyer, "is operated like the Lehman banks. It is practically one organization and spreads all over the country." Reles compares Murder, Inc., to a "tree with all its branches branched out," and in a less idyllic mood to the "airplane trust." He emphasizes that it extends from coast to coast, with headquarters in cities like New York, Chicago, New Orleans, Detroit, and Los Angeles. In the entire United States there are hundreds of thousands of people in the Combination, and in the five boroughs of New York alone there are several thousands. According to Reles, the nation-wide crime syndicate is an outgrowth of the fierce competition in the alcohol racket during the era of needled beer and bathtub gin. "There was no price regulation," Reles told O'Dwyer. "The rule was, I'll do you and you'll do me." Profits ran into the millions, and that was bound to create war. Prohibition gang shootings are now part of American legend, like the predatory excursions and killings of the frontier cattle rustlers. Reles looks aback on that era with horror, but for other reasons than the public. He feels that machine-gun competition was in the long run unprofitable for the racketeer.

"Nobody cared how he moved around," he said. "I looked to kill you and you looked to kill me. Somebody did something out of the way and got shot, and then his friends went gunning for the man who did the killing, and *he* got shot. There was no sense in that. So the leaders of the mob said, Why not stop this crazy competition and go out and make money instead? So six or seven of the leaders got together and said, 'Boys, what's the use of fighting each other? Let's put our heads together, all of us, so that there can't be a meeting without one another.' That's how they all got together, to make no fighting."

Reles claims that the crime trust was from the beginning organized on a nation-wide basis. Modern means of communication and transportation made this logical. The syndicate developed its own hierarchy. Gradations in income, power, and authority were based on original accumulations of capital. When prohibition went out, the gangs had to seek other sources of income—race tracks, cabarets, gambling joints, bordels, policy games, the corrupt sections of the labor movement, the fur and poultry industries, the trucking business. Everywhere the mobs "muscled in" and chiseled off "a piece."

The ordinary small-time mobster was in no position to muscle in. In crime, as in other modern enterprises, the day of the small entrepreneur was over. He might have "brains" as Reles put it, but "he didn't have a chance because he didn't have a dime." He needed capital or credit to start a racket. Failing that, he was forced to become a "worker" for wages, employed by the bigger racketeers. That is how the hierarchy started. In the prohibition era Tim Murphy, a witty Chicago labor racketeer, used to say that Smith and Wesson made all men equal. Now the racketeer with the money had the last word.

A gangster who wanted to run his own racket had to borrow money. He would go, let us say, to Henry (Dutch) Goldberg. During prohibition, Dutch had done quite well running beer; he had wiped out rivals and piled up millions. After the great show was over, he invested some of his money in legitimate distilleries. He also became, according to Reles, head of the Broadway syndicate known as the Big Six. Dutch Goldberg has a police record in New York of four convictions for grand larceny and manslaughter and has served time in Elmira and Sing Sing.

Secure in his millions, Dutch acted as banker for other racketeers; he financed gangsters who started various legitimate and illegitimate enterprises, and received in return a big slice of the racket. In the credit system of the crime trust Reles sees the operation of a natural law. "If you haven't got any money," he remarked philosophically to District Attorney O'Dwyer, "you can't go any place. So the main thing is, you must have money." It was this credit system which first gave wealthy racketeers like Dutch Goldberg, Frank Nitti, and Joe Adonis their leadership in the crime trust. After that, rule was maintained by rigid organization and discipline, with murder the ultimate instrument of control.

As Reles describes it, the racketeers in each zone are governed by an "inner circle" of overlords whose decisions are law. These are the big shots who direct the various "business" enterprises, arrange murders, and acquire heavy bank accounts. Below them are "vice-presidents," like Happy Maione, Pittsburgh Phil Strauss, who is to be tried separately for the Rudnick murder, and Abe Reles. The word "mob" is no longer used to designate the rank and file. They are now "troops" or, less glamorously, "punks," in the employ of the top men. Big shots operate in terms of profits—all the traffic will bear. Secondary leaders and punks work for wages. Reles emphatically denies that Murder, Inc., triggermen have committed murder for as little as $5. "That's just newspaper stuff," he says indignantly. "You don't get paid for that kind of work. When you kill, it's duty. When you work in a shop, and the boss wants you to do something, he doesn't say, 'I'll give you five or ten dollars.' He is paying you a salary, and you've got to do what he tells you." Similarly, the triggerman is on the pay roll of the Combination; any work he does is "part of the routine."

The salaries of Murder, Inc., employees vary from $100 to $250 a week. In addition, some of them are given small rackets of their own: running slot machines or collecting tribute from storekeepers and pool parlors. If the income from these is small, the "trooper" may keep it all: if it runs into real money, he has to kick back part of the take to gangsters higher up. Salaries are paid regularly all the year round, according to Reles, and all the boys make a "good living."

That is the optimistic view natural to a foreman; he resents any implication that his men are underpaid. "Punks" like Pretty Levine and Duke Maffetore, now caught in the O'Dwyer net, tell another story. They say that "troopers" make little money. They are often broke; they are compelled to borrow at fantastic interest rates from the syndicate; and they commit murders for as little as $5, or even for coffee and cake. They have no choice, because once they are in the gang they can't quit. And Reles admits that nine times out of ten when a mobster wants to quit he is killed. The widow is not told what happened to her husband, though she may learn about it from the newspapers. However, she receives his salary as long as his gang is making money. This is Murder, Inc.'s own form of life insurance.

In his confession Reles has insisted that the Combination is a "business" outfit, an economic syndicate whose main object is not murder but money. The murder is incidental to the struggle for money, just as in the moral world wars may be incidental to the struggle for markets. Since Murder, Inc., obtains its money by illegal means, it must purge rivals, code violators, and renegades by illegal means. Under the laws of the community this is murder; from the viewpoint of the crime trust it is just execution.

The economic setup of Murder, Inc., apes big business; its "troops" ape the military machine; its internal justice fantastically mimics our official courts. Charged with violating mob law, a gangster may under certain circumstances demand and obtain a trial by his peers. Here the leaders are judges, and various gangsters appear as prosecutors, witnesses, and "lawyers" for the defense. On several occasions, Reles will tell you proudly, he appeared as counsel for fellow-gangsters on trial before a Murder, Inc., court. He has a flair for legal jargon; he has had plenty of opportunity to hear it in the forty-three times that he has been brought into the official courts. He has defended fellow-gangsters by arguing, "This ain't admissible evidence," or "There ain't no corroboration for this."

Verdicts of Murder, Inc., courts and executions ordered by its leaders are accepted without question by the membership. Loyalty to the group transcends all friendships, all blood ties. The big shots may inform a gangster: "Your brother was a rat; we had to shoot him." The gangster, knowing what is best for him, accepts his brother's execution in silence. Fifteen years ago Louis Capone's own gang killed his brother. Louis, no relation to Al Capone but a powerful figure in the Brooklyn underworld, has known this all along and has done nothing about it. It all happened within accepted mob regulations.

The crime trust, Reles insists, never commits murders out of passion, excitement, jealousy, personal revenge, or any of the usual motives which prompt private, unorganized murder. It kills impersonally, and solely for business considerations. Even business rivalry, he adds, is not the usual motive, unless "somebody gets too balky or somebody steps right on top of you." No gangster may kill on his own initiative; every murder must be ordered by the leaders at the top, and it must serve the welfare of the organization.

A murder by the crime trust can be arranged only by one of the big shots. An ordinary citizen cannot hire Murder, Inc., to do away with someone he does not like. You may, of course, approach a minor triggerman with a proposition to bump off someone for $5,000. But if he did that, Murder, Inc., would kill him. Such a triggerman, Reles says, is not safe to have around. Any member of the mob who would dare to kill on his own initiative or for his own profit would be executed. "Suppose," Reles says, "I come to a triggerman on my own hook and give him $5,000 to rub out someone I don't like. What's to stop him from taking $10,000 from someone else to rub me out?" The crime trust insists that murder must be a business matter, organized by the chiefs in conference and carried out in a disciplined way. "It's real business all the way through," Reles explains. "It just happens to be that kind of business, but nobody is allowed to kill from personal grievance. There's got to be a good business reason, and the top men of the Combination must give their okay."

In support of this contention, Reles gives examples of "good business reasons." George Rudnick, whom Happy Maione and Frank Abbandando are accused of having removed from this earth, had turned police informer—a simple instance of cause and effect. Willie Weber, the policy racketeer, rated death because he bucked the Combination's attempt to organize the policy racket along trust lines. All other policy men entered the Combination. They had one boss, Lucky Luciano; they all turned in their profits to him, and he paid them a salary. Weber held out for the old laissez faire system; he kept his own policy bank and insisted on continuing in business for himself. The Combination decided to execute him. Weber turned out to be tough; he escaped death, though they managed to blow his shoulder off with shotguns. Pittsburgh Phil Strauss was bitter about the failure to rub out Weber. It was a great financial loss to the Brooklyn mob. Under the verbal contract with Luciano the killing of Weber would have given them 50 per cent of his policy racket—perhaps a million dollars clear.

Another clear case cited by Reles was that of Walter Sage. The boys liked Sage. "He was like one of us," Reles explained, "hanging around the corners of East New York making a living this way and that." Pittsburgh Phil staked him to the peanut-machine racket on a percentage basis. But Sage disappointed everybody. He doublecrossed his patron and ran away with Strauss's share of the profits. Accordingly his friend Big Gangi was detailed to visit him in Sullivan County. Later handsome, green-eyed Pretty Levine, an unfeeling triggerman, was sent up to meet the boys. They took the unsuspecting Sage for a pleasure trip through the woods in a 1937 Oldsmobile sedan. Without warning Big Gangi and Pretty Levine stabbed Sage with an icepick fifty-four times, tied a slot machine around the corpse, and threw it into Swan Lake. "There's the motive," Reles added, "when you have no respect."

Under syndicate rules it is "illegal" to kill a man outside your own territory. If New York wants a man rubbed out and he escapes to St. Louis, the job must be done through the St. Louis branch. The St. Louis leaders must give their okay and choose the killers. For strategic reasons they may call in triggermen from out of town, "so the man who will be killed won't know them," Reles explains, "and they can put him on the spot. You go to St. Louis and you don't know a thing about the man you are going to kill or why he is being killed. When you get there, you are told what to do."

Often the killer has to read the newspaper to find out whom he has executed. Then he goes into hiding, usually in Detroit. There is a special fund to take care of him, to cover his living expenses in hiding, to defend him if he is caught. Every branch of Murder, Inc., contributes to it.

Reles insists that any murder committed in the United States that has not been solved within a reasonable length of time is a murder committed by the Combination. It has got to be, he says; a private killing is broken sooner or later by the police, usually within six months or a year. If a killing remains unsolved for five or ten years, you may be sure it was the work of Murder, Inc.

Published in The Nation, *May 25, 1940, copyrighted by The Nation Associates, Inc.*

The Dodgers

BROOKLYN, which claims for itself such distinctions as Olive Packing Center of the World, is probably best known for containing Ebbets Field, the home stadium of the Dodgers and the people who cheer them on.

The team and its rooters have always been noisy, strange, and with tendencies toward argument and battle. The people who watch the games at Ebbets Field are probably the best-informed fans in any baseball park. They applaud other teams as well as their own, too. They prefer to keep to themselves the privilege of riding the Dodgers. Bill Terry once asked, "Is Brooklyn still in the league?" and he sure found out.

There have been we don't know how many million words written about the Dodgers and their fans. Many of these essays have been either of the Oh-my-God or the cute school of writing and quite dull. We are using some sections from Ring Lardner's Lose with a Smile and Frank Graham's The Brooklyn Dodgers, an Informal History, as our favorite material on the subject. Any anthologist in his right mind will use Lardner on baseball if

given any chance at all, and in Lose with a Smile Lardner gives
us baseball and his affection for the old Dodgers. He was a good
friend of Max Carey, manager of the team at the time these
scenes were laid. Frank Graham's books, as readers of his sports
columns could guess, is a pleasant, honest, accurate story of the
team, the people who ran it, the stands that watched, and the
fellows who played.

The team originally was named the Trolley Dodgers—then
the Superbas; Dodgers again; Robins after Uncle Wilbert Robinson, for years its manager; and again Dodgers. The name will
probably stay that for a while.

from . . .

THE BROOKLYN DODGERS

by FRANK GRAHAM

All his life Larry MacPhail had taken his fun, as he had
taken his education, where he found it. But where business was
concerned, he never fooled around but had a head as long as the
next one, or longer. Mark that clause in his agreement with
the Dodgers' directors:

"He will have full and complete authority over the operations
of the club . . ."

He walked into the office early on a March morning (he'd
spent a month going over the list of players the Dodgers owned
or had any title to, however slim) and said to the directors,
whom he had asked to meet him there:

"We need a first baseman and I know where I can get one."

"But we have Buddy Hassett," one of them said.

A pained expression flitted across Larry's face.

"He will cost us—this first baseman I am talking about—fifty
thousand dollars, possibly," he said.

Fifty thousand dollars! The very mention of the sum caused

the directors' heads to whirl. Fifty thousand dollars . . . and they didn't have fifty dollars they could call their own . . . and here was a man talking about spending a sum like that for a first baseman when they had Hassett to play first base. They all began to talk at once. Larry listened for a moment, then cut them short.

"It was very nice of you to have come here this morning," he said. "Thank you."

He got up and walked out and went directly to the Brooklyn Trust Company.

"George," he said to George V. McLaughlin, the president, "I want fifty thousand dollars."

George's eyebrows went up.

"For a first baseman," Larry said. "You're putting up the dough, so you're entitled to know his name. It's Dolf Camilli, and he is with the Phillies. They want more for him, but I know I can swing it for less."

"Have you—"

"Have I talked to the directors? Yes. As a matter of form."

McLaughlin's face was overtaken by a smile of understanding. He had talked to the directors, too, at one time and another. Larry got up, reaching for his hat and coat.

"Put the fifty grand on the tab," he said. "And, by the way, those improvements in the park I was talking to you about the other day: I'll need about $150,000 or $200,000. Better make it $200,000. So long, George."

McLaughlin looked after him thoughtfully. A sound banker, guarding his bank carefully, he knew a good risk when he saw one. At the moment, he saw one walking out the door of his office, headed for Philadelphia. That one, McLaughlin said to himself, could write his own ticket.

Within two hours MacPhail, who moved swiftly when there was something on his mind, was in Philadelphia. Less than an hour after that, he had Camilli. Gerry Nugent, president of the Phillies, had talked about a price tag of $75,000 on his first baseman, but Larry had knocked a third of it off and the deal was settled, signed, and sealed. The Phillies also wanted a ball-player. Larry gave them an outfielder named Eddie Morgan.

That was March 6. Larry returned to New York, had his dinner, and went to bed early. He wanted to be at Ebbets Field in the morning to continue with the plans he had for refurbishing the park. He was dressing to go to breakfast when John McDonald called him.

"Mr. McKeever just died," John said.

Larry was sorry to hear it. He hadn't known the old Judge well. He'd met him, of course, back in the days when he was new to the National League, and had seen him off and on in the years between, and they had talked briefly once or twice when he had come to Brooklyn to discuss the details of the offer the club had made to him. He had caught the Judge at the end of the old man's career and had liked and admired him. Liked him for the man he was and admired him for the man he had been in his youth.

"Why, in his youth, the old man must have been just like me," Larry could have said. "Tough and robust and standing on his own feet and not being afraid of anybody."

And so, of course, he had been. There were many who would miss the old Judge. Sitting up in back of the stand; or in the club office; or around the league meetings. The old Judge with his heavy gold watch chain and his blackthorn stick and his ready smile and his:

"How're you, Judge? You look like a million dollars! How're the wife and kids?"

Now the last of the three who for so long had guided the affairs of the Dodgers was gone. First Ebbets, and then Ed McKeever, and now Steve.

"There is not enough money in New York City to buy me out of baseball," he had said, a long time before.

Nor had there been.

"I'll hold my share as long as I live, and my family will carry on after that," he had said.

And now he was dead and his stock had passed to his daughter, Mrs. Mulvey.

Steve dead and Mrs. Mulvey holding his stock and MacPhail running the Dodgers . . . and the Dodgers moving on. The Dodgers training at Clearwater under Burleigh Grimes, and

MacPhail in Brooklyn getting the park ready for the opening of another season. MacPhail knowing what had to be done and doing it.

The stands were in bad shape. They were old now, and rusty and dusty and in need of paint, and there were broken seats that had to be replaced. The dugouts were crumbling, and the clubhouses needed cleaning and freshening, and all the equipment that a modern ball club demanded and that the Dodgers never had had. The Dodger team along with all the other ballplayers in the league had complained of stones in the infield and ruts in the outfield, and no one had paid any attention to them; but MacPhail had gone over the field in person, stone by stone and rut by rut, and he was paying attention now. Under MacPhail's watchful eye, workmen toiled now at Ebbets Field, in the stands, the dugouts, and the clubhouses, and on the ground.

There was another matter that had caught, or been called to, his attention: Not all the ushers at Ebbets Field had been grafters or hoodlums and not all the special cops had been thugs; but you could have said that, in the main, you were in the hands of grafters or hoodlums when you sought the seat you had paid for, and that you would be mauled by thugs if, however innocently, you attracted the professional attentions of one of the gray-clad "Specials."

Only the summer before, a baseball writer, entering the park late, as baseball writers sometimes will, saw three Specials dragging a man down one of the ramps, slugging him every step of the way.

"What's he been doing?" the baseball writer asked, visions of a stickup or, at the least, a job of pocket-picking flying through his mind. One of the Specials turned on him fiercely.

"He stoled a ball!" he said.

It seemed that a ball had been fouled into the stand, and the poor wight, having caught it, and thinking, perhaps, to take it home as a souvenir for his little boy, had stuck it in his pocket.

Larry, determined that his customers should enjoy a reasonable expectation of getting the seat for which they had paid and of being immune from assault if they "stoled" a ball, had engaged Andy Frayne of Chicago to bring on, or recruit in Brooklyn, a corps of intelligent, courteous young men to serve as ushers—a corps such as Frayne had supplied for the Chicago ball parks, the Kentucky Derby, and other sporting events in the Middle West. Also, he had changed the brand of Specials.

Both ushers and Specials were to have their difficulties that first year of the MacPhail regime at Ebbets Field, if for no other reason than that some of the customers were slow to accustom themselves to the change. Having been pushed around for so many years, they were prepared to keep right on pushing back. But time was to heal that situation, too.

Other improvements already in blueprint form and soon to become realities were a decent press box, and a press club in what had been a part of the ball club's offices back of the grandstand. There was to be a lounge and a bar, with bar service before, after, and even during a ball game, and a radio over which the play-by-play story of the game would come in the dulcet tones of—well, who but Red Barber?—so that if the reporters were bored by the game, they could sit at the bar, sip a beer, and listen to Red, who at Larry's bidding gladly had cut his moorings in Cincinnati and was on his way to Brooklyn.

That, by the way, was another detail. The three New York clubs—the Dodgers, the Giants and the Yankees—had agreed, before the coming of MacPhail, that they would not broadcast their ball games. Larry, not having been a party to the agreement, had laughed, tossed it out the window, and beckoned to Barber.

Meanwhile, what of the Dodgers at Clearwater? Well, Grimes was hard at work with them there, and soon enough Larry would be bouncing in on them, looking them over and bouncing back to New York. But this time it was not the happy camp for Grimes that it had been in 1937, and the optimistic glow in which he had worked the year before had been shot through with the rains of doubt and disillusionment.

"I am tickled to death," Burleigh had said, at his home in New Haven, Mo., a short two months ago, when he had learned of the appointment of MacPhail.

But after Larry's visit to the camp, Burleigh wasn't at all tickled. Whatever it was MacPhail said to him, he must have sensed then that his number was up, and he went grimly about the task of drilling his ball club from then on. Maybe what Mac-Phail had said to him had really opened his eyes to the exact spot he was on. Sure, the team had been strengthened some-what. He had got Durocher from St. Louis, and MacPhail had got Camilli from Philadelphia, but those two players practically summed up between them the improvement in the club that had finished sixth the year before. Lavagetto might improve at third base after one season in the majors, but Hudson was no bargain at second base, and his understudy, a kid named Pete Coscarart from Portland, would need another year of minor league seasoning, Burleigh was sure. With the arrival of Camilli, Grimes had switched Hassett to the outfield; he had Goody Rosen out there, too. But who else? Ernie Koy . . . Gil Brack . . . the rapidly aging Heinie Manush . . . Oris Hockett, a busher . . . and the ancient Hazen Cuyler whom he had salvaged when the Reds had given him an outright release.

No longer (and it was with good reason) did Grimes regard Van Lingle Mungo as a better pitching prospect than Dizzy Dean. No longer (with equally good reason) did he think highly of Blimp Phelps as a catcher. The only real big-league pitcher that he had on his staff was Fred Fitzsimmons; the only young-ster of promise, Luke Hamlin.

The Dodgers wound up their stay at Clearwater and started north, playing exhibition games along the way. They had lost six games in a row when the reporters asked Grimes where he thought his club would finish. Now, even the least optimistic and most cautious managers usually say, when that question is broached with the opening of the season in the offing:

"Well, I certainly am not claiming the pennant, but our club will give the others a battle all the way."

Imagine, then, the shock to the reporters—regardless of what their own opinions of the Dodgers might be—when Burleigh said:

"This club? I think it will finish last."

When they had recovered from the shock, one of them said: "Remember, Burleigh, the Phillies are still in the league." Grimes laughed, but with no mirth.

"Oh, yes," he said. "The Phillies. I had forgotten about them. Just say we'll finish seventh."

No one could miss reading between the lines of the stories sent out that night: MacPhail and all his works . . . and the manager of the Dodgers picking the team to finish seventh . . . eighth, until he had been reminded of the Phillies' presence in the league. Was Burleigh taking a backhand poke at the Master Mind a desperate Dodger directorate had imported from Cincinnati?

In Brooklyn, MacPhail read the stories and didn't miss the implications.

"If the Dodgers are in seventh place on May 15," he told the newspapers that called him up, "there will be some changes made."

The stories, and the sequel, bounced back on Grimes when the Dodgers reached Richmond, Va. A local sports writer called on him at the hotel and asked him what it was all about, heard his side of it, and returning to his office, wrote a story in which he said that Grimes swore he had been misquoted; he added that the reporters traveling with the Dodgers were a lot of heels.

The paper containing that story hit the ball park in the afternoon just about the time the reporters from Brooklyn and New York did, and having read it, the young men of the press bore down on Burleigh in the dugout, demanding to know just what he meant, anyway. Grimes glanced at the paper they handed to him, handed it back and said:

"That's a —— ——— lie! I never said anything of the kind."

The Dodgers pulled themselves together sufficiently to beat the Athletics that day (they had won four games in a row just before that, but all from minor league clubs, and hadn't beaten another major league club in two weeks) and left right after the game for Brooklyn, but Grimes didn't go with them. MacPhail, having jumped down to Greensboro, N.C., where two of the Dodger farm teams were training, had summoned Grimes for a conference there, and the Dodgers resumed their northward journey in command of Andy High, now one of the coaches. No one has yet discovered just what Larry said to Burleigh at their meeting in Greensboro. Whatever it was, Grimes never again—at least in public—cast aspersions on the athletes in his charge.

In justice to Grimes, however, it must be said that he had made a sound appraisal of the team, as forthcoming events were to prove. He had been guilty only of speaking his mind, and on that score, as the umpires could testify, he was an old offender.

With the launching of the season, MacPhail had more on his mind than Grimes's frankness and the obvious weaknesses of the team. He had said, on taking over at Ebbets Field, that while night baseball had been successful and profitable in Cincinnati, he saw no need for it in Brooklyn: all Brooklyn needed was a winning team. Between then and the opening of the season he had undergone a change of mind. Had he, on close inspection of his team, privately agreed with Grimes that it would finish seventh, and realized that, pending the development of a winner, he had to have something with which to coax the customers through the gates—and decided that night baseball was the answer?

Whatever the motive that impelled him, he had talked Mc-Laughlin into another cash advance, surveys of the field and stands had been made, and the lights soon would go up over Ebbets Field. Ed Barrow, in the Yankees' office, swore again, and across Forty-second Street, where the Giants make their headquarters, Horace Stoneham and Leo Bondy echoed his curses. Radio. And now night baseball. They had wanted neither, and they were wroth at MacPhail for introducing both in greater New York. And as they swore, Larry chuckled. He didn't have to answer to them. He didn't even have to answer to anybody in Brooklyn. This was his show, and he was going to run it his way.

The season was only a few days old when the Dodgers started their plunge for the second division. Third . . . fourth . . . fifth . . . sixth . . . down they went. As if following a script, they were in seventh place on May 15. Remembering MacPhail's threat, the baseball writers were eager to see what kind of "changes would be made"; but they waited in vain, for he did nothing. His head was too crammed with lamps and towers and all the other gadgets having to do with night baseball; and if he noticed where the team rested on that date, he gave no sign, one way or another.

The first night game was played at Ebbets Field on June 15, and the response of the mob was terrific. Long before dark the park was jammed. Latecomers, holding reserved seats, and already accustomed to the niceties of the Frayne service, were shocked to find that in many cases their seats already were occupied. Furthermore, they were occupied by rugged and determined young men who had no intention of yielding them. Fights broke out all over the stands, and some were not halted even by the progress of the ball game.

"I will never forget one fellow," Tom Meany recalls. "He had grabbed a front row seat in an upper tier box, and at the end of the game he still had a firm grip on the rail and sat there with his head bowed while the rightful owner of the seat kept belting him on the base of the skull. I don't know how much of the game he saw, but at least he scored a moral victory."

Larry had dressed up the occasion with a pre-game show that included foot races in which Jesse Owens, 1936 Olympic champion, starred. Then came the ball game, touched with what observers of the man's progress were bound to believe was Mac-Phail's luck. The Dodgers were playing the Reds, and Johnny Vander Meer, the Reds' pitcher who had hurled a no-hit game in Boston in his last time out, four days before, hurled another. No pitcher ever before had turned in two consecutive no-hit games. No pitcher ever is likely to do so again. But Vander Meer did it to mark the beginning of night baseball in Brooklyn. It must be that only in Brooklyn could such a thing have happened.

Three days later MacPhail pulled another trick out of his bag. For three years, or since the inevitable conclusion of Babe Ruth's *opera bouffe* engagement as "vice-president and assistant manager" of the Braves, sentimental fans had been asking why a place could not be found for the Babe in the game for which he had done so much over so long a span of years. They had called the club owners harsh and ungrateful because none would give the Babe a chance as manager or coach, and the Babe himself had indicated all too plainly that he, too, felt he had been shabbily treated. And now:

"Babe Ruth belongs in baseball," Larry MacPhail declared. "To prove that I mean what I say, I have signed him as a coach, and he will be in uniform at Ebbets Field tomorrow."

The first appearance of the Babe as a Dodger pulled a good crowd through the turnstiles and provided a field day for the sports writers and photographers. The Babe seemed happier than he had been since he had left the Yankees; he was sure, he said, that he could help the Dodgers. There were headlines and pictures in the papers, the fans were delighted, and MacPhail was taking bows in his new Press Club.

Only one writer took a slam at the new arrangement. Reviewing the Babe's sorry experience in Boston, and bearing in mind the unpleasantness between Grimes and MacPhail in the spring, he wrote:

"Now that the Babe has gone to Brooklyn as a lieutenant to Burleigh Grimes, the belief is that Burleigh's days are numbered and that the Babe soon will be boss of the dugout at Ebbets Field. This may not be so, but no one can think otherwise. Nor can anyone believe that it was Grimes who wanted the Babe. For Grimes to have asked for the Babe or even for him to have submitted voluntarily to his presence would have been a sign of surrender on Burleigh's part, a definite admission that, unaided, he was incapable of managing the team."

As a matter of fact, MacPhail had put the Babe in there to study him as a managerial possibility, and he had not consulted Grimes. Grimes knew, of course, that something of the sort was in Larry's mind, but he couldn't prove it. For once, tact got the better of him and he kept his mouth shut. It was too much to expect of him that he would be cordial to the Babe, but he was civil to him. He went over the signs with Ruth every day, and sometimes he went through the motions of consulting him on his choice of pitchers or his batting order. Actually, the Babe's duties were limited to giving signs from the third base coaching line or flagging down impetuous base runners headed for disaster at the plate.

It was an awkward situation, but Grimes bore it well. One day, after another game had been lost, he trailed his players into the clubhouse and came upon a lively row between the Babe and Durocher, who was captain of the team.

"Why, you big stiff!" Durocher was screaming. "You can't even remember the signs long enough to get from the bench to the coaching line! No wonder we're getting piled up on the bases and balling up hit-and-run plays!"

The Babe wanted to fight. So, naturally, did Durocher. Grimes, who could have licked both of them, wearily pulled them apart and told them to take their showers and go home. He said nothing of the incident to MacPhail, but somebody else did. Larry shook his head. His test of Ruth as a managerial possibility was at an end. He'd keep the Babe for the balance of the season, for to release him now would be to incur the displeasure of the fans, to whom the Big Guy was a hero. Worse, it would be to admit, no matter what anybody thought his motive had been in hiring the Babe, that he had made a mistake. He would keep the Babe until the end of the season, and when he let him go, he'd do it in a manner that would make the Babe look good. Make him feel good, too.

A little excitement, some laughs, some disappointments in that year of 1938. Tragedy, too; and although it did not involve the Dodgers directly, in a way it was of their making.

On the night of July 12 there was the usual group of neighborhood customers in Pat Diamond's bar and grill at Ninth Street and Seventh Avenue. The Dodgers had lost to the Giants that day, and they were talking about the ball game. One of them, Robert Joyce, stared gloomily at his beer.

"The Dodgers!" William Diamond said.

William, son of the proprietor, and a Dodger fan, of course, was having fun with Joyce, who took the Dodgers' ball games, and particularly their defeats, with dreadful seriousness. Sometimes, even if you were a Dodger fan, it was fun to tease Joyce when the team lost.

"The Dodgers!" young Diamond said again. "Whoever first called them bums was right. Don't you think so, Frank?"

He turned to Frank Krug, whose home was in Albany but who was spending his vacation with relatives in the neighborhood. Frank was a Giant fan.

"Certainly," Krug said. "It takes the Giants to show them up as bums, too. Ha-ha! What our guys did to them today! Why don't you get wise to yourself, Bob? Why don't you root for a real team?"

The bartender grinned. Joyce was a nice young fellow, but nobody should get hipped on a ball club, not even the Dodgers, like he was. It would do him good to take a little kidding about them. Some of the others joined in the fun.

Suddenly Joyce straightened up, his eyes blazing.

"Shut up!" he screamed. "Shut up, you ———! You lay off the Dodgers, you ── ── ───!"

They laughed.

"Why Bob!" Diamond said. "You don't mean to say you're mad at us boys, do you?"

And Krug grinned at Joyce and said:

"Don't be a jerk."

"A jerk!" Joyce was hysterical now. "I'll show you who's a jerk!"

He rushed from the saloon and the crowd along the bar laughed.

"Jesus," the bartender said. "He's got it bad, ain't he?"

Three minutes later Joyce was back, a gun in his hand.

"A jerk," he said. "A jerk, hey?"

Suddenly frightened, they stared at him. He shot Krug through the head, then turned his gun on young Diamond and shot him in the stomach. Krug had sprawled across the brass rail, falling with a crash, his head, with its gaping wound, striking the floor. Young Diamond sagged slowly to the floor and sat there looking up at Joyce, his hands clawing at his stomach, blood welling from his mouth.

The bartender was the first to find his voice.

"Jesus, Bob," he said. "Looka what you done to Willie!"

Joyce hurled the gun from him and ran. The patrons, recovering from the shock, pursued him, yelling for the police. Officers in a cruising radio car caught the fugitive and brought him back. He was wildly hysterical again, sobbing, screaming that he hadn't meant to harm anybody but he had been taunted too long about the Dodgers. Young Diamond, rushed to a hospital, recovered from his wound, but there wasn't anything anybody could do for Krug. He had died as the slug tore through his head.

The Dodgers stumbled on. MacPhail, still looking about him for a manager, saw little of Grimes, save when it was absolutely necessary. He seemed to feel that, in all decency, he couldn't make a pal of a man he had marked for dismissal. One candidate he had lined up in his mind was Frank Frisch, who then was managing the Cardinals but, Larry had heard, was not going back to St. Louis in 1939.

Another was Jimmy Wilson, who hadn't been able to get the Phillies higher than seventh place in four years but had given signs of being a good enough manager to get somewhere if he had any players. There was Billy Herman, too. Herman, second baseman of the Cubs, had had no managerial experience, but there were many baseball men who believed that, given an opportunity to lead a club, he would do well.

He talked these men over with McDonald. John shrugged and said:

"They're all right, I guess. But you've got a fellow right on the ball club who would make a good manager if somebody would just give him a crack at it."

"Who?"

"Durocher."

"Durocher!"

It was more than an exclamation. It was almost an explosion.

"Durocher never could manage a ball club for me!" Larry roared. "Never!"

The season ended. The Dodgers had made Grimes look good

in one respect. They finished seventh. The only starting pitcher who won more games than he lost was Fitzsimmons, with twelve victories and five defeats. Vito Tamulis, used principally as a relief pitcher, had a record of twelve and six. Hamlin had a good year, winning twelve games; but mainly because of poor support, he lost fifteen. Mungo, who was a source of irritation for Grimes all season—he jumped the club once in Pittsburgh, and Grimes was in favor of letting him go home and stay there —pitched only six complete games and wound up with a record of four victories and eleven defeats. No one on the team had hit .300, Ernie Koy being tops with .299. Camilli, who had hit .329 in Philadelphia the year before, had hit .251 as a Dodger. Around the league, critics were wondering audibly if Dolf was just another "Philadelphia ballplayer," i.e., one who goes like a house afire when there is no pressure on him and folds up when there is. If MacPhail wondered the same thing, he kept his mouth shut.

LARRY PICKS HIS MAN

The World Series was on: the Yankees and the Cubs, opening in Chicago. MacPhail, riding back from the ball park with Mc-Donald after the opening game, said suddenly:

"John, I've got a great idea."

McDonald turned to him slowly. McPhail was always having great ideas.

"What is it this time?" he asked, trying not to seem bored.

"I'm going to make Leo Durocher the manager of the Dodgers!"

John stiffened in his seat and, for a split second, was speechless. Then he said:

"Larry, that's great! That's a great idea! . . . How'd you happen to think of Leo?"

Larry didn't answer. He was gazing out the window of the cab, already visualizing his plans for 1939.

The World Series ended on the ninth of October. On the tenth

MacPhail announced that Burleigh Grimes no longer was manager of the Dodgers. On the thirteenth he announced the appointment of Durocher as Burleigh's successor.

There had to be, of course, a proper setting for the announcement of Leo's succession. Larry chose to make it at a luncheon in Parlors F and G at the Hotel New Yorker. Rumors had got about that Leo had been tapped for the job, so that none of the sports writers invited to the luncheon was surprised, exactly, to find Leo at Larry's side at the private bar where earlier arrivals were taking aboard Martinis, Old-fashioneds, and Manhattans. Indeed, even before the announcement was made officially, the boys were congratulating Leo on his accession and Larry on his wisdom. Then they all sat down to lunch; Larry broke the news; the evening newspapermen present dashed for the telephones and then came back and sat down and caught up with the others, who were halfway through their soup.

"Have you signed a contract yet, Leo?" somebody asked.

"No," Leo said, "but don't worry about that, because I'm not worrying. When Larry offered me the job, I told him I would sign a blank contract and he could fill in the figures."

"How about Ruth?" they asked MacPhail.

Larry cleared his throat.

"Ruth never was considered by us for the post as manager," he said. "He could have remained with us as coach, but he told me that he would not be available."

Durocher didn't say anything.

"Who are going to be the coaches?"

"Leo," Larry said, "has picked two coaches. One is Charley Dressen, who, as you know, used to manage the Reds and was manager at Nashville last year. The other is Bill Killefer, who has managed Sacramento in the Coast League for the last three years."

Now the inquisitors turned again to Durocher.

"What do you think of your team?" they asked.

"Well," he said, "in the first place, I would like to say that, in my opinion, Burleigh Grimes deserves a lot of credit for what he did for us last season."

Some of those at the table glanced quickly at MacPhail. He was impassive.

"We finished seventh, of course, but I know the Dodgers were a better ball club in 1938 than they were in 1937," Leo said. "I am even more confident that they will be better in 1939."

There was a small voice from one end of the table:

"Why?"

Leo picked that one up quickly.

"Camilli is sure to hit better next year," he said. "Lavagetto is getting better all the time. Coscarart, Dressen tells me—Dressen had him in Nashville after we turned him back for schooling, you know—Coscarart is ready now for the big leagues. We need some help in the outfield and on the pitching staff, and we may be able to make some trades."

Inevitably the name of Van Lingle Mungo popped up.

"Mungo," Durocher said, "positively will not be traded or sold. I still think the guy can win twenty or thirty games."

"In how many years?" somebody asked, and everybody else laughed.

"In one year," Leo said. "Maybe next year."

"And you'll continue to play shortstop?"

"Naturally," he said.

Since he never had managed a team, some of them were curious to know what his slant on his new job was.

"I am going to try to manage a club as Miller Huggins did," he said. "Huggins was, and always will be, my hero. Nobody ever has got as much out of his ballplayers as Miller did. If I can get half as much, I'll be a success."

They finished eating and sat around talking. Tommy Holmes of the *Brooklyn Eagle* said to MacPhail:

"Why was your choice Durocher, rather than the other men that, I know, you considered for the job?"

"It was this way," Larry said. "It seemed to me that Leo could better supply the thing that our club lacked mostly during the past season."

"Meaning?"

"Well, call it morale, if you like. Call it anything you want.

Whatever you call it, our club didn't have it. I think it's important. You can laugh at me, if you will, for trying to put the old college spirit into a team of professional ballplayers—but show me a big league team that ever got by without it. I think that's the spirit that Durocher can promote better than anybody else I know. Look at his record. He's never been a manager, but he's been a hustling, standout guy on every team he ever played with —the Yankees, the Reds, the Cardinals, and us."

"But he'll need more than that to win with the Dodgers," Holmes said. "He'll need better ballplayers than Grimes had— and better than Stengel or Carey had."

MacPhail nodded.

"He'll be as good a manager as we can make him," he said.

With his new manager installed and his eyes on 1939, Mac-Phail was moving fast. None of his moves were spectacular, and some of them didn't mean anything, but at least he was stirring up the breeze, and with it, a few ballplayers.

He had drafted Hugh Casey, a pitcher, from Memphis at the draft meetings during the World Series. In December, Tony Lazzeri was released outright by the Cubs and Larry signed him, thinking he might help out as an infield replacement, and wanting a little of that old Yankee spirit on his team. He got Jimmy Outlaw, a catcher, from St. Louis, and sent him and Buddy Hassett to Boston for Gene Moore, an outfielder, and Ira Hutchinson, a pitcher. The same day he made another deal with Boston, trading Fred Frankhouse for Joe Stripp. The White Sox asked for waivers on Luke Sewell, the veteran catcher, and Larry claimed him. All this before the first of the year.

Early in 1939 he bought Whit Wyatt from Milwaukee. This didn't look like a bargain at the time, but it was. Wyatt had been moving in and out of the American League for ten years, first as the property of the Tigers, then as White Sox chattel, finally winding up—but not for long—with the Indians. In 1937 he had managed to win two games for the Indians while losing three, and had been released outright to Milwaukee. He was thirty years old, and the only major league magnate who had any interest in him was MacPhail.

February was a lively month for Larry. He bought pitchers Kemp Wicker and Jack LaRocca, and catcher Chris Hartje, Yankee farmhands; released Stripp to Chattanooga, and fired Durocher.

The firing of Durocher took place over the telephone from New York to Hot Springs, Ark., where Leo had gone for a couple of weeks' limbering up before working out in Clearwater. Some of the Dodger pitchers and catchers also were there, and this advance training was covered by a corps of newspapermen who, with nothing much else going on, concentrated on the doings of Durocher on and off the field, with accent on the latter. Their first story was that Leo had won $750 playing bingo in a gambling joint; their second that he had had a fight with his caddy on the hotel golf course.

MacPhail swallowed hard when he read the first and exploded at the second. Within a few minutes he had Durocher on the telephone.

"Gambling! Fighting! You're fired!" he yelled.

"But Larry, if you'll give me a chance—"

"Give you a chance! Why, you ————! I gave you a chance when I made you manager! You're through!"

He slammed the receiver down, leaving Leo to talk to himself. As this was the first time he had been fired by MacPhail—he was to get used to it later, of course—Leo didn't know quite what to do. Having heard nothing further by the next morning, he was starting to pack his stuff and look up trains to St. Louis, where he made his home, when his telephone rang. It was Mac-Phail again. Larry wanted to ask his opinion of a ballplayer on whom he had got a tip. He didn't mention the firing, and Leo didn't bring the matter up, either.

On April 4, while the team was at Clearwater, MacPhail was elected president of the club, filling the vacancy that had been created by the death of Steve McKeever the year before. Durocher called up to congratulate him; Larry wanted to know how he was doing. Leo said he was doing very well: as, indeed, he was. He had a firm grip on his players and was absolute boss of the camp. Some of the newspapermen present who hadn't thought much of MacPhail's choice of Durocher as manager were revising their opinions. They began to believe that, given sound material, he would accomplish something.

The Dodgers started slowly as the season opened, hit seventh place, then bobbed up as high as second in May. Sewell, who hadn't caught a game, was released. Lazzeri, who had played little, soon followed. Casey, Wyatt and Hamlin were pitching well. Durocher picked up Lyn Lary as a utility infielder following the ditching of Lazzeri, taking on one old Yankee in place of another.

MacPhail, an old newspaperman fighter from away back, had had no trouble in that direction since arriving in Brooklyn, but he was to have some now. Not that it bothered him very much, if any. Such brush-ups never did. But it indicated that, on occasion, he could revert to form.

Harold Parrott of the *Eagle*, looking over some out-of-town newspapers, came across a Milwaukee paper carrying a story which set forth that the president of the Milwaukee club was threatening to demand the return of Wyatt. MacPhail, according to this story, had not yet come through with four players he had promised Milwaukee as part of the deal, although demands for them had been made upon him since the opening of the season.

This, of course, was news in Brooklyn, since Wyatt rapidly was becoming a favorite at Ebbets Field. Parrott rewrote the story and it was slapped on the front page of the *Eagle*'s first edition. Before the game that afternoon, he was on his way to the press box at Ebbets Field when MacPhail suddenly lunged out of the milling fans in the back of the stand to confront him.

"You —— liar!" Larry roared. "You little —— — — ——!"

Parrott's attempts to defend himself against this verbal onslaught were useless, because when MacPhail is angry, he leaves few openings for his opponent. He continued to berate Parrott at the top of his voice as a ring of curious fans gathered about them.

"I'll have you barred from the park!" he yelled. "I've got a

good mind to have you thrown out right now, you———! I'll
show you whether or not you can lie about me in your lousy
paper! You'll never get in this ball park again!"

Parrott, unable to make a stand before this blast, beat an
orderly retreat in the direction of a telephone and called Ford
Frick to give him a first-hand report of the battle and seek
his advice.

"Keep away from him for the rest of the afternoon," Ford
counseled. "I'll get him on the phone as soon as I can and
straighten him out. And I can assure you, you won't be barred
from the park."

The next day Parrott called Frick again.

"It's all right," Ford said. "I spoke to Larry last night. I cooled
him off, and he said that while he had left word at the press
gate not to admit you, he would rescind the order this morning.
When you get out there, you'll find you'll have no trouble getting in."

So Parrott hied himself to the park. When he reached the
press gate the attendant said:

"Sorry, Mr. Parrott, but Mr. MacPhail left word that you
were not to be admitted."

Parrott smiled.

"I know he did," he said, "but he told Ford Frick that he
would rescind the order."

The gatekeeper shrugged.

"He didn't tell me," he said.

However, after some discussion and some backstage telephon-
ing to the office upstairs, Parrott was allowed to enter.

He reported the situation to Edwin Wilson, the editor of the
Eagle, and Wilson called it to the attention of George Barnewall of the Brooklyn Trust Company, who was, and still is, a
director of the ball club. Barnewall, eager to see the Dodgers
prosper if for no other reason than that his bank held the club's
notes, naturally was anxious to re-establish friendly relations between the club and the town's most important newspaper. To
that end he arranged a luncheon at which Wilson, Parrott, Mac-

Phail, and himself could bring the matter to an amiable conclusion.

The four sat down at the luncheon table a day or so later. MacPhail was in high good humor, greeted Parrott pleasantly, ordered cocktails, and began to discuss some deals he had in mind. After a second round of cocktails, he was still talking about the deals. Wilson said:

"That's very interesting, Mr. MacPhail, but let's get down to business. You know the purpose of this luncheon."

MacPhail grinned.

"Oh, that!" he said, with a generous wave, "I am willing to forget the whole thing."

He went right back to talking about his deals, and no more was said about the row. Parrott left the table at the end of the luncheon wondering whether MacPhail considered he had given —or received—an apology. The only tangible result of the whole affair was that MacPhail settled the claim of the Milwaukee club and retained title to Wyatt.

At Boston in June 27, those long-winded rivals, the Dodgers and the Braves, almost duplicated their twenty-six-inning struggle of 1920. They were headed strongly in that direction but ran out of daylight a little short of the mark, darkness closing in at the end of the twenty-third inning and forcing Umpire Babe Pinelli to call the the game. The score was 2-2, the Braves having got their two runs in the second inning, the Dodgers having picked up one in the third inning and the other in the eighth. This time neither manager was foolish enough to permit only one of his pitchers to carry the full burden, although Wyatt, who started for the Dodgers, went sixteen innings. Lou Fette went the first nine for the Braves. The Braves could have won in the thirteenth except that Otto Huber, a pinch runner, who was headed for the plate, stumbled just off third base and had to scramble back, and his mates never could get him home. The chief sufferers in the game were, naturally, the hitters, and many a batting average took a frightful beating through that long afternoon. Koy and Camilli, for instance, each made only one hit in ten times at bat, while Melo Almada, in center field for the Dodgers, made no hits in nine trips to the plate.

July was a lively month for the Dodgers. They began to fight their way back from the depths; Durocher was thrown out of two ball games and fined each time; and Dixie Walker made his bow at Ebbets Field.

Leo was desperate, in July. It looked as though the Dodgers would wind up in seventh place again, and some of the critics, having done another turnabout in their judgment of Leo as a manager, were intimating that if he were not to be marked a flop, it was high time he proved his case. Up to then, Leo had got along so well with umpires (with whom he had battled furiously the year before) that Frick was inclined to believe he had reformed, and actually had complimented him on his attitude. Goaded by the lowly plight of his team, nagged by Mac-Phail, and, for the first time, sensitive about some of the cracks the baseball writers were taking at him, he began to rip and tear in the old Durocher manner at umpires, rival players, any who stood in his way.

In the second game of a double-header at the Polo Grounds on July 2—the Dodgers had won the first game but were losing the second—Leo was bandying insults with the entire Giant team, including the bench warmers, when the row developed from the verbal stage into the physical. Hal Schumacher, pitching for the Giants, ripped a fast ball close to Durocher's head and Leo, hitting the dirt unharmed, came up screaming.

"So that's the way you want to play, is it?" he screamed at Schumacher. "All right, you ———!"

He dug himself in again, hit the next pitch sharply to Jurges at shortstop, and raced to first base. He was an easy out, but as he flashed across the bag he spiked big Zeke Bonura. Enraged, the Giant first baseman threw the ball at him, trying to hit him in the head, then rushed after him. Durocher whirled to meet him and they swapped punches until they were pried apart.

There were more than fifty thousand in the stands that day, many, if not most, of them Dodger fans, and the Brooklyn rooters were violently upset when Leo was tossed out of the game by

Umpire Tom Dunn, who, by the way, was new to the league and making his first appearance at the Polo Grounds. They yelled encouragement to Durocher, who had shaken off the players separating him from Bonura, and now was raging at the umpire. They threatened Dunn, and the game was delayed for some time. When it was resumed, Durocher, peering out of a clubhouse window and wigwagging instructions to Dressen, saw his team beaten, 6 to 4.

Frick, receiving Dunn's report the next morning, promptly changed his mind about Leo's reformation and slapped a $25 fine on the culprit. Dodger fans, still incensed at the ejection of their manager, collected twenty-five hundred pennies, put them in a bag, and sent them to Leo with the message:

"Pay your fine with these."

Leo, recalling a tale he had heard, of a trick a minor league player once had pulled on an umpire who was the cause of his being fined, said to MacPhail:

"Do you know what I'd like to do? I'd like to stall on paying this fine until we catch up with Dunn again and then take this bag of pennies to the plate with me and dump it on the ground and say:

" 'There's your fine. Pick it up.' "

That appealed to MacPhail's sense of humor.

"Swell!" he roared. "Do that."

One or the other must have told somebody about the plan. The next day the telephone in the Dodgers' clubhouse rang. Ford Frick was on the wire, calling Durocher.

"I wouldn't advise you to do that," he said to Leo.

"Do what?"

"You know what," Ford said, and hung up.

The pennies went to the bank and a check went to the league headquarters.

Two weeks later Leo was in the bucket again. This time he had Wyatt for company. During a night game with the Reds at Ebbets Field, Leo and Whit squawked so long and so loud over a ball called on a Cincinnati hitter that they were both thrown out. Frick fined Durocher $50 and Wyatt $25. Maybe MacPhail thought Leo was getting somewhat out of hand, and that if he were to continue to antagonize the umpires, the effect on the ball club might not be good.

"It's silly to fine ballplayers for things like that," he cracked. "That doesn't stop them from beefing, because the ball club in most cases, pays the fine. Frick should suspend them."

For at least a while after that, Leo was on his very good behavior. He was afraid Frick might take Larry's tip.

But the main event in July was, of course, the engagement of Dixie Walker, although at the moment it seemed no more important than the purchase of Wyatt some months before. Dixie's history, taking it over all, was similar to Wyatt's, for he, too, had failed to make a permanent place for himself in the American League and had been tossed around from one club to another. Although he was only twenty-eight, he had been in professional baseball for ten years, spending much of his time in the minors as the property of the Yankees, who had bought him from the Greenville club of the South Atlantic League in 1930. He had come up with the Yanks in the spring of 1931, but there was no room for him in the plans of the then new manager, Joe McCarthy, and he had been sent back to the International League for two years. Up again in 1933, he had got off to a good start and then had suffered an injury to his right shoulder, which hampered him for the next couple of years. McCarthy, most patient of managers, was patient with him, but he couldn't quite prove, in the circumstances, that he was a big-leaguer. Joe sent him to Newark in 1935, brought him back in 1936 and then, definitely having given up on him, released him to the White Sox. Dixie had a reasonably good year with the Sox in 1937, hitting .302, but the following winter he was traded to Detroit. He hit .308 for the Tigers in 1938, but his shoulder was troubling him again, and now, in July of 1939, the Tigers asked for waivers on him. All the other American League clubs promptly waived. MacPhail, needing help in the outfield and willing to gamble on a fellow who could hit, picked Walker up.

There was something about the guy—big, blond, smiling affable—that caught the fancy of the mob at Ebbets Field almost

as soon as he went to the plate for the first time. They yelled to him when he was in the line-up—and yelled for him when he wasn't. A new hero, whose popularity in time would rival that of Nap Rucker, Zack Wheat, and Casey Stengel, had arrived on the scene.

As the National League teams swept into August, the Dodgers were coming with a rush. They were at their best when Durocher played, and fell off a little when Hudson, a second baseman by trade, was used at shortstop, but Leo felt the strain, now and then, of his role as player-manager and had to take a rest. Casey, Hamlin, Presnell, and Wyatt were effective in the box. Fitzsimmons would step in and win one. Walker was hitting. So was Lavagetto. Camilli had cleared up all notions that he might be just another "Philadelphia ballplayer" and, slugging the ball hard, was in a three-cornered race with Johnny Mize of the Cardinals and Mel Ott of the Giants for the home-run-hitting leadership.

The Reds, having taken over first place late in May and never having been dislodged, even for a day, were making a straight run for the pennant. The Cardinals had so firm a grasp on second place there was no hope that the Dodgers could shake them loose. But the Dodgers were the most exciting club in the league, and as MacPhail had dreamed when he put Red Barber in the radio booth, were winning new friends all over the country as a result of Red's broadcasts. Ladies' Day had been instituted at the Flatbush ball park, and the shrill cries of the female rooters pierced the ears of passers-by blocks away. (Five years later, Homer Bigart of the *New York Herald Tribune* was to quote an American soldier who had just come through a Banzai charge by the Japs on Leyte: "They make the weirdest sound as they rush at you, screaming. It sounds like Ladies' Day at Ebbets Field.")

The Dodgers had to knock the Cubs off to finish third. They achieved that feat in the last two days of the season.

Durocher had proven himself as a manager and was taking bows all over the place. MacPhail was hailed as a wonder worker and took a few bows himself. Everybody was happy, including the club directors and George McLaughlin and his associates in the Brooklyn Trust Company. The Dodgers not only had finished third but had drawn over a million customers at home, and MacPhail was paying back some of the loans made by the bank.

Not all the profits reaped at Ebbets Field were going to the bank, however. Some of them were going into the farm system that MacPhail was building up. A firm believer in finding ballplayers young and developing them under managers of his own choosing, as Branch Rickey was doing for the Cardinals and George Weiss for the Yankees, Larry had welded a chain of Dodger-owned or -controlled clubs in leagues from Class AA to D. By the end of 1939 the Dodgers owned Elmira in the Eastern League, Dayton in the Middle Atlantic, Pine Bluff in the Cotton States, Olean in the Pony, and Americus in the Georgia-Florida. They had working agreements with Montreal in the International, Nashville in the Southern, Macon in the South Atlantic, Paducah in the Kitty, Reidsville in the Bi-State, and Superior in the Northern. Tryouts for young ballplayers were held at Ebbets Field and at other places around the country. Dodger scouts roamed the sticks. Three hundred and fifty embryonic major-leaguers were tied up in this chain.

In direct charge of the manipulations of these players was Branch Rickey, Jr., who had joined MacPhail's staff that year. Young Rickey had learned the baseball business by apprenticing himself to his father a year or two before, and MacPhail, having observed him in action and marked him as a budding executive, had said to him one day, early in 1939:

"Why don't you leave your old man and come with me?"

"Do you mean it?" the young man asked.

"Sure I do," Larry said. "I'll give you a job. I don't know just yet what it will be, but I will find a place for you."

So Branch, with his father's consent, quit the Cardinals and joined the Dodgers. The day he walked into the Dodger office on Montague Street, Larry showed him the files on the farm clubs.

"These may be a little mixed up and some of the data on the players may be missing," he said. "I've had so many things to do lately I haven't been able to give as much time to them as I'd like to. Go over them and bring them up to date. It will give you something to do until I can find the right spot for you."

Unknowingly, he had found the right spot. Branch, Jr. has done nothing else since.

There had been one other change in the Dodger organization that year, although it went unmarked by the general public. Hymie Green resigned.

Hymie was the bartender in the Press Club, which had become known to the regular on-the-cuff patrons as Larry's Saloon. No one but Hymie had tended bar there since the room had been opened, and as time passes quickly in any bar room, he already was regarded as an institution. Legends were being built up around him.

One day, with the Dodgers playing the Cardinals, Hymie was listening to Barber's broadcast of the game, coming over the cabinet radio in one corner of the room. MacPhail, who had come down from his box for a quickie and then had lingered for another, was the only other person present. And before the inning was over—it had begun just as MacPhail came in—MacPhail was alone.

"It was this way," Hymie explained, later. "Crespi comes into third base and Lavagetto puts the ball on him and Barber says:
" 'He's out!'

"Naturally, I am glad to hear that, and I bang the bar and yell:
" 'He's out!' just like Barber done.

"Then Barber says:
" 'Oop! I'm sorry! He's safe.'

"And then Larry gets tough all of a sudden. He says to me:
" 'You tend bar and let Barber announce the ball games.'

"Just like that. So I says:
" 'You can't talk that way to me.'

"So I quit. I take off my apron and walk out and get a job in Flynn's, across the street, and MacPhail can go to hell."

Somehow, Larry's Saloon never seemed quite the same with Hymie gone.

There was a kid from the farm system at Clearwater in the

spring of 1941 that Dodger fans were to hail, before the year was out, as the best young ballplayer to come up in a long time. His name was Harold Reiser and he was from St. Louis, and the boys called him Pistol Pete because of his fondness for Wild West movies. The name stuck; always he would be called Pete. He had played in Superior and Elmira and Montreal, and had been up briefly, as an infielder, with the Dodgers the year before.

Durocher had wanted to keep him then, thinking to train him as his own successor at shortstop, but MacPhail had thought the boy should go out for another year's schooling in the minors. There had been quite a row about that, and MacPhail had fired Durocher. Of course Durocher stayed on. MacPhail, though, had had his way, and Pete had gone out for another year. Now he was back, and Durocher switched him to the outfield.

He made the switch because there also was in the camp a kid who knew so much about playing shortstop that he needed very little training in that direction from Durocher or anybody else. His name was Harold Reese; he was a little guy and they called him Peewee. Reese had been with Louisville, which was controlled by the Boston Red Sox, and Tom Yawkey could have had him for the asking, but Joe Cronin, the Red Sox manager, still was playing shortstop and he said he didn't want the boy. Later some of the Boston critics said Joe didn't want him because he knew the boy would take his job in the infield away from him. Joe hotly denied this. At any rate, the Red Sox had passed Reese up and MacPhail had bought him.

Joe Vosmik was there, too. Vosmik had been with Cleveland and with Boston in the American League and was getting old, as the ages of ball players are measured. But the Dodgers still were shy on outfield strength; MacPhail thought Leo might be able to use him, and Leo agreed. Among the pitchers was another castoff, named Tex Carleton, who had been with the Cardinals back in the Gashouse days, then had gone to the Cubs, and at length had slipped out of the majors. Carleton had done a fair job with Milwaukee in 1939, and a Dodger scout thought he might have at least one more year of big league pitching left in his system.

Otherwise the team was about the same. Once the writers got past Reese and Reiser—gliding swiftly over Vosmik and Carleton—they centered most of their attention on MacPhail and Durocher. With reason, too. Larry and Leo were expanding, sartorially and otherwise. The solid places they had made for themselves in the league, Larry as an executive and Leo as a manager, were reflected in their clothes, which were of the latest cut and, so far as their sport raiment was concerned, blinding to the eye. They were seen at all the beaches and in all the night spots. They were really rolling.

There was another development. Brash before, they were even more so now. They were flip, high-handed at times, often provocative. That phase of the MacPhail regime which some of the writers jocularly referred to as the Reign of Terror had set in. Meanwhile, nobody ever worked harder to get a team ready for a fast break when the season opened than Durocher did that spring, and nobody ever succeeded to a greater degree. The Dodgers were hot when the bell rang, and they rolled up nine victories in a row before they were halted, tying the league record in that respect set by the Giants in 1918. They followed that with a dizzy whirl through the West in which they clung to the league lead, and for a while it seemed that Durocher couldn't do anything wrong.

In Cincinnati he threw the presumably washed-up Carleton against the second-place Reds, pennant winners of the year before, and Carleton pitched a no-hit game, which was won by the Dodgers in the fifth inning when, with Dixie Walker and young Herman Franks, the catcher on base, Pete Coscarart hit a home run off Jim Turner.

The swing through the West ended with a 12-2 triumph over the Cubs, and MacPhail, making a grand gesture, had the team flown back to Brooklyn in twin airliners. The dramatic appeal was terrific. The Dodgers, leading the league by two games, were flying back by night—and when the planes put down at Floyd Bennett Field, thirty thousand wildly excited fans were there to greet the players.

As many were at Ebbets Field the next day to see the Dodgers play their arch rivals, the Giants; but, with characteristic cussedness, the Giants spoiled the show by belting the local heroes all over the lot. That, however, could only check, not stop, this rush of the Dodgers. They continued their dingdong race with the Reds, the mob in Brooklyn hollering louder each time the lead changed hands.

The great hue and cry over the team at home set a vision dancing before MacPhail's eyes: a vision of the pennant. He honestly hadn't expected to win that year. He still was building for the future, picking up young players such as Reese and Reiser where he could, taking old ones like Vosmik and Carleton and Jimmy Wasdell (whom he claimed on waivers from Washington in May) as stopgaps along the way to an eventual flag-winning. Now a new plan virtually had been set for him by the cheering, screaming crowds at Ebbets Field and the echoes that came from the enthusiasm of Dodger fans through the country.

The outfield still was one weak spot; the pitching staff another, for Wyatt, Casey, and the aging Fitzsimmons were carrying the burden in the box, with little help from the others, including Carleton, who had been no great shakes since that no-hitter in Cincinnati. Walker, whose popularity (somewhat galling to MacPhail, for some reason or other) had reached such bounds that he was known as "the People's Cherce," was hitting, but he wasn't in the line-up all the time. Reiser was thumping the ball, too, and so was Camilli. But the Dodgers needed another fleet, strong-armed outfielder, one who could hit and run and throw, and who had been around long enough to maintain the pace of this fast-traveling club.

The first one Larry thought of was Joe Medwick of the Cardinals. Joe was a holdover from the Gashouse Gang and a great pal of Durocher's. The pair had roomed together when Leo was with St. Louis, and now, when the Dodgers were in St. Louis or the Cardinals in Brooklyn, they were inseparable companions off the field. There might be a chance to get him. Everybody in the league knew that the rest of the Cardinals had soured on Medwick, blaming him for their failure to win the pennant the year before; for although he had hit over .300, as usual, they said he had played solely for himself, and his lack of team spirit had held them back in spots where they might have headed off the Reds. MacPhail made cautious inquiries in that direction, but Branch Rickey indicated there was no chance of a deal.

Larry then began to look elsewhere. He had plenty of money to spend and was in a mood to spend it.

"The Brooklyn fans deserve the best I can get for them," he said. And to some of the other club owners: "What's the best you have to offer? Speak up. I'm shopping."

On June 11, his telephone rang. Branch Rickey was calling.

"I hear you're shopping," Branch said.

"You know damned well I am," Larry said. "Whom will you sell?"

"Anybody."

"Anybody! Does that go for Medwick?"

"Yes," Branch said.

"I'll be right out," Larry yelled.

That night he got off a plane in St. Louis. On June 12 he had Medwick. He paid $125,000 for him and threw in Ernie Koy, two young pitchers, Carl Doyle and Sam Nahem, and a young utility player, Berthold Haas. Not to be outdone, Rickey threw in Curt Davis, a thirty-three-year-old pitcher. Medwick and Davis flew back to Brooklyn with MacPhail to join the Dodgers, just returning to Ebbets Field from a western trip.

The deal was hailed in Brooklyn. This was it. This was the pennant. The newspapers joined in the acclaim. One writer added a sardonic note to his comments.

"It's about time the Dodgers got Medwick," he wrote. "He and Durocher have been holding hands so long that it has verged on the scandalous."

MacPhail was in high humor. The cheers at Ebbets Field hit a new high in volume. Then, a frightening thing happened. Playing against his old teammates for the first time, in a game at Ebbets Field on June 19, only a week after he had become a Dodger, Medwick was hit in the head by a fast ball pitched by Bob Bowman.

As Medwick fell, unconscious, at the plate, the Dodgers tumbled out of their dugout to wreak vengeance on Bowman, who, they believed, had beaned the outfielder deliberately. Some tried to punch him. Others, with bats in their hands, wanted to brain him.

"You said you'd get him!" Durocher was yelling.

Thrust away repeatedly by the umpires and St. Louis players, who had rushed to the pitcher's defense, Leo was swinging wildly at Bowman's chin. The crowd seemed about to boil out of the stands. MacPhail darted from his box, where he had been viewing the game, and raced madly down a ramp to the field, where, in an almost incoherent rage, he mouthed curses at Bowman. Mrs. Medwick, who had arrived from St. Louis that morning and was seated in a box just back of the Dodgers' dugout, sobbed in her fright.

Medwick was rushed to the near-by Caledonian Hospital, where it was found that while the blow had been severe enough to cause a concussion, there was no fracture. In a short time he regained consciousness.

Manager Billy Southworth of the Cardinals withdrew Bowman from the game, and the pitcher, shaken by the injury to Medwick, the attack upon him by the Brooklyn players, and the cry for his blood that beat down upon him from the stands, was escorted by policemen to the clubhouse. A short time later, still guarded by policemen, he was taken from the park to the New Yorker Hotel in Manhattan, where the Cardinals were quartered.

MacPhail, having seen Medwick removed to the hospital, dashed back to his office and got Ford Frick on the telephone. Still wildly excited, he demanded that the league president bar Bowman for life, nor could he be appeased by Frick's belief that the beaning had been accidental.

"You ask Durocher if it was accidental!" Larry bellowed. "He'll tell you that Bowman threatened him and Medwick this morning!"

Durocher's story was that he and Medwick, both living at the New Yorker, had met Bowman in an elevator in the hotel as they were leaving for the ball park about noon.

"We figured he was going to pitch this afternoon," Leo said, "and we were needling him. He took it all right for a minute or so, and then he got mad, and he said:

" 'I'll take care of you! I'll take care of both of you!'

"And I said:

" 'Why, you bum, you'll be out of there before Joe and I get to bat.'

"Don't tell me he didn't do it on purpose."

MacPhail wanted to have Bowman arrested for assault; he talked of going to the district attorney and having him indicted, but as Medwick's condition rapidly improved, Larry's anger cooled. Medwick remained in the hospital for five or six days and then returned to the line-up. Naturally, it took him a little time to regain his hitting form, and he was bat shy for the rest of the year. But in spite of that, he finished with an average of .301.

Early in July, the fate of the Dodgers was sealed. They didn't know it then, and a little later on, when they must have suspected it, they continued to struggle against it. But at the end of the first week in July they were in second place, and no matter how hard they tried, they couldn't overtake the Reds. The Reds had gathered World Series money the year before, and they wanted more of it, and nobody was going to pull them back now. They were riding to another pennant on the pitching of Bucky Walters and Paul Derringer.

But the Dodgers tried, every day. They hung on and battled for every ball game as the mob yelled. Durocher drove his players to the limit and the umpires to distraction. MacPhail was enjoying it thoroughly. The battle was on. The lid was off. He battled with Durocher almost as much as Durocher battled with the umpires; but if anybody made a hostile crack at Durocher, he was at Leo's shoulder.

It just was not, as Brooklyn fans had thought, their year. The Dodgers could pile up victories over the Giants, the Phillies, the Braves, and the Pirates, but they couldn't hold their own with the Reds, the Cardinals, the Cubs. Then in mid-August, Reese suffered a fracture of two small bones in his left heel and was out for the rest of the season; in Cincinnati on the last western trip, Lavagetto was trundled off to a hospital to have his appendix removed; and the absence of those two young men just about put the finishing touches on whatever chance the Dodgers still had to win. Durocher, who had broken Reese in as his understudy and then virtually retired to the dugout to let the boy play all the time (that was the reason for some of his more violent quarrels with MacPhail) now climbed back into action and played superbly, yet to no avail so far as the flag was concerned.

The last western trip was thrilling for some of the players, nightmarish for others, since it was made almost entirely by plane. Even when they were in motion on the ground, they traveled so fast they had to have motorcycle police escorts. They raced from ball park to airport, roared through the skies, raced from airport to hotel. St. Louis to Chicago . . . Chicago to Pittsburgh . . . Pittsburgh to Cincinnati.

"The Dodgers are the only team in the history of baseball," Eddie Murphy said, "to fall out of the pennant race with a motorcycle escort."

Van Mungo said he was so plane-punchy when the team reached Cincinnati that he couldn't even bear to send a letter by air mail.

For those who didn't like air travel, there was a happy ending in Cincinnati. The two planes that bore the athletes had been chartered by the club, and the charter expired on the date set for the final game in Cincinnati. When it rained that day and the Cincinnati club insisted the Dodgers stay over to play on the following day, the planes no longer were available.

"So we'll go by train," John McDonald said.

So they did, but for a time it looked as though they would have to go by boat, bus or wheelbarrow. The railroads, irked by the Dodgers' preference for planes, reported they didn't have the necessary extra cars to accommodate them, and in the long run it was only McDonald's personal popularity in Cincinnati that enabled him to get the team out of town in time to maintain their schedule.

Back home in Flatbush, the Dodgers continued to wrestle around, keeping excitement at Ebbets Field at a high pitch. It reached its highest during a September game with the Reds that was followed by a memorable brawl.

Durocher, and most of the other Dodgers, for that matter, had ridden umpire George Magerkurth hard all afternoon. When the game was over and the official, still badgered by snarling Dodgers, was on his way off the field, he was set upon by a burly fan. Magerkurth, a powerful giant and a former heavyweight fighter, taken completely by surprise, was knocked down by the quick rush of his 200-pound attacker. They rolled on the ground, fighting desperately until umpire Bill Stewart, also a muscle man, "mugged" the fan and dragged him loose. By this time, the cops had their hands on the assailant and lugged him off to the station house.

The fan, built like Tony Galento, said his name was Frank Germano. When he was arraigned in Flatbush court, he was met by a parole officer with a warrant for his arrest on a charge of parole violation, for it seemed that he was loose on sufferance from the West Coxackie (N.Y.) Vocational Institution, where he had been sentenced for petty larceny. So the young man paid for his loyalty to the Dodgers by being returned to the sneezer.

Durocher also paid. When he showed up at Ebbets Field the following day this message awaited him:

"For prolonged argument and conduct on the field tending to incite riot, you are fined one hundred dollars payable this office and suspended five days. (Signed) Ford Frick."

Leo sent his check to Ford and spent the next five days managing the Dodgers from a box near the dugout. It was the first time in his career as manager that he was suspended.

All the tussling and all the excitement, however, couldn't get the Dodgers home. They finished in second place, twelve games behind the Reds. But they had made a great fight, had landed one notch higher than in 1939, and had further endeared themselves to the fans, particularly as they had taken sixteen of their twenty-one games from the Giants and had helped to hammer the Giants down into sixth place. Fitzsimmons had compiled, mainly at the expense of the Phillies and the Pirates, an amazing record: the thirty-nine year-old hurler won sixteen games while losing only two, setting a National League record with a won-and-lost average of .889. Walker, whose hitting was sensational through the first half of the season, although it trailed off somewhat as the season waned, was the team's leading batter with a mark of .308.

Through Flatbush, through all Brooklyn, the cry rang loud: "*Wait till next year!*"

THE SNATCHING OF KIRBY HIGBE

Larry MacPhail didn't wait till next year. The day after the end of one season was, for him, the beginning of another. He flew to Cincinnati for the opening of the World Series between the Reds and the Tigers, and he didn't go only to see the ball games. He had two deals in mind that would strengthen the Dodgers where they needed it most: in the box and back of the bat. The pitcher he wanted was Kirby Higbe of the Phillies; the catcher, Arnold (Mickey) Owen of the Cardinals.

He had to move cagily, he knew, for there were other clubs that wanted Higbe and there was good reason to believe that if it became known he was after Higbe and had a good chance to get him, he would not get Owen. And for all that he likes to bluster and to work in the open when it suits him to do so, he can work quietly, even furtively, when it suits him to do that instead.

He made his first move for Higbe, who, lightly regarded by the Cubs, his original owners in the National League, had been traded off to the Phillies and had won fourteen games with a last-place ball club in 1940. He sought out Gerald Nugent, president of the Phils, and told him he wanted to talk to him about Higbe but asked him to keep quiet about it and suggested they meet the next day and discuss terms. Nugent agreed, and Larry next called on Branch Rickey.

"How about a deal for that young punk, Owen?" he asked.

Rickey raised his eyebrows, chewed on his cigar and said

nothing. Owen, twenty-three years old, had been in the Cardinal chain since 1935 and with the Cardinals for four years. He had given promise of becoming a great catcher but had not yet fulfilled the promise. MacPhail, believing he would someday, and meanwhile liking him for his hustle and his pugnacity, was sure he would help the Dodgers, who hadn't had a good catcher since Al Lopez went to Boston in 1935.

"Well?" he asked.

"I'm not eager to sell him," Rickey said. "I like him pretty well, myself."

"You probably like him better than I do," Larry said, "but I might be able to use him if I could get him cheap."

He walked away, went to dinner, and after dinner was relaxing in the press headquarters in the Netherland-Plaza when John McDonald, who knew his plans, of course, said to him:

"You know where Nugent is, don't you? He's at a country club over on the Kentucky side of the river with Horace Stoneham, Leo Bondy, and Eddie Brannick, and they are wining and dining him. It seems the Giants want Higbe, too."

The Giants! If Larry needed any spur, that was it. The Giants, eh? He'd show them! What a laugh he'd have on Stoneham, taking the pitcher right out from under his nose! And after Horace had blown his dough entertaining Nugent!

The next morning he called Nugent and in mock anger accused him of giving him the runaround. Gerry protested he had done nothing of the sort and hadn't mentioned to Stoneham that MacPhail was after Higbe. But after all, he said, Higbe was his ballplayer and he had a perfect right to listen to all propositions for him.

"I was just kidding," Larry said. "I'll come right down to your room and you can listen to mine."

In Nugent's room, he asked, abruptly:

"How much do you want for Higbe?"

"A hundred thousand dollars," Nugent said, hopefully.

"You got a deal," Larry said.

Nugent almost fell off his chair.

"Well," he managed to say, "that's great with me, but before

I can make the deal, I have to have the approval of my directors."

Larry pointed to the telephone. Nugent nodded, picked up the phone and called Philadelphia. He had no trouble getting the necessary approval, of course. Putting that price on Higbe, he had shot at the moon—and hit it. The directors, always hard pressed for money for even the barest operating expenses, were delighted.

"Now," Larry said, "you've still got to keep quiet about it, because if Rickey hears I have Higbe, he won't sell me Owen because he doesn't want to strengthen my club and help me to beat out the Cardinals again next year."

Nugent feared Judge Landis might not like a deal made in secrecy. Now Larry grabbed the telephone and called Landis. The Judge said it would be all right if all the information on the transaction were sent to him in regular form, so that in due course it could be included in the bulletins sent out from his office to the club owners. That satisfied MacPhail. He simply was stalling for time, and this would give him time enough. He knew the bulletin wouldn't be sent out at least until Landis returned to his office in Chicago after the series.

"By the way," he asked Nugent, "how much did Stoneham offer you for Higbe?"

"Sixty-five thousand dollars," Nugent said. "I was waiting to hear what you said, so I turned him down."

MacPhail howled. He knew what Horace thought: Since the Phillies were in need of money, Nugent would come back with a counter offer, and they could go on from there.

Now, being careful to make it appear as though it were an accident, Larry contrived to meet Rickey.

"What's this I hear about Nugent being willing to sell Higbe?" Branch asked.

"He's crazy!" Larry scoffed. "Do you know what he wants for Higbe? A hundred thousand dollars!"

Rickey laughed, too.

"How about Owen?" Larry asked.

"He'll come high."

"How high?"

"Sixty thousand dollars and two ballplayers—and one of them must be a catcher."

"You're on," Larry said.

And so, with Rickey unaware that Higbe belonged to the Dodgers, the deal was made: $60,000, Gus Mancuso, and a young pitcher named John Pintar that nobody ever heard of— nor has yet, so far as his performances are concerned.

Larry got a bang out of seeing the Reds win the series, for they were, by discovery, his players. They had been beaten and humiliated by the Yankees the year before, but now they had vindicated themselves.

The series over and the deals for Owen and Higbe concluded, there was another matter that claimed Larry's attention.

Leo Durocher's contract had expired (Leo worked on a year-to-year basis), and there were strange stories about town concerning Leo and Larry. Strange, in view of the fact that under Durocher the Dodgers had jumped from seventh place to third, then to second, and might, with a little luck, hit the top of the league in 1941. The stories were that Leo's contract might not be renewed.

Tales were told here and there, in the bars and grills in Brooklyn, in the newspapers, around and about the town, of the quarrels between Larry and Leo. Of Larry's bitterness because Leo had not played shortstop regularly during the season just past. Of Larry screaming, on one notable occasion:

"I'm paying you to see some of that sparkling infield play I've been reading about in the papers! You don't think I'm paying you just to manage the ball club, do you? With the players I've dug up for you, I could manage the club myself and do a damned sight better job than you have!"

And of how Leo had screamed back at him:

"You manage the ball club! Don't make me laugh!"

And MacPhail:

"You're fired!"

And Durocher:

"All right, I'm fired! Get somebody else to manage your lousy ball club."

And so on.

Some of the tales undoubtedly were true. All of them may have been. But they were a couple of fellows who could say things like that to each other one minute and forget them the next and when MacPhail returned to Brooklyn from Cincinnati, he had a contract for 1941 signed by Durocher in his pocket.

Back in New York a few weeks after the series, Larry laughed out loud when he picked up the newspapers one day. The bulletin on the sale of Higbe had not yet been issued from the Commissioner's office, so that no one but Larry, Nugent, and their directors knew of it—and here was Horace Stoneham telling some newspapermen in Toots Shor's the night before that the Giants were about to close a deal for the pitcher. Larry's scheme had worked even better than he could have hoped. Not only had he beaten the Giants to the pitcher, but Horace had put himself in a spot from which he could not extricate himself without considerable embarrassment. How the newspapers—and, more important, the Brooklyn fans—would eat up the story he had to tell!

No time like the present to tell it, either. He notified all the newspaper offices that he had an important announcement to make that afternoon, and when the reporters gathered, he beamed smugly and said:

"In spite of what Mr. Stoneham says, the Giants are not going to get Kirby Higbe."

"Why?" one of them wanted to know.

"Because," Larry said triumphantly, "he belongs to the Dodgers. I bought him in Cincinnati during the World Series, and if you doubt me, look at this."

He threw on his desk before him a copy of his agreement with Nugent.

"If you still doubt it," he added, "you can call Nugent or Judge Landis."

In New York, Stoneham called Nugent and MacPhail everything he could think of. In Brooklyn, MacPhail's popularity climbed.

This was the year. Everybody knew it. MacPhail . . . Durocher . . . the ballplayers . . . the fans . . . the experts, who, especially in Brooklyn and New York, almost unanimously picked the Dodgers to win, even before the training season opened. The fact that the Reds had won the pennant and the world championship the year before was no deterrent. "Next year" had arrived.

Even those who did not go out on a limb for the Dodgers had to admit there was a pretty good basis for this surge of optimism. Third in 1939, second in 1940, now strengthened by the addition of Higbe and Owen, the Dodgers could win. On top of that, there was more good news: Peewee Reese was coming back, sound again, and on January 31 MacPhail signed Paul Waner, who had been released outright by the Pirates. Doctors said Reese's fractured heel had mended and would give him no trouble; which meant that the Dodgers once more would have the best infield in the league. Waner had slowed down in the field, of course, but he would be a handy guy to have around when a pinch hit was needed. He still could walk up to the plate and hit one for two bases.

MacPhail set a new high in pre-season programs by scheduling fifty exhibition games that would take the Dodgers from Havana, where they would train for the first four weeks, as far into the Southwest as Houston and Fort Worth.

"This trip," Jack Miley wrote in the *New York Post*, "will make the Lewis and Clark expedition seem like a short walk."

The players blanched at news of this schedule, but MacPhail hastened to add that the squad would be split into A and B teams, so that each would have to make only half the jumps listed after the young men had returned to the mainland and established a base at Clearwater on April 1.

Miami was the gathering point at the outset of the training season, and from there the Dodgers launched a full-scale invasion of Havana by plane. On their arrival, they were met by an official reception committee which included Mike Gonzales,

Adolfo Luque, and Joe Rodriguez; a band; and a large crowd of ebullient fans, while across the administration building at the airport was stretched a huge sign reading:

"*Bienvenido el Club Brooklyn.*"

None of the players knew what it meant, but they guessed it was all right. They piled into cabs and, with the band blaring in front of them and the mob trailing behind, proceeded into town and through narrow streets to the Prado and on to the Palace, where they were received by aides of President Fulgencio Batista. The amenities having been observed there, they were driven to the Hotel Nacional, their headquarters.

Mungo was the only survivor of the hilarious visit of the Dodgers in 1931; he had a good memory for things like that and showed the players some of the better spots: Prado 86, kept by Otto Precht; the Florida, Sloppy Joe's, and all the others. This time, however, there was no carousing. This was a different kind of ball club. Even Van didn't take so much as a beaker of the famed Tropical brew.

Durocher went right to work with the players at Tropical Park (hard by the brewery of the same name), for there was little time to be wasted, as the Giants were coming over from Miami in two weeks and Leo wanted to be ready for them. Neither Phelps nor Owen was in camp, Phelps pleading illness and Owen not yet having signed, so Leo had to borrow some Cuban catchers for batting practice. Casey wasn't on hand for the first workout, but the other pitchers were there. Hugh came in four days late, and MacPhail slapped a fine of $100 on him. Since the ballplayers aren't paid during the training season, the money would come out of Hugh's first pay check. He grumbled about that, naturally, but soon was hard at work.

A few days later Owen signed and reported. Phelps remained at his home, and at a press conference in the Nacional a wrathful MacPhail boomed:

"Now I forbid him to come here! He's no sicker than I am. I have ordered him to report at the Montreal club's training camp at Macon."

It had been suspected all along that Babe had shied away

from Havana because he had an equal dislike for travel by air or by water, and that he would obey Larry and go promptly to Macon. But he didn't.

"Let him stay home," Durocher said. "The hell with him."

Leo had intended to align his outfield with Medwick in left field, Reiser in right, and Walker and Gilbert alternating in center, but a new development caused him to change his mind. Waner, who had fished, golfed, and taken excellent care of himself through the off season, not only smacked the ball around the park, but on defense, in the practice games, covered ground like a strong-legged kid just up from the bushes.

"I'm playing Waner in right field from now on, with Reiser in center, and of course Medwick in left," Leo told the reporters just before the advent of the Giants.

The reporters looked shocked.

"Where does that leave Walker?" they asked.

"On the bench," Leo snapped.

The news, received in Brooklyn, caused an ominous rumble among the faithful.

"What's the matter with Leo?" they asked in the bars and grills. "Has he blown his topper?"

The phrasing was more polite in the homes and the clubs on the Heights, but the sentiment was the same. Yet the reporters on the scene, although disliking the benching of Walker, confessed that Waner was hot. He was as hot as Dixie had been in 1940, and maybe Leo was right.

The coming of the Giants stirred the fans in Havana. For the most part, the Dodgers were the popular favorites, but the Giants did not lack for support from those who looked back to the days when they had played there under John McGraw or to the spring of 1937, when they had been there under Bill Terry. The three-game series drew well, the betting was brisk, and it was a little like seeing the teams play at Ebbets Field. It was a great series for the Dodgers: they swept the three games.

On March 9 there was a slight disturbance in the camp. It was precipitated by Mungo, whose behavior had been excellent and whose form had matched his behavior, so that when he predicted he would win twenty-five games that year, few were inclined to disagree with him seriously and most were of the opinion that he would win eighteen or twenty, anyway. But on the night of March 9, when the other ballplayers had gone to bed, Van showed up at the bar in the Nacional, which was lined with tourists. He obviously was in a happy and expansive mood, and throwing a twenty-dollar bill on the mahogany, said to the bartender:

"See what the folks will have."

The bartender nodded toward one end of the bar.

"How about those two folks?" he asked.

"See what they'll have, too," Van said.

Then he looked in the direction indicated. At the end of the bar were Durocher and Dressen, having a bedtime toddy. They saw him at the same instant. Leo beckoned, Van joined them, and Leo said:

"Do you know what time it is?"

Van looked at his watch.

"Nearly twelve o'clock," he said.

"All right," Leo said. "Scram. You know you should be in your room—and that you shouldn't be in here, of all places. How about those promises you made? Get to bed and I'll forget all about this, though—and the fact that you've had a few snifters."

Van was reluctant to go, but Leo and Charley, after a mild scuffle, escorted him to his room, saw him getting ready for bed, and went to their own rooms. A little later, round two got under way. Van had left his room and got tangled up with a Cuban dance team entertaining in the hotel's supper room. It must have been a lively round, for Van came out of it with a black eye. This time Leo not only returned him to his room but made sure that he had retired before he left him.

The Dodgers were playing the Cleveland Indians the next day; or, to be more precise, at 2:30 that day; and Mungo had been slated to pitch. The other players were in their uniforms and about to go out on the field when he walked into the clubhouse.

"Leave me at them Indians," he said.

He had taken his coat off and was hanging it in his locker when Durocher caught up with him.

"No," Leo said. "Put that coat on again. You're not going to pitch against the Indians or anybody else around here. You're fined two hundred dollars and John McDonald has a ticket for you on the afternoon plane. You're going to Macon and work out with the Montreal club."

Mungo protested, howled, threatened. A policeman loomed in the doorway, and Durocher nodded. Turning to Mungo, Leo said:

"Will you go to the airport yourself or do you want this cop to take you?"

Mungo put on his coat and walked out.

The stay in Havana drew to a close. The Dodgers were in great shape. Never had a more confident club moved toward the final phase of its training and the opening of the season. Even MacPhail, sometimes strangely cautious in his predictions, said he was sure the Dodgers would win. Durocher was even bolder. He said that, bar accidents to some of his key players, it was practically a cinch. The newspapermen with the team felt the same way.

The Dodgers pitched their camp at Clearwater, and MacPhail engaged Max Carey to teach some of the young players—and some of the older ones, too—how to run bases. Wyatt and Higbe were going great, Owen was just what the Dodgers had needed back of the bat. Coscarart, after a good beginning, was not doing so well, but Camilli and Lavagetto were clicking, and Reese was as nimble as he had been before he was hurt. Durocher had no doubts about Coscarart. Pete would regain his stride. Waner still looked like a youngster in right field.

One day Leo received a telegram from Brooklyn. It was, certainly, the most remarkable wire Western Union ever handled.

"Put Walker back in right field or we will boycott the Dodgers!" it read. And it bore the duly attested signatures of five thousand fans!

When MacPhail saw it, his anger flamed.

"Keep Waner in there!" he yelled at Durocher. "If you play Walker, I'll fire you!"

The Dodgers went about the South and the Southwest playing their exhibition games with Waner in right field on Team A. MacPhail went back to Brooklyn, heading into the storm raised by the demotion of Walker.

"Let them holler!" he snorted. "I'll show them who's running this ball club!"

When Durocher reached Atlanta with the A team on April 7, he found Mungo in the lobby of the hotel.

"What are you doing here?" Leo demanded.

"MacPhail told me to report to you today," Van said.

"He didn't tell me anything about it."

Mungo shrugged.

"Call him up and find out," he said. "All I know is he told me to report."

Leo angrily followed the bellhop carrying his bags to his room. He knew it would be a waste of time to call MacPhail because Mungo must be telling the truth. He called the reporters to his room.

"Mungo's back," he said. "Larry has reinstated him. But I'll tell you this, and I'll tell it to Mungo and to MacPhail, too: If I ever see Mungo take a drink again, he'll go off this ball club to stay or I'll quit!"

"This is a great ball club," one of the reporters said to another on the way out. "The manager's always either quitting or being fired."

Now, at last, the season opened, the season for which Dodger fans had waited so eagerly. Forgotten, of course, was the threat of the five thousand admirers of Dixie Walker to boycott the club; or, if any of them had remembered, they were not missed in the mob that packed Ebbets Field to see the Dodgers open the campaign against the hated Giants.

But alas, there was a rude jolt at the very beginning. The Giants not only won the opening game but the two other games of the series. Brooklyn was devastated. More, it was disillusioned. The Dodgers were, in all truth, nothing but bums. Where was

Dixie Walker? Why didn't they get somebody who could play second base? Durocher? MacPhail? Boo!

Almost overnight the skies cleared. The Dodgers began to win. They had it, after all. Only one sore point remained: While Walker was not chained to the bench, he got into the line-up only once in a while. Even when Reiser became ill, Durocher put a kid named Tom Tatum, just up from Nashville, in center field while Dixie rode the pine. But Tatum was no ball of fire, and Reiser recovered quickly, and the Dodgers moved on.

Now the pace was beginning to tell on Waner. Maybe he had worked too hard at Havana and through the South. Maybe, as they say in the prize fight business, he had left his fight in the gymnasium. He had started the season brightly, but as he ploughed through May, his steps lagged and his hitting fell off. There came a day when MacPhail could hold out no longer against the demands of the mob: Paul was benched and the People's Cherce was in right field.

Equally electrifying was another switch made by MacPhail and Durocher in May. Coscarart simply couldn't keep up with Camilli, Reese, and Lavagetto, and MacPhail made a deal with the Cubs for the veteran Billy Herman, giving $65,000 for him. Herman was thirty-two years old and had been with the Cubs for ten years; but he still was agile and would be a big help to young Reese around second base, and he was a dependable hitter.

Dodger fans hailed him with joy and he found the lively atmosphere of Ebbets Field to his liking.

"Every day, it's like a World Series game around here," he said to Eddie Murphy. "What a town!"

Phelps rejoined the team, caught a few games, and then went home again in June, complaining once more of his health. MacPhail ordered him to return, asserting there was nothing the matter with him except a strange reluctance to play with the Dodgers, and when Phelps refused to do so, Larry referred the case to Landis and the Judge put Phelps on the inactive list. That, so far as the Dodgers were concerned, was the last of the Blimp. The following winter he was traded to the Pirates.

The Dodgers battled on. Their chief foes were not the champion Reds but the Cardinals, striking back at the top of the league after a seven-year lapse. There were times when the Brooklyn pitchers were hard pressed, although Wyatt, Higbe, and Curt Davis were winning regularly. On July 14, Durocher pulled Higbe through to victory in a game marked by a rousing pitching duel between Kirby and Verne Olsen of the Cubs. Higbe had yielded only two hits, but the Dodgers had been unable to hit Olsen, and when they reached the last half of the ninth inning they were bound up in a scoreless tie. They filled the bases, and it was Higbe's turn to hit. He started for the plate, but Leo motioned him back, picked up a bat, and had himself announced as a pinch hitter. The crowd roared its disapproval, wanting to see Higbe, who had pitched so magnificently, have an opportunity to win his own game.

But Leo had a plan and he believed that he, better than Higbe, was qualified to carry it out. He was putting himself on a spot, of course. He knew that if he failed, the wrath of the crowd would descend upon him violently. But it was characteristic of him that he should take the chance. It panned out as Leo deserved. On the second pitch he rolled a bunt past the box and Medwick raced in from third base with the winning run.

As July waned, Wyatt weakened and the Dodgers slumped. Desperate, MacPhail claimed Johnny Allen, on whom the St. Louis Browns had asked waivers. Because of a hair-trigger temper that had made him a storm center in the American League, Allen had been shunted about from the Yankees to the Indians to the Browns. But there was no doubt that he could pitch and that he was hard-boiled and stubborn and game under fire. In a clutch like this he was the kind of pitcher Larry and Leo wanted. The kind of pitcher who, when somebody once asked him if it was true that he would throw at his grandmother's head if she went to bat against him in a pinch, could grin and say:

"No, but I might loosen her up with one around the knees."

Now it was August and the Dodgers were driving hard for the pennant. All over the country, fans listening to Red Barber's descriptions of their games—reported in person from Ebbets Field or off the ticker in the studio when the team was on the road—were rooting for them. At home, every day was, as Herman had said, like a day in a World Series. Brooklyn rapidly was becoming delirious. At the Lefferts Bar, at Flynn's, at the Ball Field Tavern, in hundreds of bars, restaurants, and cafés, the radio brought tidings of the games by day or night, brought on celebrations or moments of despair, brought on arguments, invective, praise.

One Tony Grimeli, whose place at Fifteenth Street and Fifth Avenue was a popular spot with the fans, made it even more popular with a startling innovation. Anyone—up to the number of sixty—who paid him three dollars across the bar before a game could drink all the beer he wanted, would be hauled to Ebbets Field, provided with a reserved seat back of first base, hauled back, and permitted to wind up the evening drinking all the free beer he could hold.

"I got a waiting list of 241," he boasted to Tom O'Reilly of New York's *PM* one day, "but I got to keep the limit to sixty because that's all the joint will hold."

"But how do you expect to make any money this way?" Tom asked.

Tony winked.

"Only the beer is free," he said, "and I know these people. The Dodgers make them very excited, and when they come back here after a game and start to argue, they forget about the beer and buy whisky."

He winked again.

"Grimeli will get rich," he said.

The fans fought their way into the park on the big days, and sometimes kept right on fighting. One broiling hot day, during a double-header with the Reds, a fan muscled his way through a jam in the aisle just back of the Dodgers' dugout.

"Let me by," he said to a man who was slow to give him headway.

"Where are you going?" the man demanded.

The other was irate.

"I don't have to take that guff from you!" he roared, and slugged the obdurate one.

Even the ballplayers, rapidly becoming used to such scenes, stopped to watch the fight that, all too soon, was broken up by the cops.

Winning most of the time, losing here and there, the Dodgers were alternately cheered and maligned. One day when they were playing the Phillies (they had lost to the Phillies the day before and the attendance had fallen off somewhat), Toots Shor and Bill Corum were seated in the upper tier back of first base. Camilli, who was in a batting slump, started for the plate, and a fan seated in front of Shor bawled:

"Sit down, you bum!"

"Watch me have some fun with this fellow," Toots said to Bill.

He leaned over and tapped the fan on the shoulder.

"I wish you wouldn't call Camilli a bum," he said. "He's a friend of mine and a very nice fellow. If you knew him, you wouldn't call him a bum."

The fan glowered.

"All right," he said, grudgingly. "If he's a friend of yours, I'll lay off him."

Even when Dolf popped out, the fan restrained himself; but when Walker, the next hitter—and there were days when even Dixie wasn't immune from verbal punishment—moved up to the plate, he bawled:

"You bum! Put that bat down and let somebody hit that can hit!"

Toots tapped him on the shoulder again and he whirled.

"Is Walker your friend, too?" he yelled.

Toots nodded.

"Are all these bums your friends?"

Toots nodded again.

The fan got up and started across the aisle, headed for a seat in another section.

"I'm gettin' the hell away from you," he said over his shoulder. "You ain't going to spoil my afternoon!"

But on days when the sun shone bright—meaning on days when the Dodgers won—the fans were rapturous in their joy.

Four of them composed a band which played every day, marching back and forth through the stands during the game, marching off the field with a dancing mob behind them when the game was over. In the center field bleachers Hilda (The Bell) Chester, gained sports page prominence. Hilda, a middle-aged woman, was a veteran Ebbets Field fan; with her bell, which she rang loudly every time the Dodgers rallied or she thought they needed encouragement, she long had been a familiar figure to the ballplayers, the newspapermen, and the other regular fans. Now she became a symbol of the Dodgers' pennant charge and, as such, saw her picture in the papers and her name in the headlines.

Harold Parrott, who had been one of the first to write about her, went out to see her one day, and found her, armed with her bell as always, regally ensconced in the seat reserved for her, even on the biggest days, by a group of her strong-arm friends. They chatted for a while and Harold, about to leave for the press box, said:

"Hilda, wouldn't you like to sit in the grandstand, right back of the dugout? I'll have a place reserved for you every day if you would."

Hilda was scornful.

"Did any of those plush seat bums come near me when I was in the hospital?" she asked. "Not one! But the ballplayers did, and they sent me cards and letters and flowers, and the boys and girls out here were dropping in all the time. No, sir. I'll stay right here, thank you!"

Dan Parker, sports editor of the *Daily Mirror*, who took great delight in needling MacPhail in his column (Larry would counter his thrusts by calling him on the telephone every hour on the hour all through the night after one of the pieces had appeared) contributed to the hilarity raging in Brooklyn with his epic poem, "Leave Us Go Root for the Dodgers, Rodgers":

Murgatroyd Darcy, a broad from Canarsie
Went 'round with a fellow named Rodge.
At dancing a rumba or jitterbug numbah
You couldn't beat Rodge—'twas his dodge.

The pair danced together throughout the cold weather
But when the trees blossomed again
Miss Murgatroyd Darcy, the belle of Canarsie
To Rodgers would sing this refrain:

Leave us go root for the Dodgers, Rodgers,
They're playing ball under lights.
Leave us cut out all the juke jernts, Rodgers,
Where we've been wastin' our nights.
Dancin' the shag or the rumba is silly
When we can be rooting for Adolf Camilli,
So leave us go root for the Dodgers, Rodgers,
Them Dodgers is my gallant knights.

Bud Green and Ted Berkman later collaborated in setting the poem with a few changes to music and it became the marching song of all the little Murgatroyds and Rodgers in the borough.

The Dodgers packing them in at home, packing them in on the road, sweeping through—or being hurled back in—critical series, and all the time drawing nearer to the pennant. And now that they were within range of the prize, MacPhail and Durocher getting jittery and, when a game or two was lost, reaching out for reinforcements.

On August 20 the Cubs asked for waivers on Larry French, veteran southpaw, and MacPhail quickly claimed him, for Kemp Wicker had not fulfilled early promises; Vito Tamulis, picked up from the Phillies, hadn't, either, and the team was weak on left-handers. Five days later a deal was made with the Los Angeles club, which is owned by the Cubs, for Augie Galan, who had been with the Cubs from 1934 until the end of the 1940 season. On July 31, 1940, Augie had suffered a broken knee as he crashed into a wall at Shibe Park; at the Cubs' training camp in the spring of 1941 there had been grave doubt of his ability to continue as a major league outfielder, and the Cubs had released him to Los Angeles. Augie had refused to report to the Angels, but, through the summer, had kept himself in shape. Now Mac-Phail wanted him for insurance on the picket line.

The Dodgers tore through a final, winning western trip with a row at the end of it. In the last game in Pittsburgh, on September 18, Umpire Magerkurth called a balk on Casey and threw Durocher into a tantrum. Leo whirled out of the dugout, all guns blazing, and was joined by a half dozen of his players, who held the game up for five minutes or more, until Magerkurth threw most of them out.

That night the Dodgers left for Philadelphia, and on their arrival the next morning Durocher was notified by Ford Frick that he had been fined $150 for abusing the umpire, while lesser fines were levied on Medwick, Camilli, Franks, Wyatt, and Coscarart. Leo, still steaming over what he deemed an injustice, walked out of the hotel to take the air for a few minutes and encountered Ted Meier, an Associated Press reporter, who wanted a statement from him on the tangle with the umpire. That, it seemed was the last subject on which to question Leo at the moment and expect a civil answer. One word led to another, and manager and reporter adjourned to an alley alongside the hotel, where Leo, although outweighed some thirty pounds, flattened Meier three times with punches on the chin. Just as Meier was getting to his feet after the last knockdown and onlookers were pulling Durocher away from him, a cop appeared on the scene.

"What's going on here?" he demanded.

"Nothing, officer," said Jerry Mitchell of the *New York Post*. "It's only that the Dodgers are in town."

"Oh!" the cop said, and walked away.

Quiet having been restored, peace followed immediately; Durocher and Meier shook hands and apologized to each other. Leo gave Ted the story he wanted, and Ted started back to his office.

"You got a good left hook, Leo," he said.

There was a Sunday double-header in Philadelphia on the visit of the Dodgers, the last of the season, and all unexpectedly, thousands of Brooklyn rooters descended upon the town by train and bus and car. Vastly outnumbering the Philadelphia rooters, they took command of Shibe Park and, brushing cops and ushers out of their way, swirled out on the field while the Dodgers were at batting practice to talk to the players or get their autographs on score cards or baseballs. This cut the batting practice down virtually to a bunting drill, for none of the Dodgers wanted to take a chance on hitting a line drive that might maim or kill one of the boys from home. Besides, the pitchers who were shagging flies were fenced in by the eager Brooklynites.

Fitzsimmons, who was standing just back of the box feeding baseballs to the pitcher, turned to find a fan, clutching a ball, at his elbow.

"Sign this for me, will you, Fitz?" the fan asked, holding out the ball and a fountain pen.

"Sure," Fitz said, obliging him. A few moments later the same fan had another ball to be autographed, and shortly thereafter, a third.

"Where are you getting all these balls from?" Fitz asked.

The fan grinned and pointed to the ball bag, almost at Fitz's feet.

"From there," he said.

"Hey!" Fitz yelled to the other Dodgers. "Hey! That's enough! This business is going too far!"

The Dodgers, eager to clinch the pennant as quickly as possible, attacked the Phils vigorously and won the first game. Leo, entering the clubhouse between games, found Ted McGrew, the scout, waiting for him. McGrew, a former umpire in whose judgment (strangely enough!) Leo had a great deal of confidence, said:

"Leo, do you know who I'd pitch in the second game?"

"Who?"

"Hamlin."

"Hamlin! Oh, no. Not Luke in a spot like this. I want to sew this pennant up as quick as I can, and Luke hasn't been going so good lately."

"He can beat these fellows," McGrew said.

Leo hesitated for a moment.

"Well," he said, "maybe you're right. I'll take a chance on him. But I know the guys won't like it."

They didn't either. They wanted somebody, almost anybody, but Hamlin. But Leo went through with it. Luke did all right until Danny Litwhiler hit one over the fence, and that was the ball game. Leo was furious. So were the rest of the Dodgers as they trudged into the clubhouse.

Dressing quickly, Leo met some friends and got into a cab with them to go downtown to dinner. He still burned over the defeat as they sat down at a table in a Chestnut Street restaurant, and, chancing to glance at a picture on the wall, he saw a photograph of Abraham Lincoln posing with a man he didn't recognize. Looking closer, he read the faded inscription:

"Mr. Lincoln with his Vice-President, Mr. Hannibal Hamlin."

"Hamlin!" he shrieked. "Hamlin! Jesus! They shot the wrong guy!"

Squabbles, fights, flare-ups in the clubhouse now and then. But now the Dodgers had the pennant in their grasp, and in Boston on September 25 they clinched it. Wyatt shut the Braves out. The Dodgers, winning 6 to 0, made a long-held dream come true.

MacPhail, in New York, tried to get Durocher on the telephone to congratulate him, but the only one he could reach was McDonald; he was incoherent in his joy. The Dodgers, hurriedly packing for the trip to New York, for their victory had been scored in the last game, were walloping each other and yelling wildly. The emotional Durocher, with the strain over at last, was almost in tears.

In the WOR studio in New York, Red Barber, taking the details of the game off the ticker, had relayed them to a frenzied populace. Then, thoughtlessly, he announced the time of the Dodgers' arrival at the Grand Central. He regretted it several hours later when, reaching the Grand Central for a spot broadcast of the reception for the players, he was almost torn apart by the delirious mob that surged and swirled through the station.

Meanwhile the Dodgers were having a wild ride home, with training rules off for the evening. Bulletins on their progress were flashed from Providence, New London, New Haven, Bridgeport, Stamford. MacPhail leaped into a cab and was driven to the One Hundred and Twenty-fifth Street station, the last stop out of Grand Central, to meet them. He waited impatiently on the station platform for the train. Now, locomotive headlight gleaming, it roared into the station—and roared on its way without even hesitating. Durocher, knowing there would be a crowd at Grand Central and that the fans would be disappointed if all their heroes didn't come up the ramp from the train, had asked that no stop be made at One Hundred and Twenty-fifth Street, fearing that if the train did stop there, some of the shyer athletes, wishing to duck the crowd, would get off and make the trip downtown in cabs.

MacPhail, sorely disappointed, the joyful noises he had been making suddenly turned to growls, went to the New Yorker Hotel, thus missing the shoving, mauling, hauling, deafening scene at Grand Central. As soon as Durocher could extricate himself, by the aid of a half dozen cops, from the grasp of the crowd, he went to the New Yorker, knowing he would find Larry there.

"Larry!" he cried, rushing into his suite. "Mitt me, boy! Mitt me! We're champions!"

And then he stopped short, for MacPhail, his jaw thrust out and his face colored with rage was glaring at him.

"Why, Larry," Leo asked. "What's the matter?"

"What's the matter? Did you tell them not to stop that train at One Hundred and Twenty-fifth Street?"

"Why, yes. I—"

He had no chance to explain.

"You're through!" Larry yelled. "You're fired!"

MacPhail stalked from the room. Durocher, hurt, bewildered, feeling worse, perhaps, than he ever had felt in his life—and this at the end of a day marked by his greatest triumph in baseball—sank into a chair. He still was there, staring dully out a window, when McDonald came in.

"Leo," John began, "I wondered if you wanted to have the players at the park in the morning. I thought I would tell them now and—"

Leo looked up at him and said wearily:

"Go see the manager of the club about it, whoever he is."

But the next morning, of course, everything was all right. MacPhail had got over his disappointment, and his anger had died away.

"I guess I was a little rough on you last night," he said. "I found out, later, why you gave orders not to have the train stop at One Hundred and Twenty-fifth Street. Well, the hell with it. Now let's concentrate on licking the Yankees."

Borough President John Cashmore proclaimed September 29 Dodger Day in Brooklyn. The feature of the day was a parade of sixty thousand with the Dodgers riding at the head of it, and, of course, MacPhail and Durocher at the head of the Dodgers. It was estimated by the police that a million persons, hugging the curbs or in the windows or on the rooftops of the houses along the line of march, cheered the heroes. Old-timers said it was Brooklyn's biggest parade since the Fourteenth Zouaves and the Twenty-third Regiment returned from the Civil War.

ONE HIT, ONE ERROR, ONE LEFT

from LOSE WITH A SMILE

by RING W. LARDNER

Clearwater, fla., march 3

Dear Jessie well kid here it is the 3 of march and I am still in the big league but kidding on the square things is beggin to look pretty rosey as mgr Carey has now got Casey Stengel rooming with me and I guest I all ready told you about Stengel he is a kind of asst mgr and coach of the club and kind of took me in toe the 1st day we beggin to work out and now mgr Carey has got him rooming with me so it looks like there takeing a special interest in how I get a long as Stengel sets and talks to me by the hr about the fine points and gives me pointers about the fine points of the game that comes up durn practice.

I guest that sounds pretty good hay kid on account of the promise I give you the day I left home so you better get ready to pack up the old bag and all a board for Brooklyn or maybe you better wait a wile as maybe I will run a cross some kid I like better. No danger hay kid.

Stengels name aint Casey but that is just a nick name witch he says they call him that because he come from Kansas City but that dont make sense but some of the boys has got nick names like wear they come from like 1 of the pitchers Clyde Day but they call him Pea ridge Day because he come from a town name Pea ridge and he was the champion hog caller of Arkansaw and when he use to pitch in Brooklyn last year he use to give a hog call after every ball he throwed but the club made him cut it out because the fans come down on the field every time he give a call and the club had to hire the champion of iowa to set up in the stand and call them back. Then there is a infielder Tommy Thompson but some times they call him Fresco and I thought it was because he come from Frisco but Stengel says his hole name is Al Fresco and his folks give him the name because he was born out doors like restrants where they got tables under a tree and 1 of the boys was asking if they call Wilson Hack because he was born in a hack but Stengel says it was 2 of them and they had to sell them to a junk dealer.

Wilson is the man who the Cubs had and 2 yrs ago he led both leagues in home runs but last yr he had a bad yr and they trade it him to St Louis for Grimes but the St Louis club found out that the Cubs had been paying him a salery so they give him to Brooklyn as the St. Louis players works on a commission base and what ever amt you get out of the world series the club leaves you keep it. Hack takes a good cut at the ball and if he meets them square it is no wonder they go for a ride as he ways as much as your piano but I can hit them just as far and maybe farther as I got more strenth in my rist but any ways we both hit right hand it and who plays center field depends on witch is socking them the hardest tho of course we will both be in there at the same time if any mgr is crazy enough to pitch a left hander. I says to Stengel last night I says to Stengel if any mgr is crazy enough to pitch a left hander again this club they would put them in a silium and Stengel says they are all ready there.

We was talking about nick names and Thompson says to me wear do you come from Warner and I says Centralia and Stengel says well we cant call him all that because he would be back a sleep before you was half threw and we all ready got a Jack Warner on the club so we better call this one bench but that was the night before last and last night we was out in front of the hotel and a couple of the boys beggin to sing and I joined in kind of soft and ever since then they dont call me nothing but Rudy on account of Rudy Valet and Thompson says if I could groon like you I would not be plain base ball and Stengel says he aint but any ways they all call me Rudy and keep asking me wear did I lern to groon.

Will close for this time kid as am all tarred out as they had me chason fly balls all day and not only that but mgr Carey makes all the boys go threw a case of calsthenics and part of it is wear you lay on your back and push your ft up in the air like you are rideing a bycycle and I says to Stengel what is the idea of that kind of practice because when we get to Brooklyn I hope to live some wear wear I wont have to ride a bycycle to the ball pk and even if I did I wouldent never get there laying on my back and pushing my ft up in the air. Any ways am all tarred out. . . .

Danny

Brooklyn april 15.

Dear Jessie well kid it took me a long wile to break in to this league and the past 3 days I beggin to think mgr Carey had forgot old Rudy and I ought to get my card print it and give him my card but he dident forget old Rudy this pm and I guest the Boston club won't forget me all season specialy there left hander Sherdel and I bet when we visit Boston next wk he will be lade up with the flu till wear safe out of town but dont supose you will see no paper so will tell you what I done. The past 3 days I beggin to think Carey had forgot my name and I was going to ask Stengel to tell him my name but Stengel act it like he had forgot me to but I wont be no secret after to-day. The game beggin like we would murder them and we seen all their pitchers in the 1st 4 innings and had them beat 7 to 1 and it looked like I might as well curl up and fall a sleep on the bench like I been doing but in the 7th innings our pitchers beggin to put on there own parade and when the 8th innings beggin the score was 7 and 7 and it was Jack Quinn again this here Sherdel and they both pitch like they was trying to kid somebody but they couldent no body kid them back and we went in to extra innings for the 1st time and come to the 14th innings with the score still 7 and 7 and a cinch they would call the game on account of darkness unlest some body broke it up and of corse this would be the time to have your fireball pitcher in there but the fires had all been put out.

Well old Jack had a tough break in the 14th and Odoul lose a fly ball and I dont blame him as it was to dark to see but anyways the Boston club got a run and it looked like we was threw and all of a sudden Lopez with 1 out hit for 2 bases and Quinn was up next and all of a sudden I herd Carey holler Rudy and I jumped out and grabbed a bat and Carey come up to me from the 1st base coachers box and says remember this guy is a left hander but he will try and slow ball you to death so dont over swing and just remember you are supose to hit left handers and they cant take him out because they aint got nobody left only judge Fuchs and the sun is set so you are back in Bloom-ington in the moon light league and I went up and the crowd cheered and Stengel was on the 3d base coach lines and he yelled come on Rudy your at home in a night club and Sherdel throwed a curve but it was so far inside that even the empire called it a ball.

Then he throwed a dink ball and did I give it a ride hay kid a ft hire and we could of both walked around but am glad it dident because it would have spoiled the show and it hit the fence in right center and Lopez run faster than he can and slid a cross the plate 5 ft a head of the throw and I was on second base with the score 8 and 8.

Well I herd Carey say wait a minit and I was scarred he was going to put some one on to run thinking I dont know nothing but he changed his mind and says go a head and Stengel hollered there just beggin to play out in Bloomington but I dident need no advice because you see kid there was only 1 out and if the man next hit a long fly what good was I on 2nd base and of corse Sherdel dident give me no start but I went any ways and there catcher was so surprise that he throwed a 2 base ball over there 3d base mans head and Stengel yelled stay up keep going like he thot I was libel to stop and talk things over with him and I slid a cross the plate but they dident even make a play and the crowd would of tore me to pieces if I hadent dove in to the bench and a way from them and I wisht you could have been in the club house and herd the noise.

It was Rudy this and Rudy that and Stengel says to Carey he says what did I tell you Max all you got to do is start the games after supper and Rudy will hit 500 and steal there bench and if we could only play a double header every night beggin at 8 we would break up this league by the middle of July and then Lopez says well you give me a run a round but it was worth it and Carey shook hands and says thats a boy I was going to pull you off 2nd base and put on a runner not because you aint fast but I wasent sure you had sense enough to make the play and I would rather seen you make that play than hit 60 home runs what you done today wont hurt how you stand with me and I says I thot you had forgot me and he says I wont forget you again but that dont mean I am going to use you regular but it does mean that I can stick you in there and know you aint going to doze off and Glenn Wright says I am glad I dident do it because I am the captain and they cant no body fire me only Max and the men that owns the club but you showed you can think and you will have a tough time getting off this club now because novelty is what the fans likes.

Then they all insist it I should groon but I says I was too tarred and I left the pk but late as it was they was a crowd hang out side waiting for I and Lopez and only for Stengel telling them to get the hell out of there and give these young fellas a chance to get

home and sleep we would of been shakeing hands the rest of the
night and Lopez left us and Stengel walked a long home with me
and I ast him to come up and see my rm and he says aint you
going to eat nothing and I says I forgot all about it and he says
that is what I thot when I seen you steal 3d base that you must
have been out of your head all day and go and eat some thing
and then write a letter to that little girl in Centralia because
you certainly got enough to tell her tonight and I says she dont
understand base ball. . . .

Well kid what do you think of me now and I will send yo' 1
what the Brooklyn and n y papers say in the am.

Danny

Boston april 23

Dear Jessie your letter come today witch was just in time for
me to get it here as we leave for home at midnight and play
the Giants tomorrow and dont you never worry kid about me
getting mad at you as I know that you all ways got my interest
at heart and never your self. I am sorry you been worring over
Stengels remarks but thot you would under stand that he was
just kidding as mgr Carey wouldent never stand for the boys
selling there seats on the bench because in the 1st place it is
again the rules for any body to set on the bench unlest you
are in a uniform for 1 thing and be sides that they aint enough
money in the world specialy this yr to make me forget my duty
to mgr Carey and the Brooklyn ball club.

I only got in 1 game here but that was enough to spoil the
day for the Boston club just like I done to them in Brooklyn
last wk and pretty near the same play. . . .

We was 1 run behind going in to the 8th innings and Carey
sent me up to hit for Clark with 1 out tho there pitcher was
a right hander named Seibold. He is an other 1 of these here
pitchers that cant hardly get the ball up to the plate and you
can count the seems on there fast ball and there curve beggins
to break before it leaves there hand. Well it was the same catcher
that throwed the ball a way when I stole 3d base in Brooklyn
and he says well busher I hope you hit for 2 bases and I will dare

you to steal 3d base and I says well you will proudly get your hope as it dont look like a man could hit for lest then 2 bases again this kind of pitching.

So he says I bet he strikes you out and I says that will tie up the game as you will drop the 3d strike and throw the ball over the right field stand. You see I was rideing him for the crazy throw he made in Brooklyn. Well Seibold throwed a round house curve and I was going to leave it go by and then change my mind and kind of half struck at it and hit it and the ball went over Maranvilles head and him and Bergert either I should of catch it in there cap but they both lose it and I come into second base standing up. Maranville was sore as hell and I says what is the matter is they to much day light and he called me some more names. . . .

He says are you going to steal 3d base and I says no I never pull the same play twict and he says all right I wont try and hole you up so he walked a way and I led off a few ft and all of a sudden Seibold turned and throwed and there short stop had snuck up behind me and he had me but drop the ball. Well I thot Maranville would go crazy and Stengel yelled watch your self Rudy and I says dont worry and then Seibold throwed again but I was standing on the bag. Then Seibold got ready to pitch and some thing told me he was going to pitch and I just went and I dont know if I would of been out or not but there 3d base man made it sure by dropping the ball and Stengel turned a summer salt and I looked at Maranville and he was lane on the ground kicking his ft in the air. You ought to seen Carey and the boys on our bench and Frederick come threw with a fly ball so far out that I was a cross the plate before it was back in the infield and in the 9th innings Wilson and Wright got in a couple of real socks and we win the game 6 and 4.

Well I dident have no chance to get in there today but we beat them and they still kept on trying to ride me and Maranville made faces at me on the bench but all I done was waggle my thumbs in my ears and holler rabbit at him and sqeek at him like I was a rabbit. . . .

Danny

Dear Jessie I got the both of your letters warming me to not sell my seat on the bench and you are a great kid worring your head off about me and pretty soon I will get mad at you for worring about me doing some thing out of the way.

Stengel was right about the crowd yesterday and it was the biggest crowd that ever seen a game in Brooklyn and it was Hubbell again Dazzy but all I side it so they was no chance for me to get in there. But I seen what this guy calls his screw ball witch is just like a nuggle ball or any of them other fancy names and I been in this league now for 2 wks and the only pitcher I seen so far that throws a fire ball and a curve ball and a change of paste is Dazzy and that dont do me no good as he is on our club. Today it was another nuggler a right hander name Fitzsimmons and he beat us and tomorrow it will be Walker who is left handed it and maybe they will be a spot for me.

Well kid I know you dont like for me to call my self Rudy but that is what the boys calls me and never seem to get enough hearing me groon but the other day in the club house up in Boston they ast me for a song and I says I am a shame to keep sing the same old songs over and over and Stengel says dont worry about that because the way you sing them they dont sound like nothing anybody ever herd before. Then Carey says your name sake writes his own songs meaning Rudy Valet and why dont you write 1 your self and I says I might write the words but how about the music and Carey says just fix up some words for music you all ready know and Stengel says why dont you write life is just a bold of cherrys only make it some other fruit or even a vegetable. So Carey says life is just a game of base ball would be a good title and you all ready got the tune and Stengel says but dont make it Brooklyn base ball unlest you want a torch song.

Well kid I dident say nothing but I went up in my rm after supper that night and set down with a pencil and paper and went to work and I had to keep groon the music over to my self so as I could make up words to fit it and after a wile when Stengel come in I had it all wrote out and read it out loud to him and he says it was great but you only got the chorus and you ought to write a verse and then you will have a song hit and I says I never herd the verse and he says that dont matter as it is just the same like any other verse and cant help from fitting.

So he promise to keep a secret till I had the hole song fix up and today I sprang it on the boys in the club house and I had to just read the verse out loud as I don't know the tune but I grooned the chorus and the boys went wild and pet it me on the back and they all want it a copy. But Carey says wait till you see a publisher and get the copy rights as some of the boys will try and beat you to it so the day after tomorrow we got a day off before we go to Phila and I am going over to New York and see witch publisher will offer me the most money and wont it be funny if I turn in to a song writer as I never thot of writeing them only groon them. Well kid I know you wont cheat me so will write out the hole song and see what you think of it and will start with the verse.

> Some people take life serious
> in stead of a game to play
> If they would only not take it so serious
> But more like a game to play.
> I try and laugh at the hard knocks
> like you get in a base ball game
> so wether your with St. Louis or the red Sox
> smile and dont be a shame.

Then comes the chorus.

> Life is just a game of base ball
> If you get in it
> you want to win it
> But some times the mgr dont give you a chance
> But leave you setting there on the bench.
> Just give me a left handers fast ball
> and I will sock it a mile

And if the empire calls it a foul
laugh and dont say your blind as a owl
Life is just a game of base ball
So win or lose with a smile.

I know you know the tune to the chorus and last night I
was down to Frank Earls apt and his wife played it as good as
she can and she says there is a couple spots where it dont come
out even but Frank says the publishers will tend to that and he
says he wisht he could do some thing like write a song hit be
sides just pitch a base ball. So I will let you know how I come
out with the publishers but I dont see how I can mist and
maybe it means that I can make more money off writeing songs
than plain base ball and you know kid what that means.

Danny

Chi may 8.

Dear Jessie well kid that is surely good news and will be
tickled to death to see you and your father and will try and see
that you have a good time. I am going to pay your expenses kid
you and your father both wether you like it or not as I know
I can ford it better than you. I will stick to my promise and
not make you meet mgr Carey and Stengel tho they wouldent
never notice how you look and you all ways look good to me.
You wont upset no plans as I havent made no plans and you
wont only have to meet 1 person out side of me and that is
Frank Earls wifes sister but she is just a girl about your own
age and you wont care how you look in front of her.

I think I told you about Frank as him and his wife live in
the same bldg with me in Brooklyn and I been down to there
apt a couple times to supper and his wife plays the piano or
trys to and I groon a few songs for them. He is a young pitcher
and still with the club but not on this trip and I guest mgr
Carey will send him to the Jersey City club witch our club has
just boughten as a farm. Well any ways his wife come from St
Louis and her kid sister lives there yet and I give my wd that I
would look her up and treat her to lunch and take her to the

ball game and Mrs. Earl wired her what day would be best and she wired back Tuesday so the 4 of us will have lunch and maybe she will set with you at the ball pk but you wont mind that and after words we can shake her off. As for wear will I meet you I will be down to the station when your train gets there and it don't make no difference if its early or not. . . .

Well kid I wrote the lyrics to the Dad song chorus on the train comeing out here and Stengel help me with them and he says I have got to end up with the wd Pop to make it the opp of Mom but I like Dad better my self and maybe will change it.

Well here is the chorus.

> My dad I love him.
> My mom she loves him.
> My sister Edna she loves him my dad.
> He is a wonder
> Will live to be a hundred
> And never made a blunder my dad.
> When I was a lad
> If I act it bad mom would scold me.
> Then I would go to him
> And on his lower limbs he would hold me.
> Theys no one greater
> Then my old pater.
> He is my alma mater my pop.

Stengel made me put Ednas name in and told me about alma mater but he says the line about never made a blunder dont ring true. Alma mater and pater are greek and means the same thing. . . .

Danny

Brooklyn june 15

Dear Jessie well kid here I am threw and don't know yet if I am comeing home or stay in n y and groon songs for the radio people and wont know for a wk as the man I got to see is out of town. Who ever wrote that song knowed more than I did but

I will fool him and Carey and Stengel and the rest of them by not shown up at no Jersey City or no other miner league. . . .

When I went in the club house yesterday some of the boys was dressing and Carey was there and he called me over in a corner and set down. He says well Rudy tomorrow is the limb it wear we got to cut down to 23 men and I am going to send you over to Jersey City. Well I was so choke up that I couldent say nothing back. He says you will have a chance to get in the game every day regular and that is what you need is be in there every day under a good mgr and lern the things that you cant lern only by plain every day. I says I could play here every day if you say the wd but he says no I cant bench none of my outfield and be sides you make to many mistakes. . . .

He says if you hanent kind of act it like your mind was logey the last couple wks I might keep you in place of 1 of the other boys but I think you need every day work to be at your best and may be next yr I will be able to start you every time they pitch a left hander again us. So I says what if I dont want to go to Jersey City. He says that will be an other of your mistakes and the biggest 1 you made yet. I says what if I dont dress this pm and he says I dont care if you dress or not and I dont care if I see you again till you get out of your present state a mind. He says I am giveing you a chance and you better take it. I says yes you surly are giveing me a fine chance and I walked out of the club house and dident even stay and watch the dam game. I come right here to my rm and laid down on the bed and cride like I was a baby or some thing. It wouldent be so bad kid if I hadent thot Carey and Stengel and the rest of the boys was my friend but I guest I got no friends around here. . . .

I was still lain here at 9 a clock tonight when the door rapt and I dident pay no tension and Stengel walked in like it was his own home. He says well Rudy your 1 of the lucky boys. I dident anser him and he says Caldwell goes to Hartford and Max had to sell Richards right out but you go to Jersey City wear he can call you back and you will have a pal Tommy Thompson a long with you. I says I dont want to be no place wear Max can call me back after what him and you done. Stengel says well may be I can fix it so as he can send Richards to Jersey and sell you right out. Then if you look good why you will proudly land with the red sox wear all men is free and eagle and some even worst. You ought to play your best base ball for them because when you feel like running from 1 base to an other you wont never fine no class mates all ready there.

I says did Carey get wafers from the Giants. Stengel says they offered him some but he dont like wafers but the Giants is full up and McGraw cant even use you in the office because he dont dictate musicle notes. I says I am threw with base ball and you can tell Carey that when you see him. Stengel says I wont have to tell him as he has thot that way for 2 or 3 wks. He says what are you going to do and I says I dont know yet so Stengel says well I will tell you. Your going to get your last check tomorrow and then your going to take that southren eye sore over to n y and both of you get lit up and bat a round till your moneys all shot and then you wont need to go to Jersey City because they all ready got there coda of bums. I says may be that is just what I will do is like you say.

Then Stengel says what is the name of that little girl in Centralia and I says what of it. He says well you dont have to tell me her name because its Jessie Graham but whats her dress and I says just Centralia and he says in a town wear they can have a half a million dollar fire they must have a street. But any ways why dont you wire and ask her to come east and see Jersey City and may be go threw with that business witch I ast you to call off last spring. I says she aint libel to want me now that Brooklyn says I aint good enough and Stengel says she is just the kind of a girl that would want you all the more and what ain't good enough for Brooklyn is good enough for any body. And he says be sides that they feel different about there young ball players been married in Jersey City. I says well I aint going to no Jersey City and I aint going to ask her to marry a man that cant hole a big league job and she aint got no money to come east. . . .

Well dear you see I aint no good after all and the people who I thot they was friends is turn out different. I dont care what the base ball world thinks about me as I am threw with the game but am sorry on your a count as you thot I would make good and I have felt down on the job and aint no good after all.

Good by dear and may be will see you in 10 days or may be never but will all ways feel tords you like I all ways done and only wisht I had some thing to offer but cant offer you nothing now only my love.

Danny

Centralia, Ill. June 15.

Dearest Danny—Well dear I wrote to you yesterday and here I am writing to you again today, but this time I have got some news to write and I only hope it wont be bad news to you as that would make it bad news for me.

I read in the paper today that you are going to be with the Jersey City nine where you can be one of the regular fielder men and play every day and I know that you will like that better than not being active all the time. Well Danny it just happens that Jersey City has always been one of my favorite towns because papa has talked about it so much and what an interesting town it is there on the river seeing the big boats come in and go out. Dear it makes me blush to write this kind of a letter, but I am writing it just the same and taking a chance that you wont hate me for it.

Well Danny papa got some money from some one who owed him it and he asked me if I wanted to take a trip and I said yes and he said he wished that I would go to Jersey City where his step brother lives and where he paid him such a pleasant visit once.

Well dear I am coming and will arrive at the Penn station at 9:40 in New York Saturday morning and please meet me as I will be scared to death if you dont. If you still feel like you felt last winter and spring, well dear this is leap year. So goodbye till Saturday morning and don't fail me dear.

Yours,

Jessie.

Reprinted from Lose with a Smile *by Ring Lardner; copyright 1933 by Charles Scribner's Sons; used by permission of the publishers.*

Ships, Bridges, Trolleys, and Subways

ITS ISLAND POSITION has always been somewhat of a problem to Brooklyn. Fortune made its neighbor, Manhattan, the place that Brooklyn people had to go to, and once they got a bridge in, Manhattan people started coming to Brooklyn to live, and the problem became how to get around Brooklyn. "It is," one man said, "a very problematical place to live in."

The history of transportation in Brooklyn has been one damn thing after another. In the early days the problems were to get across East River to New York and to get by stage to other parts of Long Island; as time went on there was a third added: that of getting around the borough itself.

There have been rowboats, sailboats, horse-powered boats, steamboats, bridges, tunnels, stages, horsecars, electric street-cars, buses, steam-powered elevated trains, electric elevated trains, subways, bicycles, taxicabs, and private automobiles.

And it has been one long fight. New York got the first ferry "corporation," and for years Brooklyn fought it. The fight was not only over finance, control, and timetables, it also went into definitions of high and low water and of made land. For years after Robert Fulton had built his steam ferries it was still more economical to use those where horses, walking on treadmills, turned the paddle wheels.

Brooklyn Bridge was originally financed by private corporations, which were taken over by the municipalities when they ran out of money. The subway systems were the reverse. The cities built them; some transportation companies got them, and then the city eventually got them back. The streetcar lines spent about as much money on bribery as on track, and for years caused horror in the town. The Dodgers were called originally the Trolley Dodgers because even New Yorkers were amazed at the foolhardiness of people of Brooklyn going out of doors where the things careened along. Syrett tells of a restaurant keeper in Yellowstone Park who would tell his guests that he didn't leave Brooklyn until after the trolleys had killed off all his family. Syrett also found this poem about the old steam elevateds:

> When the evening shades are falling,
> Or the morning sun is high
> Comes a hot and blazing cinder
> Straight into your upcast eye.
>
> When your sweetheart shopward wanders,
> Mingling deep in fashion's stream,
> Overhead the fireman ponders
> And lets off a cloud of steam.
>
> Then the jovial iron worker,
> While your fears you fondly lull,
> Swiftly drops a ton of metal
> Down upon your hapless skull.

Up above are myriad dangers,
Underneath a helpless crowd;
Everywhere, both friends and strangers
By monopoly are cowed.

Blinded visions, ruined dresses,
Broken heads and thoughts of—well,
Are among the mad distresses
Wrought upon the Brooklyn "L."

But we must have rapid transit
In this town at any cost.
Take a walk—but if you chance it
Count yourself among the lost.

The borough, a series of towns and real-estate developments, all built according to varying exigencies and theories, looks as though it were laid out by an idiot. Lewis Mumford in a chapter called "The Insensate Industrial Town" in his Culture of Cities mentions Brooklyn: "The indifference to geographical contours in the application of the formal gridiron to the land surface, was nothing short of sublime: the engineer's streets often swept through swamps, embraced dump-heaps, accepted piles of slag and waste, climbed cliffs, and ended up a quarter of a mile beyond the low water mark of the waterfront."

We like a description in a guidebook of 1871: bounded ". . . on the north by Newtown Creek; on the south by the towns of New Lots, Flatbush, and New Utrecht; on the east by the Kings County line; and on the west by the East River and the Bay of New York. Precise as all this may seem, we challenge anyone to keep any sort of track of the points of the compass while travelling the streets of the city, for with the exception of Boston, there is no American city whose streets so bid defiance to the rules of regularity. . . . It is deemed worth mentioning, as a caution to strangers, who receive frequent directions impossible to follow except on wings."

If you ask a traffic cop in this borough how to get to a certain

*spot, he won't tell you. He'll just let you know whether you
are headed in the right direction.*

The following pages from Theodore Dreiser's Sister Carrie
tell of the bitter Brooklyn transit strike of 1895. The men, who
were demanding $1.50 to $2.25 for a ten-hour day, lost the
strike. Hurstwood, whose adventures are told, was the second of
Carrie's men, and in the book he eventually goes to pieces, becoming a Bowery bum, while Carrie reaches success in the
theater.

THE STRIKE

from SISTER CARRIE

by THEODORE DREISER

The barn at which Hurstwood applied was exceedingly
short-handed, and was being operated practically by three men
as directors. There were a lot of green hands around—queer,
hungry-looking men, who looked as if want had driven them to
desperate means. They tried to be lively and willing, but there
was an air of hang-dog diffidence about the place.

Hurstwood went back through the barns and out into a large,
enclosed lot, where were a series of tracks and loops. A half-
dozen cars were there, manned by instructors, each with a pupil
at the lever. More pupils were waiting at one of the rear doors
of the barn.

In silence Hurstwood viewed this scene, and waited. His companions took his eye for a while, though they did not interest
him much more than the cars. They were an uncomfortable-
looking gang, however. One or two were very thin and lean.
Several were quite stout. Several others were rawboned and sal-
low, as if they had been beaten upon by all sorts of rough
weather.

"Did you see by the paper they are going to call out the
militia?" Hurstwood heard one of them remark.

"Oh, they'll do that," returned the other. "They always do."

"Think we're liable to have much trouble?" said another, whom Hurstwood did not see.

"Not very."

"That Scotchman that went out on the last car," put in a voice, "told me that they hit him in the ear with a cinder."

A small, nervous laugh accompanied this.

"One of those fellows on the Fifth Avenue line must have had a hell of a time, according to the papers," drawled another. "They broke his car windows and pulled him off into the street 'fore the police could stop 'em."

"Yes; but there are more police around to-day," was added by another.

Hurstwood hearkened without much mental comment. These talkers seemed scared to him. Their gabbling was feverish—things said to quiet their own minds. He looked out into the yard and waited.

Two of the men got around quite near him, but behind his back. They were rather social, and he listened to what they said.

"Are you a railroad man?" said one.

"Me? No. I've always worked in a paper factory."

"I had a job in Newark until last October," returned the other, with reciprocal feeling.

There were some words which passed too low to hear. Then the conversation became strong again.

"I don't blame these fellers for striking," said one. "They've got the right of it, all right, but I had to get something to do."

"Same here," said the other. "If I had any job in Newark I wouldn't be over here takin' chances like these."

"It's hell these days, ain't it?" said the man. "A poor man ain't nowhere. You could starve, by God, right in the streets, and there ain't most no one would help you."

"Right you are," said the other. "The job I had I lost 'cause they shut down. They run all summer and lay up a big stock, and then shut down."

Hurstwood paid some little attention to this. Somehow, he felt a little superior to these two—a little better off. To him these were ignorant and commonplace, poor sheep in a driver's hand.

"Poor devils," he thought, speaking out of the thoughts and feelings of a bygone period of success.

"Next," said one of the instructors.

"You're next," said a neighbour, touching him.

He went out and climbed on the platform. The instructor took it for granted that no preliminaries were needed.

"You see this handle," he said, reaching up to an electric cut-off, which was fastened to the roof. "This throws the current off or on. If you want to reverse the car you turn it over here. If you want to send it forward, you put it over here. If you want to cut off the power, you keep it in the middle."

Hurstwood smiled at the simple information.

"Now, this handle here regulates your speed. To here," he said, pointing with his finger, "gives you about four miles an hour. This is eight. When it's full on, you make about fourteen miles an hour."

Hurstwood watched him calmly. He had seen motormen work before. He knew just about how they did it, and was sure he could do as well, with a very little practice.

The instructor explained a few more details, and then said: "Now, we'll back her up."

Hurstwood stood placidly by, while the car rolled back into the yard.

"One thing you want to be careful about, and that is to start easy. Give one degree time to act before you start another. The one fault of most men is that they always want to throw her wide open. That's bad. It's dangerous, too. Wears out the motor. You don't want to do that."

"I see," said Hurstwood.

He waited and waited, while the man talked on.

"Now you take it," he said, finally.

The ex-manager laid hand to the lever and pushed it gently, as he thought. It worked much easier than he imagined, however, with the result that the car jerked quickly forward, throwing him back against the door. He straightened up sheepishly, while the instructor stopped the car with the brake.

"You want to be careful about that," was all he said.

Hurstwood found, however, that handling a brake and regulating speed were not so instantly mastered as he had imagined. Once or twice he would have ploughed through the rear fence if it had not been for the hand and word of his companion. The latter was rather patient with him, but he never smiled.

"You've got to get the knack of working both arms at once," he said. "It takes a little practice."

One o'clock came while he was still on the car practising, and he began to feel hungry. The day set in snowing, and he was cold. He grew weary of running to and fro on the short track.

They ran the car to the end and both got off. Hurstwood went into the barn and sought a car step, pulling out his paper-wrapped lunch from his pocket. There was no water and the bread was dry, but he enjoyed it. There was no ceremony about dining. He swallowed and looked about, contemplating the dull, homely labour of the thing. It was disagreeable—miserably disagreeable—in all its phases. Not because it was bitter, but because it was hard. It would be hard to say one, he thought.

After eating, he stood about as before, waiting until his turn came.

The intention was to give him an afternoon of practice, but the greater part of the time was spent in waiting about.

At last evening came, and with it hunger and a debate with himself as to how he should spend the night. It was half-past five. He must soon eat. If he tried to go home, it would take him two hours and a half of cold walking and riding. Besides, he had orders to report at seven the next morning, and going home would necessitate his rising at an unholy and disagreeable hour. He had only something like a dollar and fifteen cents of Carrie's money, with which he had intended to pay the two weeks' coal bill before the present idea struck him.

"They must have some place around here," he thought. "Where does that fellow from Newark stay?"

Finally he decided to ask. There was a young fellow standing near one of the doors in the cold, waiting a last turn. He was a mere boy in years—twenty-one about—but with a body lank and long, because of privation. A little good living would have made this youth plump and swaggering.

"How do they arrange this, if a man hasn't any money?" inquired Hurstwood, discreetly.

The fellow turned a keen, watchful face on the inquirer.

"You mean eat?" he replied.

"Yes, and sleep. I can't go back to New York to-night."

"The foreman'll fix that if you ask him, I guess. He did me."

"That so?"

"Yes. I just told him I didn't have anything. Gee, I couldn't go home. I live way over in Hoboken."

Hurstwood only cleared his throat by way of acknowledgment.

"They've got a place upstairs here, I understand. I don't know what sort of a thing it is. Purty tough, I guess. He gave me a meal ticket this noon. I know that wasn't much."

Hurstwood smiled grimly, and the boy laughed.

"It ain't no fun, is it?" he inquired, wishing vainly for a cheery reply.

"Not much," answered Hurstwood.

"I'd tackle him now," volunteered the youth. "He may go 'way."

Hurstwood did so.

"Isn't there some place I can stay around here to-night?" he inquired. "If I have to go back to New York, I'm afraid I won't——"

"There're some cots upstairs," interrupted the man, "if you want one of them."

"That'll do," he assented.

He meant to ask for a meal ticket, but the seemingly proper moment never came, and he decided to pay himself that night.

"I'll ask him in the morning."

He ate in a cheap restaurant in the vicinity, and being cold and lonely, went straight off to seek the loft in question. The company was not attempting to run cars after nightfall. It was so advised by the police.

The room seemed to have been a lounging place for night workers. There were some nine cots in the place, two or three wooden chairs, a soap box, and a small, round-bellied stove, in which a fire was blazing. Early as he was, another man was there before him. The latter was sitting beside the stove warming his hands.

Hurstwood approached and held out his own toward the fire. He was sick of the bareness and privation of all things connected with his venture, but was steeling himself to hold out. He fancied he could for a while.

"Cold, isn't it?" said the early guest.

"Rather."

A long silence.

"Not much of a place to sleep in, is it?" said the man.

"Better than nothing," replied Hurstwood.

Another silence.

"I believe I'll turn in," said the man.

Rising, he went to one of the cots and stretched himself, removing only his shoes, and pulling the one blanket and dirty old comforter over him in a sort of bundle. The sight disgusted Hurstwood, but he did not dwell on it, choosing to gaze into the stove and think of something else. Presently he decided to retire, and picked a cot, also removing his shoes.

While he was doing so, the youth who had advised him to come here entered, and, seeing Hurstwood, tried to be genial.

"Better'n nothin'," he observed, looking around.

Hurstwood did not take this to himself. He thought it to be an expression of individual satisfaction, and so did not answer. The youth imagined he was out of sorts, and set to whistling softly. Seeing another man asleep, he quit that and lapsed into silence.

Hurstwood made the best of a bad lot by keeping on his clothes and pushing away the dirty covering from his head, but at last he dozed in sheer weariness. The covering became more and more comfortable, its character was forgotten, and he pulled it about his neck and slept.

In the morning he was aroused out of a pleasant dream by several men stirring about in the cold, cheerless room. He had been back in Chicago in fancy, in his own comfortable home. Jessica had been arranging to go somewhere, and he had been talking with her about it. This was so clear in his mind, that he was startled now by the contrast of this room. He raised his head, and the cold, bitter reality jarred him into wakefulness.

"Guess I'd better get up," he said.

There was no water on this floor. He put on his shoes in the cold and stood up, shaking himself in his stiffness. His clothes felt disagreeable, his hair bad.

"Hell!" he muttered, as he put on his hat.

Downstairs things were stirring again.

He found a hydrant, with a trough which had once been used for horses, but there was no towel here, and his handkerchief was soiled from yesterday. He contented himself with wetting his eyes with the ice-cold water. Then he sought the foreman, who was already on the ground.

"Had your breakfast yet?" inquired that worthy.

"No," said Hurstwood.

"Better get it, then; your car won't be ready for a little while."

Hurstwood hesitated.

"Could you let me have a meal ticket?" he asked with an effort.

"Here you are," said the man, handing him one.

He breakfasted as poorly as the night before on some fried steak and bad coffee. Then he went back.

"Here," said the foreman, motioning him, when he came in. "You take this car out in a few minutes."

Hurstwood climbed up on the platform in the gloomy barn and waited for a signal. He was nervous, and yet the thing was a relief. Anything was better than the barn.

On this the fourth day of the strike, the situation had taken a turn for the worse. The strikers, following the counsel of their leaders and the newspapers, had struggled peaceably enough. There had been no great violence done. Cars had been stopped, it is true, and the men argued with. Some crews had been won over and led away, some windows broken, some jeering and yelling done; but in no more than five or six instances had men been seriously injured. These by crowds whose acts the leaders disclaimed.

Idleness, however, and the sight of the company, backed by the police, triumphing, angered the men. They saw that each day more cars were going on, each day more declarations were being made by the company officials that the effective opposition of the strikers was broken. This put desperate thoughts in the minds of the men. Peaceful methods meant, they saw, that the companies would soon run all their cars and those who had complained would be forgotten. There was nothing so helpful to the companies as peaceful methods.

All at once they blazed forth, and for a week there was storm and stress. Cars were assailed, men attacked, policemen struggled with, tracks torn up, and shots fired, until at last street fights and mob movements became frequent, and the city was invested with militia.

Hurstwood knew nothing of the change of temper.

"Run your car out," called the foreman, waving a vigorous hand at him. A green conductor jumped up behind and rang the bell twice as a signal to start. Hurstwood turned the lever and ran the car out through the door into the street in front of the barn. Here two brawny policemen got up beside him on the platform—one on either hand.

At the sound of a gong near the barn door, two bells were given by the conductor and Hurstwood opened his lever.

The two policemen looked about them calmly.

"'Tis cold, all right, this morning," said the one on the left, who possessed a rich brogue.

"I had enough of it yesterday," said the other. "I wouldn't want a steady job of this."

"Nor I."

Neither paid the slightest attention to Hurstwood, who stood facing the cold wind, which was chilling him completely, and thinking of his orders.

"Keep a steady gait," the foreman had said. "Don't stop for any one who doesn't look like a real passenger. Whatever you do, don't stop for a crowd."

The two officers kept silent for a few moments.

"The last man must have gone through all right," said the officer on the left. "I don't see his car anywhere."

"Who's on there?" asked the second officer, referring, of course, to its complement of policemen.

"Schaeffer and Ryan."

There was another silence, in which the car ran smoothly along. There were not so many houses along this part of the way. Hurstwood did not see many people either. The situation was not wholly disagreeable to him. If he were not so cold, he thought he would do well enough.

He was brought out of this feeling by the sudden appearance of a curve ahead, which he had not expected. He shut off the current and did an energetic turn at the brake, but not in time to avoid an unnaturally quick turn. It shook him up and made him feel like making some apologetic remarks, but he refrained.

"You want to look out for them things," said the officer on the left, condescendingly.

"That's right," agreed Hurstwood, shamefacedly.

"There's lots of them on this line," said the officer on the right.

Around the corner a more populated way appeared. One or two pedestrians were in view ahead. A boy coming out of a gate with a tin milk bucket gave Hurstwood his first objectionable greeting.

"Scab!" he yelled. "Scab!"

Hurstwood heard it, but tried to make no comment, even to himself. He knew he would get that, and much more of the same sort probably.

At a corner farther up a man stood by the track and signalled the car to stop.

"Never mind him," said one of the officers, "He's up to some game."

Hurstwood obeyed. At the corner he saw the wisdom of it. No sooner did the man perceive the intention to ignore him, than he shook his fist.

"Ah, you bloody coward!" he yelled.

Some half dozen men, standing on the corner, flung taunts and jeers after the speeding car.

Hurstwood winced the least bit. The real thing was slightly worse than the thoughts of it had been.

Now came in sight, three or four blocks farther on, a heap of something on the track.

"They've been at work, here, all right," said one of the policemen.

"We'll have an argument, maybe," said the other.

Hurstwood ran the car close and stopped. He had not done so wholly, however, before a crowd gathered about. It was composed of ex-motormen and conductors in part, with a sprinkling of friends and sympathisers.

"Come off the car, pardner," said one of the men in a voice meant to be conciliatory. "You don't want to take the bread out of another man's mouth, do you?"

Hurstwood held to his brake and lever, pale and very uncertain what to do.

"Stand back," yelled one of the officers, leaning over the platform railing. "Clear out of this, now. Give the man a chance to do his work."

"Listen, pardner," said the leader, ignoring the policeman and addressing Hurstwood. "We're all working men, like yourself. If you were a regular motorman, and had been treated as we've been, you wouldn't want any one to come in and take your place, would you? You wouldn't want any one to do you out of your chance to get your rights, would you?"

"Shut her off! shut her off!" urged the other of the policemen, roughly. "Get out of this, now," and he jumped the railing and landed before the crowd and began shoving. Instantly the other officer was down beside him.

"Stand back, now," they yelled. "Get out of this. What the hell do you mean? Out, now."

It was like a small swarm of bees.

"Don't shove me," said one of the strikers, determinedly. "I'm not doing anything."

"Get out of this!" cried the officer, swinging his club. "I'll give ye a bat on the sconce. Back, now."

"What the hell!" cried another of the strikers, pushing the other way, adding at the same time some lusty oaths.

Crack came an officer's club on his forehead. He blinked his eyes blindly a few times, wabbled on his legs, threw up his hands, and staggered back. In return, a swift fist landed on the officer's neck.

Infuriated by this, the latter plunged left and right, laying about madly with his club. He was ably assisted by his brother of the blue, who poured ponderous oaths upon the troubled waters. No severe damage was done, owing to the agility of the strikers in keeping out of reach. They stood about the sidewalk now and jeered.

"Where is the conductor?" yelled one of the officers, getting his eye on that individual, who had come nervously forward to stand by Hurstwood. The latter had stood gazing upon the scene with more astonishment than fear.

"Why don't you come down here and get these stones off the track?" inquired the officer. "What you standing there for? Do you want to stay here all day? Get down."

Hurstwood breathed heavily in excitement and jumped down with the nervous conductor as if he had been called.

"Hurry up, now," said the other policeman.

Cold as it was, these officers were hot and mad. Hurstwood worked with the conductor, lifting stone after stone and warming himself by the work.

"Ah, you scab, you!" yelled the crowd. "You coward! Steal a man's job, will you? Rob the poor, will you, you thief? We'll get you yet, now. Wait."

Not all of this was delivered by one man. It came from here and there, incorporated with much more of the same sort and curses.

"Work, you blackguards," yelled a voice. "Do the dirty work. You're the suckers that keep the poor people down!"

"May God starve ye yet," yelled an old Irish woman, who now threw open a nearby window and stuck out her head.

"Yes, and you," she added, catching the eye of one of the policemen. "You bloody, murtherin' thafe! Crack my son over the head, will you, you hard-hearted, murtherin' divil? Ah, ye——"

But the officer turned a deaf ear.

"Go to the devil, you old hag," he half muttered as he stared round upon the scattered company.

Now the stones were off, and Hurstwood took his place again amid a continued chorus of epithets. Both officers got up beside him and the conductor rang the bell, when, bang! bang! through window and door came rocks and stones. One narrowly grazed Hurstwood's head. Another shattered the window behind.

"Throw open your lever," yelled one of the officers, grabbing at the handle himself.

Hurstwood complied and the car shot away, followed by a rattle of stones and a rain of curses.

"That — — — —— hit me in the neck," said one of the officers. "I gave him a good crack for it, though."

"I think I must have left spots on some of them," said the other.

"I know that big guy that called us a — — — ——," said the first. "I'll get him yet for that."

"I thought we were in for it sure, once there," said the second.

Hurstwood, warmed and excited, gazed steadily ahead. It was an astonishing experience for him. He had read of these things, but the reality seemed something altogether new. He was no coward in spirit. The fact that he had suffered this much now rather operated to arouse a stolid determination to stick it out. He did not recur in thought to New York or the flat. This one trip seemed a consuming thing.

They now ran into the business heart of Brooklyn uninterrupted. People gazed at the broken windows of the car and at Hurstwood in his plain clothes. Voices called "scab" now and then, as well as other epithets, but no crowd attacked the car. At the downtown end of the line, one of the officers went to call up his station and report the trouble.

"There's a gang out there," he said, "laying for us yet. Better send some one over there and clean them out."

The car ran back more quietly—hooted, watched, flung at, but not attacked. Hurstwood breathed freely when he saw the barns.

"Well," he observed to himself, "I came out of that all right."

The car was turned in and he was allowed to loaf a while, but later he was again called. This time a new team of officers was aboard. Slightly more confident, he sped the car along the commonplace streets and felt somewhat less fearful. On one side, however, he suffered intensely. The day was raw, with a sprinkling of snow and a gusty wind, made all the more intolerable by the speed of the car. His clothing was not intended for this sort of work. He shivered, stamped his feet, and beat his arms as he had seen other motormen do in the past, but said nothing. The novelty and danger of the situation modified in a way his disgust and distress at being compelled to be here, but not enough to prevent him from feeling grim and sour. This was a dog's life, he thought. It was a tough thing to have to come to.

The one thought that strengthened him was the insult offered by Carrie. He was not down so low as to take all that, he thought. He could do something—this, even—for a while. It would get better. He would save a little.

A boy threw a clod of mud while he was thus reflecting and hit him upon the arm. It hurt sharply and angered him more than he had been any time since morning.

"The little cur!" he muttered.

"Hurt you?" asked one of the policemen.

"No," he answered.

At one of the corners, where the car slowed up because of a turn, an ex-motorman, standing on the sidewalk, called to him:

"Won't you come out, pardner, and be a man? Remember we're fighting for decent day's wages, that's all. We've got families to support." The man seemed most peaceably inclined.

Hurstwood pretended not to see him. He kept his eyes straight on before and opened the lever wide. The voice had something appealing in it.

All morning this went on and long into the afternoon. He made three such trips. The dinner he had was no stay for such work and the cold was telling on him. At each end of the line he stopped to thaw out, but he could have groaned at the anguish of it. One of the barnmen, out of pity, loaned him a heavy cap and a pair of sheepskin gloves, and for once he was extremely thankful.

On the second trip of the afternoon he ran into a crowd about half way along the line, that had blocked the car's progress with an old telegraph pole.

"Get that thing off the track," shouted the two policemen.

"Yah, yah, yah!" yelled the crowd. "Get it off yourself."

The two policemen got down and Hurstwood started to follow.

"You stay there," one called. "Some one will run away with your car."

Amid the babel of voices, Hurstwood heard one close beside him.

"Come down, pardner, and be a man. Don't fight the poor. Leave that to the corporations."

He saw the same fellow who had called to him from the corner. Now, as before, he pretended not to hear him.

"Come down," the man repeated gently. "You don't want to fight poor men. Don't fight at all." It was a most philosophic and jesuitical motorman.

A third policeman joined the other two from somewhere and some one ran to telephone for more officers. Hurstwood gazed about, determined but fearful.

A man grabbed him by the coat.

"Come off of that," he exclaimed, jerking at him and trying to pull him over the railing.

"Let go," said Hurstwood, savagely.

"I'll show you—you scab!" cried a young Irishman, jumping up on the car and aiming a blow at Hurstwood. The latter ducked and caught it on the shoulder instead of the jaw.

"Away from here," shouted an officer, hastening to the rescue, and adding, of course, the usual oaths.

Hurstwood recovered himself, pale and trembling. It was becoming serious with him now. People were looking up and jeering at him. One girl was making faces.

He began to waver in his resolution, when a patrol wagon rolled up and more officers dismounted. Now the track was quickly cleared and the release effected.

"Let her go now, quick," said the officer, and again he was off.

The end came with a real mob, which met the car on its return trip a mile or two from the barns. It was an exceedingly poor-looking neighbourhood. He wanted to run fast through it, but again the track was blocked. He saw men carrying something out to it when he was yet a half-dozen blocks away.

"There they are again!" exclaimed one policeman.

"I'll give them something this time," said the second officer, whose patience was becoming worn. Hurstwood suffered a qualm of body as the car rolled up. As before, the crowd began hooting, but now, rather than come near, they threw things. One or two windows were smashed and Hurstwood dodged a stone.

Both policemen ran out toward the crowd, but the latter replied by running toward the car. A woman—a mere girl in appearance—was among these, bearing a rough stick. She was exceedingly wrathful and struck at Hurstwood, who dodged. Thereupon, her companions, duly encouraged, jumped on the car and pulled Hurstwood over. He had hardly time to speak or shout before he fell.

"Let go of me," he said, falling on his side.

"Ah, you sucker," he heard some one say. Kicks and blows rained on him. He seemed to be suffocating. Then two men seemed to be dragging him off and he wrestled for freedom.

"Let up," said a voice, "you're all right. Stand up."

He was let loose and recovered himself. Now he recognised two officers. He felt as if he would faint from exhaustion. Something was wet on his chin. He put up his hand and felt, then looked. It was red.

"They cut me," he said, foolishly, fishing for his handkerchief.

"Now, now," said one of the officers. "It's only a scratch."

His senses became cleared now and he looked around. He was standing in a little store, where they left him for the moment. Outside, he could see, as he stood wiping his chin, the car and the excited crowd. A patrol wagon was there, and another.

He walked over and looked out. It was an ambulance, backing in.

He saw some energetic charging by the police and arrests being made.

"Come on, now, if you want to take your car," said an officer, opening the door and looking in.

He walked out, feeling rather uncertain of himself. He was very cold and frightened.

"Where's the conductor?" he asked.

"Oh, he's not here now," said the policeman.

Hurstwood went toward the car and stepped nervously on. As he did so there was a pistol shot. Something stung his shoulder.

"Who fired that?" he heard an officer exclaim. "By God! who did that?" Both left him, running toward a certain building. He paused a moment and then got down.

"George!" exclaimed Hurstwood, weakly, "this is too much for me."

He walked nervously to the corner and hurried down a side street.

"Whew!" he said, drawing in his breath.

A half block away, a small girl gazed at him.

"You'd better sneak," she called.

He walked homeward in a blinding snowstorm, reaching the ferry by dusk. The cabins were filled with comfortable souls, who studied him curiously. His head was still in such a whirl that he felt confused. All the wonder of the twinkling lights of the river in a white storm passed for nothing. He trudged doggedly on until he reached the flat. There he entered and found the room warm. Carrie was gone. A couple of evening papers were laying on the table where she left them. He lit the gas and sat down. Then he got up and stripped to examine his shoulder. It was a mere scratch. He washed his hands and face, still in a brown study, apparently, and combed his hair. Then he looked for something to eat, and finally, his hunger gone, sat down in his comfortable rocking-chair. It was a wonderful relief.

He put his hand to his chin, forgetting, for the moment, the papers.

"Well," he said, after a time, his nature recovering itself, "that's a pretty tough game over there."

Then he turned and saw the papers. With half a sigh he picked up the "World."

"Strike, Spreading in Brooklyn," he read. "Rioting Breaks Out in all Parts of the City."

He adjusted his paper very comfortably and continued. It was the one thing he read with absorbing interest.

THE GREAT MANTA

by EDWIN CORLE

Mr. Gagus had a job. It was a good job, too. He said so and his wife said so. They were both very happy. Mr. and Mrs. Gagus lived in Brooklyn, almost as far out as New Lots, but not quite. They used the Van Sicklen Avenue subway station.

One of the best things about the job was that Mr. Gagus didn't have to be at work until ten o'clock in the morning. Of course that meant he got home late at night, but even so, it was pretty nice to be able to start the business day at ten. There was something aristocratic about it. It gave him an air.

But in spite of that fact, Mr. Gagus had to get up at 7:30 every morning. It took him an hour to shave and dress and eat his breakfast. While he did these things, Mrs. Gagus packed his lunch. Occasionally in this interval he had time to glance at a newspaper, but usually he reserved that for his subway ride.

At 8:30, he left his tiny flat and walked along Livonia Avenue to the subway entrance. At 8:38, he boarded a Broadway-Seventh Avenue express. Then occurred his customary perusal of the affairs of the world at large, which lasted until 9:27, when he arrived at the Times Square subway station. Here he changed to a Broadway-Seventh Avenue local, and at 9:30 he left it at the Fiftieth Street subway station, where he ascended to the street. Eastward on Fiftieth Street he walked to Sixth Avenue and his establishment of business, arriving there more often than not (provided, of course, that the weather was fair) at 9:35. In bad weather, he might be as late as 9:38, but certainly never any later than that.

The first thing he did when he reached his place of business was to take off his suit and shirt and collar, tie, and shoes. These he placed in a locker. Then he put on a pair of trousers that resembled riding pants, but were not. They were marvellous trousers—a nice light blue with red stripes running down the sides. On his feet, he put a pair of black leather boots, and into the tops of the boots he tucked the legs of the trousers. Over his head he slipped a plain shirt of the type usually known as a sweatshirt. Over this he placed a white waistcoat with gold braid adorning its visible parts. Adjusting these garments with the skill of familiarity, he then took from a hanger a heavy coat with a cutaway tail. This coat was blue with red-and-white decorations, and the entire lining was a brilliant red. There were golden epaulets on the shoulders and several medals on the breast and a stiff brocade collar that fitted tightly under the chin. With the coat resting correctly on his back and shoulders and showing just the proper amount of waistcoat and none of the sweatshirt, he placed on his head a hat. This hat was all of a foot in height and was faced with black fur, adorned with a red plume and a gold band and a gold tassel. It was held in place by a strap under the chin and gave him an appearance of tremendous height and imperious dignity. He took a last look of·self-inspection as he pulled a pair of white gloves onto his hands. It was 9:57. And, dressed as a captain of the Grenadier Guards of the First Empire, Mr. Gagus of Brooklyn, and doorman of the Greatest Picture Palace in the World, was ready to go to work. He would close the locker containing his own clothes, walk out of the building, and appear before it on the street at ten o'clock, on the job.

There wasn't much for him to do the first hour but look important and impressive and keep beggars away from the foyer. An occasional taxicab or private car would drive up and he would open the door, and close it after the occupant or occupants had got out. But by eleven o'clock the automobiles arrived with more frequency, and from then until two o'clock he was kept pretty well concentrated on the business of opening and closing automobile doors.

At two o'clock, after four hours on duty, he was relieved by Mr. Parkinson, whom he addressed below in the locker room as Otto, but who, in public, was a captain of the Grenadier Guards, like himself. Mr. Gagus, turning over his duties to Mr. Parkinson, then retired to the locker room preparatory to eating his lunch—sandwiches, an apple, cheese, sweet chocolate, and coffee kept hot in a small thermos bottle. Before he could eat, he had first to remove his white gloves, his high fur hat, his dignified and decorated coat, and his gold-braided waistcoat. The trousers and the boots he was allowed to leave on if he were careful not to soil or scuff them, but if he wished to appear on the street, he had to change completely back to his own clothes. As this was a great nuisance and as he had no desire to walk anywhere after four hours on his feet, he almost invariably spent his relief period in his undress uniform. He ate and read and dozed, and sometimes he just sat.

At 6 P.M. Mr. Gagus, again attired in full regalia, relieved Mr. Parkinson. By 9 P.M. things began to get a little easier. Fewer and fewer automobiles arrived, though he was occasionally obliged to summon taxicabs for departing patrons. At 10 P.M., he had reached the end of his day's work.

Again he descended to the locker room, and again he took off the white gloves, the high fur hat, the dignified and decorated coat, the gold-braided waistcoat, and this time the plain sweatshirt, the black leather boots, and the red-striped trousers. All of these he placed in the locker in exchange for his own unimpressive clothes, and by 10:22 he was ready to walk west on Fiftieth Street. At 10:28, he entered the Fiftieth Street subway station. At 10:31, he transferred to an express at Times Square. At 11:20, he arrived at the Van Sicklen Avenue subway station in Brooklyn. At 11:28, he unlocked the front door of his apartment building. At 11:29, he entered his tiny flat. At 11:35, he drank a cup of coffee and followed it with a supper of stew or vegetables or cold meat, or perhaps a bit of chicken and a piece of pie, and finished off with another cup of coffee. Mrs. Gagus might inquire as to whom he had this week, and he would laconically reply with a mouth full of meat, "John Barrymore," or "Katharine Hepburn," or "Will Rogers," or "Claudette Colbert," or some other name. Mrs. Gagus saw all of the big pictures at a neighborhood theatre in Brooklyn, but Mr. Gagus, being in the business, never went to the movies at all.

Between 12 and 12:15, they went to bed. Then, at 7:30 the next morning, Mr. Gagus arose once more in order to get to work on time. It was good to have a job that began at ten o'clock in the morning, and that required him to wear such impressive garments and that made him an integral part of the greatest theatre playing the greatest pictures in the greatest city for the greatest audiences in all this great world. He said so and his wife said so.

Then came The Great Manta.

At first Mr. Gagus wasn't concerned with it, didn't even notice it, and hadn't the remotest idea of what a manta was. But across Sixth Avenue from the Greatest Picture Palace in the World came this Great Manta and Mr. Gagus spent eight hours a day standing before it. The Great Manta—the largest devilfish ever exhibited, the most terrifying of marine monsters, and a barker with a line of wisecracks, who invited the public to come in and see it for ten cents, a thin dime, the tenth part of a dollar —was not at all out of place on Sixth Avenue, even directly across from the great cinema palace that provided a captain of the Grenadier Guards of the First Empire simply to open your carriage door. Sixth Avenue is an ambiguous street.

At first the attachés of the Greatest Picture Palace in the World were moved to smile and even laugh at this cheap Coney Island sideshow attraction. Its price was enough to belittle it. Ten cents to see a big devilfish. Why, they were charging a top price of a dollar sixty-five to see Katherine Hepburn. The Great Manta was beneath them. But Sixth Avenue, a street of heterogeneous shops, has also a heterogeneity of people. Men stood before the flashy advertisements of The Great Manta and read them. Of course at the beginning only a few men did so, but when four or five men stand still in New York and look at something, there is a crowd doing the same thing in a very few minutes. Then a few of the men went in, and before long most of the crowd managed to find a mere ten cents, and went in also. The Great Manta became a hit.

In time, the super-film with Katherine Hepburn left the Greatest Picture Palace in the World, and Anna Sten took her place in a super-super-production, but The Great Manta across the street stayed on. Four colossal, staggering, sensational super- and sometimes super-super-film went by, and still across the street The Great Manta stayed on.

Mr. Gagus, though he had no interest whatsoever in the fate of The Great Manta, could not help noticing this. A taxi-driver who had his stand near the entrance of the Greatest Picture Palace in the World once spoke to Mr. Gagus about it.

"Many people go see that damn thing?" he asked.

"Well, yes," admitted Mr. Gagus. "Quite a few."

And even as they looked over at this oddity, people were offering dimes to the ticket-teller and the barker was barking about The Great Manta, the largest devilfish ever exhibited, taken at the risk of a dozen lives. Usually he said it was the largest devilfish, but sometimes he made it the oldest, sometimes the meanest, occasionally the ugliest, and once in a while the heaviest. But always he came back to the point that it was the largest.

After some weeks of this, the thought, ever so casual, but nevertheless a thought, flickered through Mr. Gagus's mind to the effect that he had no idea what a great manta really looked like. The livid pictures outside the place were stirring but unsatisfying. He almost felt that he would like to see it. But the thought was so silly that he slammed a taxicab door a little harder than usual just to assert himself. Then one day, in his relief period in the locker-room, Mr. Gagus learned that Fritz, the assistant superintendent, and Joe, the first engineer, had both paid ten cents apiece to see The Great Manta.

"What's it like?" asked Mr. Gagus.

"Hell of a lookin' thing," said Joe.

"It is a great pig t'ing vot they got out of the ocean," said Fritz.

Mr. Gagus nodded, but experienced no feeling of satisfaction.

A few days later, Mr. Gagus learned that his alternate, Mr. Parkinson, had, during his rest period, paid ten cents and visited The Great Manta. Mr. Gagus did not deign to discuss the subject at the time, but some hours later, when Captain of the Grenadier Guards Gagus replaced Captain of the Grenadier Guards Parkinson, Captain Gagus caught Captain Parkinson's eye and, nodding his head toward the opposite side of the street, Captain Gagus said quietly out of the corner of his mouth, "What's it like?" Captain Parkinson did not reply. His face grew serious, he shook his head ever so slightly, winked one eye and raised his eyebrows, and then, without a word, marched off to the locker room.

And with the suspense at this high pitch, Mr. Gagus had to go to work for four hours, while across the street, when the roar of the "L" did not drown it out, came the rasping voice of the barker: "Here y' are, folks—step right up, one and all—the sensation of the age . . ."

At 10:22 that night, when Mr. Gagus walked west on Fiftieth Street to the Fiftieth Street subway station, he could still hear ringing in his ears "Step right up, folks—the sensation of the age," but he put it out of his mind and wondered what Mrs. Gagus would have ready for his supper.

At 11:35, he drank his first cup of coffee, and followed that with some pigs' knuckles and sauerkraut. And while he was eating with his mind on other things, Mrs. Gagus said, "Who do you have next week?"

"Oh, we got George Arliss."

"Oh, I like him," said Mrs. Gagus.

"And a Silly Symphony, too," added Mr. Gagus.

"My, my!" said Mrs. Gagus.

And at 12:15 they went to bed.

The days went by and Mr. Gagus continued his work. More and more of his casual acquaintances who worked at the Greatest Picture Palace in the World had succumbed to their instincts for romance and adventure and had gone to see The Great Manta. George Arliss and the Silly Symphony came and went. A musical talking-picture review with a blackface star and one hundred of the most beautiful girls in the world came to the Greatest Picture Palace in the World. In time it passed away and a foreign film, the greatest, naturally, that had ever been produced in Europe, took its place. The Great Manta stayed on. Every day, for four hours in the morning and four hours in the evening, Mr. Gagus heard the adjurations of the barker across the street and saw the crowds entering to see The Great Manta.

And as regularly as the earth turned, he stopped work at 10 P.M. And as regularly, at 10:22 he was ready to walk west on Fiftieth Street to the Fiftieth Street subway station. But hand in hand with regularity goes inevitability. Something had been going on in the environment of Mr. Gagus that made a reaction on his part inevitable. Through no really conscious control of his whatsoever, there came the inevitable night when, for the first time, he failed to walk west on Fiftieth Street at 10:22 P.M. Instead, without thinking much about it, and acting as if it were perfectly normal, he walked across Sixth Avenue and stopped at the ticket-seller of the attraction ballyhooed as The Great Manta. He paid ten cents and walked inside. Fifteen minutes later, he walked out. He had seen The Great Manta. He knew what it looked like. He was completely satisfied and he walked west on Fiftieth Street to the Fiftieth Street subway station.

That night it was 10:46 instead of 10:31 when he transferred to an express at Times Square. And it was 11:35 when he arrived at the Van Sicklen Avenue station, instead of 11:20. It was 11:43 when he unlocked his front door, and 11:44 when he entered his tiny flat, and 11:50 when he drank his first cup of coffee. Over the supper of corned-beef hash, Mrs. Gagus commented that he was fifteen minutes late, and she wondered why.

"Stopped to see The Great Manta," he explained.

That meant nothing to Mrs. Gagus. Naturally, she inquired what it was. Mr. Gagus swallowed more coffee, and she asked again, "What is The Great Manta?"

Mr. Gagus paused and looked at his empty plate.

"It's a devilfish," he said finally.

"What's it look like?" asked Mrs. Gagus.

"Oh, funny-lookin' thing," he answered. "Kind of a big fish that they got out of the ocean."

"Huh," sniffed Mrs. Gagus, which meant she couldn't possibly see why anybody should ever want to waste time to go see a big fish that somebody had pulled out of the ocean.

And that night they went to bed at 12:30 instead of 12:15—all on account of a big fish. But Mrs. Gagus used her self-control and said nothing more about it. Next morning Mr. Gagus got up at 7:30 on schedule, so everything was back in order again. He shaved and dressed and ate his breakfast. While he did this, Mrs. Gagus packed his lunch. At 8:30, he left his tiny flat. At 8:38, he boarded a Broadway-Seventh Avenue express. . . .

The Harbor

There are 108.6 miles of "commercially developed" water front in Brooklyn, a region of warehouses, piers, and drydocks; a place of romantic smells and also murder, of raucous diners and quiet drinking dens. Years ago Clipper ships spread their great sails under the Heights and sailed out to California, China, and the Indies. Now, the working ships of every nation with a merchant navy put in to Brooklyn docks. The big, fancy ships, like the Elizabeth, the Mary, and the America, tie up at the huge piers along the Hudson River, but the working ships, the cargo vessels, discharge and load in Brooklyn.

The sea lanes of the world end at Brooklyn piers; there are spices and coffee, cocoa, quinine and beeswax, in the warehouses. Brooklyn has been called "America's biggest grocery store," and it could be named, too, the biggest corner drugstore. On West Street in Manhattan, you can walk along, dodge trucks, and see nothing but the façades of the huge piers. In Brooklyn, the ships are at hand, and you can smell the stuff in the jute bags, and look at the crates of automobiles and airplanes marked for shipment to Argentina.

The shape-up at this moment persists along the water front, and in the mornings stevedores pick from a semicircle of longshoremen the men they want to work that day. There are rackets and thieving, and now and then people discuss the fate of Peter Panto, who led a rebellion in the International Longshoreman's Association against the Joe Ryan regime. Panto got into a car with four men one night and a year later was found in quicklime. There are seamen, too, Americans, British, Norwegian, Lascar, Puerto Rican, South and Central American, and Chinese. Before December 1941, the Japanese docked some of the biggest, and certainly the neatest and cleanest, vessels on the borough's water front.

Some of the country's largest battleships, and innumerable destroyers, cruisers, and smaller craft, have been built in the New York Navy Yard, known generally as the Brooklyn Navy Yard, and during the war many of our own vessels and those of our allies were repaired there. The historians of Greenpoint recall, at the slightest provocation, that the Monitor was built in Thomas F. Rowland's shipyard there. Her keel was laid in October 1861. On January 30, 1862, she was launched; she was commissioned on February 25 of that year, and on March 9 fought the Merrimac and caused her to retire. The Monitor went out into the open sea again in December 1862, and on December 29 floundered in a gale of wind off Cape Hatteras.

Sands Street runs from Brooklyn Bridge to a Navy Yard gate, and is known to every chief petty officer in the American Navy. Its dance halls were closed during the war, and, what with the

Broadway traps again patriotically welcoming sailors, it lost a little—not much—of its color. It's a sailor street, a rowdy place of tailor shops, pressing establishments, eating places, saloons, and the Navy Y.M.C.A. Before the war, when Tony's Square Bar and the Oval Bar had their dance halls running, it was a wonderful street of swaggering sailors and their Navy girls, who were attracted from all parts of the continent by the peculiar charm of sailors. The bartenders and waiters were tough and adept, and could spot and stop a fight before it even started. To the amazement of the hard-bitten gin-mill proprietors the place became somewhat fashionable for slummers, and Tony's Square Bar and the Oval now and then received favorable notices in Vogue.

Yet with all this color, excitement, and down-to-the-sea-in-ships air about the place there has been surprisingly little good stuff written about the Brooklyn water front or the ships which leave it. Ernest Poole's The Harbor is about the only book that readily comes to mind. In his autobiography, The Bridge, My Own Story, he told how he came to write the book.

. . . on a spring evening in 1912, my wife and I went to dine with some friends in their stately old house on Brooklyn Heights. After dinner we had coffee in their garden, looking down on the twinkling river below. Suddenly I noticed a thin blue column of smoke that rose between two flower beds close by. Then I saw that it came from a chimney, and our smiling hostess explained.

"You see, this garden is on the roof of an old warehouse down below."

Abruptly I drew into myself and heard nothing for a while. What a garden for a little boy! My thoughts leaped back to those early years of my life in Chicago, when with my wild gang I'd explored the lumberyards and the river and lake front. How much grander this place here, upon the threshold of the sea! How it would be to try a story about just such a little boy in just such a garden as this, with the harbor around him and even beneath, for his father would own that warehouse and pier and even the sailing ships that came. The boy would grow up and, as he grew—through good times, bad times, death, love, marriage, hope, despair, success and failure, pride, revolt—the harbor would keep changing, each time that he looked at it with his new eyes, changing like the boy himself, changing like this world I'd seen and through these forces I had seen; for wealth and poverty, labor, rebellion, and a whole world of trade and commerce, travel and adventure, were here! A harbor now wonderful, all romance, but again all grim and dull and flat; now friendly, now hostile! . . . My thoughts raced on, my excitement grew as I felt the possibilities. I have written many novels since then but never one that leaped together so quickly in my mind at the start.

The story of The Harbor *is laid in all the New York water front, and we have taken a scene having to do particularly with Brooklyn. The plots in the book, as in so many good books, are quite simple: the development of a young man into a fighter for the oppressed and the decline of an old man's fortunes matching the decline of American shipping being two of the stories told.*

from . . .

THE HARBOR

by ERNEST POOLE

As I walked home from church with my mother that day the streets seemed as quiet and safe as her eyes. How suddenly tempting it seemed to me, this quiet and this safety, compared to the place where I was going. For I had decided to run away from my home and my mother that afternoon, down to the harbor to see the world. What would become of me 'way down there? What would she do if I never came back? A lump rose in my throat at the thought of her tears .It was terrible.

"All the same I am going to do it," I kept thinking doggedly. And yet suddenly, as we reached our front steps, how near I came to telling her. But no, she would only spoil it all. She wanted me always up in the garden, she wanted me never to have any thrills.

My mother knew me so well. She had seen that when she read stories of fairies, witches and goblins out of my books to Sue and me, while Sue, though two years younger, would sit there like a little dark imp, her black eyes snapping over the fights, I would creep softly out of the room, ashamed and shaken, and would wait in the hall outside till the happy ending was in plain view. So my mother had gradually toned down all the fights and the killings, the witches and the monsters, and much to my disappointment had wholly shut out the gory pirates who were for me the most frightfully fascinating of all. Sometimes I felt vaguely that for this she had her own reason, too—that my mother hated everything that had to do with the ocean, especially my father's dock that made him so gloomy and silent. But of this I could never be quite sure. I would often watch her intently, with a sudden sharp anxiety, for I loved my mother with all my soul and I could not bear to see her unhappy.

"Never on any account," I heard her say to Belle, "are the children to go down the street toward the docks."

"Yes, ma'am," said Belle. "I'll see to it."

At once I wanted to go there. The street in front of our house sloped abruptly down at the next corner two blocks through poorer and smaller houses to a cobblestone space below, over which trucks clattered, plainly on their way to the docks. So I could go down and around by that way. How tempting it all looked down there. Above the roofs of the houses, the elevated railroad made a sharp bend on its way to the Bridge, trains roared by, high over all the Great Bridge swept across the sky. And below all this and more thrilling than all, I caught glimpses of strange, ragged boys. "Micks," Belle sometimes called them, and sometimes, "Finian Mickies." Up here I had no playmates.

From now on, our garden lost its charms. Up the narrow courtway which ran along the side of the house I would slip stealthily to the front gate and often get a good look down the street before Belle sharply called me back. The longest looks, I found, were always on Sunday afternoons, when Belle would sit back there in the garden, close to the bed of red tulips which encircled a small fountain made of two white angels. Belle, who was bony, tall and grim, would sit by the little angels reading her shabby Bible. Her face was wrinkled and almost brown, her eyes now kind, now gloomy. She had a song she would sing now and then. "For beneath the Union Jack we will drive the Finians back"—is all I can remember. She told me of witches in the Scotch hills. At her touch horrible monsters rose in the most surprising places. In the bathtub, for example, when I stayed in the bath too long she would jerk out the stopper, and as from the hole there came a loud gurgle—"it's the Were-shark," Belle would mutter. And I would leap out trembling.

This old "Were-shark" had his home in the very middle of the ocean. In one gulp he could swallow a boy of my size, and this he did three time each day. The boys were brought to him by the "Condor," a perfectly hideous bird as large as a cow and as fierce as a tiger. If ever I dared go down that street and disobey my mother, the Condor would "swoop" down over the roofs, snatch me up in his long yellow beak with the blood of the last boy on it, and with thunder and lightning would carry me off far over the clouds and drop me into the Were-shark's mouth.

Then Belle would sit down to her Bible.

Sunday after Sunday passed, and still in fascinated dread I would steal quietly out to the gate and watch this street forbidden. Pointing to it one day, Belle had declared in awful tones, "Broad is the way that leadeth to destruction." But it was not broad. In that at least she was all wrong. It was in fact so narrow that a Condor as big as a cow might easily bump himself when he "swooped." Besides, there were good strong lampposts where a little boy could cling and scream, and almost always somewhere in sight was a policeman so fat and heavy that even two Condors could hardly lift him from the ground. This policeman would come running. My mother had said I must never be scared by policemen, because they were really good kind men. In fact, she said, it was foolish to be scared by anything ever. She never knew of Belle's methods with me.

So at last I had decided to risk it, and now the fearful day had come. I could barely eat my dinner. My courage was fast ebbing away. In the dining-room the sunlight was for a time wiped out by clouds, and I grew suddenly happy. It might rain and then I could not go. But it did not rain nor did anything I hoped for happen to prevent my plan. Belle sat down by the angels and was soon so deep in her Bible that it was plain I could easily slip up the path. Sue never looked up from her sand-pile to say, "Stop Billy! He's running away from home!" With a gulp I passed my mother's window. She did not happen to look out. Now I had reached the very gate. "I can't go! I can't open the gate!" But the old gate opened with one push. "I can't go! There is no policeman!" But yes, there he was on my side of the street slowly walking toward me. My heart thumped, I could hardly breathe. In a moment with a frantic rush I had reached the nearest lamp-post and was clinging breathless. I could not scream, I shut my eyes in sickening fear and waited for the rushing of enormous wings.

But there came no Condor swooping.

Another rush—another post—another and another!

"What's the matter with you, little feller?"

I looked up at the big safe policeman and laughed.

"I'm playing a game," I almost shouted, and ran without touching another post two blocks to the cobblestone space below. I ran blindly around it several times, I bumped into a man who said, "Heigh there! Look out!" After that I strutted proudly, then turned and ran back with all my might up the street, and into our house and up to my room. And there on my bed to my great surprise I found myself sobbing and sobbing. It was a long time before I could stop. I had had my first adventure.

I made many Sunday trips after that, and on no one of them was I caught. For delighted and proud at what I had done I kept asking Belle to talk of the Condor, gloomily she pried on the terrors, and seeing the awed look in my eyes (awe at my own courage in defying such a bird), she felt so sure of my safety that often she would barely look up from her Bible the whole afternoon. Even on workdays over her sewing she would forget. And so I went "to destruction."

At first I stayed but a little while and never left the cobblestone space, only peering up into the steep little streets that led to the fearsome homes of the "Micks." But then I made the acquaintance of Sam. It happened through a small toy boat which I had taken down there with the purpose of starting it off for "heathen lands." As I headed across the railroad tracks that led to the docks, suddenly Sam and his gang appeared from around a freight car. I stood stock-still. They were certainly "Micks"—ragged and dirty, with holes in their shoes and soot on their faces. Sam was smoking a cigarette.

"Heigh, fellers," he said, "look at Willy's boat."

I clutched my boat tighter and turned to run. But the next moment Sam had me by the arm.

"Look here, young feller," he growled. "You've got the wrong man to do business with this time."

"I don't want to do any business," I gasped.

"Smash him, Sam—smash in his nut for him," piped the smallest Micky cheerfully. And this Sam promptly proceeded to do. It was a wild and painful time. But though Sam was two years older, he was barely any larger than I, and when he and his gang had gone off with my boat, as I stood there breathing hard, I was filled with a grim satisfaction. For once when he tried to wrench the boat from me I had hit him with it right on the face, and I had had a glimpse of a thick red mark across his cheek. I tasted something new in my mouth and spit it out. It was blood. I did this several times, slowly and impressively, till it made a good big spot on the railroad tie at my feet. Then I walked with dignity back across the tracks and up "the way of destruction" home. I walked slowly, planning as I went. At the gate I climbed up on it and swung. Then with a sudden loud cry I fell off and ran back into the garden crying, "I fell off the gate! I fell on my face!" So my cut and swollen lip was explained, and my trips were not discovered.

I felt myself growing older fast. For I knew that I could both fight and tell lies, besides defying the Condor.

In the next years, for weeks at a time my life was centered on Sam and his gang. How we became friends, how often we met, by just what means I evaded my nurse, all these details are vague to me now. I am not even sure I was never caught. But it seems to me that I was not. For as I grew to be eight years old, Belle turned her attention more and more to that impish little sister of mine who was always up to some mischief or other. There was the corner grocer, too, with whom I pretended to be staunch friends. "I'm going to see the grocer," I would say, when I heard Sam's cautious whistle in front of the house—and so presently I would join the gang. I followed Sam with a doglike devotion, giving up my weekly twenty-five cents instead of saving it for Christmas, and in return receiving from him all the world-old wisdom stored in that bullet-shaped head of his which sat so tight on his round little shoulders.

And though I did not realize it then, in my tense crowded childhood, through Sam and his companions I learned something else that was to stand me in good stead years later on. I learned how to make friends with "the slums." I discovered that by making friends with "Micks" and "Dockers" and the like, you find they are no fearful goblins, giants bursting savagely up among the flowers of your life, but people as human as yourself, or rather, much more human, because they live so close to the harbor, close to the deep rough tides of life.

Into these tides I was now drawn down—and it did me some good and a great deal of harm. For I was too little those days for the harbor.

Sam had the most wonderful life in the world. He could go wherever he liked and at any hour day or night. Once, he said, when a "feller" was drowned, he had stayed out on the docks all night. His mother always let him alone. An enormous woman with heavy eyes, I was in awe of her from the first. The place that she kept with Sam's father was called "The Sailor's Harbor." It stood on a corner down by the docks, a long, low wooden building painted white, with twelve tight-shuttered, mysterious windows along the second story, and below them a "Ladies' Entrance." In front was a small blackboard with words in white which Sam could read. "Ten Cent Dinners" stood at the top. Below came, "Coffee and rolls." Next, "Ham and eggs." Then "Bacon and eggs." And then, "To-day"—with a space underneath where Sam's fat father wrote down every morning still more delicious eatables. You got whiffs of these things and they made your mouth water, they made your stomach fairly turn against your nursery supper.

But most of our time we spent on the docks. All were roofed, and exploring the long dock sheds and climbing down into the dark holds of the square-rigged ships called "clippers," we found logs of curious mottled wood, huge baskets of sugar, odorous spices, indigo, camphor, tea, coffee, jute and endless other things. Sam knew their names and the names of the wonder-places they came from—Manila, Calcutta, Bombay, Ceylon. He knew besides such words as "hawser," "bulkhead" and "ebb-tide." And Sam knew how to swear. He swore with a fascinating ease such words as made me shiver and stare. And then he would look at me and chuckle.

"You think I'll go to hell for this, don't you," he asked me once. And my face grew hot with embarrassment, for I thought that he assuredly would.

I asked him what were heathen lands, and he said they were countries where heathen lived. And what were heathen? Cannibals. And what were they?

"Fellers that eat fellers," he said.

"Alive?" I inquired. He turned to the gang:

"Listen to the kid! He wants to know if they eat 'em alive!" Sam spat disgustedly. "Naw," he said. "First they roast 'em like any meat. They roast 'em," he added reflectively, "until their skin gets brown and bubbles out and busts."

One afternoon a carriage brought three travelers for one of the ships, a man, his wife and a little girl with shining yellow pig-tails. "To be et," Sam whispered as we stood close beside them. And then, pointing to some of the half-naked brown men that made the crew of the ship near by—"cannibals," he muttered. For a long time I stared at these eaters, especially at their lean brown stomachs.

"We're safe enough," Sam told me. "They ain't allowed to come ashore." I found this very comforting.

But what a frightful fate lay in store for the little girl with pig-tails. As I watched her I felt worse and worse. Why couldn't somebody warn her in time? At last I decided to do it myself. Procuring a scrap of paper I retired behind a pile of crates and wrote in my large, clumsy hand, "You look out—you are going to be et." Watching my chance, I slipped this into her satchel and hoped that she would read it soon. Then I promptly forgot all about her and ran off into a warehouse where the gang had gone to slide.

These warehouses had cavernous rooms, so dark you could not see to the ends, and there from between the wooden columns the things from the ships loomed out of the dark like so many ghosts. There were strange sweet smells. And from a hole in the ceiling there was a twisting chute of steel down which you could slide with terrific speed. We used to slide by the hour.

Outside were freight cars in long lines, some motionless, some suddenly lurching forward or back, with a grinding and screeching of wheels and a puffing and coughing from engines ahead. Sam taught me how to climb on the cars and how to swing off while they were going. He had learned from watching the brakemen that dangerous backward left-hand swing that lands you stock-still in your tracks. It is a splendid feeling. Only once Sam's left hand caught, I heard a low cry, and after I jumped I found him standing there with a white face. His left hand hung straight down from the wrist and blood was dripping from it.

"Shut up, you damn fool!" he said fiercely.

"I wasn't saying nothing," I gasped.

"Yes, you was—you was startin' to cry! Holy Christ!" He sat down suddenly, then rolled over and lay still. Some one ran for his mother, and after a time he was carried away. I did not see him again for some weeks.

We did things that were bad for a boy of my size, and I saw

things that I shouldn't have seen—a docker crushed upon one of the docks and brought out on a stretcher dead, a stoker as drunk as though he were dead being wheeled on a wheelbarrow to a ship by the man called a "crimp," who sold his drunken body for an advance on its future pay. Sam told me in detail of these things. There came a strike, and once in the darkness of a cold November twilight I saw some dockers rush on a "scab," I heard the dull sickening thumps as they beat him.

And one day Sam took me to the door of his father's saloon and pointed out a man in there who had an admiring circle around him.

"He's going to jump from the Bridge on a bet," Sam whispered. I saw the man go. For what seemed to me hours I watched the Great Bridge up there in the sky, with its crawling processions of trolleys and wagons, its whole moving armies of little black men. Suddenly one of these tiny specks shot out and down, I saw it fall below the roofs, I felt Sam's hand like ice in mine. And this was not good for a boy of ten.

But the sight that ended it all for me was not a man, but a woman. It happened one chilly March afternoon when I fell from a dock into water covered with grease and foam, came up spluttering and terrified, was quickly hauled to the dock by a man and then hustled by Sam and the gang to his home, to have my clothes dried and so not get caught by my mother. Scolded by Sam's mother and given something fiery hot to drink, stripped naked and wrapped in an old flannel night-gown and told to sit by the stove in the kitchen—I was then left alone with Sam. And then Sam with a curious light in his eyes took me to a door which he opened just a crack. Through the crack he showed me a small back room full of round iron tables. And at one of these a man, stoker or sailor I don't know which, his face flushed red under dirt and hair, held in his lap a big fat girl half dressed, giggling and queer, quite drunk. And then while Sam whispered on and on about the shuttered rooms upstairs, I felt a rush of such sickening fear and loathing that I wanted to scream—but I turned too faint.

I remember awakening on the floor, Sam's mother furiously

slapping Sam, then dressing me quickly, gripping me tight by both my arms and saying,

"You tell a word of this to your pa and we'll come up and kill you!"

That night at home I did not sleep. I lay in my bed and shivered and burned. My first long exciting adventure was over. Ended were all the thrills, the wild fun. It was a spree I had had with the harbor, from the time I was seven until I was ten. It had taken me at seven, a plump sturdy little boy, and at ten it had left me wiry, thin, with quick, nervous movements and often dark shadows under my eyes. And it left a deep scar on my early life. For over all the adventures and over my whole childhood loomed this last thing I had seen, hideous, disgusting. For years after that, when I saw or even thought of the harbor, I felt the taste of foul, greasy water in my mouth and in my soul.

So ended the first lesson.

MOM, MURDER AIN'T POLITE

from THE EIGHT MILLION

by MEYER BERGER

Anna Lonergan came to our house for dinner one night. She brought her fourteen-year-old son. Between the soup and the chicken courses, Anna fell into a dreamy mood and started talking about her brother and her husbands and all the nice fellas she had known and how hardly any were left, now, what with all the shooting in her neighborhood.

The boy grew restless. He said, "Mom, it ain't nice to talk about murder when you're eating. It ain't polite."

Anna's clear white skin ebbed red. She glared at her son. She turned indignantly to us.

"You got an encyclopedia?" she said.

We had the *Britannica*. Anna seemed highly pleased. She ordered the boy to leave the table.

"You go in the next room," she told him in sharp maternal reproof. "You stay there and read the encyclopedia and you don't get no dessert."

The boy suddenly left the table.

Anna turned back to us happily. "I always do that," she explained. "When he talks back to his mother I make him go out and read the encyclopedia. That's the way to train children."

And Anna eagerly took up again the story of how many men her husbands had killed.

It is not often that Anna yields to the philosophical mood, but sometimes she talks wistfully of what a funny thing life is; how, when she was a little girl in yellow pigtails, she used to trot around the religious-goods store on Barclay Street with the sisters from St. James' because she wanted to be a nun, and how she turned out, instead, to be Queen of Brooklyn's Irishtown Docks.

This mood never lasts very long. Anna would rather tell about the sixteen years' dock war and how she won dower rights to the queenly title through the strong arms and the good trigger work of her two husbands, Wild Bill Lovett and Matty Martin, and her brother Richard ("Peg-Leg") Lonergan. She estimates that before they died (all three of them of bullet wounds) they killed about twenty men between them in order to gain and hold the water-front leadership and the graft that went with it. This estimate may sound extravagant but it is really conservative. Records in the Medical Examiner's office show, for instance, that in the ten years from 1922 to 1932 there were seventy-eight unsolved murders in the section of Brooklyn called Irishtown—the rough-cobbled area between the Brooklyn Navy Yard and Fulton Ferry, under and around the approaches to the Brooklyn and Manhattan bridges. The prosecuting officials always fretted about this but were never able to do anything about it. The police usually knew who the killer was but they could never get any witnesses, and without witnesses an indictment was not obtainable, much less a trial. Exactly how many of the seventy-eight unsolved murders in that decade are attributable to dock wars, and how many to incidental motives, nobody really knows.

Anna's men were hard-working fellows who kept pretty regular hours. Six mornings a week they would go down to the docks for the stevedores' roll call. They had to be there to make sure that no stevedore was working who was not paying a share of his salary to the dock leadership. Sometimes a stevedore would argue about paying tribute and he would have to be beaten up or maybe his skull would have to be cracked. Men like that were not shot unless they were exceptionally obstinate. But when some superstevedore, with a gang of ten or twelve supporters, would try to take the leadership away from Anna's men, somebody usually got killed.

When Anna claims that Wild Bill, Matty, and Peg-Leg murdered about twenty men between them, she does not count neighborhood killings attributable to such things as honor, bad temper, and misunderstanding. Murders directly attributable to the racket of extorting a portion of stevedores' salaries were discussed at her dinner table, and she remembers most of them distinctly. She recalls only the more spectacular of the family murders that fall within the noncommercial or amateur category. Back in the twenties, every time there was a killing in Irishtown, the newspaper would label it "dock-war murder," but Anna says that was a lot of journalistic prittle-prattle. When Jim Gillen was killed on Jay Street in 1921, for example, his death was attributed to dock trouble, but the motive was something entirely different. Wild Bill Lovett killed Gillen for pulling a cat's tail. "Bill always hated to see anyone hurt a animal," Anna says.

It has been Anna's experience that you become accustomed to murder if you see enough of it. She didn't like it at first, but as time went on it became more or less routine. Sometimes a sensitive ear may detect a bit of pride in Anna's voice as she tells how many times she has gone to the morgue to identify her own dead or the neighbors'. She started when her father was killed by her mother, and went again when Bill got his. When her brother Peg-Leg was shot to death with Aaron Harms and Needles Ferry, his pals, Anna identified the three of them at one time. Later, Charlie Donnelly disputed the dock leadership with Matty Martin, who was Anna's second husband, and she made another trip to the morgue as a friendly gesture to Mrs. Donnelly, who was afraid she couldn't stand the ordeal of identifying her own husband. Eddie McGuire, murdered on the docks on May 16, 1928, was officially identified by Anna, too, and finally she did the honors for Matty, who had been accused (wrongfully, according to Anna) of the McGuire killing. Anna probably has an all-time record for morgue identifications, but she hasn't checked up on it. She never dreams about any of the killings and never cries when she thinks of them. Detectives say the only time they ever saw her cry was when she claimed Peg-Leg's body.

Anna was the first of fifteen children. Her father, John Lonergan, was red-haired, six feet two inches tall, a second-rate prize fighter when he married Mary Brady over on Cherry Hill on the East Side of Manhattan in 1898. There is some family legend that he once sparred with John L. Sullivan, but Anna wouldn't swear to it. Anna was born with a caul, which is supposed to bring good luck, but her Uncle Nelson, who was a captain on one of Jay Gould's yachts, bought it from Anna's mother. Sailors, you know, believe you can't drown if there's a caul aboard ship. Uncle Nelson had three, which he'd picked up here and there, just to make sure. He couldn't swim.

As a little girl, Anna attended St. James' parochial school on the East Side, the same one that Al Smith went to when he was a boy, and Al's wife sponsored Anna's enrollment in the Sacred Heart sodality. Anna admits, though, that the children were sponsored in groups and that she didn't know Mrs. Smith "real well." The Lonergans moved to the Brooklyn water front when Anna was about ten years old and took a house on Johnson Street. During this period Anna was extremely devout, trudged everywhere with the sisters, and, to use her own expression, "was in church morning, noon, and night." At about this time, too, she had her first contact with murder. Margaret Doran, one of her classmates, asked her one day after school to visit the Doran home on Pacific Street, in the same neighborhood, and in the basement they stumbled over the body of Margaret's mother. Margaret's pa, a motorman on the Smith Street trolley line, had chopped off Ma Doran's head. Some dock workers found his body in the river next day. He had jumped off the wharf, after the killing, in a fit of remorse. Anna doesn't remember any other details, and she doesn't think the incident bothered her for any length of time. She says most people have a wrong idea about murder from books and movies, and it doesn't really haunt you and affect your sleep.

Anna is close to forty now, by her own count. She is still fussy about her blonde, bobbed hair, never misses a Saturday appointment at the neighborhood beauty parlor, and is extremely proud of her white hands. She is careful with her fingernails, too. She never uses red nail polish because she thinks it's cheap and vulgar, but she does do a rather professional job on her face with lipstick and eyebrow pencil. Her experience as a Broadway show girl is responsible for that. She danced at Rector's and Churchill's when she was eighteen and had a non-speaking part with Fay Bainter in *The Kiss Burglar*. Since leaving the stage, she has been shot twice and stabbed once, and when she mentions these things she always crosses herelf and thanks God that none of the scars show. Dressed for the street, she is still a good-looking woman. "My mother was beautiful, too," she'll tell new acquaintance. "She was the pitcher of me when she was a girl; a natural blonde, the same as me, only her hair turned gray overnight after Richard [she hates to have her brother called Peg-Leg] got his."

The first casualty in the Lonergan family was Boy, the family's pet spaniel. Boy was a cop hater, like most of the residents of Irishtown. The elder Lonergan had a special trapdoor in this bicycle-repair shop on Bridge Street, leading into a hole in which the dog could hide after he had nipped a patrolman, but one day a mounted officer, quick on the draw, fired a shot at the Lonergan pet and Boy died in what was to become the traditional Lonergan manner.

Anna was out walking with Laura Rich at dusk on April 16, 1923. She was still in the show business then, and so was Laura, who was from Irishtown too. As they passed the bicycle shop, they saw two other Irishtown girls ("tramps," Anna calls them) talking with old man Lonergan and Peg-Leg. Anna told her mother about it when she got home and then forgot about it.

But Anna's mother didn't forget about it. She went down to the shop, and before she got through telling John Lonergan what she thought of him and the loose women he was entertaining, the cop had to come in off his beat to restore peace and quiet. A half-hour later Mrs. Lonergan went back to the bicycle shop and within a few minutes after she got there, her spouse was dying from bullet wounds. Anna heard about it and rushed down to the store. She pushed her way through the crowd and got in before the cops came. The old man was sprawled out on the floor and Mrs. Lonergan was kneeling over him, screaming. Anna sent for a priest and got her mother into a chair. "Mamma," she said, "what have you done to Papa?"

Peg-Leg wasn't in the store when the old man was killed. He showed up at the station house as his mother was being booked for murder, and tried to take the blame. That's why the rumor got around, later, that he actually committed the murder. Anna admits that Peg-Leg told the desk lieutenant, "The old lady didn't do it; I did," but she says there was no truth in his confession. "It was Mamma done it," she says explicitly.

The two girls who started the whole business came to John Lonergan's wake and made Anna furious, but she restrained herself until they left her house. Then she went after them with a boy's baseball bat which had been parked in the umbrella stand in the hall for some years. She caught up with one of them, a girl named Kate, and knocked her out cold. Anna thinks now that perhaps it wasn't ladylike, but, as she says, "I was berling mad at the time."

Big Ed Reilly, who was famous in Irishtown as a deliverer of oppressed gunmen and beautiful ladies with homicidal tendencies long before the Hauptmann case, was hired by Bill Lovett as Mrs. Lonergan's attorney. Reilly's oratory at the trial made short work of the case against Mrs. Lonergan. It pictured Anna's mother as the patient drudge, beaten and kicked by her brute of a husband every day of their married life. With a quavering voice the lawyer depicted Mrs. Lonergan moved to great anger when the old man sent Anna home from the bicycle shop bleeding at the mouth because she had asked him to give her money for the family supper. Mrs. Lonergan had gone to the shop to reproach her husband for this and in the course of the argument which resulted the elder Lonergan had pulled a gun. Mrs. Lonergan, naturally, had tried to take it away from him and had shot him, accidentally. Anna was the star witness for her mother. She talked convincingly, and the jurymen seemed sad and turned Mrs. Lonergan loose.

Sometimes when Anna recalls her wedding to Bill Lovett, on July 28, 1923, she grows melancholy. She would have liked a church wedding with a misty veil and long train, and maybe some orange blossoms and organ music, but she had to stand up before City Clerk McCormick in ordinary street clothes. A formal wedding would have been out of place, in the circumstances. The ceremony came off only a month after Anna's mother had been freed of the murder charge; Peg-Leg, her brother, had just been arrested in connection with another killing (the murder of Eddie Hughes in a Sands Street speakeasy), and the bridegroom himself was out on bail on a charge of carrying concealed weapon.

Anna had known Bill since they had been kids together on Catherine Street on the East Side, but had never thought much of him. He was shy around women and he was short—only five feet seven inches in height—and his face was a peculiar gray, owing to a lung condition. His black hair accentuated the pallor. The family had liked Bill though, and the elder Lonergan had encouraged the match. Peg-Leg was for it, too, because he and Bill had been in Cumberland Hospital once at the same time— Peg-Leg with a bullet wound he'd acquired in a brawl in a Gold Street speak-easy, and Bill with five bullet wounds inflicted by the Frankie Byrnes gang of Irishtown.

Bill's courtship was almost mute. He used to sit around the

Lonergan home by the hour, pretending he was calling on Peg-Leg, and he would stare at Anna. The old man pleaded with Anna to talk to Bill. "I don't talk to fellers who go around shooting people," she said one time.

That made the old man mad. "Your brother shoots people, too," he argued.

"Yeh," said Anna, "and he ought to be ashamed of himself."

Bill finally compelled Anna's admiration, though, by assuming ownership of a loaded .25-caliber automatic that was found on the elder Lonergan when detective raided a Greenpoint speak-easy where he and Peg-Leg and Bill were having some of their favorite needle beer. "It was only a little gun," Anna says when she tells about it, "but I always thought it was a swell thing for Bill to do."

Bill promised to give up homicide as soon as he and Anna were married. They moved out to Ridgefield Park, New Jersey, to a little house with a garden around it, and Anna buckled down to the mean job of reforming Bill completely. It was even harder than she thought it would be. He was to have gone to work in a Paterson silk mill, but never quite got around to it. He had a few hundred dollars left after the house was furnished, and coasted along on that. They had been married about a month when Bill came home late one night, sat down in a parlor chair, and yanked out his automatic. (Anna had let him keep that one, out of his collection, for self-protection.) He told Anna to get into the far corner of the room. "I want to see if you can take it," he said. She had an idea what was coming, but she started for the corner, hoping he'd change his mind before she got there. He didn't, though. If Anna knows you well enough, she'll take the shoe off her left foot and show you where Bill shot away part of her big toe.

Anna was proud of Bill's marksmanship, of which the toe shooting is an example, but he did embarrass her sometimes by showing off with his automatic. He never did any shooting unless he was very drunk. Once, before they moved to New Jersey, he shot out all the lights in a Smith Street trolley car. Anna was humiliated, to hear her tell it, but she got a laugh out of the passengers. They all looked so scared. Another time, when Anna and Bill were visiting friends in Irishtown, Bill shot two pork chops out of the friend's frying pan. It was good shooting, but it was a social error. They were never invited to that house again. On another occasion, at an Easter Sunday party in Bridge Street, before they were married, their host put on a derby hat and gave an imitation of Charlie Chaplin. It wasn't a good imitation, and Bill fired a shot at the hat. Someone jiggled his arm and the slug caught the host in the shoulder. Bill was all for a second try, but he was talked out of it.

Bill was very proud of Anna and bought her the best clothes he could find. He liked to be seen with her, and was pleased when other men eyed her, but was apt to get nasty if they looked at her too long. He shot one man just for that. It was over on the Chelsea docks, in Manhattan, where he'd gone to visit his father, who was a stevedore there. An inoffensive French chef on a liner, stuck his head out of a porthole for a breath of air. Anna came into his line of vision and he let his eyes rest on her for a few seconds. This annoyed Bill. "He thought this Frenchman was trying to make me," Anna explains, "so he gets his gun out and shoots the poor feller's right ear off."

During the courtship period in Brooklyn, Anna could always tell when Bill was primed for a killing. A spot in the center of his pale forehead would grow dark when the urge came on. His stevedore pals knew that spot, too, and would excuse themselves from Bill's presence when they saw it blooming. Still, to hear Anna tell it, Bill wasn't really vicious, because the fiercest dogs would make up to him, and in her opinion that is an infallible sign of something basically gentle in a man's nature. Bill liked babies, too. He proved that the night of March 31, 1920, when he killed Dinny Meehan, who was Irishtown dock leader at the time. As he walked through the Meehan flat on Warren Street, Brooklyn, he stopped in the parlor to pat little Dinny, Jr., on the head before he went into the bedroom and put two slugs into big Dinny. One of the shots ricocheted and wounded Mrs. Meehan, who was sleeping with her husband, but she recovered. Three years later Mrs. Meehan showed Anna the scar as an argument against her marrying Bill, but it didn't change Anna's mind.

Outside of shooting off Anna's big toe to see whether she could take it, Bill made an ideal husband, for a while. He stayed in the Jersey cottage at night and read a lot. Anna says he was a sucker for anything penned by Arthur Brisbane, and for all kinds of history. He was a great Bible reader, too, and could quote long passages from the Scriptures. He didn't care much for the movies, but he knew they were Anna's favorite form of entertainment and he'd take her whenever she asked. Today Anna prefers Wallace Beery and John Barrymore films. She likes Broadway shows, too, but not as much. She seldom comes to Broadway now at all. Stage pathos leaves her cold unless a child is involved; the spectacle of kids getting a dirty deal, on the stage or off, always makes her cry.

Three months after she started to reform Bill, Anna noticed that he wasn't paying much attention to his history books, his solitaire, and two-handed pinochle. He was off form in his checker game, too, and seemed tired of Paterson. He sometimes spoke wistfully of Irishtown. One night, when he couldn't bear the nostalgia, he blurted that he was going to Brooklyn. "Just for a little visit, Doll," he told Anna. She decided to go over, too, and he arranged to meet her later that night near her favorite Irishtown beauty parlor, at Jay and Fulton Streets. When he didn't come, Anna went to his mother's house on Bath Beach and asked Bill's brother George, who was studying for the priesthood, to help her search for Bill. George didn't like the idea, but he agreed to go along. When they had made the round of all the waterfront speak-easies and home-brew joints, George suggested they try the Dockloaders' Club at 25 Bridge Street, but Anna vetoed that. She said Bill had been shot once at that address, and was superstitious about returning to any place where he'd once been hurt. They gave up the search then, but it was at the Dockloaders' Club that Bill was found by the police some hours later, filled with bullets, his head bashed in with a stevedore's bale hook.

Bill was buried in the National Cemetery in Cypress Hills with full military honors. He had served with the Seventy-seventh Division in France and had won the D.S.C. After he got back from the other side, he had been shot on five separate occasions and had been formally arrested seven times (but never tried) for killing people. His death left Anna penniless. The insurance companies had considered him a poor risk. Anna closed the house in New Jersey and moved back to her mother's.

She was rather proud of the long homicidal record of her first husband. A newspaper reporter once asked her how she ever came to marry a man who, during his career, had been officially accused of seven murders. Anna bristled so fiercely that the journalist shrank. "The papers only gave Bill credit for seven," Anna said bitterly. "He killed nearer twenty-seven in Brooklyn." In her indignation, Anna went on to say that Bill never got credit, either, for the half-dozen murders he added to his list during the two years that he was hiding out in Chicago after he had killed Dinny Meehan, the dock leader. The Chicago murders were strictly amateur, though, she says now, and perhaps deserve only a footnote in his record. He did the Chicago jobs as a favor to friends who gave him shelter.

Another thing that stirred Anna to anger was any newspaper reference to her as "gun moll." She has never fired a revolver or automatic, and is a little afraid of them. It isn't that she's a softy. She has taken loaded weapons from many a truculent drunk, and she often had to pick guns up during housecleanings at home. But she has never really used one in her life.

Anna doesn't consider herself tough. As a young girl, she shied away from the more raucous neighborhood elements because the he-men of the Irishtown section along the Brooklyn water front didn't conform to her ideals of what true gentlemen should be. She has been arrested only once. When she was fourteen years old, she was shopping one night with some older Irishtown girls when an Italian storekeeper, as she puts it, "made passes at us with their eyes." All Italians—called "ginzoes" by the 'Towners—were poison to an Irish girl like Anna. She fished a slab of liver off the street counter of a butcher shop next door and smacked the shopkeeper's face with it. It splashed his shirt with red stains and he thought he had been stabbed. His screams brought the police, and Anna and her friends were taken to the

Poplar Street police station. She might have gone free because she was a minor, but a sort of grim loyalty is one of her virtues, and she gave her age as eighteen. She and her friends were released next day after a night in jail.

After that the only fighting Anna did was in behalf of Peg-Leg, her brother, who was red-haired and pugnacious like her father. Anna loves to recall how Peg-Leg held on to the groceries and change the night he lost his left leg under a Smith Street trolley car. The accident happened when he was stealing a ride on the way back from the store, she remembers, and he was carried into Conley's saloon. He wouldn't get into the ambulance until he had handed the package over to his mother. Anna likes to tell the story because it illustrates what stuff the Lonergans were made of. Papa Lonergan gave the boys free rein as they grew up, but was strict with the girls. Until she was eighteen, Anna had to be in bed every night before the Navy Yard bells bonged at nine o'clock, or feel her father's horny hand. Later, when she was in show business, the curfew didn't apply. The family needed the money. Even Mrs. Lonergan worked, scrubbing offices in the Borough Hall district, to keep the family going.

While Anna was light-footing it on Broadway, Peg-Leg was helping his father run his bicycle shop. They had the Telephone Company trade. In those days, the repair men rode bicycles instead of Fords. Peg-Leg had a lot of interests outside of the shop, too. Despite his wooden leg he managed to get around, and became pretty handy with an automatic. He was a good man in a speak-easy brawl, and got an early start on his long string of homicides. He never went to prison for any of them, but neither did Anna's husband, Bill Lovett, or any other Irishtown trigger men. That seems to puzzle most people when they hear about it, but it's quite simple, as Anna explains it. Most of the killings were done when there were no witnesses around. Even when there were witnesses the cops couldn't get anything out of them. The neighborhood code forbade squealing, and in Irishtown an informer was rated twenty degrees lower than an Italian policeman.

By the time he was twenty, Peg-Leg was a holy terror along the docks and in the Irishtown speak-easies, but Anna will not admit it. She will concede that he killed a lot of men, but will insist that he was good at heart. He took up homicide, she contends, not from choice but by accident. It seems that when Peg-Leg was seventeen, Giuseppe Bonanzio, a Navy Street drug peddler, tried to get him to handle narcotics in the bicycle shop as a sort of sideline. Peg-Leg refused and Bonanzio pulled a gun. Peg-Leg grabbed the weapon, according to Anna, and it went off. Bonanzio dropped with a bullet in the heart. The killing made Peg-Leg a neighborhood big shot, and pretty soon he was taking on killing jobs for his friends on the docks. "He wasn't a professional killer," Anna says. "He'd just do these jobs to help his friends out."

After Bill died, Peg-Leg teamed up with Matty Martin, who was to be Anna's second husband. Matty was what might be called the coleader of the Irishtown stevedores. With his partner, Charlie ("Cute Charlie") Donnelly, and a gang of supporters, he dominated the docks and exacted tribute from all the dockworkers. Peg-Leg would meet Matty on the docks every day and help him with his work. Then the two of them would go to Anna's house for dinner and relaxation.

It wasn't long before these evenings took on a romantic tinge. Like Bill, Matty went in for mute courtship. Anna has found that rather a common trait among men who do a lot of shooting. They're hard-boiled and fearless among men, but practically tongue-tied around women. "It used to be real pitiful to watch Matty trying to get out a word, every now and then," she remembers. It took every bit of courage he had. Matty was taller than Bill, but, like Bill, he was a heavy drinker. He could hold even more than Bill could, though, and no one could ever tell when he was drunk. Bill had liked publicity, but Matty hated it. When Matty finally proposed to Anna, he persuaded her to get married at Saugerties, New York, so the newspapers wouldn't make a fuss about it. They were married in February, 1924, three months after Bill had been killed and buried. Right after the wedding they returned to Brooklyn to live with Anna's mother in the Bushwick district, which is a long way from the water front.

It was Anna's idea the family should move out of Irishtown. She thought people were getting to know too much of the family affairs, what with the publicity that came with every fresh shooting. Besides, she hoped Bushwick would be a safer place for Matty. They moved, but it didn't turn out that way. Two weeks after the wedding, when she was walking down the street with Matty, not far from the house, one of the aspirants for the stevedore crown on the Irishtown docks stepped out of a doorway with a revolver and aimed at Matty. Anna jumped for him, caught his shooting hand, and tried to pull the weapon away from him. One shot went off, and the powder burned Anna's right temple. It left no scar, for which she is grateful. She thinks that if the burn had left a mark people *would* think she was a gunwoman. She never tells the name of the man who tried to shoot Matty, which may be taken as indication that he is still alive.

Anna found that Matty didn't care much for food. He lived on booze most of the time. The only thing he really cared for in the way of solids was home-baked bread. His poor appetite didn't bother her, however. Bill hadn't been much of an eater, either. Matty was more easily domesticated, on the whole, than Bill had been. He preferred tinkering with radios to going out and he bought every new gadget for eliminating static or getting more distance. At one time, he owned and tinkered with five radio sets. None of them worked very well.

The chief reason for Matty's radio tinkering late at night was insomnia. Sometimes, when he did get to sleep, he would wake up screaming. It wasn't conscience, Anna says; Matty's mother said he used to do it even when he was a baby. Besides being an insomniac, Matty was a somnambulist. One hot night, when the Lonergans were asleep on mattresses on the parlor floor, he got up and walked to the rear window. Anna, who happened to be awake, was amazed at the ease with which he stepped between the sleepers in the dark. On another of his walks in his sleep Matty went downstairs, ate everything in the icebox, and took up the *Brooklyn Daily Eagle* that lay on the table. An hour later Anna went down with her mother to look for him. When Mrs. Lonergan became convinced that Matty wasn't shamming, that he was actually reading in his sleep, she told Anna to get him out of the house. "Take him away," she ordered, terrified. "He gives me the horrors."

Anna and Matty then took up housekeeping in a one-family frame house in the Bushwick district. Anna never liked apartment houses, because she has found apartment-house dwellers nosy. Another advantage of the one-family house was the flower garden. Anna had always been fond of flowers, and she found Matty was, too. He had a "green thumb"—a way with plants—as well as a supple trigger finger. He was tender with guppys, too, and in sentimental moods played the zither well.

Peg-Leg, while Anna and Matty were living the quiet life in Bushwick, didn't find enough activity or competition on the docks to satisfy his craving for target practice, so he ventured into the Gowanus area for frequent ginzo-baiting expeditions. He focused his attention on the Adonis Social Club, an Italian cabaret in Twentieth Street where Al Capone, as an unknown dance-hall bouncer, had perfected his marksmanship by shooting necks off beer bottles when there was nothing else to do. Peg-Leg and two of his stooges, Needless Ferry and Aaron Harms, swilled and guzzled liberally in the cabaret the night before Christmas, 1925, sneered at Jack ("Stickem") Stabile, the bartender, and insulted Italian patrons individually and in groups. They chased all the Irish girls out, just as they used to do in Fort Greene Park, and told them to "come back with white men." Then Peg-Leg and his friends went on drinking.

On Christmas morning, Anna made another excursion to Kings County Morgue and identified Peg-Leg, Ferry, and Harms. All three had been shot through the back of the head as they stood at the Adonis bar. Detectives made twenty arrests in the case, but ran into the customary thing—none of the men or women who were in the club when the shooting started knew who had fired the shots, and no amount of persuasion by the police, physical or oral, could convince them that they did.

Among the twenty prisoners was Capone, and he was turned loose along with the others. Anna says she knows who did the job in the Adonis Club and that she knows who killed Matty and who killed Bill, but she says she won't tell.

Anna arranged Peg-Leg's burial. She was in the habit of taking charge of all family burials. She has always been the family spokesman, too, whenever any member of her family figured in a shooting. She never tells the police much. "The way I look at it," she says, "is this: those who live by the gun, they die by the gun. It's in the hands of God." Anna is extremely religious, and always has been. Through all the shooting and the frequent murders in which her husbands and brother figured, she never missed a Mass. Her mother, who is still living, is just as steady in church attendance. Anna makes special novenas to pray for her mother's health. Her favorite saint is Saint Teresa, the Little Flower, to whom she pleads for safe guidance for her brothers and sister. "I always pray they'll have good company and not go bad," she says.

Things stayed quiet for Anna a long time after her brother Peg-Leg was buried. Matty was arrested at Peg-Leg's wake for carrying a loaded revolver and did six months on the charge. After he had finished his prison term, he went back to the docks and resumed his coleadership. He would come home from the docks every night around six o'clock and fiddle with his rheostats and verniers, and his life seemed secure and relatively peaceful. He gave Anna all she needed to run the house and a liberal clothing allowance besides. He even took her to the movies once a month, much as he disliked the cinema. But by the end of 1929 Matty's share of the money extorted from the stevedores and truckmen on the water front had dropped from an average of two hundred dollars a week to around fifty. The depression had hit shipping hard. Anna noticed, however, that "Cute Charlie" Donnelly, who shared the leadership of the stevedores with Matty, was still able to keep his wife in good clothes and seemed to have as much money as ever. She must have mentioned it to Matty. On the morning of January 29, 1930, Matty had a business conference in the loaders' shack on

Dock Street and flatly accused Donnelly of double-crossing him. After the conference, Donnelly was found dead on the floor of the shack. No witnesses. Anna felt sorry for Mrs. Donnelly. She identified the body at the morgue and helped with the funeral plans.

After the Donnelly killing, for which Matty had to make the customary trip before the magistrate to get his usual dismissal, Anna kept hearing rumors that Matty was marked for the next "out." The night of December 13 she had a bad dream, and with it her first and only premonition that death was in the offing. She explains it now as "a funny kind of feeling" and clutches in the general vicinity of her heart when she tells about it. She awakened Matty and told him about the dream, but he wasn't impressed. He didn't come home to dinner the next night, though. A police car called instead, and took Anna to Cumberland Hospital. Matty had been wounded in a De Kalb Avenue speak-easy. He lived two days. When the cops asked him who had shot him, he wouldn't discuss it. They had three men in custody, they told him—were they the ones? "Turn them guys loose," said Matty, and died.

There is every reason to believe that Matty told Anna who had shot him before he died.

Anna is especially proud of the confidence reposed in her by her husbands and their friends in all matters pertaining to homicide. Whenever there was a fresh killing, the men would tell her about it immediately. That wasn't true in the homes of other warring dock leaders. Few women could be trusted as Anna was. She did not, however, get all her information about the murders from her immediate family. The underworld has a system of its own, called "the kite," which brings murder bulletins to those who can be trusted with them. Anna used to get them long before the police or newspapers did. Sometimes they would come by telephone, sometimes by messenger. "It's like a magazine subscription," she says. "You don't ask for it, but it keeps right on coming." Anna has an idea that she is cut in on the kite line because occasional newspaper articles and a mention, now and then, in some book (there's a whole chapter about her, for instance, in "Not Guilty," the book about Sam Leibowitz) keep her name fresh in the minds of people along the water front who are close to the warring stevedore gangs and who get murder news while it's hot.

Anna is quite proud, too, of her popularity at Sing Sing. She has made several trips to the death house to console friends, and all the boys up there seem to like her. The late Leonard Scarnici, bank robber and murderer, was, in spite of being an Italian, one of her friends. After he was put to death in the electric chair, she felt pretty bad about it. "Maybe he buried a man alive up in Connecticut, like they say he did," she said recently, "and maybe he did all the killings they gave him credit for, but I knew him and I still think he had a heart of gold."

Anna lives alone, now, in a little one-family house in the Bushwick section. She devotes a lot of time to keeping the place neat. She is fussy about little details; it makes her uncomfortable if a guest so much as nudges an antimacassar out of place. She keeps about two hundred books in the house, most of them slightly out of date. She has read all of Victoria Cross, and her favorite novel is *One Night of Temptation,* by that author. There is a copy of Herbert Asbury's *Gangs of New York* in her collection, but she keeps it only out of sentiment for Matty, who liked it. Anna never cared for it very much, because it's about tough people. At least that's what she says. In the next breath, though, she's apt to point out that both Bill and Peg-Leg are mentioned in it, as well as her Uncle Jake Brady, who was a noted brawler on Cherry Hill.

Anna doesn't think she will ever marry again, although she has had some attractive offers. She says she may, of course, change her mind any day. There was a report, after Matty died, that she intended to marry Edward (Red) Patterson, a South Brooklyn holdup man who had done time in Sing Sing Prison, but that was not true. Anyway, Patterson is dead now. He was killed in a brawl by Jim Cahill, an ex-cop.

Anna keeps hoping for better times. She has an idea she may find a future in politics, and to get started in the right direction has joined a Democratic club in her neighborhood. She thinks she might be a coleader some day. She learned how to smoke at the club, and picked up a passing knowledge of bridge there. She hasn't been near the docks for a long time. She cut down her water-front visits after one of the lads stabbed her in the left arm because she demanded a cut on the meager, present-day graft. For a time after Matty's death the boys who inherited the water-front leadership saw to it that she got thirty dollars a week, but later they cut that off. "There's only a few of the old crowd left down there, anyways," she says, "and they're a bunch of heels."

ALICE AND THE AQUITANIA

by CHRISTOPHER MORLEY

Shipping business is bad; it is grievous to see so many good vessels laid up in the Erie Basin and in the alcoves of the Gowanus Canal. But *Alice M. Moran*, "of 29 net tons measurement," says her certificate, still puts in a lively twelve-hour day.

We were talking to Buck McNeil at the Battery Pier. If you have ever fallen—or jumped—overboard from the Battery seawall, you know Buck. He is the fellow who pulled you out. In his 26 years as boatman at that pier he has rescued 290 people. At least he has been credited with 290; the number is really more than that, for Buck has a habit of walking away when he has got the pessimist ashore. He keeps in his pocket the certificate of the U.S. Life Saving Medal of Honor, "for acts of Unusual Heroism," and on his watch-chain is the gold medal of the Dock Department, given him by Mayor Hylan. But in spite of hard times, people don't seem to go off the deep end so much nowadays. Buck hasn't had to go into the harbor for anyone in the last two years. He's just as pleased, for he says there are occasional twinges of rheumatism. We wanted to ask Buck whether the Carnegie Medal committee knew about all this, but just then *Alice M. Moran* came streaming across from Jersey City with a bone in her teeth. This was the Club's first chance in many years to go tugboating, and we hastened aboard.

We are not the first to raise a small chantey of praise in honor of *Alice*, for her skipper, Anton Huseby, proudly showed us an admirable article written about her by Roy Crandall in *Gas Logic* of last September. No one could improve on Mr. Crandall's excellent story, which Captain Huseby keeps in the pilot house, and which includes also a lifelike photograph of *Alice's* snug galley with the skipper, and Mr. Banks, the mate, and Mr. Anderson, the chief, and I think also Selverson, the rope-artist on deck, sitting down to chow, with Bill Paton, the Scotch cook, in the background. The deck-hand is the lad who can toss a four-inch hawser so that it loops itself right round the big iron cleat when *Alice* comes alongside a pier. And Bill Paton is still a real Scot though he admits it's a long time since he tasted haggis. We apologize to Bill for having thought he said he came from Canarsie. It wasn't Canarsie but Carnoustie, which is near Dundee. This record of the Three Hours for Lunch Club's visit doesn't attempt to compete with Mr. Crandall's narrative. But all days on a tugboat are different, and this one happened to be our own.

We were remembering that it was just 45 years ago this month that the Lords of Committee of Privy Council for Trade granted to a certain Conrad Korzeniowski his "Certificate of Competency as Master." For that reason I was the more interested in Captain Huseby's own license. It reads that he "can safely be entrusted with the duties and responsibilities of master of freight and towing steam vessels of any gross tons upon the waters of bays, sounds and rivers and to Dumping Grounds off Scotland Light, and Pilot of any Steamer of any tonnage upon New York Bay and Harbor to Yonkers, Staten Island Sound, South Amboy, Newark Bay and tributaries of the East River to Stepping Stones." The commander of a tug is a more important navigator than a lubber perhaps realizes. He is a seaman to his finger-tips, and performs dexterities of manoeuvre that astound any lover of craft. And when he takes a steamship in or out of dock he climbs to the big fellow's bridge and takes charge up there. Even if she's as big as the *Aquitania*, it's the tugboat captain who is up aloft giving the word to his leash of soft-nosed whelps, nuzzling like beagles under her tall side.

Alice had already done a good five hours' work when we boarded her. She left her berth in Brooklyn at 6 A.M. First she went to Pier 57 North River and brought the *Jacques Cartier* to Pier 3, Army Base. Then she docked the steamer *Tergestea*, and the transport *St. Mihiel* just in from Honolulu. Then she took the barge *Dwyer* 17 across to Pier 7, Central Railroad of New Jersey. It was there, I suppose, that she got the surprising news from her home office that four members of the Club had received permission to come aboard. In older days the owners of tugboat fleets sometimes signalled their captains by intricate codes of waving from the office windows in Battery Place. Perhaps there still is an emergency signal that means Visitors for Lunch.

We were hardly in the roomy pilot house before sturdy *Alice* was again about her affairs. The first thing one noticed was that tugboats, by old tradition, steer backward: unlike social craft the wheel preserves the old theory of the tiller. When the wheel is turned to starboard, the tugboat turns to port. So the ordinary merchant seaman or yachtsman is a dangerous fellow at a tugboat helm until he has learned this difference by instinct.

We went down past Governor's Island, which seemed empty and peaceful. A solitary officer was riding on a horse beside the big polo field. Captain Huseby recalled with some amusement a thing that happened (but not to his own clients), a few years ago. A big cattle-barge for the Union Stock Yards was rounding the Battery when someone hit her amidships, "right in the belly." She began to founder and the nearest safety was the army pier at Governor's Island. She was got alongside just in time and drove off several hundred terrified steers and sheep who fled in panic among barracks and parade grounds, putting major generals and polo players to flight. That day Governor's Island's dignity was badly shaken. It must have looked like a Wild West show. We had always wondered at the origin of the name Buttermilk Channel for the strait between Governor's Island and Brooklyn. Did it imply that mariners of softer temper kept in that sheltered reach while men of strong gizzard plowed up the main slot? No; Captain Huseby thinks it was named when the Brooklyn shore was all farmland and there was a rustic refreshment stand for thirsty boatmen near where the Hamilton Avenue ferry is now.

At Erie Basin and along the Gowanus Inlet one observes the curious transition in the naming of ships. There we saw old-timers like the *Buccaneer*, romantic names like *Silver Sandal*, *Western Ocean*, *Munamar*, alongside the *Commercial Guide*, the *Bird City*, the *Commercial Trader*, the *Cities Service Empire*. The *Eastern Temple* is a sulphur trader from Louisiana. The *Gibraltar* of Glasgow, a sturdy British tramp with salmon and black funnel, showed an active riffle of steam from her escape. The *West Isleta* was canted far over to starboard so we supposed she was loading. Among many idle bottoms it was encouraging to see these signs of activity. The *Cities Service Empire* was evidently very much on the job, but some of her neighbors lay rusting and forlorn. What a setting for a mystery story, one of these grim idle freighters.

We lay off Owl's Head, an old mansion on the hill at Bay Ridge, waiting for the *Alaskan*. Two old wooden hulks are on the beach there, surely a disgrace to the pride of New York Harbor. They have been there many years, and boatmen are sensitive about these things. Why doesn't the Port Authority destroy them?

In the sunny noon, which seemed more like April than November, we tarried for our client. The great heights of Manhattan showed faintly through soft haze. Along that Brooklyn shore one is aware of the enormous auxiliaries of power and service that lie behind the tall frontages of the office world. The Bush piers, the Edison plant, the Long Island Railroad freight terminal, give one plenty to think about. The incredibly vast warehouses of the Army Base add a vibration of anxiety. Then the *Alaskan* of the American-Hawaiian Line came striding up the Narrows, in light from Boston. We had thought she might be the original *Alaskan*, whom F. R. had met years ago in the Straits of Magellan. But she must be a younger vessel, and her bow showed traces of a previous name, *Wheaton*. It was fine to see *Alice* slide alongside of her, running parallel and at exactly the same speed, and gently edge in with hardly a creak from the log fenders. Bill Banks took the wheel, Captain Huseby ran up the tall green ladder *Alice* carries at her side. With unbelievable address she was swung and pushed to her berth. Her neighbor there was a well-known Bermudian friend, the *Fort St. George*. Not far away were the handsome *Eastern Prince* and *Japanese Prince* with their emblems on the Prince of Wales's three feathers. Just above was the pier of the Brazilian Lloyd, and a very handsome ship, the *Niel Maersk* of Svendborg. A few hours round the waterfront make geography very real.

Now it was time for lunch. Tugboat meals are a noble tradition, and Bill Paton, even though four guests had been put upon him unexpectedly, was ready for the test. No one ever tasted better corned beef and cabbage, boiled potatoes, spinach, coffee with condensed milk. The bowl of apples had been polished until they glittered. Bill's doughnuts, little balls of crisp fluff, compare to the average doughnut of commerce as Bacon's essays to a newspaper editorial. When we asked him if he ever gave his crew a Scotch haggis he replied that there was hardly enough room to compound one in that galley, where the stove warms the backs of the eaters as they sit. But I think he could do it if it were laid upon him. His eyes shone as we recalled how Captain Bone has the haggis played in with pipers aboard the *Transylvania*, and the cook is honored for his art with a tumbler of neat Highland elixir. The next time *Transylvania* comes up the harbor I think if Bill Paton happens to see her he will look out from his galley, see her commander high aloft in gold stripes and yellow gloves, and say to himself "Yon's the skipper wha kens aboot a haggis."

What's our next job? we asked, already feeling that for one day *Alice's* affairs were our concern. We were to take out the *Ashburton* of London, said Captain Huseby. We had noticed her at Pier 2, flying her Blue Peter, and her house-flag, with the emblem of a swan. "The Hungry Goose they call it in the Old Country," said Bill Paton.

But the *Ashburton* wasn't quite ready for us yet, so we tied up and lay comfortably in a warm drowse. Gray gulls were squealing, New York shone faintly through a yellow veil of sun. The radio in the pilot house was turned on, and through peaceful siesta some humorist from Newark was singing hunting songs about view hallos and gentry in scarlet "galloping, galloping, galloping." We ourselves felt more like snoring, snoring, snoring. Another member of the *Moran* family, *Eugene F.*, sidled in and lay alongside us with calm brotherly affection. One man sat on the stringpiece of the pier, sketching the pair. Others walked along beneath *Ashburton's* comely stern, watched the last of her cargo going aboard, learned from her mate that she was bound for Newport News and then Australia. A Diesel barge called *Corning* went buzzing fussily in and out of various piers, carrying only one huge case which looked like a crated automobile. It was like a small dog with a bone he hasn't decided where to bury. *Corning* barked every now and then with a loud and very unshiplike-sounding horn. From *Alice's* pilot house we heard the radio cry "This quaint minuet is redolent with the atmosphere of bygone days."

Then suddenly there was a hail from *Ashburton's* stern. We woke from our drowse on the pierhead. *Alice* and *Eugene F.* sprang to life. One of the Club's own members, master mariner himself, cast off *Ashburton's* stern lines from the big iron cleat. Water boiled under her counter. We took her out and swung her toward open sea, feeling we had done well. But our greatest adventure was still to come.

We came up harbor again in the pink light of late afternoon, too wise even to try to match words against that cluster of stalagmites that will never be described by deliberate intention; only, if ever, by accident. Perhaps James Bone came as near it as anyone: "The City of Dreadful Height." It is a much steeper view from the deck of a tug than from the high terraces of a liner. We steered for the deep notch of Broadway, as the big ships do, and rounded the bend of the island. F. A. remembered that the last time we had come up the bay in a tug was the night President Harding died, when some great building in

Battery Place had left its lights burning toward sea in the pattern of a huge cross. "I'm afraid they wouldn't do it again for poor old Harding," was someone's comment. Yet no man need be grudged whatever light he can get as he heads down those dark Narrows.

We passed the *American Farmer* at her pier: a merchantman of letters in spite of her bucolic name. The other day she brought over from London the new edition of Sir Thomas Browne; and is it not her commander, good Captain Myddleton, who told us long ago that he always keeps the General Catalogue of the Oxford University Press in the chart-room, for momentary relief during hours of fog or soundings? But our minds were on other matters. The *Aquitania* was now at Quarantine and would be up shortly—a full day late, after a bad voyage. *Alice* was to help dock her.

At Pier 42 is a little rendezvous where the *Moran* family and their friends the *Barretts* wait for the prima donnas to come in. We tarried there in a plain, undemonstrative family group. From the various errands of the day these stout workwomen of the harbor came puffing in. They seemed to wipe their hands on their aprons and sit rocking gently on beamy bottoms to talk things over before the big job. They filled water coolers, the men took a sluice at the fresh-water hose. There was *Joseph H. Moran*, bigger than ourself; and *Helen B. Moran* with a small white dog on board, very alert and eager of eye, much aware of his responsibility as the only dog among so many informal human beings. He stood up with front paws rigid against *Helen B's* bulwarks and watched the other kinsmen arrive with critical attention. Oliver (who notices everything) says the small white dog was furiously annoyed when in the middle of his supervisions one of the men sprayed him humorously with a mouthful of drinking water. Certainly it was a liberty, and the more so if it was done by someone on the *Howard C. Moore* or the *Downer X.*, who were not *Morans* or *Barretts*. But I did not see this myself, for at that moment F. R. was telling me of his excitement in reading Defoe's *Journal of the Plague Year* and asking me (so it seemed to my morbid mind) why none of us could write as well as Defoe.

We lay in a knot, haunch to haunch, at the end of Pier 42. *Eugene F. Moran* had followed us faithfully from Brooklyn. *Grace Barrett* was there, and *Richard J. Barrett*, and *R. J. Barrett*. It must be fun to have a big family and a tugboat to name after each of them. *John Nichols*, however, kept a little in the offing. He was too proud to join our little gab, for it is *John Nichols's* captain who goes aboard the big liner and commands the whole fleet of tugs. The rest of us sociabled our soft noses together, our upward poking bows muzzled with the big fenders that look like a brown bear climbing aboard. Above the soft aroma of the North River was a good smell of cooking. We lay in an eddy of it, for all galleys were busy.

Aquitania loomed up in the haze. Only someone very important could arrive so quietly, so steadily, so sure of herself. We had the oblique profile of her, best for both women and ships. Every slant of her seemed to accept homage. She took it as her due, yet not wholly unconscious of it, for she was still a little sore from discourtesies outside. At sea, alone with gray trigonometry, she is only a little thing. Here she was queen. In that soft light she did not come, she grew. But these were the thoughts of lubbers. The urchin tugs (I am sorry to switch metaphors so often) have no time for awe. They swarm about her skirts and hustle her with sooty grasp.

Our little fleet throbbed into action. It was like letting a pack of well-trained beagles out of a kennel. No one needed to be told anything. The routine has been perfected in every detail. *John Nichols* turned downstream to meet her. *Joseph H.* and *Helen B.* shot up ahead of us with a scurry of froth. *Grace Barrett*, pirouetting on her solid heel, twirled across our bow and took the inside track along the pierheads. Behind this interference *Eugene* and ourself and *Howard Moore* followed upstream. There was a very strong ebb, Captain Huseby had told us. But there was no difficulty of wind, a gentle breeze from S.W. It was pink November dusk at its mildest.

Alice and *Eugene* went outward to join her. She came huge above us, steadily increasing. Now we had no eyes to note the movements of the other tugs, only to study this monstrous nobility of a ship. It must have been a bad voyage, for she looked dingy, rusted and salted from water-line to funnels. High on her sloping stacks were crusts of salt. Her white-work was stained, her boot-topping green with scum. The safety nettings were still stretched along her steerage decks, even high on the promenade we could see them brailed up. Passengers at her rails looked down incuriously as we dropped astern. Just one more landing, they supposed.

We passed the notice board—*Propeller 8 feet beneath surface, Keep Clear*—and with *Eugene* slid in under her magnificent stern. Her bronze fans, turning unseen, slipped her cleanly along; we nosed busily into the very broth of her wake. Almost beneath the overhang we followed, dipping in the great swelling bubbles of her shove. It was like carrying the train of an empress. AQUITANIA, LIVERPOOL! Only the sharks have followed her closer than that. She was drawing 33½ feet at the rudderpost. The smooth taper of her hull, swimming forward ahead of us, made her seem suddenly fishlike. Beneath that skin of metal you could divine the intricate veinings and glands of her life: silvery shafts turning in a perspiration of oil, hot bulbs of light, white honeycombs of corridor, cell-like staterooms suddenly vacated. All the cunning structure of vivid life, and yet like everything living so pitifully frail. Then Bill Banks the mate went forward with a boathook. He stood under her colossal tail with his rod poised like a lance. "My God," said Oliver, "he's going to harpoon her." We looked at *Eugene F.* and there, too, stood one with boathook pointed. Like two whaleboats we followed *Moby Dick*.

She swam steadily. A uniformed officer and two sailors looked down at us from the taffrail far above. There was superiority in that look. But *Alice M.* takes condescension from none. "Give us your rope," she cried. They said nothing. We continued to follow. A breath of anxiety seemed to pass over Captain Huseby and Bill Banks. For now we were almost abreast of the pier. Perhaps that ebb tide was on their minds. To deal with that ebb was our affair. They repeated the invitation. "Wait till we get word from the bridge," replied the officer calmly. The devil with the bridge, we could see *Alice* thinking. Her job is to get hold of a line and the sooner the better. At last it came, snaking downward. Bill Banks caught it, partly on the boathook and partly on his neck. The big hawser drooped after it, five inches thick of new rope. There was fierce haste to get it looped on the towing bitts astern. It was *Alice* who took *Aquitania's* first line, from the port quarter. "You've got to be careful taking a rope under way like this," said Captain Huseby spinning his wheel. "These big ships have a powerful suction."

Eugene F. took the second line. The next thing we realized a quick hitch-up had taken place, and we were towing in tandem. *R. J. Barrett* was coupled ahead of *Alice*, *Richard Barrett* was in line with *Eugene*. The quartet headed diagonally upstream. The big hawsers came taut and creaked. *Alice* trembled. Up at *Aquitania's* port bow were three other tugs pushing downward, side by side. Seven of us altogether on the port side. There must have been half a dozen to starboard, but what was happening there we couldn't see.

Alice shook with life. The churn from *R. J. Barrett* boiled past us. The mass of *Aquitania's* stern plus the flow of the whole Hudson watershed hung on a few inches of splice hooked over the bitts. The big ship stood unmoved as a cliff, while our quartet strained and quivered. *Morans* and *Barretts* dug their twirly heels into the slippery river and grunted with work. Steam panted with hot enjoyment. *Aquitania* didn't seem to care. She wasn't even looking at us. Her port side was almost deserted. Passengers were all to starboard looking for someone to say hullo to. Lights began to shine from the ports. One was blocked with a wooden deadlight, proof of smashing weather. A single steward looked out calmly from the glory hole. It was all old business to him. For several minutes nothing seemed to happen. In midstream a big Socony tanker, almost loaded under with weight of oil, stood by to bring in fuel as soon as she was docked. John D. ready for business, we thought. There was no time to lose: she must sail again only 31 hours later. And in this, the very stress of the battle, they asked us, "How about some supper?" *Alice* had hold now. Apparently she could do practically all the rest of it herself. Captain Huseby was surprised when we said we were too excited to eat.

Gradually the big hull swung. The downward sweep of the tide crisped in a smacking surf against her side as she straightened out across the river. Her great profile brightened with lights in the thickening dusk. Now she was straight onto the opening of the pier. She blew once, very short, a deep, mellow rumble. Thanks! We all answered in chorus, with equal brevity. Sure! Our quartet slackened the pull, wheeled off at wider angles to safeguard her stern as she warped in. She had pivoted round the corner and was slowly easing against the camels, those floating rafts that keep her from rubbing. Captain Huseby now did his steering from the wheel at *Alice's* stern. The rest were at supper.

It was blue dark, 5:10 P.M. New Jersey had vanished except for the bright words LIPTON'S TEA. *Aquitania's* stern was flush with the outer end of the pier. Her ensign came down. We could hardly believe it was all over.

Bill Paton was a little disappointed we could not stay for supper. But we had seen too much—and eaten too much lunch—to be hungry yet. "Next time let us know a day ahead," he remarked, "and we can really give you a meal." We tried to compliment the deck-hand on his sure skill with a hawser. He was embarrassed. "I'm glad you were pleased," was his modest reply. They put us ashore at the end of the pier.

Why do people build or buy big steam yachts, we wondered. Surely a tugboat is the perfect craft. They build them on the Great Lakes—Green Bay, I think they said, was where *Alice* came from. You can get one like her for something like $100,000. A maiden voyage in a tugboat from Green Bay to New York would be a good trip to take.

Aquitania lay there, a blaze of lights, stewards busy carrying off baggage. *Alice* backed off with a curtseying motion, and vanished into the dark. She sleeps in Brooklyn.

From The Saturday Review of Literature. *Reprinted by permission of* The Saturday Review of Literature *and Christopher Morley*.

The Bridge

ON FEBRUARY 13, 1834, General Jeremiah Johnson wrote in The Star: "Between New York and Brooklyn, there is nothing in common, either in object, interest, or feeling—nothing that even apparently tends to their connection, unless it be the water that flow between them. And even those waters, instead of, in fact, uniting them, form a barrier between them which, however frequently passed, still form and must forever continue to form an insurmountable obstacle to their union."

On May 24, 1883, Brooklyn Bridge was opened, and in fifteen years Brooklyn as a city ceased to exist. It would be a highly inaccurate over-simplification to say that this bridge and the others which followed it caused the death of the town, but they were expressions of a great number of factors, mostly economic, which were making Brooklyn secondary to the island across from it.

Brooklyn Bridge was a creation of true grandeur and beauty, and one of the greatest pieces of engineering the world had seen. It remains one of the most majestic structures of any city of the world. Although called at first East River Bridge, it soon was known as Brooklyn Bridge, as well it should have been. Brooklyn men brought it about, and it was mostly Brooklyn money that paid for it.

The Bridge cost many lives, and maimed scores of men. It took the life of its creator, John A. Roebling, who died of tetanus after his foot was crushed by a ferry as he was looking over the site of some bridge pillars, and it made a suffering cripple of his son and successor, Washington Roebling. Emily Warren Roebling, wife of Washington, became a practical bridge engineer and carried her husband's orders and designs to his foremen. Washington Roebling watched his bridge go up from his bedroom in his home on Columbia Heights.

Too, there were men like William C. Kingsley, Colonel Julius Adams, James S. T. Stranahan, Judge Alexander McCure, and Henry Cruse Murphy, whose vision and financial courage enabled the Roeblings to complete the job. We might as well include here old Boss Tweed, who handled $55,000 or $65,000—he couldn't remember the exact amount—for arranging the authorization for building it.

For most of the fourteen years it took to construct Brooklyn Bridge, it was attacked on grounds of cost and practicability. It often had to shut down while wrangles went on in the legislature or the common councils. Seth Low, a man of singular civic piety, criticized the Roeblings whenever he got a chance, and he called the Bridge the "unsubstantial fabric of a dream, and beyond everything else it claims to be a suspension bridge. It has established the claim by suspending operations when it got a chance." Low contributed to these suspensions, and yet on May 24, 1883, he was able to say as mayor of Brooklyn: "It will be a source of pleasure today to every citizen that no other name is associated with the end than that which has directed the work from the beginning—the name of Roebling."

For more than sixty years the Bridge has delighted students of aesthetics and of engineering, poets and painters, and people who like exhilarating walks. Six days after it was opened, twelve people were killed in a panicky crush for which the police blamed pickpockets, and New York newspapers on Brooklyn mismanagement. Fifteen years later there was considerable discussion in newspapers and scientific journals about the likelihood of its falling down.

From the hundreds of bits of writing about the Bridge—the others that came later, the Manhattan, the Williamsburg, the Queensboro, and the Triboro, did not inspire such ardor and affection—we especially commend Lewis Mumford to you.

The best way to know Brooklyn Bridge is to hunt it out, look at it, and walk over it.

From The Brown Decades *by Lewis Mumford, copyright, 1931, by Harcourt, Brace and Company, Inc.*

from . . .

THE BROWN DECADES

by LEWIS MUMFORD

From the standpoint of art and nature, the gross ineffi-
ciencies of industrialism in its earliest stages were recorded in
the general loss of form in the landscape and in the various
works of man that appeared on it. Was industrialism synony-
mous with ugliness? Could steel be used as effectively as stone?
Up to the middle of the nineteenth century there was no sure
answer to these questions. Cast iron had been used in bridge
construction in London with a little practical success, but with
no decisive aesthetic results. The great glass and iron conserva-
tory that Paxton built for the London Exposition of 1851
seemed to promise something; but a similar building, done a
little later in New York, made the issue seem dubious.

A stunning act was necessary to demonstrate the aesthetic
possibilities of the new materials, and to give people confidence
in that side of engineering which the engineer had least concerned himself with: its human and aesthetic effect. That act
was the building of the Brooklyn Bridge—not merely one of the
best pieces of engineering the nineteenth century can show anywhere, but perhaps the most completely satisfactory structure
of any kind that had appeared in America. Coming into existence in an "era of deformation," it proved that the loss of form
was an accident, not an inescapable result of the industrial
processes.

The Brooklyn Bridge was the conception and achievement of
two men: John A. Roebling and his son Washington, loyally
supported by a corps of workers whose dangers and difficulties
they intimately shared. In order to understand the monument
itself, one must know a little of the characters and personalities
that stood behind it.

John A. Roebling was born in Mühlhausen, in Saxony, in
1806. He received his degree as an engineer at the Royal Polytech-

nic School in Berlin in 1826, after having studied architecture, bridge construction, and hydraulics: according to another biographical memoir, he studied philosophy with Hegel, "who avowed that John Roebling was his favourite pupil." After spending three years in obligatory service with the state, as Superintendent of Public Works in Westphalia, John Roebling emigrated to the United States in 1831. He had $3000 in capital, and with a few fellow immigrants he founded the village of Saxonburg, about twenty-five miles from Pittsburgh. Here Washington Roebling was born in 1837.

Those were the days when the canal boats made their way through the Alleghenies by means of long overhill portages, the whole boat being pulled up the steep incline: the ordinary ropes used in such hauls frayed too quickly, and Roebling, whose first job was that of assistant engineer on the slack-water navigation of Beaver River, invented the steel cable to take the place of the weak hemp, and set up a cable manufacturing plant. Roebling had first seen a chain suspension bride on a student tramp at Bamberg, and suspension bridges formed the subject of his graduation thesis. He presently invented a suspension aqueduct to make the portage of a canal over a river, using cable instead of chains; and he built it in record time. Another step brought him to the first cable suspension bridge at Pittsburgh in 1846. In 1849, he removed his wire-rope factory to Trenton, N. J. Without these wire-ropes vertical transportation would have come tardily and been more dangerous.

Roebling was the architect of his own plant; he designed every piece of machinery in it. Like many other early industrialists—people like Robert Gair, the paper-box manufacturer, for example—Roebling was a man of iron regularity and inflexible will: he would call off a conference with a man who was five minutes late. He disciplined his family, apparently, with equal rigour. Indeed, he anticipated the customs of Erewhon by regarding illness as a moral offence and penalizing it severely. But he was also an eager student of the new scene: in the midst of his inventions, he read Emerson and wrote a long MS. volume entitled Roebling's Theory of the Universe. His son, after being graduated from the Rensselaer Polytechnic in 1857, assisted his father on the Allegheny suspension bridge. During the Civil War Washington built suspension bridges for the Union Army and did balloon observation.

Manhattan Island needed a bridge connection with Long Island to supplement the ferries. The bitter winter of 1866-67, which froze over the East River entirely and blocked ferryboat traffic, brought to a head the plan for a bridge, which John Roebling had broached in 1857. Nothing but Roebling's experience, his personal power, and his immense authority could have made this plan go through: a suspension bridge with towers 276 feet high and almost 1600 feet in the central span had not been built anywhere in the world: Stephenson, one of the great English engineers, had declared against this form. By 1869 the design had come into existence. Unfortunately, as a result of an accident on a ferry, John Roebling acquired lockjaw and died, leaving behind little more than the outline that Washington was to work up into their masterpiece, provided he had the power to grapple with the many unsolved problems of tactics and construction.

Washington Roebling's heavy bullet head reminds one a little of Grant's: what it lacked of his father's granite intellectuality was made up for by an equally massive will. Washington threw himself into the work. In 1871 the foundations for the Brooklyn tower were sunk. The building of the New York tower involved a drastic decision: should he waste a year and possibly many lives in digging to bed rock, or should he let the sand distribute the weight of the caisson on the uneven rock, a few feet away? He risked his reputation and his fortune on the decision; but he boldly faced the possibility of seeing his tower slip into the river. That possibility cannot have been absent from his mind until the cable and span were set.

The whole work of building the bridge was full of martial decisions, heroic sacrifices: the Civil War itself had been easier on Colonel Roebling. A fire broke out in the caisson in 1871; and Roebling, who had spent more time than any other workman under pressure, and who directed the fighting of the fire, acquired the bends, or caisson disease. He retired to a house on Columbia Heights; his wife sat at the window with a telescope and reported on the progress of the work; and from his bed Washington Roebling directed every detail through letters. In 1872, fearing that he might not live to finish the bridge, and knowing how incomplete all the plans and instructions were, he spent the winter writing and drawing in all the details; and a year later, after a cure in Wiesbaden, he was still too weak to talk for more than a few minutes. Such heroism was not lost: the work went with a will: the little man on a white horse who commanded at Austerlitz never had a more devoted army. When the carriage for winding the cable was ready for trial, the first man to test it out was not a common workman, but Frank Farrington, the master mechanic. As many as 600 men were employed at one time. More than twenty were fatally hurt. Several succumbed to caisson disease. But the granite towers rose: the nineteen strands of cable were spun and anchored: the girders were riveted: the bridge stood. Cars and processions passed over it. It still stood.

In 1883 the battle was over. The bridge was opened, and the Brooklyn Bridge took its place with the Eads Bridge at St. Louis and the Pont Garabit in France as one of the victories of modern engineering. But it was more than that. If any one doubts that a bridge is an aesthetic object, if any one doubts that it reveals personality, let him compare the Brooklyn Bridge with the other suspension bridges on the same river. The first bridge is in every sense classic. Like every positive creative work, the Brooklyn Bridge eludes analysis, in that its effect is disproportionate to the visible means, and it triumphs over one's objections even when it falls short of its highest possibilities.

I know no better appreciation of the bridge than Montgomery Schuyler's contemporary estimate. His whole appraisal, in *American Architecture*, is worth examination; but here is the nub of it. "It is an organism of nature. There was no question in the mind of the designer of 'good taste' or of appearance. He learned the law that struck its curves, the law that fixed the strength of the relation of its parts, and he applied the law. His work is beautiful, as the work of a ship-builder is unfailingly beautiful in the forms and outlines in which he is only studying 'what the water likes,' without a thought of beauty. . . . Where a more massive material forebade him to skeletonize the structure, and the lines of effort and resistance needed to be brought out by modelling, he has failed to bring them out, and his structure is only as impressive as it needs must be."

Still, to say that the masonry might have been better is a different thing from being able to point out a single architect who might have done it better: the Richardson of 1885 might have qualified, but the young romantic architect of 1870 would, I fear, have made a horrible botch of it. Schuyler objected to the towers on the ground that the stone does not reflect the passage of the cables over the cushions on which they rest: but perhaps the greatest weakness is in the heavy rustication of the granite and the character of the stone cornice. But, particularly from the waterfront below, the piers are simple and convincing: at all events, they are the highwater mark of American architecture in the period between the design of the Washington Monument and the last phase of Richardson. The stone plays against the steel: the granite mass in compression, the spidery steel in tension. In this structure, the architecture of the past, massive and protective, meets the architecture of the future, light, aerial, open to sunlight, an architecture of voids rather than solids.

The Brooklyn Bridge was both a fulfilment and a prophecy. In the use of the steel in tension it disclosed a great range of new possibilities: for the great mission of steel as a building material is essentially to span and enclose space, and to remove the inconvenient bulkiness of bearing walls and stone columns. In its absence of ornament, its refusal to permit the steel to be other than its own unadorned reality, the Brooklyn Bridge pointed to the logic and aesthetics of the machine; and it did this far more rigorously than its later rival, the Eiffel Tower in Paris, with its early Art Nouveau treatment of the base. Finally, the bridge existed in its own right, independent of its influences and potentialities, as a work of art, a delight to the artist and the poet, but equally well appreciated by the man in the street.

This was not the first work of engineering to be a work of art; but it was the first product of the age of coal and iron to achieve this completeness of expression. It needed a man of John Roebling's intellectual and philosophic capacities to conceive such a clean, untrammelled work; it needed Washington's courage to make it an actuality. Washington Roebling lingered on, once his great life-work was fulfilled, a soldier who had not the good fortune to die on the battlefield: he collected minerals, and found life a little bitter and sardonic, according to reports, in the final years before his death in 1926. The firm that these men founded remains, too; but the heroism and the exploit of an untried problem has been diminished a little by routine: the new Hudson River bridge is doubtless a mighty work, but in comparison with the knowledge, experience, and mechanical powers available in 1869, the first is still the grander accomplishment.

If the lesson of the Brooklyn Bridge has been less potent in our engineering and architecture than it should have been, it is perhaps because our engineering schools have had a narrower conception of the engineer's vocation and culture than John Roebling had. Their simple factual statements, their respect for materials, their willing anonymity, are all fine qualities: in them is the making of a modern architectural vernacular. What is needed is an application of the method and attitude to something more than the bare mechanical problem. But the lesson of the Brooklyn Bridge has not altogether been lost: far from it. Dams, waterworks, locks, bridges, power plants, factories—we begin to recognize these as important parts of the human environment. They are good or bad, efficient or inefficient, by something more than quantitative criteria. The Roeblings perhaps never used the word aesthetics in this relation; but it was their distinction to have made it visible.

Unknowable Brooklyn

O N OCTOBER 14, 1916, the old Literary Digest ran a piece on Brooklyn which concluded:

"There is no hope that any one ever will know Brooklyn. The tide of population pours into its seventy-seven square miles. When they are filled Brooklyn will demand the rest of Long Island, with a five-cent subway to Montauk Point. And all the time man's knowledge of the borough will decrease. Study well its citizens when they come over to Manhattan to have a good time. They are the knowable people of an unknowable land."

How much any person will know of a town or another person is a doubtful quantity. What does a man know about a place, especially a land that extends up, to the sixth or tenth floor, and out to the waterfront or to the silky lanes of Long Island?

Most of the people of Brooklyn live in the same neighborhood, often in the same house, all of their lives. What is it then to a woman who has sent all her children to the same school, has traded with one grocer, one butcher, and, in the main, shopped the same two streets of dry goods and specialty stores, where she lives?

These are open questions, but it is a fair guess that roots in Brooklyn sink as deep as they do anywhere in the world.

*   *   *

As a curiosity, a souvenir from another day, we are giving you a couple of chapters from a book by Laura Jean Libbey, one of the most popular writers of her time. She stayed in her home in Brooklyn, a young maiden, and wrote of doings in the high life, and of titled ladies and simple country girls.

This one is Junie's Love Test. There has been considerable plot before these chapters, but most of it is gone over again in them. Junie has been betrayed a few times, and she is about to be again by a woman she trusts. We might add that although Junie has been the victim of a mock marriage, there was no consummation. That never happened to a Libbey heroine until she got her own true love, and usually some time after the book was ended.

from . . .

JUNIE'S LOVE TEST

by LAURA JEAN LIBBEY

"Poor child!" replied madame, compassionately, stroking Junie's tumbled, golden locks. "I think I understand. Good heavens!" cried the madame, bending still lower over Junie, "see how white she is—she does not breathe—the gray pallor of death is upon her!"

"That is the natural color of those suffering with that peculiar malady," returned Dolly, quickly. "You need have no apprehensions upon that score, madame."

Thus assured, madame appeared relieved, and presently asked, as she drew a day-book from her pocket, "What is the name of my patient?"

"Her name is Ida Murray," replied Dolly, boldly, "and mine," she added, "is Clara Murray. I should prefer keeping our residence a secret for the present."

"As you please," returned madame, booking the names, and, after leaving a deposit in requirement with the rules of the house, Dolly Carleton took her departure, congratulating herself upon carrying out so cleverly Irene's ingenious scheme.

· 363 ·

"Junie shall be kept there until the sensation of her disappearance and all search for her is over," she mused. "Then she shall be taken away where no human eye will ever rest upon the face of Junie Dean again. In time Harry Granger will learn to forget her. I will make it the study of my life to gain his love. He shall depend upon me for sympathy and consolation, and before the first frost blights the blossoms, I shall be his wife. As for Arthur, he will think Junie has fled from him rather than marry him. He is quick-tempered, hotly, bitterly jealous, and all his love will fall back upon his own heart with redoubled force. He would die before he would let Junie see how the iron had entered his soul. I can see how it will end. Irene's patient love will be rewarded, and he will marry her on the spur of the moment out of pique. How strange it is that both Irene's lover and mine have loved Junie Dean."

Dolly re-entered the coach and it rolled rapidly away, leaving Farmer Dean gazing after it in front of the house, with a puzzled expression on his honest, toil-hardened face.

"They have left the other one inside," he muttered, in astonishment, "and I'll stake the best cow on the farm that there's foul play here somewhere. If I wasn't in such a hurry to see my little Junie, I'd stay around here and look into this mystery a bit. I've always heard of the dark ways of city life, but I always calculated it was more than half talk; but after witnessing such a scene as this at midnight, I'm beginning to think there's some truth in it after all."

Farmer Dean gazed wistfully up at the tall granite building as he spoke, as if loath to tear himself away.

Oh! if he had but known that those grim walls closed in his Junie from the outside world, the after events which are soon to follow would never have happened.

As the door closed behind Dolly's retreating footsteps, madame crossed over to the sofa upon which Junie lay, and gazed compassionately down into her lovely face.

"She is scarcely more than sixteen or seventeen," she mused. "How terrible that one so young and so lovely should have formed a taste for opium? If she were a child of mine, I would rather see her dead than the slave of such a pernicious habit. I can scarcely believe it. Yet her cousin could have had no motive in willfully deceiving me. That grayish, unearthly pallor must have been produced by the drug. I shall be firm with her," commended the madame, half aloud, "and I will cure this lovely girl if I have to watch beside her night and day to accomplish it. But, first of all, I must see about preparing a room for her."

She walked slowly from the apartment as she spoke, and Junie was left alone. As the door closed softly, Junie sprung from the sofa with a little wild, stifled cry.

The fact is, the jolting of the vehicle and the action of the cold air upon her face had quite revived her, and by the time madame had entered the room Junie was in possession of her full faculties.

She heard with the most intense, breathless dismay the cruel falsehood Dolly Carleton uttered against her, and her cunning warning to the honest-hearted madame "to utterly ignore her pleadings." She heard the fictitious names Dolly had given, and her parting words that she was to be kept there a fortnight or more, and at the very thought of the awful conspiracy against her Junie had fainted outright in sheer terror. Junie did not stop to think how she had been brought into the house in which she now found herself—her one thought was to escape, and with the intuition that often comes to us when danger menaces us, she knew that whatever she did must be done at once, before madame had time to return.

Her head felt strangely dizzy, and it was with the utmost difficulty she could think clearly.

Hastily wrapping her cloak about her, Junie staggered toward the door.

It yielded to her touch, and like a startled bird who suddenly finds the door of its cage standing open and breathes the sweet air of freedom, Junie fairly flew down the winding corridors, past the astonished porter, and out into the street, her garments brushing against the stout, burly figure of Farmer Dean, who stood under the gaslight glancing up at the house.

"What was there in that slight, swaying, girlish figure so

familiar to him?" he asked himself, blankly, and again that unerring impulse prompted him to follow in close pursuit.

But young feet are more nimble than old ones. With every step the distance between them grew greater, until at length the little figure disappeared in the darkness altogether.

"Alone—at midnight—on the streets of New York," muttered Farmer Dean, compassionately. "Thank God, my little Junie is not in such peril!"

Oh! wicked city of New York—cruel, mysterious city of New York—where crime peeps forth with the setting sun and on-coming night, and stalks boldly abroad under the dim, flickering light of the stars!

As the last vibrations of the midnight hour died away in the tall towers and belfries, Junie threaded her way swiftly through the dark streets, trembling at every step, little heeding whither she went. In the distance the dark towers of the Brooklyn Bridge were dimly outlined against the dark, frowning heavens, toward which Junie unconsciously bent her steps.

"One leap from that bridge and all my troubles in this world would be over," she sighed—"my enemies could not track me beyond the gates of death."

A cold, drizzling rain was falling, and a thick gray mist was slowly curling up from the dark water.

Owing to the lateness of the hour and the storm, the bridge was almost deserted by all pedestrians, save the patrolmen slowly pacing their beats to and fro, who took little heed of the dark-robed, slender little figure gliding quietly along stealthily as a shadow.

About midway on the bridge she paused, casting quick, furtive glances to the right and to the left.

The words of Fanny still rang like a death-knell in her ears.

"If you do not marry Arthur Seymour to-morrow, and go far away, I will give forth on the morrow your shameful story. Who will believe you innocent and guiltless when the world hears of that week you spent with Harry Granger, nearly a year ago, yet you were not his wife? The world will scoff at you, and you will bring shame and disgrace upon us all. Your honor will be at stake, and ere the sun sets on the morrow your story will be blazoned before the world unless you marry Arthur Seymour at once, and go far away from here. This alone will purchase my silence for evermore."

"I see that I could never have married Arthur to-morrow," she sobbed, wringing her little white hands together, "for in spite of all the cruel wrong I have suffered, my heart is Harry's still. I have done no wrong knowingly, yet I am hunted down. There is no room for me in the great, cold, cruel world; it has narrowed down—to a grave.

"Oh, Harry, my love! my love!" she cried, "perhaps you will pity me when they tell you how I died, and, dying, loved you still, cruelly, bitterly, false though you were. No one knows of the dark secret I have guarded so well. The terrible truth can not be wrung from lips sealed in death. I forgive you, Fanny, for all your cruelty, and Irene and Dolly, I forgive you too."

She took the photograph of Harry Granger from her pocket and kissed it with such passionate, hungry, clinging kisses. "Let the world say I died in the cold, dark water; but you must not believe it, Harry; it is false, all false. I died of a broken heart! How can one live when one's heart is broken!

"Father," she murmured—"poor old papa, you, of all the world, will pity your heart-broken, miserable Junie. Good-bye, Harry," she wailed, and with the name of the love whom she believed so false upon her lips, Junie plunged madly from the Brooklyn Bridge. There was a splash and a plaintive cry; then the waters of the East River flowed onward, without a ripple to show where they had closed over Junie's golden head.

The steamer "Alaska" was nearing port; but, owing to the rules and regulations of ocean life; it would not reach the wharf until late on the following morning.

A young man on board, impatient at the delay, which he could illy brook, had taken advantage of the permit he possessed to leave the vessel and board a small skiff, which was to land him at his destination many hours in advance of the time the "Alaska" was due. The little skiff fairly danced over the dark water, despite the adverse wind and waves and the cold, drizzling rain which had just set in.

Louis Arnold—for it was he—sat in the bow of the boat, watching with eager admiration the Brooklyn Bridge, which he was fast nearing, that rose dark, majestic, and silent, spanning the shadowy East River and clasping the two slumbering cities in its dark embrace.

The skiff swept under the great dark arch, and at that very instant a swift, startled cry broke the awful stillness of the hour, quickly followed by a dark-clad figure which leaped from the towering height of the great bridge suspended between water and sky down into the turbulent, seething waters of the East River.

"My God!" cried Louis Arnold, with a terrible cry, "a woman has leaped from the bridge, and she will come up directly under this skiff!"

In an instant the brave fellow had divested himself of both coat and hat and leaped into the dark, angry waves to the rescue of the would-be suicide. One terrible, thrilling moment followed; another, and still another; then the dark, angry waves, as if loath to give up their prey, sullenly parted, and brave Louis Arnold, with the dark-robed figure held high in his arms, struck manfully out for the boat. Another moment and they were both aboard, rapidly nearing the New York shore.

The clear white light from the electric lamps shone full upon the upturned face, and an exclamation of intense surprise burst from Louis Arnold's lips as he noted how young and how gloriously beautiful this little creature was who was so bitterly tired of life—life which should have held such golden beauty for her.

They neared the shore rapidly, and Louis gathered up the slender little figure in his arms, and bore her into the waiting-room of the ferry-house just as Farmer Dean, panting and puffing with his long chase, reached the spot.

He recognized the slim little figure as the one he had been following, and at one glance at the water-soaked, dripping garments the truth flashed across his mind—the poor girl, whoever she was, had attempted to drown herself, and some one had rescued her.

The honest old farmer had a tender spot in his heart for all young girls on account of his Junie, and with a sympathetic tear coursing down his toil-hardened cheek for the sorrows of this forlorn little creature, he silently drew near.

They were just removing the folds of the cloak from about her, and the clear, steady rays of the gas-light fell full upon her white face.

For one instant the eyes of the old farmer rested upon her, then a hoarse, piercing, piteous cry echoed through the room that those who heard it never forgot to their dying day.

"Oh, my God!" cried the agonized old man, flinging himself upon his knees beside that still form. "God pity me! It is my little Junie! Junie, Junie!—little Junie!" he cried, utterly ignoring the by-standers in his terrible agony, "look up and speak to your poor old father, little pet! God help me, my heart is broken, Junie! This is more than man can bear!"

Strong-hearted men who stood around him, who, perchance, had children of their own whom they loved just as dearly, turned away with tears coursing down their cheeks, whispering to each other that this was the most pitiful scene they had ever beheld.

The old farmer would let no one approach his child; he gathered her up, just as he had done in her babyhood—gathered her up in his shaking arms, straining her close to his heart, all cold and wet, with the dripping river-water trickling from her clothing in little rills, calling upon her by every endearing name to open her pretty blue eyes and speak to him.

"Leave me alone with my child," he wailed. "My grief is too great for the eyes of strangers to witness."

"See, she is not dead!" they whispered, one to the other; "she is reviving, her eyelids quiver, her hands move!" And they all silently quitted the room, leaving the poor old farmer alone with his beloved child, still calling her name and entreating her to speak to him.

It almost seemed as though that agonized, familiar voice had the power to draw her back from the very brink of death.

Suddenly the white, golden-lashed lids flashed open wide, and Junie gazed up into his face with a soft, low, contented sigh;

then, with a terrible sob, she shrunk away from him, struggling from his arms and cowering on her knees at his feet.

"Do not touch me, papa," she sobbed, wildly, drawing back from his honest, toil-hardened, outstretched hands. "You must not touch me, papa," she whispered, "for I have committed a great sin. I was so innocent that I did not know. Yet Fanny says that will not excuse the fault—it was still a sin. I tried so hard to repent of it, papa, and I could not, and that was a double sin; and, to atone for it, I tried to die and end it all—oh, why, why did they not let me die?"

The face of the old farmer had grown strangely pale, as he listened to little Junie's wild, disconnected story.

"No matter what you have done, little Junie, your father will always find pardon for you in his heart," he cried, brokenly, lifting up the shrinking figure again, and holding her close in his arms. "You must tell your poor old father what has happened. No sin has touched my little Junie," he muttered, plaintively. "No, no, you are as pure as an angel, little Junie; you do not know what sin is; why should you speak such a word? Where is your husband, Junie?" he asked, suddenly, a new dread foreboding of coming evil chilling his heart like a blasting frost.

Junie sprung again from his encircling arms, and stood pantingly before him, the color coming and going on her lovely young face, as she nerved herself for the awful confession.

"Promise me you will not curse Harry, or wreak your vengeance on him, and I will tell you all, truthfully, papa," she said.

The farmer's lips twitched convulsively, and Junie believed he had promised.

The farmer scarcely breathed in his intense wrath, as the poor child cowered down at his feet and told him all her pitiful story; surely, the saddest that was every wrung from a young girl's lips.

"I believed so truly in our marriage," she sobbed, piteously, "that when he came to me that day at the hotel, and told me it was only a mock marriage we had gone through, I fell on my knees and begged him to take then and there the life he had so cruelly destroyed; but he turned on his heel, and, with a mocking laugh on his lips, left me alone, to live or to die of a broken heart."

LAURA JEAN LIBBEY

by LOUIS GOLD

Nearly a quarter of a century ago, when I was seventeen, I was typist for a while for Laura Jean Libbey, and she dictated to me a long series of plays and articles. I had called at her husband's law office in answer to an advertisement. He accepted me, apparently, on my appearance, for he asked me none of the usual questions regarding my experience and references, and not even my name. I was sent to his home in the Park Slope section of Brooklyn and told simply that his wife needed my services. At the start I did not know who she was and she did not reveal her identity. I knew her only as Mrs. Stilwell.

She was at that time about forty-two years old, and inclined to stoutness. Her complexion was florid, her nose aquiline, and her lips full and firm. She carried herself with dignity, and spoke in a pleasant, unhesitating contralto voice. Her hair puzzled me; it was short, perhaps six inches long, and showed a curious riot of colors, except at the back, where it was a fine dark brown. In her younger days, I learned later, it had been chestnut all over, and she had worn it in a mass of curls piled over her forehead, and rather long in the back.

I took dictation from her for a few days, wondering who she might be, and then I began to suspect that she was Laura Jean Libbey, for I had read a number of her novels when I was a few years younger, and I recognized her style. She was surprised and pleased that I had discovered her identity, and asked if the picture in the front parlor had caused me to guess who she was. When I told her I had not seen the picture she made me go down to look at it. It was a full-sized oil painting by Benjamin Eggleston, and showed her in a dazzling white satin dress and pearl necklace. She was in her early twenties when it was done. She was very proud of it, and showed me favorable articles in the newspapers regarding it.

Laura Jean Libbey wrote her first romance when she was seventeen, in the early eighties. When she completed it, she took the manuscript to New York, walking over the Brooklyn Bridge with a friend. She presented the work to a publisher who said it was wonderful, and gave her $25 for it. She was overjoyed and decided to celebrate the event in a fitting manner. She had a very strict upbringing and had not been able to get much candy. Near the Brooklyn Bridge was a confectionery store. She bought five pounds of marshmallows, and on the way home, with the aid of her friend, finished them. Both girls had severe attacks of indigestion.

The style of her first book and of all the succeeding ones was essentially the same; they showed the mentality of seventeen, and were addressed mainly to an audience of the same age. Miss Libbey claimed to be the first author of the paper-bound novels that were once so popular, and she told me that all the subsequent writers of them, such as Charles Garvice, Bertha M. Clay, Mrs. E. D. E. N. Southworth, Charlotte Braeme and Caroline Hart, were her imitators and plagiarized her stories, and that a good many dramatists used her plots. The plan of action was always the same, and it could be said of her books what Cabell says of women, that their names alone varied. A virtuous young man met a similarly blessed young girl and there was love at first sight, which was displeasing to the villain or villainess, or both. From then on the characters moved on joined circles or figures of eight; where the lines of movements met there was a collision, with favorable or undesirable consequences; then they separated and again circled until another meeting. This was repeated for two hundred pages, when the lovers were abruptly united, misunderstandings were cleared up, the bad characters suddenly discomfited, and the book ended happily. The conclusion was always a wedding.

Only once did she write a story with an unhappy ending; the storm of protesting letters she received discouraged her from making another such blunder. In this story the poor girl died of a broken heart, and was buried in a lonely grave. One night, during a terrible snow-storm, the hero, who had learned where she was buried, dragged himself to the grave and wept bitterly over it. He was found the next day, frozen dead, and was buried beside his sweetheart.

In her novels the bride of the hero was always a virgin, even though she had married the villain of the story. Miss Libbey often had to stretch probability to extremes to accomplish this. Sometimes the villain-husband was jailed immediately after the ceremony, or kidnapped, or had to flee from the police, and the separation continued until his first wife, from whom he had not had a legal separation, appeared on the scene to permit a happy ending. At other times, the bride fell ill of brain-fever, which lasted until the death or exposure of her wicked husband. In every case the virtuous young man of the story was assured of a virgin bride.

It was generally impossible to judge the contents of a given story by the title, for most of them could be used, like the characters, interchangeably. There were "When His Love Grew Cold," "He Loved Her but Was Lured Away," "Had She Loved Him Less," "Was She Sweetheart or Wife?" "Beautiful Florabelle's Lover," "The Abandoned Bride," "The Loan of a Lover," and so on. The chapter headings were usually long and romantic. The following, for example, were the first three in "The Girl He Forsook":

Chapter 1. *Why should Heaven let those meet who might learn to love each other, if there is an insurmountable barrier between them which can never be beaten down? I say it is cruel—it is unjust!*
Chapter 2. *Oh God, can nothing save us from being dispossessed—turned out into the street, with our little all, this bitterly cold Winter day?*
Chapter 3. *In the great battle between love and duty, which would win? He was only human.*

II

Laura Jean Libbey wrote all of her novels before her mother died, when she was still unmarried. Her mother, she told me, loved to read them as she wrote the pages in her fine firm penmanship, making hardly any elisions or corrections, the story flowing from her in a steady stream. Her mother was of French extraction, of which fact she appeared to be proud. Laura Jean described her as quite an aristocratic little lady. She would never go into the dining-room in the basement of the family house, but insisted that meals be served in the back parlor. Laura Jean had been very fond of her mother and revered her memory; she showed me a photograph of a granite shaft she had erected to her in Greenwood Cemetery. But there were times when she spoke with regret of the demands that her mother had made—for example, that she remain single. She declined a number of proposals when she was young, one of them from a man who is now a noted editorial writer. She never told me anything about her father, although there was a large picture of him on the wall of her bedroom; he must have died when she was quite young.

She married a few years after her mother's death, when she was about thirty-six. Her husband, when I knew him, was a taciturn lawyer. The only other member of her family that I ever saw or heard of was a sister, somewhat older than Laura Jean. She was married, with an adult son, and often came for visits of days or even weeks. She was immensely proud of Laura, telling me constantly how popular she had been at the height of her career, and how she had been greeted and acclaimed all over this country and in Europe. I never liked the way this sister called me. It was "Lou-ass, Lou-ass," with very definite emphasis on the second syllable.

A red tom-cat called Teddy and its mother, a coal black cat, were Laura Jean Libbey's pets. The tom-cat was rather bad tempered and often gave its mistress scratches, but that did not diminish her fondness for him. The black cat regularly presented her with a litter of kittens, all of which were taken away by the S.P.C.A.

About ten years after she had written her last novel, and before her popularity had entirely waned, Miss Libbey blossomed once more into public notice. The theatrical manager, Charles E. Blaney, who was then staging a series of melodramas, dramatized and produced one of her books, "Parted On Her Bridal Tour." She was overwhelmed with delight and immediately considered her possibilities as a dramatist, finally deciding that she could write plays as well as books. Her ambition led to my employment.

In the morning I would arrive at about half past nine. A few minutes later her husband would leave to walk to his office in the Borough Hall section of Brooklyn. Laura Jean would kiss him good-bye, usually asking him to come home early, or not to go to his club. His reply was regularly polite but non-committal.

She would dictate to me in the back parlor behind the billiard room, or in the music room on the floor above. In the former place there was a door to a stairway which went down to the kitchen. In the early part of the playwriting period, Laura Jean would now and then tip-toe over to the door, continuing to dictate to me, and pull it open quickly. Once she caught her Irish maid listening, and at other times there was a sound of scurrying feet. The maid did not continue this very long, however, for it must have been trying to be chased away at an interesting point in a play, leaving the outcome in doubt.

Usually, Laura Jean wore a house dress or apron when dictating, and nearly always stood up. She seldom paced the floor, and rarely was at a loss for words. Her usual pose was to stand with her left arm across her waist, resting her right elbow in the palm of her left hand, with her right hand at her chin. Sometimes she would stand at a window, looking out as she dictated.

She began a play by looking in the morning newspaper for names. She never made an outline or had notes, saying that she did not have the full plot in mind, but would work it out as she proceeded, just as she had written her books. She dictated for a few hours in the morning and a few hours in the afternoon, taking sometimes a holiday of an afternoon or at the end of a week. It usually took two days to write a play, and two plays a week was the rule, but occasionally there were three plays a week. Each play filled from sixty to ninety pages of legal paper size. In a year and a half she finished in this manner about a hundred and twenty plays.

As in her books, there was a great deal of repetition, and none of the characters was drawn very clearly. As plays, they frankly bored me, for they exhibited no originality, and lacked the action of the books. Whenever I ventured to point out that she had used a given situation or joke in a previous play she said she would make the necessary changes in whichever play was produced last; she was certain that all of them would be staged.

Two jokes were her favorites, and she used them in every other play. One had to do with a widower who was chided for remarrying too soon after the death of his first wife. He answered: "Well, isn't she as dead now as she ever will be?" The other came from "Parted On Her Bridal Tour"; it was not in her book, but was put in by the man who dramatized it. A woman sat on a man's straw hat, crushing it completely. The woman then presented the hat to the man, saying: "I think I sat on your hat." The man looked at the hat and replied: "You *think* you sat on my hat? You know damn well you did!"

When the one hundred and twenty plays were all finished, she named them. She came down one day with a list of one hundred and twenty names, similar to those of her books, and I made out the title sheets, using one name to a sheet. I thought that we would have a hard time locating the plays to which the titles belonged, but she had a quick solution for that problem. According to her instructions, I placed a title page on each play in the order in which they came to my hand without regard to the contents, and that was the way they were copyrighted. I imagine the names fitted the plays pretty well. She made a trip to Washington for the occasion, and received quite a bit of publicity, which she hoped would create a demand for the production of the plays. But in the twenty-odd years that have followed since the last of them was written, not one of them, so far as I know, has ever been produced. Perhaps the rise of the movies is to blame; they were becoming popular at the time she finished, and beginning to take over the theatres formerly devoted to melodrama.

She did very little entertaining and went out seldom. I remember there was only a single visitor in the daytime in over two years, and the maid informed me there were very few in the evenings. I imagine she would have made an entertaining hostess or guest. Once she read a paper on Ouida before a women's club, laying emphasis on Ouida's death, which she described in minute detail. After the reading, she told me, tears were streaming and handkerchiefs were wet.

After I had been working for her about a year, I asked for a raise in salary. She said she would speak to her husband. She told me later that he was opposed to it, but said that she would give me the usual check weekly and add the raise I wanted in cash, but I was not to mention it to anyone.

Now and then there would be periods of a few days or a week when she could not think of anything or felt indisposed. On such days I showed up as usual in the morning, but left immediately after her husband did; or if he delayed his departure, occupied myself in making lines on pages or in appearing busy in some other fashion.

The bedrooms in the house were all on the third floor. There was an iron gate at the head of the stairs which went up to the ceiling and was locked every night. During a short period when she was suffering from lumbago I carried my typewriter to her bedroom, and took dictation there. Once she showed me a small box full of jewelry, mostly unset diamonds, which she kept in a small safe in the room. At the same time, perhaps purposely, she also showed me two of the longest barrelled .45 revolvers that I have ever seen, even in the movies, which were kept near the safe.

When the plays were completed, I was given an extra week's pay and told there was no further use for my services.

III

The following Winter Laura Jean Libbey appeared as a vaudeville performer at the American Theatre in West 42nd Street in New York. She wore a large bonnet with wide ribbons underneath her chin. She carried a parasol and skipped to the center of the stage with stiff swaying movements. She had adopted a high-pitched falsetto voice for the stage, and with a wide fixed smile she gave humorous anecdotes of what would now be called the love racket, ending each one with a little laugh, a long indrawn breath, and a long "Ye-e-es" before going on to the next.

The audience was not in a receptive mood and there was hardly any applause. After the performance, she held a reception on the stage to greet those who came to shake hands with her. Letters could then be handed to her requesting advice on love matters, or they could be dropped into the boxes set up in different parts of the theatre. Her sister was there also, bustling about. Laura Jean never again appeared on the stage. Evidently she was not a success.

I wrote a letter to her saying that I had enjoyed her performance, and that she looked and acted youthful, girlish and splendid. She wrote back, requesting me to call at her home, which I did with alacrity, as I had lacked a steady job since I left her employ six months before. She told me she had a contract to conduct a column of love advice for a syndicate of newspapers and needed a typist again.

Shortly afterward, huge billboard advertisements, and a series of interviews in the New York *Mail* announced her appearance as a special writer for that newspaper. She was to conduct a department called "Cupid's Red Cross: First Aid to Wounded Hearts." I do not know who picked the title; it sounds a good deal like her own choice. F. P. A. was at that time conducting his column, "Always in Good Humor," in the same newspaper.

The method used in preparing these articles was different from that used for the plays. She would write them out in longhand on legal length paper, two full sheets to an article, and I would copy them on the typewriter. The written sheets, as she presented them to me, were quite neat and showed practically no corrections or erasures.

The articles, in contents and outlook, were a generation behind their times, and showed a lack of worldly knowledge that could have come only from one who had lived a secluded life. She hinted to me once that she had to write down to the level of her audience, but she gave many evidences that she believed in the greater part of what she wrote.

On the first day of the appearance of the articles there were two of them, with a large photograph of her taken about twenty years previously. The type was large and the two articles with the picture filled half a page. The titles were "What's the World to One Who Has No Dearie?" and "Where May Girls Who Toil Meet Men to Marry?" The articles following bore such titles as "Are Women Ever Loved Too Well?" "Do Men Cast Off by Society Make Good Husbands?" "Wiles of Wedded Flirts," "Is a Wife a Husband's Heart Partner Only?" "Can Love Become a Mockery?" "A Wife's Broken Love Dream," "Do Men Admire Gayly Attired Women?"

I considered one article so bad that I made bold to comment upon it unfavorably. It was entitled "The Heart of a Working Girl," and appeared in the *Mail* with the others. It told with pathos of the trials and tribulations of poor working girls, particularly those who had to stand behind department-store counters and wait upon snappish insulting customers. One pretty girl unwittingly made a customer angry. The floor-walker was called and in spite of the poor girl's pleadings and tears, and a pathetic story of the family dependent upon her support, with sick members and the possibility of being dispossessed, she was brutally discharged. She received her tiny pay from the cashier and staggered out of the door into the slush and snow, so crushed by the blow that she did not notice the traffic. A large automobile knocked her over. Immediately a handsome young man sprang out and picked up the poor little victim. He was overjoyed at finding her unhurt and took her to her home. He was the son of the owner of the department-store. Soon he married her. Therefore, continued the article, let not the poor working girls become disheartened, for something similar may happen to them.

Laura Jean Libbey received many letters asking for advice. They were of the kind one would expect. Some were from flippant smart-alecks, and a few were unprintable. But in order to fill up her space, she sometimes had to make up letters. These were good enough, but she made up only a few of them, leaving to her sister the job of concocting the rest.

In those days Laura Jean received a number of letters proposing marriage. One writer claimed he was the son of a former Governor of Mississippi. They all thought that she was single and that her present appearance was like the photograph at the head of her column.

Apparently the column was not successful. At first it was placed prominently in large type near the front page of the newspaper. In a very short while her picture disappeared, and the type became smaller. Page by page it retreated until it reached the last page. In a few months there were days when there was no article. Long before the end of the year, the articles disap‚ peared altogether.

About three years ago there was a brief announcement in the Brooklyn *Daily Eagle*, occupying barely half an inch, which said that Laura Jean Libbey had died. I read a number of metropolitan newspapers. No other newspaper that I saw carried the news and I did not see any editorial comment.

From The American Mercury, *September, 1931. Reprinted with permission of the author.*

On the other hand, there has probably been no more bitter picture of a hack writer than Irwin Shaw's "Main Currents of American Thought."

MAIN CURRENTS OF AMERICAN THOUGHT

by IRWIN SHAW

"Flacker: All right now, Kid, now you'd better talk," Andrew Draper dictated. "Business: sound of the door closing, the slow turning of the key in the lock. Buddy: You're never going to get me to talk, Flacker. Business: sound of a slap. Flacker: Maybe that'll make you think different, Kid. Where is Jerry

By permission of the author. Copyright 1939, Irwin Shaw. Originally published in The New Yorker. *In* Welcome to the City, *Random House.*

Carmichael? Buddy (laughing): Wouldn't you like to know, Flacker? Flacker: Yeah. (Slowly, with great threatening in his voice) And I'm going to find out. One way or another. See? Business: siren fades in, louder, then fades out. Announcer: Will Buddy talk? Will Flacker force him to disclose the whereabouts of the rescued son of the Railroad King? Will Dusty Blades reach him in time? Tune in Monday at the same time etcetera etcetera—"

Andrew dropped onto the couch and put his feet up. He stretched and sighed as he watched his secretary finish scratching the dictation down in her shorthand notebook. "There's another thirty bucks," he said. "Is it the right length?"

"Uh huh," she said. "Eleven and a half pages. This is a very good one, Andy."

"Yeah," Andrew said, closing his eyes. "Put it next to 'Moby Dick' on your library shelf."

"It's very exciting," she said, standing up. "I don't know what they're complaining about."

"You're a lovely girl, Lenore." Andrew put his hands over his eyes and rubbed around and around.

"Tomorrow? At ten o'clock?"

"At ten o'clock. Dig me out of the arms of sleep. We shall leave Dusty Blades to his fate for this week and go on with the further adventures of Ronnie Cook and his friends, forty dollars a script. I always enjoy writing 'Ronnie Cook' much better than 'Dusty Blades.' See what ten dollars does to a man." He opened his eyes and watched Lenore putting her hat on in the mirror. When he squinted, she was not so plain-looking. He felt very sorry for Lenore, plain as sand, with her flat-colored face and her hair pulled down like a rope, and never a man to her name. She was putting on a red hat with a kind of ladder arrangement up one side. It looked very funny and sad on her. Andrew realized that it was a new hat. "That's a mighty fine hat," he said.

"I thought a long time before I bought this hat," Lenore said, flushing because he'd noticed it.

"Harriet!" the French governess next door screamed, in the

alley outside, at the next door's little girl. "Harriet, get away from there this minute."

Andrew turned over on his stomach on the couch and put a pillow over his head. "Have you got any ideas for 'Ronnie Cook and His Friends' for tomorrow?" he asked.

"No. Have you?"

"No."

"You'll get them by tomorrow," she said. "You always do."

"Yeah," said Andrew. "God-damn Ronnie Cook and his god-damn friends."

"You need a vacation," Lenore said. "Goodbye. Get a good night's sleep."

"Anything you say."

Andrew watched her with one eye as she went off the porch on which he worked and through the living room and dining room toward the stairs. Then he closed his eyes and tried to sleep. The sun came in through the open windows, and the curtains blew softly over his head, and the sun was warm and comforting on his closed eyes. Across the street, on the public athletic field, four boys were shagging flies. There would be the neat, pleasant crack of the bat and a long time later the smack of the ball in the fielder's glove. The tall trees outside, as old as Brooklyn, rustled from time to time as little spurts of wind swept across the baseball field.

"Harriet!" the governess called. "Stop that or I will make you stand by yourself in the corner all afternoon! Harriet! I demand you to stop!"

The little girl cried, "Mamma! Mamma! Mamma, she's going to hit me!"

The little girl hated the governess and the governess hated the little girl and they continually reported each other to the little girl's mother.

"You are a little liar!" the governess screamed. "You will grow up and you will be a liar all your life. There is no hope for you."

"Mamma!" wailed the little girl.

They went inside the house and it was quiet again.

"Charlie," one of the boys yelled, "hit it to me, Charlie!"

The telephone rang four times, and then Andrew heard his mother talking into it.

"It's a man from the bank," she called to him. "He wants to talk to you."

"You should've told him I wasn't home," Andrew said.

"But you are home," his mother said. "How was I to know that—"

"You're right." Andrew swung his legs over the side of the couch and sat up. "You're perfectly right." He went into the dining room to the telephone.

"You're a hundred and eleven dollars overdrawn," said the man at the bank.

Andrew squinted at his mother, sitting across the room on a straight chair with her arms folded in her lap, her head turned just a little, so as not to miss anything.

"I thought I had about four hundred dollars in the bank," Andrew said into the phone.

"You're a hundred and eleven dollars overdrawn."

Andrew sighed. "I'll check it." He hung up.

"What's the matter?" his mother asked.

"I'm a hundred and eleven dollars overdrawn," he said.

"That's shameful," his mother said. "You ought to be more methodical."

Andrew started back to the porch.

"You're awfully careless," his mother said, following him. "You really ought to keep track of your money."

"Yes." Andrew sat down on the couch.

"Give me a kiss," his mother said.

"Why?"

"No particular reason." She laughed.

"O.K." He kissed her and she held him for a moment. He lay back on the couch. She ran her finger under his eye.

"You've got rings under your eyes," she said.

"That's right."

She kissed him again and went away.

He closed his eyes. From the rear of the house came the sound of the vacuum cleaner. He got up and went to his mother's bedroom. She was down on one knee and bent over, running the machine back and forth under the bed.

"Hey!" Andrew yelled. "Hey, Mom!"

She turned off the machine and looked up at him. "What's the matter?"

"I'm trying to sleep," he said.

"Well, why don't you sleep?"

"The vacuum cleaner. It's shaking the house."

. His mother stood up, her face setting into stern lines. "I can't use it while you're working. I can't use it while you're reading. I can't use it until ten o'clock in the morning because you're sleeping." She started the machine. "When am I supposed to clean the house?" she called over the noise of the cleaner. "Why don't you sleep at night, like everybody else?" And she put her head down low and vigorously ran the machine back and forth.

Andrew watched her for a moment. Then he went out of the room, closing the door behind him.

The telephone was ringing again, and he picked it up and said "Hello."

"Ahndrew?" his agent's voice asked. His agent was from Brooklyn, too, but he had a very broad "a," with which he impressed actors and sponsors.

"Yes, this is Ahndrew." Andrew always made this straight-faced little joke with his agent, but the agent never seemed to catch on. "The 'Dusty Blades' scripts are all through. You'll get them tomorrow."

"I called about something else, Ahndrew. The complaints're piling up on the 'Blades' scripts. They're as slow as gum. Nothing ever happens. Ahndrew, you're not writing for the *Atlantic Monthly*."

"I know I'm not writing for the *Atlantic Monthly*."

"I think you've rather ran out of material," his agent said lightly, soothingly. "I think perhaps you ought to take a little vacation from the 'Blades' scripts."

"Go to hell, Herman!" Andrew said, knowing that his agent had found somebody to do the scripts more cheaply for him.

"That's hardly the way to talk, Ahndrew," Herman said. "After all, I have to stand in the studio and listen to the complaints."

"Sad, Herman," Andrew said. "That's a sad picture," and hung up.

He rubbed the back of his neck reflectively, feeling the little lump behind his ear. Then he went into his own room and sat at his deck, looking blankly at the notes for his play, which lay to one side, neatly piled, growing older. He took out his checkbook and his last month's vouchers and arranged them in front of him.

"One hundred and eleven dollars," he murmured as he checked back and added and subtracted, his eyes smarting from the strain, his hands shaking a little because the vacuum cleaner was still going in his mother's room. Out on the athletic field more boys had arrived and formed an infield and were throwing the ball around the bases and yelling at each other.

Dr. Chalmers, seventy-five dollars. That was for his mother and her stomach.

Eighty dollars rent. The roof over his head equalled two "Ronnie Cook and His Friends." Five thousand words for rent.

Buddy was in the hands of Flacker. Flacker could torture him for six pages. Then Dusty Blades could be speeding to the rescue with Sam, by boat, and the boat could spring a leak, because the driver was in Flacker's pay, and there could be a fight for the next six pages. The driver could have a gun. It could be used, Andrew decided, but it wouldn't be liked, because he'd written at least four like it already.

Furniture, a hundred and thirty-seven dollars. His mother had always wanted a good dining-room table. She didn't have a maid, she said, so he ought to get her a dining-room table. How many words for a dining-room table?

"Come on, baby, make it two!" the second baseman out on the field was yelling. "Double 'em up!"

When Andrew was still in college he used to go out on a Saturday at ten o'clock in the morning and shag flies and jump around the infield and run and run all day, playing in pickup games until it got too dark to see. He was always tired now, and even when he played tennis he didn't move his feet right, because he was tired, and hit flatfooted and wild.

Spain, one hundred dollars. Oh, Lord!

A hundred and fifty to his father, to make up the deficit in his payroll. His father had nine people on his payroll, making little tin gadgets that he tried to sell to the dime stores, and at the end of every month Andrew had to meet the payroll. His father always gravely made out a note to him.

Flacker is about to kill Buddy out of anger and desperation. In bursts Dusty, alone. Sam is hurt. On the way to the hospital. Buddy is spirited away a moment before Dusty arrives. Flacker very smooth and oily. Confrontation. "Where is Buddy, Flacker?" "You mean the little lad?" "I mean the little lad, Flacker!" . . .

Fifty dollars to Dorothy's piano teacher. His sister, Dorothy. Another plain girl. She might as well learn how to play the piano. Then one day they'd come to him and say, "Dorothy is ready for her début. All we're asking you to do is rent Town Hall for a Wednesday evening. Just advance the money." She'd never get married. She was too smart for the men who would want her and too plain for the men she'd want herself. She bought her dresses in Saks. He would have to support, for life, a sister who would only buy her dresses in Saks and paid her piano teacher fifty dollars a month every month. She was only twenty-four. She would have a normal life expectancy of at least forty years. Twelve times forty, plus dresses at Saks and Town Hall from time to time . . .

His father's teeth, ninety dollars. The money it cost to keep a man going in his losing fight against age.

The automobile, nine hundred dollars. A nine-hundred dollar check looked very austere and impressive, like a penal institution. He was going to go off in the automobile, find a place in the mountains, write a play. Only he could never get himself far enough ahead on "Dusty Blades" and "Ronnie Cook and His Friends." Twenty thousand words a week, each week, recurring like Sunday on the calendar. How many words was "Hamlet"? Thirty, thirty-five thousand?

Twenty-three dollars to Best's. That was Martha's sweater for her birthday. "Either you say yes or no," Martha had said last Saturday night. "I want to get married and I've waited long enough." If he got married, he would pay rent in two places, light, gas, telephone.

Flacker played with something in his pocket. Dusty's hand shoots out, grabs Flacker's wrist, pulls his hand out. Buddy's little penknife, which Dusty had given him for a birthday present, is in Flacker's hand. "Flacker, tell me where Buddy Jones is or I'll kill you with my bare hands." A gong rings. Flacker has stepped on an alarm. Doors open and the room fills with his henchmen. . . .

Twenty dollars to Macy's for books. Parrington's "Main Currents of American Thought." How does Dusty Blades fit into the "Main Currents of American Thought"?

Ten dollars to Dr. Faber. "I don't sleep at night, Doctor. Can you help me?"

"Do you drink coffee, Mr. Draper?"

"I drink one cup of coffee in the morning. That's all."

Pills, to be taken before retiring. Ten dollars.

If he married, he would take an apartment downtown, because it would be silly to live in Brooklyn this way, and he would buy furniture, four rooms full of furniture, beds, chairs, dishrags, relatives. Martha's family was poor and getting no younger and finally there would be three families, with rent and clothes and doctors and funerals.

Andrew got up and opened the closet door. Inside, stacked in files, were the scripts he had written in the last four years. They stretched from one wall of the wide closet across to the other—a million words. Four years.

Next script. The henchmen close in on Dusty. He hears Buddy screaming in the next room . . .

How many years more?

The vacuum cleaner roared.

Martha was Jewish. That meant he'd have to lie his way into some hotels if he took her to them at all and he never could escape from one particular meanness of the world around him.

He sat down at his desk. One hundred dollars again to Spain. Barcelona had fallen and the long, dusty lines had beaten their ways to the French border with the planes over them. And out of a sense of guilt at not being on a dusty road himself, bloody-footed and in fear of death, he had given a second hundred dollars, feeling at the same time that it was too much and nothing he ever gave could be enough. Three and a third "The Adventures of Dusty Blades" to the dead and dying of Spain.

The world loads you day by day with new burdens that increase on your shoulders. Lift a pound and you find you're carrying a ton. "Marry me," she says, "marry me." Then what does Dusty do? What the hell can he do that he hasn't done before? For five afternoons a week now, for a year, Dusty has been in Flacker's hands, or the hands of somebody else who is Flacker but has another name, and each time he has escaped, but now how?

The vacuum cleaner roared in the hallway outside his room. "Mom!" he yelled. "Please turn that thing off!"

"What did you say?" his mother called.

"Nothing."

He added up the bank balances. His figures showed that he was four hundred and twelve dollars overdrawn instead of one hundred and eleven dollars, as the bank said. He didn't feel like adding the figures over. He put the vouchers and the bank's sheet into an envelope for his income-tax returns.

"Hit it out, Charlie!" a boy called on the field. "Make it a fast one!"

Andrew felt suddenly like going out and playing with them. He changed his clothes and put on a pair of old spiked shoes that were lying in back of the closet. His old pants were tight on him. Fat. If he ever let go, if anything happened and he couldn't exercise, he'd get as big as a house. Maybe Dusty has a knife in a holster up his sleeve. How plant that? The rent, the food, the piano teacher, the people at Saks who sold his sister dresses, the nimble girls who painted the tin gadgets in his father's shop, the teeth in his father's mouth, the doctors, the doctors, all living on the words that would have to come out of his head. . . . See here, Flacker, I know what you're up to. Business: Sound of a shot. A groan. Hurry, before the train gets to the crossing! Look! He's gaining on us! Hurry! Will he make it? Will Dusty Blades head off the desperate gang of counterfeiters and murderers in the race for the yacht? Will I be able to keep it up? Andrew asked himself. The years, the years ahead. . . . He would grow fat and the lines would become permanent under his eyes and he'd drink too much and pay more to the doctors because death was nearer and there was no stop, no vacation from life, because in no year could he say, "I want to sit this one out. Kindly excuse me."

His mother opened the door. "Martha's on the phone."

Andrew clattered out in his spiked shoes, holding the old, torn fielder's glove. He closed the door to the dining room to show his mother this was going to be a private conversation.

"Hello," he said. "Yes." He listened gravely. "No," he said. "I guess not. Goodbye. Good luck, Martha." He stood looking at the phone after he had put it down. His mother came in and he picked up his glove and started down the steps.

"Andrew," she said, "could you spare fifty dollars?"

"Oh, God!"

"It's for Dorothy. She's going to a party, a very important party—"

"Do the invitations cost fifty dollars apiece?" Andrew kicked the top step and a little piece of dried mud fell off one of the spiked shoes.

"No, Andrew. It's for a dress. She can't go without a new dress, she says. There's a man there she's after."

"She won't get him, dress or no dress," Andrew said. "Your daughter's a very plain girl."

"I know," his mother said. Her hands waved a little, helpless and sad. "But it's better if she at least does the best she can. I feel so sorry for her, Andrew."

"Everybody comes to me!" Andrew yelled, his voice suddenly high. "Nobody leaves me alone! Not for a minute!"

He was crying now and he turned to hide it from his mother. She looked at him, surprised, shaking her head. She put her arms around him. "Just do what you want to do, Andrew, that's all. Don't do anything you don't want to do."

"Yeah," Andrew said. "Yeah. I'm sorry. I'll give you the money. I'm sorry I yelled at you."

"Don't give it to me if you don't want to, Andrew."

He laughed a little. "I want to, Mom, I want to."

He patted her shoulder and went down toward the baseball field, leaving her standing there, puzzled, at the top of the steps.

The sun and the breeze felt good to him on the baseball field and he forgot for an hour, but he moved slowly. His arm hurt at the shoulder when he threw, and the boy playing second base called him "Mister," which he wouldn't have done even last year, when Andrew was twenty-four.

When nine-year-old Nathalia Crane's verse was first printed in 1922 it caused a poetical furore. Newspaper men, poetry critics, and article writers journeyed out to Brooklyn to talk to the child prodigy. The Brooklyn Eagle "exposed" Nathalia Crane, as Nunnally Johnson tells in the following piece, and altogether it was a nine-day, Sunday-supplement wonder.

As a footnote to the charge of fakery, Nathalia Crane has had several volumes of poetry and novels published since then.

NATHALIA FROM BROOKLYN

by NUNNALLY JOHNSON

One day last Fall a Brooklyn newspaper came to the conclusion that its distinguished young fellow-citizen, Nathalia Crane, could not possibly be anything short of a hoax. This conclusion was based, at the outset, on a sort of plain, common, hard horse-sense. It simply didn't stand to reason that a child of twelve could have written the lines to be found in "The Janitor's Boy and Other Poems" and "Lava Lane." The day of miracles had passed. More specifically, the managing editor and the two women reporters who prosecuted the newspapers' "investigation" of Nathalia's integrity had this in mind: that in the two collections there were manifestations of a scientific erudition impossible in a child of her environment. They found in them, they said, indications of a familiarity with the theories and substances of such varied and adult matters as chess, counterpoint, the nebular hypothesis, navigation, military tactics, zoölogy, the manual of arms, botany, and atheism. There was nothing in all that they could learn of Nathalia, they said, to show that she had ever been exposed to more than, say, one or two of these occult arts and sciences.

Nor were they alone in their conviction. In the course of their "investigation" they rallied to their support Indignant Reader, Edwin Markham, Just a Mother, John V. A. Weaver, Wot A. Guy, of 2763 Rugby Road, Brooklyn, and a score or more of Old Subscribers. They succeeded in arousing numberless private controversies. The discussion spread over the entire country and made Nathalia almost as widely known as Gerald Chapman. In point of fact, there was an understandable justification for most of this skepticism. The poems credited to Nathalia were unquestionably distinguished, and frequently breath-taking in their bold originality. They were in them, as the investigators said, traces of an extraordinary wisdom. The poem, "Lava Lane," was undeniably based on Laplace's theory of the beginnings of matter. And there were at least suggestions of the other mysteries mentioned.

As in all other cases of child prodigy, there remained also the stubborn theory that the scope and potentialities of the child mind are everybody's huckleberry. Poetry or no poetry, mamma and papa assume to know children. Mamma may not be very far up on the fine arts but you can't fool her on children. She's seen too many. She's been a child herself. She's borne and raised three of her own. So you needn't try to tell her that any child ever wrote *that* poetry. No, sir! The newspaper published columns of such nonsense. As for Nathalia, she had been, and in all but one way still was, just such a child as mamma bore and raised. In December, 1922, when she was nine, she was living in a comfortable, homelike apartment, the rent of which was less than a hundred dollars, in that lovely and monotonous section of Brooklyn known as Flatbush. She attended a public school and was a lazy pupil. She dawdled in her studies and was satisfied with a B, or good, in most of them, and indifferent to the damning C, or fair, in mathematics. She straggled in after school and was bitter about having to wash her hands. She played inexplicable games in the court with Louise and Dorothy and Roger, the son of Mr. Jackson, the janitor, and owned a sequence of pets ranging from a chicken to rabbits.

Yet, despite her general indifference to education at that time —she applies more effort to her studies now—something of an understanding of her capabilities had evidently reached the principal of the school, for she was skipped several grades. An illness resulting from a mastoid operation prevented her entering school until she was in her seventh year, and during the five years since then she has completed eight years of grade work and will enter high-school next year.

It was in the latter months of 1922 that she began to compose her extraordinary verse. She employed for the purpose a singularly battered typewriter, on which she had learned her alphabet before entering the first grade, and she worked mysteriously behind the closed door of her room. The significance of the tappings on her machine became known to the family when her mother, in answer to an hysterical question, replied that she had sent down the dumbwaiter, along with other trash, certain sheets of badly typed paper left carelessly on the table. Trash! They were her songs—her poetry! Gone! Nathalia wailed. Her father clucked his tongue sympathetically. She could write more, couldn't she? Her mother was impatient at the fuss. How could she tell which of all the strange playthings about the place was to be treasured and which to be discarded? Why didn't Nanny put away the things she wished to save? But, anyway, she could run along now and stop crying. Mother would be more careful next time.

A few days later Nathalia brought to her father two new songs. They were "The Janitor's Boy," then named, I think,

"Romance," and one other, likewise a tribute to the fascinating Roger Jackson. Mr. Crane read them with some perplexity. They seemed to him amazingly good, but he was afraid that a father's bias flavored his view. So he warily avoided the issue by suggesting that she mail them to a newspaper man he knew slightly, the late Walter M. Oestreicher, then managing editor of the Brooklyn *Daily Times*. The next morning a reporter came to interview her. In that afternoon's *Times* Nathalia—then, loquaciously, Nathalia Clare Ruth Abarbannel Crane—emerged from obscurity.

Thus began a strange and dangerous experience for a nine-year old child. Other newspapers followed the *Times'* lead and camera men and moving picture photographers shuffled through the apartment-house court to Nathalia's door, posed her amiable person in what they considered staggering positions, and exhibited her likeness in hundreds of cities. She was asked imbecile questions: her opinions on love, on bobbed hair, on what she wanted to be when she grew up. Young women reporters smirked a saccharine affection for her, and male sob-sisters tried to carry matters off with an air under the level, amused glance of the new freak. What they wrote was lengthy, if not notably well considered. For two weeks after that first interview she was slathered with columns of praise. The miracle then was simply that she could rhyme, that her lines had a metrical swing. But she also had, it appeared, cute ideas.

In time the situation subsided to something resembling normal. Nathalia continued her absorbed interest in the battered typewriter, and what came out of it Mrs. Crane gave graciously to the newspaper folk. After dozens of poems had thus been disposed of liberally, Nathalia one day mailed one to Edmund Leamy, poetry editor of the New York *Sun*, as a contribution for which she expected to be paid. Leamy accepted it, for six or eight dollars, without having heard of her or knowing her age. He accepted it on the basis of its merit. A little later she achieved another recognition. This was the acceptance by William Rose Benét, then associate editor of the Literary Review of the New York *Evening Post*, of two poems, one of which "The

Blind Girl," is now included in "The Janitor's Boy and Other Poems."

Nathalia bore all these uncommon experiences, as well as those that followed, with admirable presence. What might have swelled another child's ego to the point where a fine, strong wallop would not be amiss has failed to disturb, even in the slightest, a naturally indifferent, though superficially pleasant, disposition. In the beginning she read the newspaper stories written by those reporters to whom she had taken a fancy. The others received from her only a glance at the head-lines. Her deportment at school, in the presence of her teachers and in the company of her playmates, remained unaltered. Re-porters calling for interviews found that she had to be brought in from the crowd of children in the court. She came in po-litely and answered their fool questions as well as she could, but it was generally plain that she was unmoved by the attention and would have been just as well pleased had they never called.

II

Nathalia's course thus continued without spectacular develop-ments until one day two women reporters and the managing editor of the Brooklyn *Daily Eagle* came to the conclusion that she was a hoax. That was on the occasion of the publication of her second collection, "Lava Lane," in November of last year. Were newspaper ethics less nebulous, the *Eagle's* ensuing dis-cussion of Nathalia's personal and professional integrity might have been questioned on the grounds of taste. But the paper's own argument was that there was widespread skepticism over the authorship of the poems and that this skepticism constituted legitimate news and an honorable justification for an "investiga-tion." Such an investigation, conducted fairly and honestly and by competent authorities, would not have been objectionable to the Cranes. Even as it was, they offered no obstacle until it be-came downright silly. Indeed, at the beginning, they gave aid.

It is over now, and I think it is safe to assume that it failed.

The *Eagle*, to be sure, is given even yet to allusions to the time it "exposed" Nathalia, but such allusions do not seem to be conclusive. No harm ever came to her from the matter. The black headlines and charges on the front page did make her sensitive and self-conscious at school among her mates, but that did not last long. Some of the aspects of the investigation, however, seem to have a definite intrinsic interest, futile though the whole thing was, and so an account of it may be of value to the student of modern journalism.

The initial spark of righteousness in the *Eagle* office burned in the bosom of a woman reporter, a spinster who, in her particular field, has the force of an ambitious district attorney. Horse-sense, she said, told her that Nathalia had not written the poems, and it needed no more than a neat little whirlwind investigation to make the fact clear. With her in this belief was the woman editor of the children's section of the paper. So strongly did the two feel this conviction that they were able to persuade the managing editor, Harris M. Crist, a man who admitted only a slight familiarity with poetry but tipped his hat to no man, woman, or child in so far as a knowledge of children was concerned, that it was the paper's duty to expose the hoax.

Not much, I fear, can be said of the competency of the investigators. One of them believed, because she had been told, that William Rose Bénet was the greatest poet in America, and the other, though she had a general familiarity with the works of Keats, a relic of her days at Vassar, was under the impression that it was Shelley who wrote "Endymion," the "Ode on a Grecian Urn," and "Hyperion." On the other hand, she was herself a poet, being the author of "R U A Rooster" and other whimsicalities published in the *Eagle's* children's section.

Thus equipped for the grapple with deceit, the investigators plunged into a strange and furious effort to prove their original conviction. A series of twelve or more long articles followed, headed first in one direction and then in another. At the outset the two women decided that the poems had been written by a syndicate composed of Mr. Bénet, Louis Untermeyer, Jean Starr

Untermeyer, Faith Baldwin, and probably Edna St. Vincent Millay. They conveyed this belief to Edwin Markham, the author of "The Man with the Hoe," who obligingly repeated it back to them for publication. A few days later the investigators parted company for a day. While one, the author of "R U A Rooster," composed a critical analysis proving that Mr. Bénet had written all of the poems, the other was, at precisely the same moment, engaged in an effort to persuade Mrs. Hugh Cuthrell, who writes under the name of Faith Baldwin, to "confess" to their authorship.

Two days later this phase of dissension passed, and the finger of suspicion was leveled at Clarence Porter Crane, Nathalia's father. There it remained to the end, although one or two other theories were raised within the *Eagle* office, the most arresting being a conviction on the part of the elder woman that it was all a gigantic Jewish plot. She pointed out—or so her argument went—that the Jews have produced no great genius since Jesus Christ, and that it was clear here that, sensing this, the mightiest of Jewish minds were pooling their products and giving them to the world through Nathalia Crane, a partly-Jewish child. Even the managing editor laughed at this, but the woman reporter became so exercised over the matter that she is said to have gone out and had herself insured against a bash on the head from some thwarted and infuriated Jewish poet.

Included in the "investigation," but never acknowledged in print, were several interviews granted the paper by Mr. Crane and several tests to which the bewildered Nathalia submitted herself. The first of the interviews was characteristic of them all. The two women reporters filed solemnly into the Crane's living-room and sat down much in the manner of a committee from the Ladies' Aid Society calling to inform a fancy lady that she must get out of town. At the Cranes' at the time were, by chance, Mr. and Mrs. Louis Untermeyer and the present word-painter. The two ladies from the *Eagle* sat down and after a few pleasantries notified the assemblage formally that they knew Nathalia had not written the poems she claimed and that they had come to prove it. Mr. Crane amiably replied that he'd heard that such a doubt existed at the *Eagle* office, but felt certain that Nathalia would answer satisfactorily any questions that burned in their breasts.

Thereupon the elder of the reporters opened her sheaf of notes and, clearing her throat, demanded of Nathalia where she had learned so perfect an exposition of the nebular hypothesis as was to be found in "Lava Lane." Had she studied science? Unfortunately the approach had been ill-considered. At the first abrupt question Nathalia's customary anxiety to be a perfect hostess disappeared. Her reply was sullen. No, she hadn't studied science. Where, then, had she got all this highly technical information? Wasn't it—Nathalia retorted nastily—correct? The reporters beamed. Yes, indeed! Entirely too correct for a child to know. Mr. Untermeyer, in an effort to establish a pleasanter tone, interrupted to point out that "Lava Lane" was not, in fact, highly technical—that it simply set forth the skeleton of the nebular hypothesis clothed in childish fancy, and that in more than one place the exposition was clearly (to the informed student, at any rate) erroneous. So, he felt, it was absurd to expect Nathalia to say she had a scientific knowledge of the subject. Then, exclaimed the reporters triumphantly, she wouldn't answer? "No," Nathalia replied shortly. Let it be explained here, if an explanation is necessary, that her concept of the nebular hypothesis, by which name, of course, she didn't know it, actually came from an "educational" moving-picture, a sequence of animated drawings shown at a theatre around the corner from her home in Flatbush.

The reporters resumed their inquiries. Did Nathalia attend Sunday-school or church? Mr. Crane, an indifferent agnostic, replied for his daughter. No. Was she atheistic? "What," Nathalia asked, "do you mean?" The reporters opened "Lava Lane" to the poem "Sunday Morning." One read the first stanza:

> God, on a Sunday morning,
>   Sits in his old armchair
> Comforting May Madonna—
>   Slip-heel who fell the stair.

That, announced one of the reporters, is plainly a charge that the Virgin Mary did something she shouldn't have done. Nathalia and the elder Cranes looked puzzled. The Virgin Mary? "Certainly," replied the reporters. "Isn't May Madonna intended to be Mary, Mother of Jesus?" Nathalia was disgusted. "May Madonna is a little girl's name," she explained; "I liked the sound of it." The reporters shook their heads with indulgent smiles. "No, no, dear, you meant the Virgin Mary. Didn't she, Mr. Untermeyer?" Mr. Untermeyer was impatient. "Nathalia," he replied, "should know what she meant." If she said May Madonna was the name of a child, then he saw no way of proving that it wasn't. But, demanded the reporter, wasn't Madonna the Italian word for mother, and wasn't it usually applied to Mary? Yes, Mr. Untermeyer admitted, but also weren't thousands of Italian children named Madonna?

It was a futile discussion, and its conclusion left the reporters unmoved. "What, then, Nathalia," they asked next, "makes a rose red?" "Don't you know?" the child countered. "Certainly we know, dear, but do you?" "If you know," Nathalia sulked, "why ask me?" Mr. Untermeyer offered again to help. What was the point of the question? The older reporter smiled grimly at him. "Excuse us, Mr. Untermeyer, but we are asking Nathalia, not you." Mr. Untermeyer apologized. The younger reporter, the author of "R U A Rooster," then asked Nathalia if she had studied physical properties of the prism, and if she was acquainted with the chromatic scale and the phenomenon of refraction. Nathalia shook her head, now obviously determined to say nothing. "Then," declared the reporter quietly, "you could not possibly have written this line:

"In the darkness, who would answer for the color of a rose—"

It was a line from "The Blind Girl," in "The Janitor's Boy." "And why," demanded Nathalia, "couldn't I have written it?" "Because, dear," explained the reporter, "you say you haven't the scientific knowledge." "But couldn't I," Nathalia asked, "have taken a rose into a dark room?" "The person who wrote that line," insisted the reporter firmly, "was thoroughly familiar with the physical basis for the statement."

So the interview continued, with the two reporters piling up points in their minds, until the elder one, for the final coup, turned to Nathalia and demanded: "Nathalia, tell us what you know about Sex." There was a brief silence. "Surely," urged the reporter, "you are not self-conscious about Sex. You could not be after having written 'The Warming Pan.'" Still no answer. "Come, dear," the reporter urged again, "you needn't be shy. We are all married—except us reporters, of course, and I have been a trained nurse." She waited, then, for Sex. She waited a minute, two minutes. And then Nathalia rose from the corner of the divan where she had been sitting throughout the interview and, going over to Mrs. Untermeyer, began to cry softly on her shoulder. "Have you got enough?" Mr. Crane asked courteously. The reporters gathered up their notes and, bidding everyone a pleasant good-evening, left.

The character of the remainder of the investigation was little different from this. Mr. Crist, the managing editor, despite the unpersuasive manner of the first interview, was later permitted to call and study the situation. The test he suggested was a two-fisted business man's, with none of this artistic whangdoodle about it. Nathalia should sit down at a typewriter directly in front of him and write a piece of poetry. Either she could write it or she couldn't, and there were no two ways about it, Nathalia tried. After about ten minutes of squirming she produced the following:

> Lo and behold, God made this starry world,
> The maggot and the mold; Lo and behold.
> He taught the grass contentment blade by blade,
> The sanctity of sameness in a shade.

Mr. Crist suspected a trick, and presently perceived it. He discovered that the idea had been used by Nathalia once before, in a letter to the present writer, who had shown it to him. So, too keen to be caught like that, he decided to say nothing in his newspaper about his call and the test.

The investigation finally began to expire. It was shown by others newspapers, which had assumed the rôles of protectors for Nathalia against the *Eagle*, that she had never met or seen Mr. Bénet or Miss Millay, that Louis Untermeyer and Jean Starr Untermeyer were in Germany at the time Nathalia began writing, and that Faith Baldwin would not, despite all promises to keep the facts secret, confess to the authorship of the poems. Mr. Crist himself printed the fact that Mr. Crane had had a volume of poems published twenty-five years before (Mr. Crane had published the collection at his own expense), and added "that efforts to find a copy in Brooklyn have failed," a statement which was somewhat shady, since a copy of the book, found in the Library of Congress, was at that moment, and had been for several days, in the *Eagle's* possession. At the end of all this Clement Wood, generally known as a poet and critic, approached the *Eagle* in the guise of an amateur psycho-analyst and wrote two lengthy discussions of Nathalia's works from the point of view of one capable of piercing the subconscious mind. He came to a great many entertaining conclusions, the most notable being that Nathalia's father was a Svengali, exercising the black arts in Brooklyn. Immediately upon the publication of Mr. Wood's report, word spread in the back alleys of Greenwich Village that the *Eagle* could be taken in for decent space rates by any free-lance worker able to advance the idea that Nathalia had not written her poems, and so the paper, for a week or so thereafter, was approached by all manner of occult practitioners, ranging from numerologists to plain, every-day clairvoyants, each bringing an authoritative article. Some of these the *Eagle* bought and published. Then the investigation died.

All of these circumstances suggested legal action of some character against the *Eagle* and Mr. Crane retained a lawyer to watch the paper's publications concerning Nathalia. The lawyer reported, when the attacks ceased, that a suit would be ill-advised, for so generally privileged is all discussion of literary matters and persons, that no adequate grounds for action could be found.

Quoting Mr. Untermeyer, who has devoted much attention and a discerning intelligence to Nathalia, it may be "the peculiar combination of the parents" that produced the child's extraordinary talent. "You have there," he says, "an oldish man and a much younger woman. You have the Puritan and the Jewess. You have the repressed New England stock and the stock of the fiery Spanish Jews. That may explain it, in part, on the basis of heredity. In part only. Genius is never entirely explicable. It always remains a marvel. The theory has been propounded that the girl is a species of medium, that in some mesmeric way her poetry comes to her, and she writes. If that means that a voice from the dead speaks to Nathalia and she repeats what she hears, then of course I don't believe anything like that. But in another sense she *is* a medium. She is a medium for the transmission of the experience, the wisdom of the race, which, like other children, she has inherited, but which other children, having nothing of genius about them, are unable to express."

Clarence Crane is now fifty-four years of age. Born in Sherbrooke, Quebec, he is a member of the Crane family of Massachusetts, and through him Nathalia traces her ancestry to John and Priscilla Alden. He was educated in the public schools, by private tutors, and, beginning with the Bryant School at Roslyn, Long Island, of which George B. Cortelyou, later Secretary of the Treasury, was head, in several private preparatory schools. Foregoing college, he knocked about the country until the outbreak of the Spanish-American War, when he enlisted in a Massachusetts regiment of infantry and saw service in Cuba. Following this war, he enlisted in the Ninth Infantry, United States Army, and was shipped to the Philippines. In that regiment and the Eighth Infantry, he saw service about Peking during the Boxer Rebellion and finally was returned to Governors Island. Upon his discharge he succeeded in achieving the rim of a copydesk on a Brooklyn newspaper. He lasted in this calling, with indifferent success, for several years, occasionally with the New York City News Association and occasionally on Brooklyn newspapers. When the United States entered the World War he went to Governors Island and managed, at the age of forty-five, to reënlist as a drill sergeant. Subsequently he was transferred to the Tenth Field Battalion, Signal Corps, and served in France, where he was gassed and wounded near Mons.

He is a short, deceptively robust man, prematurely aged by lingering traces of gas, who sits with the moody fatalism of a Buddha in the centre of his small family. To company he discourses in a hopeless monotone, dismissing impatiently all such minor vexations as the attacks on Nanny in order to concentrate on vaster pessimisms. "The trouble is, Brother Johnson," he sums up, "it's all too civilized. Everything is too elaborate. Everybody is hustling, hustling, hustling, and headed where? Progress! Progress! What do they mean by Progress? They don't know. All they know is that a shibboleth called Progress is the proper thing to shout. Yes, we're getting further and further away from the real things, the essentials of life. Tell me, Brother Johnson, what else do we need beside a breech-cloth, a dry cave, cigarettes, and a cup of coffee now and then? What else is there—I'd like to know." He laughs appreciatively at the tense note of seriousness which has crept into his voice. "I don't know whether I mean it or not; but it might be very nice, now, mightn't it?" The cigarettes and coffee he takes in unbelievable quantities. He tries brand after brand of coffee, making every cup as strong as his tongue can bear it. "Somehow," he explains, "I don't seem to get a kick out of it any more." He switches brands of cigarettes in the same way. To company, to reporters, he represents himself as a strange and unfathomable man, sweetly courteous and considerate, and amazingly patient and even tempered. It may be the result of bodily suffering—"I never feel well," he says—or it may be a form of misanthropy, but in any case he apparently abhors all forms of social life, never goes calling of an evening, and has, so far as I have been able to discover over three and a half years of fairly close acquaintance, no near friends.

But to Nathalia, he is a curiously fascinating fount of entertainment. At times she gives the impression that she is teasing him tenderly, but carefully, lest she hurt in some way, but as he sits evening after evening in his wicker-chair, narrating, with a sonorous perfection of rhetoric, tales of the countries he has seen, of the army, of ships, of history, of exploration, colored always with a contemptuous irony, she lies back in a chair transfixed, plucking from his discourse a strange and arresting word occasionally, to grasp its sound and to get its meaning. Subjects for them to discuss are everywhere: in an acquaintance of her father's who makes maps, in a plaster figure on the book-case, in any mythological reference, in a news account of new discoveries in the Gobi Desert, in an exhibit in the museum, in so fair and pleasant a name as Roslyn.

Nathalia's mother does not, alas, contribute greatly to her omnivorous child's appetite for facts and words. A vivid young woman, not yet thirty, she emerges from an ancient Spanish Jew family, the Abarbannels, the most distinguished member of which was prime minister at the court of Ferdinand and Isabella. Thusnelda, or Nelda, Zurich, as she made it, was born in Switzerland, brought to this country when she was a child, and educated in a Catholic convent and at Wadleigh High School, New York City, which latter institution she left to marry Clarence Crane.

A somewhat impractical person, it was she who, determined to make no second mistake such as that she fell into when she threw her daughter's poem down the dumb-waiter, set out to sell those that followed out of Nathalia's typewriter. Her method of doing it was first to write out a list of the addresses of editors, magazines, and publishers, then to give this list to a taxi-cab chauffeur and then to travel in the cab by whatever lengthy routes the chauffeur wished to take. By selling a poem for five dollars she had but to add another five dollars to pay the taxi bill.

Aside from Mr. Crane, Nathalia has one other important source of the erudition which confounded the ladies from the *Eagle*. It is ten volumes of out-dated volumes of reference. She has two two-volume sets of the Standard Dictionary issued in 1895 and six out of eight volumes of Johnson's Universal Cyclopedia, likewise a publication of 1895. The two volumes running from the last of F to Mos in this series are missing, the result of which, if skeptics care to look it up, that Nathalia's erudition is somewhat weak on matters beginning with G, H, I, J, K, and L.

Nathalia is not what is known as a great reader. A fragile, frail, elfin child, she is forced, not unwillingly, out of doors as often as may be. She does not object; she likes play, as a normal child does. Her reading is, however, specialized. She has read Kipling, Tennyson, most thoroughly his "Idylls of the King," and such novels as "Ivanhoe," but she finds vastly more to her taste in the cyclopedia, where lengthy essays on castles, ships and the pyramids hold her for hours. Such a child as the master-mind and subliminal giant described by the *Eagle* could not, of course, be the product of so haphazard an education; but Nathalia is no such monstrosity. Her intellectual scope and depth are knockouts only to those who are floored by any manifestations of unusual intelligence at all. She is simply a curious child with a rudimentary grasp and a tremendous colloquial hold on a number of uncommon matters, matters which have caught her interest. She has, in addition, a flair for obsolete and ungodly words, a flair which leads her to collect and treasure them with the zeal of any fancier, and which forces her to press them into her writings with ostentation. Thirdly, she has an impressionable, sensitive, and tenacious intelligence, a mind which holds facts as tanglefoot holds flies. Beyond these comprehensible elements, she has one talent which is mysterious in her as it always is in considerable poets, and that is the talent to assemble her material, assimilating it, and, in the end, issuing it in the curves and colors of genuine fancy. The existence anywhere of that talent is a matter for marvelling, but since it has not, so far as I know, ever been isolated and analyzed, no matter where found, there doesn't seem to be any logical reason why it shouldn't exist in a child.

Of the two poems by Nathalia Crane that follow, the first is probably the best known, while the second takes us back to a street we have heard of before.

The Janitor's Boy

Oh I'm in love with the janitor's boy,
   And the janitor's boy loves me;
He's going to hunt for a desert isle
   In our geography.

A desert isle with spicy trees
   Somewhere near Sheepshead Bay;
A right nice place, just fit for two,
   Where we can live alway.

Oh I'm in love with the janitor's boy,
   He's busy as he can be;
And down in the cellar he's making a raft
   Out of an old settee.

He'll carry me off, I know that he will,
   For his hair is exceedingly red;
And the only thing that occurs to me
   Is to dutifully shiver in bed.

The day that we sail, I shall leave this brief note,
   For my parents I hate to annoy:
"I have flown away to an isle in the bay
   With the janitor's red-haired boy."

From The Janitor's Boy and Other Poems *by Nathalia Crane. Reprinted with the permission of the author and The Haddon Craftsmen, Inc.*

Love Lane

In old Love Lane on Brooklyn Heights
There's an ebony bob from Arabian Nights;
She sings each eve of the Tom Moore rose—
And the neighbors shut off their radios.

The people who pass through Henry Street,
They presently go with lagging feet,
For in old Love Lane a cantatrice shade
Is taking the trills of Adelaide.

Shaking the sistrum—a blackberry bob,
Dulcing the treble and daring the sob;
Never a wonder that listeners perch
On the mansion steps near Plymouth Church.

They hear the birds by a waterfall,
They see the rose that was last of all;
The dim garages grow less profane,
For something with pinions is down in the lane.

From Lava Lane and Other Poems *by Nathalia Crane. Reprinted with the permission of the author and The Haddon Craftsmen, Inc.*

For a while in assembling this book we thought of scattering Whitman through it like Chartreuse in a pousse-café—or perhaps the simile might be better if we said a series of pousse-cafés. The plan was to present, say, Whitman on transit, Whitman on Henry Ward Beecher, Whitman on roast clams, and so on.

It didn't quite come off, probably because Whitman is pretty much a specialized interest. People who want to know what Whitman thought about education for women undoubtedly have read all his available works. People who want to know about education for women will wonder how in the world he ever got in the argument.

Whitman worked on Brooklyn newspapers as editor, writer, and compositor in the 1840's and 1850's. The Eagle, in what now seems to have been a fight within the Democratic party, fired Whitman, a mischance that seems to bother the paper even now. It was an age of personal journalism, and other newspapers chided the Eagle at length for getting rid of the poet—though he was not recognized as one at that time. On July 19, 1849, the Eagle, for whom for two years Whitman had knocked out some

*three or four thousand words a day in addition to culling ex-
changes and making up pages, printed this rebuttal:*

We should suppose that the *Advertizer* [a Brooklyn paper
that had been needling the *Eagle* about Whitman] had had
enough by this time, of the folly of petting Mr. Whitman. That
paper has been determined to make capital out of him from the
first and has pushed its game till it has pushed itself off from
the list of corporation papers [papers which could get advertising
from the local government] and got that job in a fix which is
certainly disgraceful enough. Mr. W. came here from the *Star*
office where he was getting four or five dollars a week; he was
connected with the *Eagle* for about two years and we think we
had a pretty fair opportunity to understand him. Slow, indolent,
heavy, discourteous and without steady principles, he was a clog
upon our success, and, reluctant as we were to make changes,
we still found it absolutely necessary to do so. Mr. W. cried
persecution, and by this means interested the *Advertizer*, the
Evening Post, the *Glove*, &c. in his behalf, and through their
good offices got a handsome place in New Orleans. How long did
he remain there?—Until they could decently get rid of him. He
then came on here and started the *Freeman* as a weekly paper. It
dragged through a few months of public existence and then
stopped. It was notorious only for its dullness. Dr. Goodrich
and the *Advertizer* then gave Mr. W. assurances that if he would
revive his paper and bring it out every day the corporation advertizing should then be taken from the *Eagle* and given to him.
He was again stirred up and, on the strength of this promise,
started the *Freeman* as a morning journal, advertized for three
or four reporters, and proclaimed his circulation to be far beyond that of the older papers. The corporation advertizing did
not, however, come as promised; and the paper began to flag and
was soon after changed from a morning to an evening journal.
It is now dragging "its slow length along," sustained chiefly by
private contributions and manifesting neither tact, talent or industry.—Mr. W. has no political principles, nor, for that matter,
principles of any sort; and all that the *Advertizer* says . . . is

totally and unequivocally untrue. Whoever knows him will laugh at the idea of his *kicking any body*, much less a prominent politician. He is too indolent to kick a musketo.

Walt Whitman had his own way of writing obituaries

SAMUEL LEGGETT

—This man is dead. He was immensely rich. He died on the night of the 5th instant. Mr. Leggett belonged to the religious denomination of Friends, and was for a great number of years a prominent merchant in New York City. He was at one time one of the largest auctioneers, and President of the Franklin Bank just previous to its failure—by which failure, under the most abominable circumstances, he acquired a splendid property, and was at his death a large owner of real estate. Among other property, he was the proprietor of the United States Hotel, one of the largest in the city. He retired, about ten years ago, from active pursuits, to his farm, where he has devoted his time to agricultural pursuits. He had some good qualities.

In preparing this book Only the Dead Know Brooklyn *comes to mind. It was about the best phrasing of an often expressed idea. But we are using only a little by Thomas Wolfe, for his stuff on Brooklyn rather irritates us. He didn't have the ear for Brooklyn speech, nor the heart for Brooklyn people. In* You Can't Go Home Again, *you run across this passage:*

But if you were to go up to this fairly intelligent looking truck driver who stands and waits there with his crowd, and if you put to him your question, and if he understood what you were talking about (he wouldn't), and if he were articulate enough to frame in words the feelings that are in him (he isn't)—he might answer you with something such as this:

"'Now is duh mont' of March, duh mont' of March—now it is Sunday afternoon in Brooklyn in duh mont' of March, an' we stand upon cold corners of duh day. It's funny dat dere are so many corners in duh mont' of March, here in Brooklyn where no corners are. Jesus! On Sunday in duh mont' of March we sleep late in duh mornin', den we get up an' read duh papers—duh funnies an' duh sportin' news. We eat some chow. An' den we dress up in duh afternoon, we leave our wives, we leave duh funnies littered on duh floor, an' go outside in Brooklyn in duh mont' of March an' we stand around upon ten t'ousand corners of duh day. We need a corner in duh mont' of March, a wall to stand to, a shelter an' a door. Dere must be some place inside in duh mont' of March, but we never found it. So we stand around on corners where duh sky is cold an' ragged still wit' winter, in our good clothes we stand around wit' a lot of udder guys we know, before duh barber shop, just looking for a door. . . ."

"Only the Dead . . .", a kind of turn-around piece in which Wolfe gives his idea of what a guy on a subway thought of Wolfe, at our latest reading, seemed somewhat snobbish.

ONLY THE DEAD KNOW BROOKLYN

by THOMAS WOLFE

Dere's no guy livin' dat knows Brooklyn t'roo an' t'roo, because it'd take a guy a lifetime just to find his way aroun' duh goddam town.

So like I say, I'm waitin' for my train t' come when I sees dis big guy standin' deh—dis is duh foist I eveh see of him. Well, he's lookin' wild, y'know, an' I can see dat he's had plenty, but still he's holdin' it; he talks good an' is walkin' straight enough. So den, dis big guy steps up to a little guy dat's standin' deh, an' says, "How d'yuh get t' Eighteent' Avenoo an' Sixtysevent' Street?" he says.

"Jesus! Yuh got me, chief," duh little guy says to him. "I ain't been heah long myself. Where is duh place?" he says. "Out in duh Flatbush section somewhere?"

"Nah," duh big guy says. "It's out in Bensonhoist. But I was neveh deh befoeh. How d'yuh get deh?"

"Jesus," duh little guy says, scratchin' his head, y'know—yuh could see duh little guy didn't know his way about—"yuh got me, chief. I never hoid of it. Do any of youse guys know where it is?" he says to me.

"Sure," I says. "It's out in Bensonhoist. Yuh take duh Fourt' Avenoo express, get off at Fifty-nint' Street, change to a Sea Beach local deh, get off at Eighteent' Avenoo an' Sixty-toid, an' den walk down foeh blocks. Dat's all yuh got to do," I says.

"G'wan!" some wise guy dat I neveh seen befoeh pipes up. "Whatcha talkin' about?" he says—oh, he was wise, y'know. "Duh guy is crazy! I tell yuh what yuh do," he says to duh big guy. "Yuh change to duh West End line at Toity-sixt'," he tells him. "Get off at Noo Utrecht an' Sixteent' Avenoo," he says. "Walk two blocks oveh, foeh blocks up," he says, "an' you'll be right deh." Oh, a wise guy, y'know.

"Oh, yeah?" I says. "Who told you so much?" He got me sore because he was so wise about it. "How long you been livin' heah?" I says.

"All my life," he says. "I was bawn in Williamsboig," he says. "An' I can tell you t'ings about dis town you neveh hoid of," he says.

"Yeah?" I says.

"Yeah," he says.

"Well, den, you can tell me t'ings about dis town dat nobody else has eveh hoid of, either. Maybe you make it all up yoehself at night," I says, "befoeh you go to sleep—like cuttin' out papeh dolls, or somp'n."

"Oh, yeah?" he says. "You're pretty wise, ain't yuh?"

"Oh, I don't know," I says. "Duh boids ain't usin' my head for Lincoln's statue yet," I says. "But I'm wise enough to know a phony when I see one."

"Yeah?" he says. "A wise guy, huh? Well, you're so wise dat someone's goin' t'bust yuh one right on duh snoot some day," he says. "Dat's how wise you are."

Well, my train was comin', or I'd a smacked him den and dere, but when I seen duh train was comin', all I said was, "All right, mugg! I'm sorry I can't stay to take keh of you, but I'll be seein' yuh sometime, I hope, out in duh cemetery." So den I says to duh big guy, who'd been standin' deh all duh time, "You come wit me," I says. So when we gets onto duh train I says to him, "Where yuh goin' out in Bensonhoist?" I says. "What numbeh are yuh lookin' for?" I says. You know—I t'ought if he told me duh address I might be able to help him out.

"Oh," he says, "I'm not lookin' for no one. I don't know no one out deh."

"Then whatcha goin' out deh for?" I says.

"Oh," duh guy says, "I'm just goin' out to see duh place," he says. "I like duh sound of duh name"—Bensonhoist, y'know—"so I t'ought I'd go out an' have a look at it."

"Whatcha tryin' t'hand me?" I says. "Whatcha tryin' t'do—kid me?" You know, I t'ought duh guy was bein' wise wit me.

"No," he says, "I'm tellin' yuh duh troot. I like to go out an' take a look at places wit nice names like dat. I like to go out an' look at all kinds of places," he says.

"How'd yuh know deh was such a place," I says, "if you neveh been deh befoeh?"

"Oh," he says, "I got a map."

"A map?" I says.

"Sure," he says, "I got a map dat tells me about all dese places. I take it wit me every time I come out heah," he says.

And Jesus! Wit dat, he pulls it out of his pocket, an' so help me, but he's got it—he's tellin' duh troot—a big map of duh whole goddam place wit all duh different pahts. Mahked out, you know—Canarsie an' East Noo Yawk an' Flatbush, Bensonhoist, Sout' Brooklyn, duh Heights, Bay Ridge, Greenpernt—duh whole goddam layout, he's got it right deh on duh map.

"You been to any of dose places?" I says.

"Sure," he says, "I been to most of 'em. I was down in Red Hook just last night," he says.

"Jesus! Red Hook!" I says. "Whatcha do down deh?"

"Oh," he says, "nuttin' much. I just walked aroun'. I went into a coupla places an' had a drink," he says, "but most of the time I just walked aroun'."

"Just walked aroun'?" I says.

"Sure," he says, "just lookin' at things, y'know."

"Where'd yuh go?" I asts him.

"Oh," he says, "I don't know duh name of duh place, but I could find it on my map," he says. "One time I was walkin' across some big fields where deh ain't no houses," he says, "but I could see ships obeh deh all lighted up. Dey was loadin'. So I walks across duh fields," he says, "to where duh ships are."

"Sure," I says, "I know where you was. You was down to duh Erie Basin."

"Yeah," he says, "I guess dat was it. Dey had some of dose big elevators an' cranes an' dey was loadin' ships, an' I could see some ships in drydock all lighted up, so I walks across duh fields to where dey are," he says.

"Den what did yuh do?" I says.

"Oh," he says, "nuttin' much. I came on back across duh fields after a while an' went into a coupla places an' had a drink."

"Didn't nuttin' happen while yuh was in dere?" I says.

"No," he says. "Nuttin' much. A coupla guys was drunk in one of duh places an' started a fight, but dey bounced 'em out," he says, "an' den one of duh guys stahted to come back again, but duh bartender gets his baseball bat out from under duh counteh, so duh guy goes on."

"Jesus!" I said. "Red Hook!"

"Sure," he says. "Dat's where it was, all right."

"Well, you keep outa deh," I says. "You stay away from deh."

"Why?" he says. "What's wrong wit it?"

"Oh," I says, "it's a good place to stay away from, dat's all. It's a good place to keep out of."

"Why?" he says. "Why is it?"

Jesus! Whatcha gonna do wit a guy as dumb as dat? I saw it wasn't no use to try to tell him nuttin', he wouldn't know what I was talkin' about, so I just says to him, "Oh, nuttin'. Yuh might get lost down deh, dat's all."

"Lost?" he says. "No, I wouldn't get lost. I got a map," he says.

A map! Red Hook! Jesus!

So den duh guy begins to ast me all kinds of nutty questions: how big was Brooklyn an' could I find my way aroun' in it, an' how long would it take a guy to know duh place.

"Listen!" I says. "You get dat idea outa yoeh head right now," I says. "You ain't neveh gonna get to know Brooklyn," I says. "Not in a hunderd yeahs. I been livin' heah all my life," I says, "an' I don't even know all deh is to know about it, so how do you expect to know duh town," I says, "when you don't even live heah?"

"Yes," he says, "but I got a map to help me find my way about."

"Map or no map," I says, "yuh ain't gonna get to know Brooklyn wit no map," I says.

"Can you swim?" he says, just like dat. Jesus! By dat time, y'know, I begun to see dat duh guy was some kind of nut. He'd had plenty to drink, of course, but he had dat crazy look in his eye I didn't like. "Can you swim?" he says.

"Sure," I says. "Can't you?"

"No," he says. "Not more'n a stroke or two. I neveh loined good."

"Well, it's easy," I says. "All yuh need is a little confidence. Duh way I loined, me older bruddeh pitched me off duh dock one day when I was eight yeahs old, cloes an' all. 'You'll swim,' he says. 'You'll swim all right—or drown.' An', believe me, I swam! When yuh know yuh got to, you'll do it. Duh only t'ing yuh need is confidence. An' once you've loined," I says, "you've got nuttin' else to worry about. You'll neveh forgit it. It's somp'n dat stays with yuh as long as yuh live."

"Can yuh swim good?" he says.

"Like a fish," I tells him. "I'm a regular fish in duh wateh,"

I says. "I loined to swim right off duh docks wit all duh odeh kids," I says.

"What would yuh do if yuh saw a man drownin'?" duh guy says.

"Do? Why, I'd jump in an' pull him out," I says. "Dat's what I'd do."

"Did yuh eveh see a man drown?" he says.

"Sure," I says. "I see two guys—bot' times at Coney Island. Dey got out too far, an' neider one could swim. Dey drowned befoeh anyone could get to 'em."

"What becomes of people after dey have drowned out heah?" he says.

"Drowned out where?" I says.

"Out heah in Brooklyn."

"I don't know watcha mean," I says. "Neveh hoid of no one drownin' heah in Brooklyn, unless you mean a swimmin' pool. Yuh can't drown in Brooklyn," I says. "Yuh gotta drown some where else—in duh ocean, where dere's wateh."

"Drownin'," duh guy says, lookin' at his map. "Drownin'."

Jesus! I could see by den he was some kind of nut, he had dat crazy expression in his eyes when he looked at you, an' I didn't know what he might do. So we was comin' to a station, an' it wasn't my stop, but I got off anyway, an' waited for duh next train.

"Well, so long, chief," I says. "Take it easy, now."

"Drownin'," duh guy says, lookin' at his map. "Drownin'."

Jesus! I've t'ought about dat guy a t'ousand times since den an' wondered what eveh happened to 'm goin' out to look at Bensonhoist because he liked duh name! Walkin' aroun' t'roo Red Hook by himself at night an' lookin' at his map! How many people did I see get drowned out heah in Brooklyn! How long would it take a guy wit a good map to know all deh was to know about Brooklyn!

Jesus! What a nut he was! I wondeh what eveh happened to 'm, anyway! I wondeh if someone knocked him on duh head, or if he's still wanderin' aroun' in duh subway in duh middle of duh night with his little map! Duh poor guy! Say, I've got to laugh, at dat, when I t'ink about him! Maybe he's found out by now dat he'll neveh live long enough to know duh whole of Brooklyn. It'd take a guy a lifetime to know Brooklyn t'roo an' t'roo. An' even den, yuh wouldn't know it all.

For a long time we wanted to use all of Daniel Fuchs' books but our publishers thought that a little impractical. At that we are taking a small section from Homage to Blenholt, a wonderful book. But we would like to see Homage to Blenholt and Summer in Williamsburg reissued one of these days. They were written more than a decade ago, and hold up beautifully.

from . . .

HOMAGE TO BLENHOLT

by DANIEL FUCHS

"Hey, Heshey, you know what?" said Goldie, intending to bring up a bitter subject, "Chink's in the dumb-waiter riding up and down for a good time."

"Don't believe it," he said nonchalantly. Joy-riding in the dumb-waiter was great shakes in Williamsburg. You had to have nerve. You kicked up the center board of the three-foot box, squeezed your body into it tightly, and manipulated the ropes from a height as much as five stories. Further, Mrs. Strudel, the janitor, would positively break the neck of any boy she caught using the dumb-waiter for purposes other than collecting garbage. Riding the dumb-waiter was a feat of great courage and Heshey's shame was that he had never done it.

"Don't believe it!" Goldie exclaimed. "He asked me to go with him."

"Then why didn't you if he asked you to go with him? Hah?"

"My mudder's children," she said primly, "don't go riding in dumb-waiters."

"Ah," said Hesh, "so what?"

"You're jealous."

"Who? Me? I'm laughing out loud. Say, listen . . ."

It fell flat. On the third floor hallway landing Goldie refused to be impressed by Hesh. Hesh hated Chink to the depth, breadth and height his soul could reach. Chink always soaked him for no good reason at all, his life work was to make Hesh continuously miserable, and every time Hesh tried to get even, something went wrong and he got the worst of it again. Take the time with the paper bag of water. His mother had bawled him out for a half hour because he had had to change every stitch of clothing he had on. Now Chink was trying to make a sap out of him in front of Goldie.

"Say, listen," Hesh said, "don't get the idea I'm scared of Chink. I got tricks, hunnerds tricks, you know yourself. If I wana I could get a hunnerd guys they should shellac Chink good. Oney I don wana. Say, listen, I ask you, what's more important, strength or brains?"

Goldie couldn't say.

"See? See?" Hesh said. But just then the dumb-waiter door on the landing flew open and there was Chink, squatting like a Chinaman. Hesh ducked down the stairs like a shot.

"Hello, Toots," Chink said. "Come on, let's go for a ride."

"I should say not! The nerve of some people's children!"

"Don't get stuck-up on me. How's your boy friend, Tarzan of the Apes?"

"Listen here, you dumb Chink," Goldie declared aggressively, "don't you think for one minute that I don't know you're the dope who wrote that dirty thing on the fence in the yard! You got a dirty, filthy mind!"

"What thing? Honest, I don't know what you're talking about." Chink was all innocence.

"You don't know nothing," she said with deep sarcasm. "It's too bad about you."

"What thing? Honest, Goldie, I ain't got the slightest idea."

"About Heshy playing doctor with me. You made it and don't think I don't know it."

"On the level, Goldie, I didn't write nothing of the kind. You want me to find out who did it? You want me to bust him one? Just tell me and I'll break his head in for him."

"You dirty, lousy liar! You stinker! As if I don't know you wrote it!" Goldie sputtered with anger. The ideeer! He was going to find the fellow and bust his head in for her benefit when she knew all the time for a positive fact that he was the one. "Listen," she concluded, "I wouldn't go riding the dumb-waiter with a filthy person like you if you was the last person in the world."

"Dry up! Dry up!" Chink closed the door in disgust. He pulled the ropes and went for a visit to the fifth floor, resuming his gay spirits. "One, two, three, four," Goldie could hear him singing, "Greta Garbo went to war. Five, six, seven, eight, Goldie wets her draws each day."

Goldie could have murdered him on the spot with the greatest of pleasure. She foamed with anger. But Hesh came back running with such a fierce light in his eyes, she had to stop.

"Listen, Goldie," he said, panting with excitement. "I bet you thought I ran away because I was scared of Chink. Ain't it? But I got tricks, hunnerds tricks. You wana get even with Chink?"

"I wana break every bone in his body," she said, clipping each word poisonously. "Revenge is sweet."

"All right. Then you do what I tell you. You go in the yard and pick up clothespins. Seven clothespins I need, unnerstand?"

"Clothespins?" Goldie asked.

"Do what I tell you. I'm in a hurry. If we don't do this trick fast it'll be too late."

Goldie went running to the yard to collect clothespins dropped by housewives hanging wash on the lines from their windows. Hesh himself returned to his house, opened up the garbage pail and found two grapefruit rinds. Carefully, fastidiously, but with speed, he selected the juiciest pieces of garbage in the pail: tomatoes, lettuce, peas, farina, oatmeal, coffee grounds, banana peels. He stuffed the dripping mess into the grapefruits until they were each a luscious soft mess. Then he swiped the ketchup bottle from the closet and emptied it over the rinds, covering the goo with a thick, rich red layer. Hesh ran back to the landing and found Goldie with the seven clothespins.

· 417 ·

"For crying out loud," she said, overcome with wonder. "What's that?"

"Ammunition," Hesh said briefly. "Wait and see. I got no time for explanations. Now listen, I want you should open the dumb-waiter door and call Chink. When he comes you have to make him stop and then you vamp him. Talk to him, say anything comes into your head, like Greta Garbo in *Mata Hari*. Keep him with you, unnerstand, don't let him get away. Once he starts moving, the whole shooting match don't work. That's important."

"All right," Goldie said. "But I'm a Russian princess if I know what you're talking about."

"Listen," implored Hesh. "If you don't keep Chink and he wants to go down on the dumb-waiter, you laugh. See, for a signal. Laugh out loud like anything so I can hear you. But if everything is all right, cough. Cough to beat the band every once in a while so I can tell. Then when you hear me sneeze, you tell Chink you go for a ride with him only on one condition, he got to meet you in the basement, else you don't go riding the dumb-waiter with him."

"Me?" Goldie protested. "Nothing doing. I wouldn't go riding the dumb-waiter with that lousy Chink if you gave me a fortune."

"You don't have to! I don wana you should go riding the dumb-waiter wid him! All you have to do is say you wana. Don't worry."

"All right. Why didn't you say so in the first place. I should call Chink now?"

"Yare, now. You know the passwords? Laugh, if bad. Cough, if good. When I sneeze you tell him the basement."

"Laugh if bad. Cough if good. You sneeze and I say the basement."

"All right. You got it."

Goldie opened the dumb-waiter door and yelled up the chute. "Hey, Chink! Hey, Chink, I wana talk to you. I got a bone to pick with you."

Heshey hid the grapefruit bombs, waited for the ropes to start moving to indicate that Chink was on his way, picked up the clothespins, and ran down to the cellar. He opened the dumb-waiter door there and heard Chink and Goldie bantering. Good! Two rings had been screwed into each dumb-waiter door to serve as a hasp, but this arrangement was seldom used. Heshey stuck a clothespin through the rings. This was No. 1. Chink couldn't get out here if he stood on his head for a year. Hesh was jittery with anticipation. Six more and success. If only Chink stayed in the dumb-waiter long enough, if only he didn't smell something rotten too soon, if nothing happened to give the plan away, if only Goldie held him long enough . . . Hesh waited for the cough. It came. Too make-believe! Chink would get on to it! Hesh prayed for luck.

He ran to the ground floor dumb-waiter. Mrs. Strudel, the janitor! She'd get on to something in a minute, she'd find Chink in the dumb-waiter, everything would be spoiled!

"Oh, Mrs. Strudel!" said Hesh. "If you only knew! You know that rotten kid Chink? What do you thinking he's doing this minute?"

Of all the kids Chink was the greatest pest in Mrs. Strudel's life and Hesh well knew it. "The little illegitimate," the janitor cried promptly. "He should only fall down and break a leg and stay in bed for a week!"

"Outside," Hesh went on, "he's chalking up the whole sidewalk to play potsy. You stink, he writes on the stoop too, all colors. It'll take a week for sure to wash them off."

"The illegitimate," the janitor gasped. She went to the stoop.

"Don't run," Hesh cried. "You go slow and catch him when he ain't looking. You run, he'll see you, you'll never catch him."

Mrs. Strudel was gone. In a moment Hesh pushed the clothespin through the rings and listened for Goldie.

"What's a matter you coughing so much today?" he could hear Chink ask, with altogether too much suspicion in his voice. "You got a cold?"

He'll catch on! Heshey ran in panic to the first floor, secured this door, and was shooting up the flight when he heard Goldie laugh. Yah! Hah! Hah! Too late! Chink smelled a rat! Heshey stopped, pinching his flesh cruelly at the chest with chagrin.

On the third floor landing Goldie stood with her hand over her mouth, but she had covered it too late. She had forgotten all about the password and now she had gone and spoiled Hesh's scheme. Chink had been so funny, she couldn't restrain herself. He had shimmied the dumb-waiter until it spinned like a top, and unawares she had let go of the signal.

"Boy! You're funny, Chink!" she yelled at the top of her voice, so that Heshey might hear her. "You're so funny I couldn't keep it in. Even though I'm sore at you, I had to laugh right out loud or bust. I didn't want to give you satisfaction but I couldn't keep it in. I had to laugh."

She coughed loudly. Chink squatting in the dumb-waiter was pleased with his success but all the same perplexed. Something fishy was going on. "Why you making such a holler?" he asked. "What's a matter with you today anyway?"

Hesh opened the second floor dumb-waiter cautiously. The ropes were quiet, Chink was still there, it had been a false alarm. Good. He stuck the pin and fastened that door. Now he had to slink noiselessly along the hall up to Goldie. He sneezed.

"What's that?" asked Chink nervously.

Heshey stopped breathing.

"What?" Goldie asked.

"I just heard somebody sneeze. You hear something?" He didn't like the looks of things. Something fishy . . .

"You must amagined it. I didn't hear a thing," she said. "Hey, Chink, it still goes you wana give me a ride in the dumb-waiter?"

"You bet," he said. "Hop in."

"Oh, not here. I can't climb in here. It's too high."

"Come on! I'll give you a shove."

"No, down in the cellar. I'll meet you in the cellar."

"Come on! I'll jump out and give you a boost."

Boy, wept Hesh pasted against the wall, here's where the whole shooting match goes busted. But Goldie kept her wits and made a dash for the cellar.

"I'll meet you in the basement," she cried, and Chink slammed the door and began lowering himself rapidly.

Hesh caught her as she made the turn in the staircase. "You stay here and watch the ammunition." She was certainly a kid who knew how to use her bean. You had to hand it to her. He galloped to the fourth and fifth floors, locked the dumb-waiter doors with the clothespins, and returned. And it was only when Goldie saw him peg the door on her landing that she first realized what Heshey's scheme was. He had Chink trapped in the shaft. Chink couldn't get out. Goldie had visions of Chink rotting in the dumb-waiter, traveling up and down, from the basement to the fifth floor, hopelessly pushing and pulling himself as he sought for the rest of his life a way out. She was aghast.

"For crying out loud," she said. "That's the limit. Gee, I hate him like poison too, but I wouldn't do a trick like that on a dog! He can die in there!"

"For all I care!" Hesh chortled. Let her see him as he really was, tough, heartless, as strong as Chink, stronger because he used his head which was always mightier than ordinary strength, a hunnerd times mightier. Horses had strength. What did it get them? "Let him rot!" Hesh said. "He's got a lesson coming to him for a long time, now."

"Well," exclaimed Goldie, "I certainly ain't going to stand here and let you kill an innercent kid. I'm going to take out all the clothespins."

Horror twisted Heshey's face. He forogt all about his strength. "Goldie! Goldie! Please!" he yelled and grabbed her arm. "Goldie, you ain't going to spoil everything after all my work? After all I done, you want to spoil my revenge?"

"Just for revenge it's better he should die?"

"He won't die, don't worry. Mrs. Strudel, she'll find him when she collects the garbage tonight."

"Still in all," Goldie said. "Still in all . . ."

"Goldie," Heshey begged. Already he could hear Chink pounding on the basement door with anger and fear. "Don't spoil everything, Goldie. Look, you want I should make you feel good like before? I know a hunnerd tricks, Goldie. Don't spoil it."

"All right," she said finally, giving in. "But don't mix me in it. I wash my hands of the whole business. I wouldn't be so mean to a dog."

Chink was traveling hysterically to the first and second floors, his terror mounting as he found the doors were closed here too. It was a trap. All his courage was leaving him. The prospect of being doomed to a lifetime in the dumb-waiter shaft rose like a black cloud to darken his mind. But every sound he uttered, of fear, of exasperation, of frenzy, was sweet music to Hesh. He placed the ketchup bombs—the grapefruit rinds with the delectable garbage—ready at his side. Chink was still at the second floor landing. Hesh opened the dumb-waiter door.

"Chinkstink," he called down blithely. "Here I am. Come and get me, you dirty lousy Chinkstink."

"You!" Chink gasped in the middle of his tears. "You did it!" Curses, dirty words, threats! What he would do to Hesh's teeth, his belly, his nose, everything! Who his parents were, what he himself was, and what kind! "I, I, I, I, I . . ." fumed Chink.

"Yare?" asked Hesh pleasantly. "Is that so? Really? You don't tell me? Chinkstink!"

Chink grasped the ropes and started pulling himself up. Hesh darted back and stuck the clothespins through the rings, locking the door. First he would make Chink eat his heart out. For ten, fifteen minutes he would let him eat his heart out. He would be so kind as to give him that little pleasure.

"Let me out, you dirty rat!" Chink screamed from the shaft. "I'm gonna break every bone in your stinking head! I'm gonna knock your lousy brains out! Let me out!"

"Well," said Heshey affably to Goldie, "if it isn't our friend Mr. Chinkstink!"

"And you, Goldie," Chink raged, beside himself, "I'll get even with you if it takes me a million years and I drop dead! You dirty, yellow, stinking rat!"

"Aw, shaddap," Hesh said toughly, his sense of chivalry touched. "You keep your filthy mouth shut or I'll fix you for real."

Hesh could have broken a blood vessel with joy. Defending

Goldie he was and he looked at her proudly. But in turning his head he saw a man. It was Max Balkan, plodding up the stairs, holding the railing. Hesh went to him at once.

"Please, mister, please," he begged. "Do me a favor. Don't move, don't say nothing. Just stay here and keep quiet for a minute. It's Chink. He's socking me again."

Balkan's ambition at this time was to find a place to lie down in and sleep. He had no energy to argue with Hesh or to find out what was going on. Bending his knees almost without taking the trouble to will this action, Max sat down on the marble steps and rested his head against the wall.

"Thanks, mister, thanks," Hesh said profusely. "Any time you want a kid he should go for something, call me. I'll go."

He crept up to the door of the dumb-waiter, silently pulling out the pin. Within Chink raged and cracked like a Red Devil firecracker ground with the heel on the pavement on the Fourth of July. Hesh moved back a pace, the ketchup bombs in each hand. Suddenly Chick found the door give. He swung it open. Wham! went the bomb from the first hand. It smacked Chink in the chest and the goo slid down into his lap. Chink's face opened with surprise. Wham! went the bomb from the right hand. This one caught him properly over the eyes. The ketchup dripped down his face. The coffee grounds, oatmeal and peas clung to him like a Coney Island mud-pack. Chink was thunder-struck and speechless, one big splotch of garbage and ketchup. Hesh slammed the door shut and fastened it with the pin before Chink could recover himself. He ran to his flat.

Hesh lay on the floor and rolled in ecstasy. For once! For once! Heshey in his way realized that in this world there were the meek and the proud. All his young life, cringing in the hall-ways, he had hated the proud and people like Chink. Torment, cruelty and meanness. Now he had done it! Hesh remembered the spectacle of Chink, the mess all over him as he sat hunched up in the dumb-waiter. He remembered that searching, mysti-fied, almost pathetic expression. Hesh writhed on the floor trum-peting until his mother came running up to him, thinking he had convulsions.

"What's the matter, Heshey baby?" she wailed. "What happened, darling?"

"Nothing. Nothing," he managed to utter. Then he thought of Mrs. Strudel and what Chink would get from her when she finally came to free him. Spasms shook his body. He couldn't control himself and abandoned himself to delirium. Heshey's mother thought her son's last moments had arrived and she uttered piercing screams of anguish.

Outside, Max rested on the steps. Even with all his weariness he had been able to appreciate Heshey's triumph. Good, he thought, good. His bruised spirit raised its feeble head like a daffodil bravely resisting the wind. Hesh was one of his, a compatriot in the army of the meek, his victory was Max's also. There it was, Max said to himself, power, the meek arisen for once among the proud. Power, victory, pride and dignity, to stand a man—all these things Balkan longed for passionately, and thinking of Heshey and Chink, he also longed for childhood and peace. He rose from the steps, feeling like an unoiled hinge, and made his way to his flat.

Homage to Blenholt by Daniel Fuchs, published by The Vanguard Press, 1936. Reprinted by permission of the author.

BOROUGH OF CEMETERIES

from SAILOR OFF THE BREMEN

by IRWIN SHAW

During the cocktail hour, in Brownsville, the cab drivers gather in Lammanawitz's Bar and Grill and drink beer and talk about the world and watch the sun set slowly over the elevated tracks in the direction of Prospect Park.

Permission of the author. Copyright 1938, Irwin Shaw. Originally published in The New Yorker. *In* Sailor off the Bremen and Other Stories, *Random House.*

"Mungo?" they say. "Mungo? He got a fish for a arm. A mackerel. He will pitch Brooklyn right into the first division of the International League."

"I saw the Mayor today. His Honor, himself. The Little Flower. What this country needs . . ."

"Pinky, I want that you should trust me for a glass of beer."

Pinky wiped the wet dull expanse of the bar. "Look, Elias. It is against the law of the State of New York," he said nervously, "to sell intoxicating liquors on credit."

"One glass of beer. Intoxicatin'!" Elias' lips curled. "Who yuh think I am, Snow White?"

"Do you want me to lose my license?" Pinky asked plaintively.

"I stay up nights worryin' Pinky might lose his license. My wife hears me cryin' in my sleep," Elias said. "One beer, J. P. Morgan."

Regretfully, Pinky drew the beer, with a big head, and sighed as he marked it down in the book. "The last one," he said, "positively the last one. As God is my witness."

"Yeah," Elias said. "Keep yer mouth closed." He drank the beer in one gulp, with his eyes shut. "My God," he said quietly, his eyes still shut, as he put the glass down. "Fer a lousy dime," he said to the room in general, "yuh get somethin' like that! Fer a lousy dime! Brooklyn is a wonderful place."

"Brooklyn stinks," said another driver, down the bar. "The borough of cemeteries. This is a first class place for graveyards."

"My friend Palangio," Elias said. "Il Doochay Palangio. Yuh don't like Brooklyn, go back to Italy. They give yuh a gun, yuh get shot in the behind in Africa." The rest of the drivers laughed and Elias grinned at his own wit. "I seen in the movies. Go back t' Italy, wit' the fat girls. Who'll buy me a beer?"

Complete silence fell over the bar, like taps over an army camp.

"My friends," Elias said bitterly.

"Brooklyn is a wonderful place," Palangio said.

"All day long," Elias said, reflectively rubbing his broken nose, "I push a hack. Eleven hours on the street. I now have the sum of three dollars and fifty cents in my pocket."

Pinky came right over. "Now, Elias," he said, "there is the small matter of one beer. If I knew you had the money . . ."

Elias impatiently brushed Pinky's hand off the bar. "There is somebody callin' for a beer down there, Pinky," he said. "Attend yer business."

"I think," Pinky grumbled, retreating, "that a man oughta pay his rightful debts."

"He thinks. Pinky thinks," Elias announced. But his heart was not with Pinky. He turned his back to the bar and leaned on his frayed elbows and looked sadly up at the tin ceiling. "Three dollars and fifty cents," he said softly. "An' I can't buy a beer."

"Whatsamatta?" Palangio asked. "Yuh got a lock on yuh pocket?"

"Two dollars an' seventy-fi' cents to the Company," Elias said. "An' seventy-fi cents to my lousy wife so she don't make me sleep in the park. The lousy Company. Every day for a year I give 'em two dollars an' seventy-fi cents an' then I own the hack. After a year yuh might as well sell that crate to Japan to put in bombs. Th' only way yuh can get it to move is t' drop it. I signed a contract. I need a nurse. Who wants t' buy me a beer?"

"I signed th' same contract," Palangio said. A look of pain came over his dark face. "It got seven months more to go. Nobody shoulda learned me how to write my name."

"If you slobs would only join th' union," said a little Irishman across from the beer spigots.

"Geary," Elias said. "The Irish hero. Tell us how you fought th' English in th' battle of Belfast."

"O.K., O.K.," Geary said, pushing his cap back excitably from his red hair. "You guys wanna push a hack sixteen hours a day for beans, don' let me stop yuh."

"Join a union, get yer hair parted down the middle by the cops," Elias said. "That is my experience."

"O.K., boys," Geary pushed his beer a little to make it foam. "Property-owners. Can't pay for a glass a beer at five o'clock in th' afternoon. What's the use a' talkin' t' yuh? Lemme have a beer, Pinky."

"Geary, you're a red," Elias said. "A red bastidd."

"A Communist," Palangio said.

"I want a beer," Geary said loudly.

"Times're bad," Elias said. "That's what's th' trouble."

"Sure." Geary drained half his new glass. "Sure."

"Back in 1928," Elias said, "I averaged sixty bucks a week."

"On New Year's Eve, 1927," Palangio murmured, "I made thirty-six dollars and forty cents."

"Money was flowin'," Elias remembered.

Palangio sighed, rubbed his beard bristles with the back of his hand. "I wore silk shirts. With stripes. They cost five bucks a piece. I had four girls in 1928. My God!"

"This ain't 1928," Geary said.

"Th' smart guy," Elias said. "He's tellin' us somethin'. This ain't 1928, he says. Join th' union, we get 1928 back."

"Why the hell should I waste my time?" Geary asked himself in disgust. He drank in silence.

"Pinky!" Palangio called. "Pinky! Two beers for me and my friend Elias."

Elias moved, with a wide smile, up the bar, next to Palangio. "We are brothers in misery, Angelo," he said. "Me and th' Wop. We both signed th' contract."

They drank together and sighed together.

"I had th' biggest pigeon flight in Brownsville," Elias said softly. "One hundred and twelve pairs of pedigreed pigeons. I'd send 'em up like fireworks, every afternoon. You oughta've seen 'em wheelin' aroun' an' aroun' over th' roofs. I'm a pigeon fancier." He finished his glass. "I got fifteen pigeons left. Every time I bring home less than seventy-five cents, my wife cooks one for supper. A pedigreed pigeon. My lousy wife."

"Two beers," Palangio said. He and Elias drank with grave satisfaction.

"Now," Elias said, "if only I didn't have to go home to my lousy wife. I married her in 1929. A lot of things've changed

· 427 ·

since 1929." He sighed. "What's a woman?" he asked. "A woman is a trap."

"You shoulda seen what I seen today," Palangio said. "My third fare. On Eastern Parkway. I watched her walk all th' way acrost Nostrand Avenue, while I was waitin' on the light. A hundred-and-thirty pound girl. Blonde. Swingin' her hips like orchester music. With one of those little straw hats on top of her head, with the vegetables on it. You never saw nothin' like it. I held onto the wheel like I was drownin'. Talkin' about traps! She went to the St. George Hotel."

Elias shook his head. "The tragedy of my life," he said, "is I married young."

"Two beers," Palangio said.

"Angelo Palangio," Elias said, "yer name reminds me of music."

"A guy met her in front of the St. George. A big fat guy. Smilin' like he just seen Santa Claus. A big fat guy. Some guys . . ."

"Some guys . . ." Elias mourned. "I gotta go home to Annie. She yells at me from six to twelve, regular. Who's goin' to pay the grocer? Who's goin' to pay the gas company?" He looked steadily at his beer for a moment and downed it. "I'm a man who married at the age a' eighteen."

"We need somethin' to drink," Palangio said.

"Buy us two whiskys," Elias said. "What the hell good is beer?"

"Two Calverts," Palangio called. "The best for me and my friend Elias Pinsker."

"Two gentlemen," Elias said, "who both signed th' contract."

"Two dumb slobs," said Geary.

"Th' union man," Elias lifted his glass. "To th' union!" He downed the whisky straight. "Th' hero of th' Irish Army."

"Pinky," Palangio shouted. "Fill 'em up to the top."

"Angelo Palangio," Elias murmured gratefully.

Palangio soberly counted the money out for the drinks. "Now," he said, "the Company can jump in Flushing Bay. I am down to two bucks even."

"Nice," Geary said sarcastically. "Smart. You don't pay 'em one day, they take yer cab. After payin' them regular for five months. Buy another drink."

Palangio slowly picked up his glass and let the whisky slide down his throat in a smooth amber stream. "Don't talk like that, Geary," he said. "I don't want to hear nothin' about taxicabs. I am busy drinkin' with friends."

"You dumb Wop," Geary said.

"That is no way to talk," Elias said, going over to Geary purposefully. He cocked his right hand and squinted at Geary. Geary backed off, his hands up. "I don't like to hear people call my friend a dumb Wop," Elias said.

"Get back," Geary shouted, "before I brain yuh."

Pinky ran up excitably. "Lissen, boys," he screamed, "do you want I should lose my license?"

"We are all friends," Palangio said. "Shake hands. Everybody shake hands. Everybody have a drink. I hereby treat everybody to a drink."

Elias lumbered back to Palangio's side. "I am sorry if I made a commotion. Some people can't talk like gentlemen."

"Everybody have a drink," Palangio insisted.

Elias took out three dollar bills and laid them deliberately on the bar. "Pass the bottle around. This is on Elias Pinsker."

"Put yer money away, Elias." Geary pushed his cap around on his head with anger. "Who yuh think yuh are? Walter Chrysler?"

"The entertainment this afternoon is on me," Elias said inexorably. "There was a time I would stand drinks for twenty-five men. With a laugh, an' pass cigars out after it. Pass the bottle around, Pinky!"

The whisky flowed.

"Elias and me," Palangio said. "We are high class spenders."

"You guys oughta be fed by hand," Geary said. "Wards of the guvment."

"A man is entitled to some relaxation," Elias said. "Where's that bottle?"

"This is nice," Palangio said. "This is very nice."

"This is like the good old days," Elias said.

"I hate to go home," Palangio sighed. "I ain't even got a radio home."

"Pinky!" Elias called. "Turn on the radio for Angelo Palangio."

"One room," Palangio said. "As big as a toilet. That is where I live."

The radio played. It was soft and sweet and a rich male voice sang, "I married an Angel."

"When I get home," Elias remembered, "Annie will kill a pedigreed pigeon for supper, My lousy wife. An' after supper I push the hack five more hours and I go home and Annie yells some more and I get up tomorrow and push the hack some more." He poured himself another drink. "That is a life for a dog," he said. "For a Airedale."

"In Italy," Palangio said, "they got donkeys don't work as hard as us."

"If the donkeys were as bad off as you," Geary yelled, "they'd have sense enough to organize."

"I want to be a executive at a desk." Elias leaned both elbows on the bar and held his chin in his huge gnarled hands. "A long distance away from Brownsville. Wit' two thousand pigeons. In California. An' I should be a bachelor. Geary, can yuh organize *that*? Hey, Geary?"

"You're a workin' man," Geary said, "an you're goin' to be a workin' man all yer life."

"Geary," Elias said. "You red bastidd, Geary."

"All my life," Palangio wept, "I am goin' to push a hack up an' down Brooklyn, fifteen, sixteen hours a day an' pay th' Company forever an' go home and sleep in a room no bigger'n a toilet. Without a radio. Jesus!"

"We are victims of circumstance," Elias said.

"All my life," Palangio cried, "tied to that crate!"

Elias pounded the bar once with his fist. "Th' hell with it! Palangio!" he said. "Get into that goddam wagon of yours."

"What do yuh want me to do?" Palangio asked in wonder.

"We'll fix 'em," Elias shouted. "We'll fix those hacks. We'll fix that Company! Get into yer cab, Angelo. I'll drive mine, we'll have a chicken fight."

"Yuh drunken slobs!" Geary yelled. "Yuh can't do that!"

"Yeah," Palangio said eagerly, thinking it over. "Yeah. We'll show 'em. Two dollars and seventy-fi' cents a day for life. Yeah. We'll fix 'em. Come on, Elias!"

Elias and Palangio walked gravely out to their cars. Everybody else followed them.

"Look what they're doin!" Geary screamed. "Not a brain between the both of them! What good'll it do to ruin the cabs?"

"Shut up," Elias said, getting into his cab. "We oughta done this five months ago. Hey, Angelo," he called, leaning out of his cab. "Are yuh ready? Hey Il Doochay!"

"Contact!" Angelo shouted, starting his motor. "Boom! Boom!"

The two cars spurted at each other, in second, head-on. As they hit, glass broke and a fender flew off and the cars skidded wildly and the metal noise echoed and re-echoed like artillery fire off the buildings.

Elias stuck his head out of his cab. "Are yuh hurt?" he called. "Hey, Il Doochay!"

"Contact!" Palangio called from behind his broken windshield. "The Dawn Patrol!"

"I can't watch this," Geary moaned. "Two workin' men." He went back into Lammanawitz's Bar and Grill.

The two cabs slammed together again and people came running from all directions.

"How're yuh?" Elias asked, wiping the blood off his face.

"Onward!" Palangio stuck his hand out in salute. "Sons of Italy!"

Again and again the cabs tore into each other.

"Knights of the Round Table," Palangio announced.

"Knights of Lammanawitz's Round Table," Elias agreed, pulling at the choke to get the wheezing motor to turn over once more.

For the last time they came together. Both cars flew off the ground at the impact and Elias's toppled on its side and slid with a harsh grating noise to the curb. One of the front wheels from Palangio's cab rolled calmly and decisively toward Pitkin Avenue. Elias crawled out of his cab before anyone could reach him. He stood up, swaying, covered with blood, pulling at loose ends of his torn sweater. He shook hands soberly with Palangio and looked around him with satisfaction at the torn fenders and broken glass and scattered headlights and twisted steel. "Th' lousy Company," he said. "That does it. I am now goin' to inform 'em of th' accident."

He and Palangio entered the Bar and Grill, followed by a hundred men, women, and children. Elias dialed the number deliberately.

"Hullo," he said, "hullo, Charlie? Lissen, Charlie, if yuh send a wreckin' car down to Lammanawitz's Bar and Grill, yuh will find two of yer automobiles. Yuh lousy Charlie." He hung up carefully.

"All right, Palangio," he said.

"Yuh bet," Palangio answered.

"Now we oughta go to the movies," Elias said.

"That's right," Palangio nodded seriously.

"Yuh oughta be shot," Geary shouted.

"They're playin' Simone Simon," Elias announced to the crowd. "Let's go see Simone Simon."

Walking steadily, arm in arm, like two gentlemen, Elias and Angelo Palangio went down the street, through the lengthening shadows, toward Simone Simon.

When Edmund Wilson's book Memoirs of Hecate County *got Boston and the Hearst papers—what they got to complain about? —quite excited, the Brooklyn Eagle* ran a headline

BANNED BOOK
PRAISES BORO

and quoted from the passage we are using.

· 432 ·

from . . .

MEMOIRS OF HECATE COUNTY

by EDMUND WILSON

. . . so I decided to go over to Brooklyn and find out what the situation was.

I had never seen her house or her family, and the journey brought a certain suspense. When I went down into the black dugout of the subway and took the train that banged and hurtled through the straight narrow tube, it was as if I were engaging myself in some logical course of procedure which would force me to a harsh recognition I had hitherto kept at a distance. We shot out of the tunnel at Brooklyn Bridge, and I looked down, through the rows of dark girders that wove back and forth like a mechanical loom, on the city shown in dark silhouette above a livid and leaden water that seemed to shine at one edge white-hot, and on those streets of the East Side, where Anna had been born, with their roofs packed tight and dingy for miles, shouting here at the escaping trains, from the walls and the tops of their buildings, their last cries to come and buy fine values—in raincoats, in furs, in candy, in laxatives, in five-cent cigars; and I was caught for a moment by a vision of that immensity of anonymous life, which, though I knew it only through Anna, had thus far come for me alive at one point like the screen in the blotted theatre that is peopled by the animated shadows of persons not really present, whom one may never see in the flesh—though in this case I knew that they existed and had the heat and the accents of life and that the dramas they acted were real; and I was moved by a kind of awe. Then we went down into the blackness again, and finally emerged from the tunnel in a raw landscape of tracks and garages, gas tanks, one-story factories and bleak little cheap brick houses in which the factory workers evidently lived. This was Anna's own country, I said to myself; I might as well accept it at once.

But I was surprised when I got out at the stop which was

closest to Anna's address. I walked along under low-columned cloisters, pale brown and a little more gracious than anything connected with the subway on the Manhattan side of the bridge; and emerged from the subway steps into the sunlight of a whole new world, which seemed to me inexplicably attractive. It was Twelfth Street just off King's Highway, not far from Coney Island and Brighton Beach; and there was space and ocean air and light, and what seemed to me—it was what most astonished me—an atmosphere of freedom and leisure quite unknown on the other side. The great thing here was that there were so few high buildings—the tallest were apartment houses that ran only to six or eight stories, and there were not very many of these; and for the rest, one found little brick shops—delicatessen stores, beauty parlors, drugstores, billiard rooms, kosher butchers, and newsstands with Italian and Jewish papers—that had been relatively newly built and that looked absolutely toylike. These cropped up in patches at intervals among streets that were exceptionally wide and that seemed to go on forever, yet, more or less of a sameness though they were, had somehow escaped from the abstract monotony characteristic of American cities. They were planted with rows of young maples, now beginning to be green with April; and the houses—double affairs though they were—placed each at a good distance from its neighbors, seemed quite independent dwellings, not unpleasantly paired, rather than cramping partitioned units, and though they were all fairly small, had been planned with rather an amiable eye to the amenities—for each had its own little backyard and garage and its little privet hedge on the street, its latticed shades in the windows, its arched doorway with a diadem of bricks that rayed out around the top, and its little flight of steps in front with an ornamental patterned stone bowl in which nasturtiums or geraniums grew. These avenues and houses were further redeemed from their tendency toward uniformity by the children with whom they were populated and who, even in this period of poverty, seemed remarkably healthy and clean. There were babies being wheeled in baby-carriages that had what seemed to be a great luxury of springs and young girls with mature round

breasts that bulged out under the surfaces of their sweaters; and there were also their ample mothers leaning out of the ground-floor front windows, and occasionally a black-browed Sicilian in suburban American clothes tinkering with his car, or an old Jew walking solemnly and stiffly, a derby hat on the front of his head, pulled down over his somber eyes.